Organised Crime, Financial Crime, and Criminal Justice

Organised crime and financial crime are pressing global problems, increasingly recognised as policy priorities both by national governments and international bodies and corporations. This proudly interdisciplinary collection is built on the premise that these topics are too often artificially separated, both in scholarship and the classroom. Bringing together scholars from law, the social sciences, and the humanities, this book showcases a diverse range of perspectives on these complex and compelling global issues, and the criminal justice challenges that they pose.

The themes discussed include legal theory and procedure; regulation and enforcement; prevention and punishment; media representation and perception. Readers are encouraged to think outside traditional disciplinary bounds and form their own connections and conclusions inspired by the juxtaposition of perspectives rarely seen together in the same volume.

Dan Jasinski is a barrister (unregistered) and Senior Lecturer in Criminal Justice at the University of Northampton. Dan's current research focuses on the criminal process, and he has previously taught skills modules on the Bar Training Course, in addition to organised crime on the LLB.

Amber Phillips is a Senior Lecturer in Criminology at the University of the West of England. Having initially trained as a translator, her career as a criminologist began in 2012 while she was living and working in Calabria, Italy, as part of the EU-funded Leonardo da Vinci scheme. Her experiences with anti-mafia organisations in Calabria inspired her AHRC-funded PhD, which she successfully defended in 2018. As a researcher, Dr Phillips is primarily interested in transnational organised crime and mafia-type groups, as well as the impact of cultural representations and media narratives on crime control policy.

Ed Johnston is an Associate Professor of Criminal Justice and Procedure at the University of Northampton. His research and teaching centres on the field of field of criminal justice and, in particular, on the law of disclosure, fair trial rights, and adversarial justice.

The Law of Financial Crime

Series Editors:
Nicholas Ryder Professor of Law, Cardiff University, School of Law and Politics, UK.
Dr. Lachmi Singh Associate Lecturer, Bristol Law School, University of the West of England, UK.

While a growing number of high profile financial crime cases have hit the headlines recently the topic of financial crime is also generating much attention amongst academics and practitioners. This series will be the first to be dedicated to the law of financial, or economic, crime and offers a platform for important and original research in this area.

Books in the series will cover traditional subjects of financial crime including money laundering, terrorist financing, fraud, market abuse, insider dealing, market manipulation, tax evasion, bribery and corruption. But broader legal and regulatory issues will also be covered as well as emerging areas of concern such as the risks to stability of the financial system posed by financial crime. Emphasis will be placed on comparative approaches to the subject considering legislation across a number of jurisdictions as well as international regulations where appropriate, giving the series a truly global outlook.

The titles in the series are primarily aimed at an audience of researchers, scholars and practitioners in the area but should also be of interest to policy makers, law enforcement agencies, financial regulatory agencies, as well as people employed within the financial services sector.

Available titles in this series include:

The Law Relating to Financial Crime in the United Kingdom
Third Edition
Nicholas Ryder and Karen Harrison

Illicit Finance and the Law in the Commonwealth Caribbean
The Myth of Paradise
Rohan D. Clarke

Organised Crime, Financial Crime, and Criminal Justice
Theoretical Concepts and Challenges
Edited by Dan Jasinski, Amber Phillips, and Ed Johnston

For more information about this series, please visit: www.routledge.com/The-Law-of-Financial-Crime/book-series/FINCRIME

Organised Crime, Financial Crime, and Criminal Justice

Theoretical Concepts and Challenges

Edited by Dan Jasinski, Amber Phillips, and Ed Johnston

Routledge
Taylor & Francis Group
LONDON AND NEW YORK

First published 2023
by Routledge
4 Park Square, Milton Park, Abingdon, Oxon OX14 4RN

and by Routledge
605 Third Avenue, New York, NY 10158

Routledge is an imprint of the Taylor & Francis Group, an informa business

British Library Cataloguing-in-Publication Data
A catalogue record for this book is available from the British Library

Library of Congress Cataloging-in-Publication Data
A catalog record has been requested for this book

ISBN: 978-0-367-89745-1 (hbk)
ISBN: 978-1-032-37333-1 (pbk)
ISBN: 978-1-003-02081-3 (ebk)

DOI: 10.4324/9781003020813

Typeset in Galliard
by Deanta Global Publishing Services, Chennai, India

Contents

Acknowledgments

Ed would like to thank his co-editors and the contributors for all their efforts and patience throughout writing this book. He would also like thank his partner, Wolfy, and their two children, Erin and Jacob, for their helpful distractions, which were much appreciated.

Dan would like to extend his gratitude to Ed, Amber, and all our contributing authors for their hard work in bringing this project to fruition. Dan would also like to thank Georgia, for her unwavering patience and unparalleled support.

Amber is grateful to her co-editors and to her co-author, Stefania Di Buccio, for her support and advice. Thanks also to her husband, James, for his endless patience.

Table of legislation

UK Primary Legislation

UK Secondary Legislation

Other Jurisdictions

Table of cases

Contributors

Samantha Bourton

Sam Bourton is a lecturer in law at the University of the West of England, Bristol, and a Fellow of the Higher Education Academy. She teaches on the LLB and LLM programmes, with modules including the Law of Financial Crime and Regulation, International Financial Crime, and Research Methods. Sam's research interests lie in the law of financial crime, particularly the law pertaining to tax evasion and money laundering. She regularly publishes and presents her research in these areas. Sam's doctoral thesis concentrated on providing a comparative analysis of tax evasion law and its enforcement in the United Kingdom and United States of America. Her research was inspired by the global and national reactions to modern tax evasion scandals, such as the revelations concerning HSBC's Private Bank in Switzerland and the Panama Papers.

Stefania di Buccio

Stefania di Buccio received her doctorate from the University of Milan in 2021, with a thesis that explored the economic dimensions of mafia power and models of prevention. Her research interests are centred on the entrepreneurial and economic dimensions of organised crime and criminal assets. Her most recent work has focused on mafia groups and labour exploitation, specifically regarding taxation. Alongside her academic work, Dr di Buccio works as a judicial administrator, a specialist legal professional responsible for the management of assets confiscated from mafia-type criminal organisations. She is currently the programme coordinator of the University of Bologna's Masters in the Management and Reuse of Confiscated Assets.

Oliver Charles

Oliver P. Charles (BSc (Hons) MA SFHEA FRSA) is solicitor and a PhD candidate at the Centre for Financial and Corporate Integrity Coventry University, UK. He has worked in general practice with experience in the areas of property, wills and probates, company commercial, taxation together with matrimonial, family and civil litigation. He holds an MA in art history and has lectured for over 27 years at universities in both the UK and the EU at undergraduate and postgraduate courses on accounting and finance, forensic accounting, civil and commercial law, the ethics and conduct of the legal profession, together with art history and art fraud. He is active in the City of London within its various charitable and business spheres.

Lucy Evans

Lucy Evans is an Associate Professor in postcolonial literature. She specialises in specialise in contemporary Anglophone Caribbean literature. She is interested in literary form and genre with much of her research focused on Caribbean short stories. Her more recent research centres on representations of crime in the Anglophone Caribbean. Her current book project, *Caribbean Fictions of Crime*, which engages with scholarship in criminology as well as crime fiction studies, is informed by my collaborative work as principal investigator on two international, interdisciplinary research networking projects.

Susan Garnett

Susan Garnett is an associate lecturer in Criminology at Bath Spa University. Susan has a PhD in law from Aberystwyth University and worked as a criminal defence solicitor for many years. She was originally admitted as a legal practitioner in New South Wales, Australia. Her areas of interest include terrorism, human rights law and the rights of suspects held in police custody.

Demelza Hall

Demelza Hall is a lecturer in law at the University of the West of England, Bristol.She teaches on the LLB and LLM programmes, with modules including Constitutional and Administrative Law, the Law of Financial Crime and Regulation and Corporate Governance and Corporate Social Responsibility. Her current research interests relate to financial crime and corporate governance, especially corporate economic crime and whistleblowing. Demelza is also a PhD candidate whose thesis aims to analyse how fraud and weak corporate governance relating to corporations within the USA contributed to the Great Depression, savings and loans crisis and the 2008 financial crisis.

Rikard Jalkebro

Rikard Jalkebro is an Associate Professor at the Anwar Gargash Diplomatic Academy (AGDA) in Abu Dhabi, UAE, where he is directing the MA programme on Humanitarian Action and Development and teaching on peace processes, conflict resolution and international security issues. Rikard's research interests include exposing the juncture between the dynamics of peace processes and terrorism, with a particular focus on Southeast Asia; organised crime and corruption; humanitarian assistance; and development. He completed his PhD, in international relations, in the School of International Relations at the University of St Andrews in 2015.

Ilias Kapsis

Ilias Kapsis is an Associate Professor of Law at University of Bradford. He teaches banking law, technology law and commercial law. His research interests include money laundering, the regulation of fintech and crypto-assets, ethics and regulation of artificial intelligence and financial inclusion.

Marnie Lovejoy

Marnie Lovejoy did her law degree at the University of Basel, Switzerland, in 2005. While working as a lecturer and researcher at the University of Basel, she obtained her PhD on 'the tracing and confiscating of assets of dictators', which was awarded *summa cum laude*. After her bar exam (Switzerland) in 2012, Marnie started to work as a solicitor in a law firm in Geneva specialising in recovering stolen assets. After moving to the UK, Marnie undertook the QLTS exams to qualify as a solicitor in the UK and started to work as a senior lecturer at the University of Portsmouth. In 2019 Marnie was appointed principal lecturer and Associate Head of Portsmouth Law School. Since September 2021, Marnie is working as the head of environmental law research for the British Association for Shooting and Conservation and remains a visiting lecturer at the University of Portsmouth.

Charlie Robson

Charlie Robson is a PhD candidate and Associate Lecturer in the Department of Law at UWE Bristol. Her research interests focus on counter-terrorism financing, in particular the financing of domestic groups. Her doctoral thesis critically considers the efficacy of the profit-driven reporting model in detecting financial flows linked to terrorism through the examination and comparison of relevant law in the United Kingdom, the United States and the Netherlands in addition to the international legal framework. The thesis examines the role of financial information sharing partnerships in the disruption of terrorism financing and makes several recommendations on how to enhance financial intelligence sharing in the selected jurisdictions. Beyond academia Charlie has delivered counter-terrorism financing training seminars to CEPOL and was recently invited to provide a summary of her research to the Federal Bureau of Investigation as part of a funded research project.

Nicholas Ryder

Nicholas has an international reputation for excellence in policy-oriented research in financial crime and has played advisory roles both nationally (Home Office, Law Commission, the Nationwide, Security Intelligence Services, Transparency International) and internationally (NATO, United Nations, Cepol, Europol, EUROMED Police, the Dutch Police, the France Telecom Group, the Law Reform Commission of Ireland and the Foreign and Commonwealth Office). His research has attracted funding (£1.61m)from InnovateUK, Economic and Social Research Council (ESRC), LexisNexis Risk Solutions, the City of London Police Force, the Royal United Services Limited, The Alan Turing Institute, ICT Wilmington Risk & Compliance, the France Telecom Group and the European Social Fund.

He created and edits Routledge's Law of Financial Crime Series and has e- published five monographs and edited books and over 50 articles in internationally recognised journals including *Legal Studies*, the *Cambridge Law Journal*, the *Journal of Business Law*, *Studies in Conflict and Terrorism* and *Contemporary Issues in Law*.

Kate Tudor

Kate Tudor is an Associate Professor at Durham University. Her research interests broadly relate to the intersections between crime, harm and political economy by looking at the ways in which offender motivations, subjectivities and business models are shaped by the wider economic and social environment. She has recently carried out research in relation to investment fraud, rural crime and organised crime.

Umut Turksen

Dr. Umut Turksen is a professor in law at the Centre for Financial and Corporate Integrity Coventry University, UK (https://www.coventry.ac.uk/research/areas-of-research/centre-for-financial-and-corporate-integrity/lrc-cluster/). He is leading an EU-funded project TRACE (https://trace-illicit-money-flows.eu) and interested in the practical application of the law in innovation, societal security and development. He has published several books and articles on energy, financial crime and international trade and economic law (https://pureportal.coventry.ac.uk/en/persons/umut-turksen/publications/). He has provided consultancy and training to prestigious organisations including France Telecom, Orange, Equas Ltd, Wilmington Plc, the Commonwealth, NATO, EUROPOL, CEPOL.Professor Turksen is also a member of the Innovation Caucus (https://innovationcaucus.co.uk). He is a reviewer for several journals and publishers including the *Journal of Banking Regulation*; *Journal of Governance and Regulation*; *World Trade Review*; *Information and Communications Technology Law*; Oxford University Press; Cambridge University Press and Routledge.

William Vlcek

William Vlcek is Senior Lecturer in global political economy with the School of International Relations at the University of St Andrews. His research explores questions of money and finance in the global political economy that interrogate the conduct of power in global finance. In addition to offshore finance and international taxation, it considers the intersections of finance and security found with money laundering, terrorist finance and sovereign debt. He has published academic journal articles and book chapters on these topics along with the monographs *Offshore Finance and Small States: Sovereignty, Size and Money* (Palgrave, 2008), *Offshore Finance and Global Governance: Disciplining the Tax Nomad* (Palgrave, 2017) and *Terrorist Financing* (Agenda, 2022).

Introduction

Amber Phillips, Ed Johnston, and Dan Jasinski

This book came about originally as a result of a number of conversations between the editors – a lawyer, a criminologist, and a lawyer respectively – on the artificiality of disciplinary boundaries when it comes to organised and financial crime. These topics, it was agreed, are profoundly and inherently interdisciplinary in their reach and impact, touching not just law and criminology, but also the wider social sciences (including economics and sociology), the arts and humanities, and even science and technology. In this volume – which is centred firmly on the premise that organised crime and financial crime do not 'belong' to any single discipline – scholars from law, the social sciences and the humanities have been brought together to showcase a diverse range of perspectives on these complex and pressing global challenges. The third 'pillar' of the book, criminal justice, concerns the various responses to these challenges and is woven throughout in chapters authored by both academics and criminal justice practitioners at the coalface of the fight against these issues.

Before outlining the book's structure, it is necessary to provide a brief note on terminology. It is not for the editors to contribute to an already overcrowded knowledge base concerning definitions of organised crime. Suffice it to acknowledge that this term has long been the subject of intense academic debate, part of which has centred on its potential obsolescence as a concept that covers such a huge variety of constantly evolving crime types and criminal activities.[1] Regardless of this, however, it must also be acknowledged that the term organised crime is, to use Levi's words, 'a unifying framework around which international police and judicial cooperation can be structured',[2] and the ambiguity of the term has not prevented it from emerging as a policy priority in many countries in recent years, including the UK. The term 'financial crime', while somewhat less mired in debate, is itself far from unambiguous, again due in part to its increasing

1 See, for example, Paoli and Vander Beken, who describe organised crime as 'a vague umbrella concept': Letizia Paoli and Tom Vander Beken, 'Organised Crime: A Contested Concept' in Letitia Paoli (ed) *The Oxford Handbook of Organised Crime* (OUP 2019) 13.

2 Michael Levi, 'Policing Financial Crimes', in Henry Pontell and Gilbert Geis (eds) *International Handbook of White-Collar and Corporate Crime* (Springer 2014) 589.

DOI: 10.4324/9781003020813-1

prevalence in policy discussions across the world in recent years.[3] The key point for the purposes of this book is that many of the offences covered by the concept of 'financial crime' are profoundly linked with what could also be termed 'organised crime' activities, including money laundering, transnational corruption, and fraud.[4] Indeed, such offences are crucial in facilitating the growth and persistence of organised crime worldwide. The chapters within this collection each adopt different approaches to defining these concepts, but the book is less interested in the distinctions between these topics than it is the blurring of the lines that separate them and the global criminal justice challenges that they pose.

The structure of the book is guided in part by the editors' firm desire to break down the artificiality of the distinctions between the three topic areas and with the goal of encouraging multidisciplinary perspectives. It is hoped that the structure will encourage the reader to think outside traditional disciplinary bounds and to form their own connections and conclusions inspired by the juxtaposition of perspectives rarely seen together in the same volume.

Chapter 1, by Dr Amber Phillips, strikes the first note of interdisciplinarity. Written by an Italianist-turned-criminologist, the text explores the importance and impact of cultural narratives and representations of crime, focusing on the 'ndrangheta, one of the world's wealthiest and most powerful mafia-type criminal organisations. Phillips highlights the porosity of the border between fact and fiction when it comes to mafia-type crime in Italy and applies an analysis of the alien conspiracy perspective to the representation of the 'ndrangheta within its own 'native' region, recasting the concept of designating organised crime groups as an 'outsider'-driven phenomenon. **Chapter 2** continues the focus on mafia-type crime but situates itself firmly at the intersection between organised crime, financial crime, and criminal justice. Authored by Dr Amber Phillips and Dr Stefania Di Buccio, a judicial administrator working in Italy, the chapter offers an in-depth analysis of Italy's pioneering asset confiscation legislation. The authors work from the premise that mafia-type crime must be understood as specific and distinct, and that a key part of this distinction rests on the mafia's ability to instrumentalise complex networks, allowing it to successfully infiltrate the 'legal' economy.

Chapter 3, by Dr Marnie Lovejoy, provides a fascinating international contrast to Italy's approach to asset confiscation, offering an analysis of unexplained wealth orders (UWOs), introduced in the UK by the Criminal Finances Act of 2017. Focusing on the privilege against self-incrimination, Dr Lovejoy explores the extent to which the procedure pertaining to the procurement and enforcement

3 For a more in-depth discussion of the concept of financial crime, see Michael Levi, 'Some reflections on the evolution of economic and financial crimes', in Barry Rider (ed), *Research Handbook on International Financial Crime* (Elgar 2015).

4 Having established that the distinction between organized and financial crime is not clear cut, this book is also necessarily concerned with the concept of 'white collar crime' (an analysis of which features in chapter nine). White collar crime is mentioned here not to dilute the focus of this collection, but to highlight once again the porosity of disciplinary and terminological boundaries.

of UWOs could lead to the inadvertent breach of the right not to incriminate oneself. Through the analysis of its jurisprudence, the viewpoint of the European Court of Human Rights is explored and evaluated. **Chapter 4** focuses specifically on money laundering, a crucial area of overlap between financial crime and organised crime. The author, Dr Susan Clark Garnett, begins by attempting to define the term 'money laundering', adopting a transnational approach and considering efforts to prevent money laundering at international level. The chapter then moves on to provide a detailed analysis of nuances applicable to anti-money laundering (AML) efforts in the context of the Vatican, offering insight into whether the new AML regime will be successful in preserving the Vatican's position as the financial centre of the Roman Catholic Church.

Chapter 5, by Charlie Robson and Professor Nicholas Ryder, provides a critical assessment of the UK counterterrorist financing reporting regime, focusing specifically on the role of public-private financial information sharing. Robson and Ryder identify a number of key weaknesses in the current system, pointing to the excessive number of terrorism financing reports being filed and a subsequent lowering of the quality of financial intelligence, which dilutes its effectiveness. Nonetheless, they remain cautiously optimistic for the future. **Chapter 6**, by Dr Rikard Jalkebro and Dr William Vlcek, interrogates the future of criminal finance with a consideration of high denomination currency (specifically 500 euro notes) and the emergence of the cashless society. Tying the discourse of 'criminal' money with terrorist finance produced the term 'bin Ladens' for the high denomination euro note. At the same time, the application of this term as a pejorative isolates the use of currency and particularly these high denomination notes. Proponents of a cashless society reinforce this pejorative connotation against currency when emphasising the anti-crime benefits from the elimination of anonymous cash. The chapter considers the perceived benefits of a cashless society and questions whether it will truly limit criminal finance or simply stimulate new avenues for criminality, using Sweden as a case study to further the analysis. Continuing the focus on currency, **Chapter 7**, by Dr Ilias Kapsis, critically reviews the issue of criminality related to crypto-assets focusing in particular on crimes related to money laundering and terrorism financing. The chapter discusses the extent of crypto-asset involvement in money laundering and terrorist financing and the sources of such criminality. It then proceeds to a critical review of the revised Financial Action Task Force framework, which incorporated crypto-assets into the scope of anti-money laundering/counterterrorist financing rules. Finally, the chapter evaluates the impact of the proposed framework on the development of crypto-assets.

Chapter 8, by Dr Kate Tudor, digs more deeply into the drivers of harmful and criminal corporate practices, applying a criminological focus to analyse fraud in the context of the neoliberal state. Focusing on the perpetrators of high yield fraudulent investment (Ponzi) schemes, Tudor considers the criminogenic nature of modern neoliberal economies, pointing to a landscape in which criminal, semilicit, and 'harmful but legal' actions carried out by the powerful are not simply tolerated, but frequently rewarded. In **Chapter 9**, Dr Lucy Evans offers a unique insight into representations of white collar crime in the Caribbean. This chapter considers longstanding definitions of white-collar crime and considers how it is depicted in film and fiction. The chapter considers how such depictions influence the way in which society perceives white collar crime, with a particular focus on the Caribbean.

Chapter 10, by Oliver Charles and Professor Umut Turksen, presents an analysis of deferred prosecution agreements (DPAs) in the fight against corporate financial crime. Using the case studies of France, the USA, and the UK, the authors reach the (perhaps unsurprising) conclusion that when it comes to wealthier corporations, the punishments do not necessarily fit the crimes. Crucially, they note that DPAs are unable to address key drivers of corporate wrongdoing, including issues around accountability, ethical behaviour, and corporate governance. **Chapter 11**, by Professor Nicholas Ryder, Dr Samantha Bourton, and Demelza Hall, closes the book by taking a UK-focused approach to organised crime, exploring money laundering and UK policy.

The editors hope that this collection sparks further interdisciplinary discussion and collaboration on these vital topics.

1 Italy's other 'other mafia'

Remediation and representations of the 'ndrangheta

Amber Phillips[1]

Introduction

It is generally agreed that public perceptions of organised crime are profoundly impacted by the mass media and popular culture and that cultural representations play a major role in constructing dominant narratives.[2] Furthermore, many scholars have observed that fictional representations of organised crime have helped shape the policies of governments and law enforcement agencies.[3] Woodiwiss, for example, points to the impact of the 'mythology' of the Italian-American mafia on organised crime control policy in the United States and internationally.[4] The Italian-American mafia has certainly cast a long shadow in this regard; Smith notes the implicit racism of many media representations of organised crime, highlighting their frequent recourse to ethnic descriptors in the portrayal of a dangerous 'other'.[5] This reflects the so-called 'alien conspiracy' myth, the nefarious and lingering perception that organised crime is 'not a part of society and shaped by society itself, but is instead a problem of "outsiders" that threaten society'.[6] The Italian-American mafia is the archetype for this myth; in the 1950s, televised Senate hearings helped to propagate the idea that organised crime in the USA was in the grip of a foreign criminal conspiracy originating in Sicily. The dominance of the alien conspiracy narrative in the USA began to recede in the 1980s,

1 Senior Lecturer in Criminology, University of the West of England. All translations from Italian are my own, unless otherwise specified.

2 Patricia Rawlinson, 'Organized Crime Mythologies' in H. N. Pontell (ed.), *Oxford Research Encyclopaedia of Criminology and Criminal Justice* (OUP 2016) 6.

3 William Chambliss and Elizabeth Williams, 'Transnational Organized Crime and Social Sciences Myths' in Felia Allum and Stan Gilmour (eds.), *Routledge Handbook of Transnational Organised Crime* (Routledge 2015).

4 Michael Woodiwiss, 'The Past and Present of Transnational Organised Crime in America' in Allum and Gilmour (eds.) *Routledge Handbook of Transnational Organised Crime* (Routledge 2015).

5 Dwight C. Smith, 'Wickersham to Sutherland to Katzenbach: Evolving an "official" definition for organized crime' (1991) *Crime, Law, and Social Change*, 16, 135–54.

6 Edward Kleemans, 'Theoretical Perspectives on Organized Crime' in Letizia Paoli (ed.) *The Oxford Handbook of Organized Crime* (OUP 2014) 1.

DOI: 10.4324/9781003020813-2

but the tendency to categorise organised crime through ethnicity and to concentrate the blame on 'outsider' groups rather than confront wider social causes has proved enduring.[7]

This chapter applies the alien conspiracy perspective to the Italian context, using it as a lens through which to explore the representation of one particular mafia. The term 'alien' must clearly be reinterpreted somewhat for this purpose – the emphasis shifting from the explicitly 'foreign' to the 'other' – but the core concept of designating organised criminal groups as a phenomenon consisting of 'outsiders', ethnically distinct from the majority, remains highly applicable. The focus of the analysis is the 'ndrangheta, the mafia organisation native to the region of Calabria, which for most of its history has been underestimated 'strategically, politically, financially, internationally, and culturally'.[8] I argue that an awareness of the 'otherness' of Calabria and its people within the Italian cultural imagination has impacted the portrayal of the 'ndrangheta in key cultural representations produced by Calabrians, with a distorting effect. In this chapter, I identify two key tendencies: the first seeks to 'reclaim' the 'ndrangheta's past, minimising its negative traits in the process of 'defending' the region from negative characterisation or externally imposed stereotypes. I have termed this phenomenon *calabresismo*, mirroring the Sicilian cultural and political movement *sicilianismo*.[9] The second, more unusual, approach is to reject the mafia itself as a foreign entity within the region; this will form the focus of this chapter. Throughout, I insist on the importance of appreciating the specificity of the Calabrian context.

The significance of cultural products should not be underestimated, particularly given their capacity to both reflect and influence discourses and their substantial role in shaping perceptions of the mafias in the cultural imaginary. Indeed, Mete suggests that one of the key battlegrounds for tackling the mafias lies in the cultural sphere, identifying a 'social imagination which glorifies the mafia by distorting the reality',[10] to which cultural representations from a range of media are primary contributors. Just as in the case of the US mafia, Italian cultural production surrounding organised crime has contributed to a highly complex network of representation and reality, within which the border between fact and fiction is highly porous. The history of Italy's mafias is filled with cultural representations that have been both produced and consumed by *mafiosi* themselves;

7 Rawlinson (n 2).

8 Anna Sergi and Anita Lavorgna, *Ndrangheta: The Glocal Dimensions of the Most Powerful Italian Mafia* (Palgrave Macmillan 2016) 2.

9 Amber Phillips, 'Corrado Alvaro and the Calabrian Mafia: A critical case study of the use of literary and journalistic texts in research on Italian organized crime' (2017) *Trends in Organized Crime,* 20(1–2), 179–95.

10 Vittorio Mete, 'Quali politiche contro quali mafie. Una proposta di classificazione delle politiche antimafia' Paper presented at the XXIV Conference of the Società Italiana di Scienza Politica, Venice, 16–18 September 2010, 3.

Dickie identifies a 'strange feedback loop which is as old as the organisations themselves',[11] while Ravveduto[12] describes the effect of a 'hall of mirrors',[13] with representations from multiple media sources intersecting, overlapping and interacting to reinforce stereotypes in a 'vortex in which reality and fiction participate equally in the creation of a sole image'.[14]

This chapter will consider this 'feedback loop' or 'hall of mirrors' through the lens of cultural memory, exploring processes of remediation in cultural representations of the 'ndrangheta's past. Given the tendency within criminology to focus on screen representations of the mafias, my analysis focuses instead on literary representations; a field that, to date, has largely been the preserve of Italianists and historians.[15] Even then, scholarly work devoted to representations of the 'ndrangheta remains scarce, although this is more of a reflection of Calabria's marginality rather than the corpus of available material.[16] My analysis is influenced by the work of Birgit Neumann, who insists on the active role of literature and, in particular, the novel, in reflecting and influencing cultural memory.[17] Neumann observes that 'fictions of memory may symbolically empower the culturally marginalised or forgotten and thus figure into an imaginative counter discourse'; a phenomenon that is highly applicable to Calabria, as illustrated below.[18] In examining fictional constructions of the 'ndrangheta's past, I draw on Erll's definitions of the terms 'remediation' and 'premediation'.[19] In terms of the former, Erll notes that what is known about a 'site of memory' – a memorable event – 'seems to refer not so much to what one might cautiously call the "actual events" but instead to a canon of existent medial constructions, to the narratives and images circulating in a media culture.'[20] Premediation, meanwhile, 'draws attention to the fact that existent media which circulate in a given society provide schemata for future experience and its representation': in short, 'depictions of earlier, yet somehow comparable events shape our understanding of later events'.[21] Evidently, the Calabrian mafia is not in itself a 'memorable event', but a constant and evolving phenomenon.

11 John Dickie, 'Historicizing Italy's Other Mafias: Some considerations' in 'Italy's Other Mafias in Italian Film and Television: A roundtable' (2013) *The Italianist* 33 (2) 201–203.

12 Marcello Ravveduto, *Lo spettacolo della mafia: Storia di un immaginario tra realtà e finzione* (Kindle edn., Edizioni Gruppo Abele 2019).

13 Ibid. ch 9, para 2.

14 Ibid. ch 9, para 3.

15 See, for example, Robin Pickering-Iazzi *Mafia and Outlaw Stories from Italian Life and Literature* (University of Toronto Press 2007); Ravveduto (n 12).

16 See Pasquino Crupi, *L'anomalia selvaggia: camorra, piciotteria e 'ndrangheta nella letteratura calabrese del novecento* (Sellerio 1992) and Phillips (n 9).

17 Birgit Neumann, 'The Literary Representation of Memory' in Astrid Erll and Ansgar Nunning (eds.) *A Companion to Cultural Memory Studies* (De Gruyter 2010).

18 Ibid. p. 341.

19 Astrid Erll, 'Literature, Film, and the Mediality of Cultural Memory' in Erll and Nunning (n 17).

20 Ibid. 392.

21 Ibid. 392–3.

Nonetheless, the concept is applicable to the ways in which individual cultural products are both premediated by existent media and discourses and themselves remediated (and, in the process, altered) in subsequent representations. This can be applied to individual cultural products – which may have been echoed and distorted in a range of subsequent media[22] – and to the remediation of specific events in the mafia's history, which can be reframed to take on new meaning.

Historical background

It is first necessary to clarify the precise meaning of the word 'mafia': a criminal organisation that, beyond its criminal activities, also seeks to provide extra-legal governance through territorial control.[23] As well as being able to infiltrate legitimate businesses and politics, such groups possess the ability to accumulate and employ social capital[24] and are, to a greater or lesser extent, tolerated by their host communities. These elements of control and consensus are of particular interest in the study of cultural production, since as Dickie notes, Italy's mafias gain consensus via directly and indirectly shaping the way in which they are represented.[25] A key element of this process is the alignment of the mafia group with the culture and traditions of the host community. As Truzzolillo observes, 'the interweaving of criminality and popular values has important implications, in terms of disguise and legitimisation, for the actual development of the criminal organisation, irrespective of whether or not this is a mythical representation'.[26] Cultural representations can reflect and reinforce this process of legitimisation, as a growing body of research has sought to explore; see, for example, Castagna's analysis of the popularity of traditional Calabrian songs featuring the 'ndrangheta.[27]

A number of mafia groups are currently active in Italy, but academic and public attention have typically gravitated towards a 'big three', comprising the Sicilian mafia, the *camorra* (associated with the region of Campania), and the 'ndrangheta, native to Calabria. While each can trace its origins to roughly around the mid-nineteenth century and each can be labelled a 'mafia' according to the criteria outlined above, the three are separate, distinct organisations each with its own characteristics and peculiarities. Of the three, the Sicilian mafia is undoubtedly the most famous, and it has produced the most substantial cultural footprint

22 Phillips (n 9).

23 Federico Varese, *Mafias on the Move: How Organized Crime Conquers New Territories* (Princeton 2011) 6.

24 Rocco Sciarrone, 'Mafie, relazioni e affari nell'area grigia' in Rocco Sciarrone (ed.) *Alleanza nell'ombra. Mafie ed economie locali in Sicilia e nel Mezzogiorno* (Donzelli 2011).

25 Dickie (n 11) 201.

26 Fabio Truzzolillo, 'The 'Ndrangheta: The current state of historical research' (2011) 13(3) *Modern Italy* 369.

27 Ettore Castagna, *Sangue e onore in digitale. Rappresentazione e autorappresentazione della 'ndrangheta* (Rubbettino 2010). See also R. Dainotto, *The Mafia: A Cultural History* (Reaktion 2015).

both within Italy and abroad. The Camorra, meanwhile, has begun to catch up: described as the 'other mafia' in reference to the traditional dominance of Cosa Nostra in the Italian and international public imagination, Campania's mafia now has a much more firmly established, distinct identity in the public consciousness, thanks partly to the huge success of Roberto Saviano's book *Gomorra* (2006) and the subsequent film and TV adaptations.[28]

The 'ndrangheta, meanwhile, might be described as Italy's other 'other' mafia: for most of its history, it has been neglected by government and media alike. The name *'ndrangheta* itself only came into widespread use in the 1950s, and for much of its history there was no public discussion of organised crime specific to Calabria.[29] Indeed, Italian authorities have been painfully slow to acknowledge the 'ndrangheta's existence as an entity in its own right: it was only officially recognised under Italian law in 2010.[30] Likewise, for a long time the wider world failed to take notice until the Duisburg massacre in 2007, when the murder in Germany of six men of Calabrian descent provoked a storm of national and international media interest in the organisation.[31] When one considers the context of the 'ndrangheta's native region, its relative marginality and anonymity becomes less surprising. Calabria has always been among Italy's poorest regions, and it lacks the geopolitical significance of Sicily or Campania; its population is also much smaller, at 1.96 million compared to Sicily's 5 million inhabitants.[32] Overall, Calabria's standing in the Italian public imaginary has historically been fractured, 'weak and evanescent', characterised by backwardness and 'otherness'.[33]

While Calabria's regional identity is substantially less well defined than that of Sicily in Italy's national consciousness, it shares the negative characterisation typically attributed to the south. Counterreformation missionaries described Calabria as being populated by 'savages',[34] while 18th-century 'grand tourists' for the most

28 Giulio Bogani et al., 'Le mafi rappresentate: a dieci anni di Gomorra' (2016), *Passato e presente,* 98, 19–53, 20.

29 Truzzolillo (n 26) 364.

30 The word "'ndrangheta" was added to Article 416-*bis* of the Italian Criminal Code (Legislative Decree modified from Law No. 50, 31 March 2010, in *Gazzetta Ufficiale* 30 March 2010, No. 78).

31 In summer 2007, six men of Calabrian origin were murdered outside an Italian restaurant in the German town of Duisburg in an attack motivated by an 'ndrangheta feud. The scale of the massacre was unprecedented outside Italy and attracted a wave of international media attention and interest in Calabrian organised crime. See, for example, S. Holmes, 'A Mafia Family Feud Spills Over' (BBC News, 16 August 2007), http://news.bbc.co.uk/1/hi/world/europe/6949274.stm, accessed 26 January 2021.

32 European Commission, 'Calabria' (Regional Innovation Monitor Plus, 2020), https://ec.europa.eu/growth/ tools-databases/regional-innovation-monitor/base-profile/calabria#:~:text=Calabria%20is%20one%20of% 20the,million%20(Eurostat%2C%202020), accessed 27 January 2021.

33 Castagna (n 27) 20.

34 Peter D'Agostino, 'Craniums, Criminals, and the "Cursed Race": Italian anthropology in American racial thought, 1861–1924' (2002) *Comparative Studies in Society and History,* 44(2), 319.

part steered well clear of its mountainous terrain and its reputation for banditry and extreme poverty. Through the work of the famous 19th-century criminologist Cesare Lombroso,[35] the negative stereotypes associated with Calabria were racialised, and the region gained a name as a land of 'atavistic criminals who had prematurely disembarked from the train of evolution'.[36] While Lombroso's biological positivism has long since been discredited, the negative associations linked with Calabria have proved enduring; as evidenced by a now infamous Wikileaks cable in which an American official in 2008 declared that 'Calabrians have a reputation as a distant, difficult people' and that this 'most problematical' region would be a 'failed state' were it not part of Italy.[37]

This marginality helps to explain the historic tendency among the media, public, government, and academics alike to fail to appreciate the specificity of Calabria's mafia and to approach it simply as an 'add-on' to the Sicilian phenomenon. It is certainly the case that the two mafias share some similarities: taking Catino's approach to organisational structure, for example, the Camorra has a 'horizontal' organisational order,[38] formed of individual groups often acting in direct competition with one another.[39] The Sicilian mafia and the 'ndrangheta, meanwhile, can be described as having a 'vertical' organisational order, with a level of centralised power and systemic decision-making processes.[40] Other similarities can also be observed between the 'ndrangheta and the Sicilian mafia: Paoli, for example, notes that both are sworn secret societies and both draw on ritual practices to help develop internal cohesion.[41]

A key difference, however, lies in the fact that the 'ndrangheta is now widely considered to be the most powerful mafia organisation in Italy.[42] Its wealth is also believed to be unmatched; it has been widely reported in the media that its turnover in 2013 amounted to a staggering 53 billion euros, although, as Mete has observed, such figures should be treated with caution.[43] At first, it might appear to be a curious paradox that Italy's wealthiest and most powerful mafia should also be its least famous. However, it is precisely this anonymity that has

35 Prior to beginning his career as a criminal anthropologist, Lombroso served as a volunteer army doctor in a campaign against brigands in Calabria.

36 Ibid.

37 Embassy Naples, 'Can Calabria Be Saved?' Wikileaks Cable: 08NAPLES96_a. Dated 2 December 2008, https://wikileaks.org/plusd/cables/08NAPLES96_a.html, accessed 26 January 2021.

38 Maurizio Catino, 'How Do Mafias Organize? Conflict and violence in three mafia organizations' (2014) *European Journal of Sociology* 55 177.

39 Felia Allum, *The Invisible Camorra: Neapolitan Crime Families Across Europe* (Cornell University Press 2016).

40 Catino (n 38) 182.

41 Letizia Paoli, *Mafia Brotherhoods* (OUP 2003).

42 See Ercole Giap Parini, 'The Strongest Mafia: 'Ndrangheta made in Calabria' in Andrea Mammone and Giuseppe Veltri (eds.), *Italy Today: The Sick Man of Europe* (Routledge 2010); Sergi and Lavorgna (n 8).

43 Mete (n 10) 3.

allowed Calabria's mafia to thrive; while the focus of law enforcement was trained on Sicily in the 1980s and 1990s, the 'ndrangheta was able to quietly capitalise on the ensuing weakness within the Sicilian mafia, overtaking the latter and growing increasingly dominant in Europe's drug trade (to the extent that it now occupies a dominant position in the European cocaine market).[44] A further manifestation of the 'ndrangheta's power lies in its unparalleled success in setting up operations abroad; 'ndrangheta clans are currently operating all over the world, including in Canada, the USA, Australia, Colombia, Switzerland, and Germany.[45]

Structurally, the organisation is complex and sophisticated. It should be noted that the 'ndrangheta has produced significantly fewer *pentiti* (defectors who collaborate with the authorities) than Italy's other mafias. A key reason for this is the fact that, unlike the Sicilian mafia, the 'ndrangheta actively capitalises on family relationships to reinforce its structure; this reduces the likelihood that affiliates will breach *omertà*, since to do so would involve betraying one's own family.[46] The extent to which the 'ndrangheta can be referred to as a single organisation is disputed; Sergi and Lavorgna reject the conception of the Calabrian mafia as a monolithic organisation, arguing instead that it should be understood as a more fragmented phenomenon.[47] While accepting the existence of some centralised coordination structures, Sergi and Lavorgna view the 'ndrangheta as a 'behavioural model', strongly linked to the 'manipulation of traditions, rituals, and social practices of communication and leadership among Calabrian individuals'.[48] The 'ndrangheta is, in other words, a phenomenon that combines cultural *and* structural elements in order to prosper. Emphasis on either cultural or structural factors has been a key feature of the academic debate on the mafias in Italy and is of direct relevance to the construction of the 'ndrangheta in the public imagination, as I will outline below.

The 'ndrangheta and culturalism

Beyond the marginality of its native region, the historic failure of the Italian state to recognise the scale of the threat posed by the 'ndrangheta is linked inextricably to wider debates and discourses surrounding the mafias in Italy. As noted already, Italy's government, academics, public, and media were for a long time focused primarily on Sicily, with little attention paid to the specificity of Calabrian organised crime. Broadly speaking, academic debate on the mafias was historically dominated by two schools of thought. The first, which prevailed until the early

44 Francesco Calderoni, 'The Structure of Drug Trafficking Mafias: The 'ndrangheta and cocaine' (2012) *Crime Law Social Change* 58, 321.

45 Europol, 'Threat Assessment: Italian organised crime' (June 2013), https://www.europol.europa.eu/ publications-documents/threat-assessment-italian-organised-crime, accessed 27 January 2021.

46 Varese (n 23) 33.

47 Sergi and Lavorgna (n 8) 3.

48 Ibid.

1980s, viewed Italy's mafias as a set of cultural attitudes and behaviours typical to the southern regions and denied the existence of organised, structured criminal groups. These 'culturalists'[49] included foreign researchers who came to Sicily to conduct fieldwork in the 1960s and 1970s[50] and Italian sociologist Pino Arlacchi, who authored an influential work in 1983 examining the so-called 'traditional mafia' of both Sicily and Calabria.[51]

Following the extensive and widely publicised judicial investigations into the Sicilian mafia in the 1980s – which revealed the structured, sophisticated nature of the organisation's activities – the culturalist position was no longer tenable and the second school of thought thus emerged; academic focus shifted to the organisation's entrepreneurial activities.[52] This more economically centred approach turned its attention to the structural conditions and operations of mafias as business actors.

To some extent, Arlacchi's 1983 book combined the two, by distinguishing between a 'traditional mafia' (individuals manifesting traditional cultural attitudes and behaviours) and an 'entrepreneurial mafia' (a more economically driven mafia phenomenon that supposedly developed alongside the economic boom of the 1960s).

The reason that these perspectives on the mafia are important is clear: the way in which a phenomenon is conceptualised by the public, academics, and the media is inextricably linked to the way in which it is conceptualised by policymakers and by those charged with tackling the mafias. Put simply: the way we understand it affects the way we choose to fight it. For example, if the mafias are interpreted as a cultural phenomenon, the state will invest more resources into educational policies, while if the strength of the mafias is understood to lie in their financial resources, repressive measures such as confiscation orders are more likely to be prioritised.[53] Thus, since the Calabrian mafia was conceptualised for much of its history as an underdeveloped, disorganised phenomenon, a violent product of a poverty-stricken region and its culture, it is unsurprising that the 'ndrangheta was for so long missing from Italy's statute books.

Evidently, neither the culturalist nor the structuralist school of thought is unproblematic. The old culturalist position was always in fact a fallacy: Lupo points out that were mafias simply a manifestation of traditional culture, they would be ubiquitous across the south, rather than being found concentrated in specific areas.[54] Furthermore, evidence firmly demonstrates the existence of

49 Paoli (n 41) 15.

50 See Henner Hess, *Mafia and Mafiosi: The Structure of Power* (Saxon House 1973); Jane Schneider and Peter Schneider, *Culture and Political Economy in Western Sicily* (Academic Press 1976).

51 Pino Arlacchi, *La mafia imprenditrice. L'etica mafiosa e lo spirit del capitalismo* (Mulino 1983).

52 Paoli (n 41) 15.

53 Mete (n 10) 5.

54 Salvatore Lupo, *Storia della mafia* (Donzelli 1993) 22.

organised criminal groups in both Sicily and Calabria at least as far back as the late 19th century, firmly countering the culturalist insistence on the absence of formal structures.[55] Meanwhile, Paoli is critical of an overly structural approach, pointing to the crucial significance of cultural codes and norms to the internal cohesion of mafia groups.[56] More recently, scholars have called for a more nuanced and holistic approach to the understanding of the mafia phenomenon, with a focus on its complexity. Mete argues that the mafias are 'formed of a web of economic, entrepreneurial, political, relational and cultural aspects, all underscored by a constant physical and psychological threat'.[57] With specific regard to the 'ndrangheta, Sergi and Lavorgna have argued that it fits neither the culturalist nor the structuralist perspective; deeply entrenched in Calabrian culture, yet also inextricably linked to Calabria's structural political and economic weaknesses.[58]

Despite these advances in the understanding of the mafias, the culturalist perspective, and in particular the trope of a 'traditional mafia' contrasting with a modern, 'entrepreneurial' mafia, has proved particularly tenacious and cultural representations hold part of the key to understanding why. The roots of the culturalist perspective can to a large extent be traced back to a 19th-century cultural and political movement known as *Sicilianismo*, which evolved in response to concerns among the island's elites that Sicily was becoming a byword for criminality in the national public imagination. This must be located within the wider context of Italy's 'southern question', which cannot be addressed satisfactorily within this chapter; suffice it to note that since Italy's unification, the south has been associated with images of 'otherness', lawlessness, and savagery.[59] In response to negative press coverage and public opinion, the *Sicilianisti* maintained that the mafia was a particular attitude developed in response to Sicily's history of colonisation and oppression; it was a set of cultural values, not a criminal organisation. Although this was untrue, the significant and long-lasting impact of *Sicilianismo* as a cultural and political movement on the academic and public understanding of the mafia is highly indicative of the porosity of the border between fact and fiction, a working illustration of the 'hall of mirrors'.

The links between the culturalist perspective and cultural representations are sometimes surprisingly direct. Arlacchi's influential 1983 work, which differentiated between a 'traditional mafia' and an 'entrepreneurial mafia' in Calabria and Sicily, is notable for its frequent recourse to Calabrian cultural products, particularly novels, which the author uses to shore up the argument that the pre-1960s Calabrian mafia was a strictly cultural phenomenon. This is an example of the

55 See Paoli (n 40); John Dickie, *Mafia Brotherhoods* (London: Sceptre, 2012); Truzzolillo (n 26).
56 Paoli (n 41) 22.
57 Mete (n 10) 3.
58 Sergi and Lavorgna (n 8) 17.
59 Enrico Dal Lago, 'Italian Unification and the Mezzogiorno: Colonialism in one country?' in Enrico Dal Lago and Róisín Healy (eds.), *The Shadow of Colonialism on Europe's Modern Past* (Palgrave Macmillan 2014).

'feedback loop' in action: fictional narratives are absorbed directly into the historiography of the mafia (although it should be noted that Arlacchi is selective in the fictional narratives he chooses, excluding those that contradict his thesis).[60] I have argued that there is a visible tendency within Calabrian cultural production to resist negative stereotyping and 'othering' by presenting a benign, fictionalised construction of the 'ndrangheta's past, in a phenomenon that can be termed 'calabresismo'.[61] A key example is the work of Corrado Alvaro, a celebrated Calabrian author and journalist who, writing in the 1950s, actively minimised the negative traits of the 'traditional' mafia, working to develop a cultural memory that disconnected the negative aspects of the 'ndrangheta from the culture and identity of the region.[62] To Alvaro, the 'enemy' was the outside influences that distorted the 'ndrangheta: consumerism and 'gangster' culture imported from America, while the 'old' mafia stood for traditional values.

This element of nostalgia is a recurring motif in representations of the Calabrian mafia across other media; Castagna has observed a similar phenomenon in the images of the 'ndrangheta contained within Calabrian traditional popular songs (*canzonette*), with an emphasis on what he terms 'the good mafia of long ago'.[63] Stressing the significance of the oral tradition to the development of the 'ndrangheta and perceptions of it, Castagna observes that 'still today there remains a widespread, nostalgic popular perception, particularly in those over the age of 70: the old mafia of the "traditional" world was "good", "it kept order", while the new mafia is a different thing, it became corrupted over time.'[64] Castagna also identifies that journalists and academics have tended to uncritically interpret the material from these songs as an 'authentic' representation of the 'ndrangheta's past, irrespective of the truth; this clearly illustrates the tendency of receivers from differing spheres to remediate fictional or stylised narratives, interpreting them as 'authentic' portrayals of the mafia's past. As Erll observes, this process 'tends to solidify cultural memory, creating and stabilising certain narratives and icons of the past'.[65]

A key element of the reworking of the past in these cultural representations of the 'ndrangheta lies in their blending of fact and fiction, which sees real episodes from history mixed into the narrative and remediated; Alvaro, for example, blends recorded history with imagination in his journalism.[66] This practice is also

60 Amber Phillips, '"Old Mafia" and "New Mafia" in the Novels of Saverio Strati, 1957–1977' [2020] 12 (2) *New Readings*, https://newreadings.cardiffuniversitypress.org/articles/abstract/10.18573/newreadings.115/, accessed 27 January 2021.

61 Phillips (n 9).

62 See Corrado Alvaro, 'I briganti', *Corriere della Sera* (18 May 1955) 3; and Corrado Alvaro, 'La fibbia', *Corriere della Sera* (17 September 1955) 3.

63 Castagna (n 27) 31.

64 Ibid.

65 Erll (n 19) 393.

66 Phillips (n 9).

replicated in the most successful recent Calabrian novel to feature the 'ndrangheta, as I illustrate below.

Reclaiming the narrative: *Anime nere*

Given that for most of its existence, the 'ndrangheta has existed outside the national and international media spotlight, it is of no surprise that Calabria's mafia is yet to star in a work of comparable international acclaim to *The Godfather* or *Gomorra*. However, representations of the organisation are gradually growing more numerous as awareness of its existence and activities increases outside its home region, particularly in the wake of the Duisburg massacre. The number of books published about the 'ndrangheta has increased cumulatively with each passing decade,[67] and with the release in 2014 of the internationally successful film *Anime nere* – arguably the most popular and widely diffused representation of Calabrian organised crime ever to be produced – the landscape of representation is evolving rapidly. The film, set and shot predominantly in Calabria, with actors speaking largely in dialect, has been distributed in over 20 countries and has won numerous awards. Its depiction of Calabrian criminality has led it to be described and interpreted by many Italian critics as the first ever 'ndrangheta movie, and while this is not technically true, it is certainly the most celebrated.[68]

The film is based on the eponymous novel by Gioacchino Criaco, published in 2008. Criaco was born in Calabria in 1965 but moved to Milan after qualifying as a lawyer. The 'ndrangheta is an inescapable element of his family history: the author's father, Domenico, was killed in a bloody feud in 1993, and his brother Pietro is a convicted *'ndranghetista*, captured in December 2008 after years spent as one of Italy's most wanted criminals. The author's birthplace, Africo, also has its own connections with the Calabrian mafia – and indeed, serves as a key setting within the novel, although it is never named explicitly.

These connections are worth briefly exploring in more detail here, given the novel's borrowing of elements of Africo's past. In fact, there are two Africos: one nestles high in the Aspromonte, the mountain massif that dominates Calabria's southernmost province. Literally translated as 'harsh mountain', the area has long held a place of infamy and notoriety in the Italian public imagination and to most is known chiefly for two things: extreme poverty and crime. In the 1970s and 1980s, the Aspromonte gained a particular place in the Italian national consciousness for its association with the so-called 'kidnapping season', a particularly dark period in the nation's history that saw hundreds of victims taken hostage – many hidden away in the impenetrable mountain villages – and held to ransom.[69] These

67 Dickie (n 11); Bogani et al. (n 28).

68 There have been several attempts to portray the 'ndrangheta on the silver screen, but none has enjoyed popular success. Notable examples include Elio Ruffo's *Una rete piena di sabia* (1967), Paolo Pecora's *Faida* (1988) and Carlo Carlei's *La corsa dell'innocente* (1992).

69 High profile victims of this wave of kidnappings included John Paul Getty III, abducted in 1973 in Rome and released after the payment of a substantial ransom.

kidnappings became a key source of income for the 'ndrangheta[70] and brought national focus on to Calabria's mafia, normally excluded from the news.[71] Africo itself was particularly notorious for the extreme poverty suffered by its inhabitants, and it featured in several early 20th-century campaigns against poverty in the south.[72] In 1951, however, the village was partially destroyed by a terrible flood, and the residents were displaced to a new settlement – also named Africo – located several miles downhill on the Ionian coast, after 12 years of living in temporary structures. The process of resettlement was a fiasco, and the former inhabitants of the mountain village found themselves severed from a way of life that had been pursued in the village for centuries. The village – both the semi-abandoned mountain Africo and the coastal settlement – thus occupy a position of unusual prominence within the Italian national public imagination.

Anime nere was Criaco's first novel, written over the course of just four days. The author has since written two further novels which deal with the 'ndrangheta – *Zefira* (2009) and *American Taste* (2011) – and these titles join a small but burgeoning subgenre of fictional literature, both Calabrian and otherwise, to feature the 'ndrangheta in recent years, particularly in the wake of Duisburg. None of these texts, however, has matched the success of *Anime nere*; Criaco's bestseller was published in a second edition in 2014, to coincide with the release of the film, and has also been translated into French, German, and English. It features three core male protagonists: the narrator (who remains nameless until the very end of the text) and his friends Luciano and Luigi. Our introduction to the trio occurs in the 1970s when they are still teenagers, living between the semi-abandoned 'old' Africo, and 'Africo Nuovo', the settlement built to replace it. The boys live in poverty and begin stealing to buy themselves schoolbooks and better clothes. Meanwhile, the so-called 'kidnapping season' in the Aspromonte is at its height, and the narrator's father, concerned by his son's crimes, agrees to shelter kidnapping victims for the mafia in order to bring in some extra money. The three boys, however, are set on pursuing their criminal ambitions, and the text follows them to 1980s' Milan, where they build themselves a small empire on the back of international heroin and cocaine trafficking. With the dawn of the 1990s, as their enemies multiply and the crackdown on organised crime sets in, their Milanese empire crumbles, and the narrator and Luciano find themselves in prison. On their release, they return home to Africo to enact their final revenge against the local mafia boss, Don Peppino Zacco, who (it is gradually revealed) arranged for the murder of Luciano's father decades earlier, as well as the brutal killing of the narrator's father and a number of their friends.

70 John Dickie, *Mafia Republic* (Sceptre 2013).

71 Ravveduto (n 12).

72 In 1910, Africo was the subject of a campaign against southern poverty led by social activist Umberto Zanotti Bianco, while in 1948, journalist Tommaso Besozzi described it in *L'Europeo* as an 'emblem of desperation'.

While *Anime nere* is undoubtedly a novel about organised criminality, the sympathetic protagonists are not *'ndranghetisti*, and instead exist in a constant uneasy, hostile co-existence with the mafia, which eventually develops into all-out war. Within the text, the mafia is represented as an antagonistic 'other', its foreignness contrasted with the values and beliefs of the protagonists. This is emphasised through the names used by the narrator; in place of the words 'ndrangheta or *'ndranghetisti*, a range of (often pejorative) terms are used, including *pungiuti* (literally, 'the pricked' or 'blood brothers') and *bruciatori di Santini* (saint-burners), both of which refer to the 'ndrangheta's macabre initiation ritual.[73] The protagonists, meanwhile, along with the generation of young Calabrian criminals like them, are identified variously as 'children of shepherds', 'children of the forest', and 'dark souls'. Significantly, the former two terms delineate the strong ancestral claim of these individuals to the land, a claim that is portrayed as more legitimate than that of the detested *mafiosi*, as I will go on to explore.

In spite of their crimes, Criaco's narrative repeatedly and firmly casts the children of the forest as morally superior to the *mafiosi*. The model for their lifestyle and ambitions, the 'greatest dark soul, who struck terror into the *mafiosi*',[74] is the character of Sante Motta, the narrator's older cousin and illegitimate son of a *capomafia*. Barred from becoming an affiliate of the mafia as a result of his illegitimacy, Motta's father urges him to steer clear of *mafiosi* at all costs; he condemns them as liars and traitors, describing them as a 'cancer' on the land.[75] Sante thus forges his own path, making a fortune for himself through drug trafficking in the north. He is idolised by the narrator and his friends and draws them more deeply into the criminal lifestyle, giving them a taste of the wealth to be made in Milan. He also, crucially, encourages and empowers the boys to distance themselves from the hypocritical *mafiosi*, pointing out that while the *pungiuti* grow wealthy, the unfortunate shepherds who help them end up in prison. Sante is characterised as decent and fair-minded and his murder at the hands of Don Zacco's men leaves the protagonists hungry for revenge. Their close relationship with Sante's widow and son serves to highlight the loyalty and close ties of kinship between the children of the forest, which is contrasted with the cynicism and selfishness of the *pungiuti*.

The portrayal of the children of the forest's moral superiority to the mafia rests substantially on a fictional construction of the latter's history as an alien, colonial entity. The narrator indicates that the mafia was created by 'the immoral Bourbons',[76] who understood that 'to maintain control over the riotous popula-

73 During the 'ndrangheta's initiation ritual, the new affiliate is traditionally cut with a knife and made to bleed on an image of a saint or *santino* (usually Archangel Michael), which is then burned. See Enzo Ciconte, *Riti criminali: I codici di affiliazione alla 'ndrangheta* (Rubbettino 2015).

74 Gioacchino Criaco, *Anime nere* (Rubbettino Editore 2008) 98.

75 Ibid. 23.

76 The Royal House of Bourbon of the Two Sicilies ruled southern Italy from the 18th century up until 1860.

tion, dispersed across hundreds of tiny mountain villages', they would need a system of 'internal control' alongside their military might.[77] This portrayal of the mafia represents a fascinating contrast to the recurring, nostalgia-glazed representation of the 'ndrangheta's past elsewhere as an upholder of traditional values and protector of the people. The mafia in *Anime nere* is cast as a foreign entity, which, *since its inception*, has worked in collusion with the authorities in order to exploit and oppress the native population. Such a portrayal is highly unusual among literary representations of the 'ndrangheta; other Calabrian novelists have certainly criticised the mafia as backward and incompatible with traditional values (see, for example, Saverio Strati's construction of the mafia in his own fictionalised version of old Africo, in the 1957 novel *La teda*).[78] However, the characterisation of the mafia as explicitly foreign is practically unprecedented.

I argue that this characterisation of the mafia represents an attempt to reclaim the positive mythologised elements of the 'ndrangheta's past and transpose them onto a new brand of Calabrian protagonist, embodied by Criaco's children of the forest. This is particularly evident towards the end of *Anime nere*, when the narrator and Luciano return to Africo with their friends to finally take on Don Zacco, launching a 'revolt' against the *mafiosi*. After their victory, Criaco depicts a near-Utopian vision of an alternative to life under the mafia:

> People began to turn to us with all kinds of problems. We helped everyone without asking for anything in return; they were our people. Petty crime ceased; we had more work than the police.[79]

In this description, Criaco has effectively absorbed a number of the tropes often associated with the 'old mafia' or 'traditional mafia' in other representations – specifically, its role in mediating disputes and helping the needy – and claimed them instead for the children of the forest. The use of the term 'revolt' is particularly significant, as the mafia are depicted as an external occupying force, aligned with the authorities and not with the interests of the people: indeed, it is by colluding with the authorities that the *pungiuti* attempt to enact their final revenge on the narrator. Criaco is thus able to retain the moral opposition to the mafia, which is essential to maintaining the sympathy of the contemporary reader and, at the same time, borrow positive aspects from its mythology and folklore, applying these instead to the 'native' or 'true' Calabrians who resist them: the children of the forest.

Throughout the novel, the author insists on the specificity of the geographical, historical, and sociocultural context of the Aspromonte to establish a case for its moral specificity and contextualise (although never explicitly defend) the criminal actions of the protagonists. A key element of this is the impact of the

77 Criaco (n 74).
78 Phillips (n 60).
79 Criaco (n 74) 235.

shared cultural trauma of the relocation of the village following the 1951 flood; an enforced breach with generations of shared history, perpetrated against the people by the state.

The protagonists' heritage and specific cultural identity is worth examining in greater detail here. Despite a good deal of the plot taking place in Milan and the characters' various trips to locations all across Europe, the novel is firmly rooted in a fictionalised, unnamed version of Africo and the mountains that surround it (the Aspromonte). Indeed, the mountain landscape surrounding the ancient village effectively acts as one of the novel's protagonists, with its myths, history, tradition, and folktales driving the plot and serving a cautionary purpose. The oral transmission of folk history is personified in the novel by the character of Bino (an elderly friend of the narrator's father), who according to the narrator, 'represented the historic memory of the mountains'. Through Bino's memories and folktales, the author effectively transmits the shared values of the area's inhabitants and constructs a moral basis for the actions of the protagonists, founded on the values of mutual support and respect for the environment and the community. There is a particular insistence on the importance of man living symbiotically with his surroundings, respecting nature, and never taking more than he needs. In one story, Bino explains that once, the shepherds of the Aspromonte lived in harmony with the wolves; one would attach itself to each flock, occasionally killing one of the weaker animals, but, in return, protecting the whole from other predators. Over time, however, shepherds became possessive and greedy, so the weak and sickly beasts now end up on the tables of 'stupid customers', while the wolves run wild, causing much greater harm.[80]

This mutually beneficial relationship ruined by greed seems to represent an allegory for criminality; in the moral universe occupied by the characters, to take what you need to survive is acceptable, but pushing too far and disrupting the natural balance leads to disaster. When the children of the forest forget their values of mutual assistance or move too far from their roots and grow greedy, their judgment clouded by cocaine, it leads to their downfall. The implication is that the children of the forest have inherited this role from the brigands evoked by Bino in his stories, which have a distinctly Robin Hood-esque sheen; according to Bino, for example, when the '1951 flood' destroyed the village, the brigands did more to feed the poor than did the state. When the army was sent in to disperse the brigands, the latter escaped to the mountains and were sheltered by grateful locals.

Crucially, the successes of the narrator's gang rest on their friendships with other Calabrians and the repayment of old kindnesses: the children of the forest are always strongest when they stay true to their origins and stick together, honouring the tradition of mutual assistance. The text thus occupies a slightly uncomfortable moral position, romanticising the children of the forest's Robin Hood approach to wealth distribution and mutual assistance and the dividends

80 Ibid. 62.

paid by their friendship and loyalty to one another. The debt to the heroic mythology surrounding infamous real brigands, not least Giuseppe Musolino, is clear, even though Musolino is never evoked by name.[81]

The narrator repeatedly states that it is right that he and his colleagues should pay for their crimes, with self-critical reflections (often related specifically to the drug trade). However, the reader is also given the very firm sense that the children of the forest represent a benign alternative to other forms of criminality, for example, the foreign groups that move in to occupy the space left when the narrator's gang lose their grip on Milan. The criminal activity of the children of the forest is contextualised in relation to the greater evils of foreign criminals, the mafia, and the state.

One element that *Anime nere* (2008) shares with previous Calabrian literary representations of organised crime in the region is this firm and repeated emphasis on the detachment of the state from the interests of the people. In the novel, as well as systematically failing the villagers in the aftermath of the flood, the state authorities represent an active antagonist, unscrupulously co-opting the services of the *pungiuti* to repress the children of the forest and end the peace and order that they have imposed. The author is keen to disrupt the reader's perceptions of morality and justice when it comes to Calabrian criminals, with particular regard to the role of the authorities, and he is not afraid to break taboos in the process. As the state-mafia conspiracy to dismantle the children of the forest's Utopia continues, the protagonists enact a desperate scheme of Luciano's devising, kidnapping a local judge, Barresi, and a Piedmontese police official. In an open challenge to the well-established narrative of anti-mafia judges as martyr-like figures, the two captives in the novel are portrayed as part of the ruling classes and firmly out for their own interests.[82] The northern police official is criticised by the characters for his arrogance and his contempt for the people of Calabria[83] and the narrator derides the hypocrisy of the two men, referring to them ironically as 'the two whining heroes'.[84] In Criaco's narrative, the anti-mafia figures are simply another element in a wider mechanism of state oppression against the children of the forest, towards whom we are consistently encouraged to feel sympathy.

Throughout the novel, the narrator demonstrates an awareness of the 'othering' of Calabrians within the Italian public consciousness and the novel appears to seek to regain control of this narrative. When the protagonists find themselves in

81 See Dickie (n 55) 196–209. Giuseppe Musolino (1876–1956) was a bandit who became known as the 'King of the Aspromonte' for his exploits.

82 It should, of course, be noted that the position of anti-mafia figures in the public imagination is far from undisputed (Leonardo Sciascia's notorious 1987 article 'I professionisti dell'antimafia', published in *Corriere della Sera*, comes to mind), but it is relatively safe to say that anti-mafia judges and prosecutors are generally depicted in positive terms in public discourse and that Criaco is actively subverting this as part of his wider goal to undermine audience perceptions of Calabrian criminality.

83 Criaco (n 74) 217.

84 Ibid. 220.

prison in the early 1990s, the narrator comments that: 'The hardship was greatest for prisoners from the South, especially if you were Calabrian.' To judges, prosecutors, and police, Calabrians were 'the scum of humanity, immoral and amoral beasts'.[85] This frustration at the simplistic, prejudiced approach to Calabrian criminality underscores the whole text. The author is keen instead to present a more complex (and substantially more sympathetic) portrait, drawing heavily on the specific social, cultural, and historical context of the Aspromonte. The 'final showdown' of the text further highlights the state's incomprehension of the situation in Calabria, as armed police officers arrive to arrest the narrator and Luciano expecting a dangerous battle, but are confronted instead with two men in their forties quietly drinking coffee with the local policeman. The implication of the scene is clear: the authorities and the public have been misinformed about the true nature of crime in the Aspromonte.

Remediation

Anime nere can be interpreted as an attempt to rewrite the history of Calabrian organised crime by offering a new perspective, a demonstration of Neumann's 'imaginative counter discourse'. As part of this process, Criaco employs and subverts real episodes from history, adapted to fit his own narrative. A striking example of this is the story of the 'salters'. In the novel, the protagonists find themselves on a train with an elderly man, who flees in fear when he learns they are from the village, shouting 'the salters, heaven help us!'[86] The narrator explains that the story involves 'our grandparents back in the 1940s', 'a group of starving village rogues' who stole some livestock from a neighbouring village.[87] Sometimes the thieves would cook the stolen meat and share it with friends, including a man named Peppe Tavilla. Unfortunately, the seven men were falsely led to believe that Tavilla had betrayed them, so they murdered him, stabbing him and covering the wounds with salt. Their subsequent infamy sullies the reputation of the whole village, but the novel's narrator recounts the tale with considerable sympathy for the perpetrators: '[T]he seven murderers were themselves victims, paying for the deed with decades of hard prison time, and discovered at the trial that their victim was innocent.'[88] The true villain of the story is identified as the woman who concocted the false rumour; described pointedly as 'a cruel, childless gossip'.[89] The narrator closes the episode by reflecting: 'Poor Peppe. A victim, like so many others, of a dissatisfied whore'.[90]

This story strikingly resembles a real event that took place in 19th-century Africo, uncovered by Dickie in his research into Calabrian court archives on the

85 Ibid. 191.
86 Criaco (n 74) 78.
87 Ibid. 80.
88 Ibid.
89 Ibid. 79.
90 Ibid.

early 'ndrangheta.[91] In 1894, a physically disabled, elderly man named Pietro Maviglia was brutally murdered. Maviglia was a member of the early 'ndrangheta who had been expelled from the group for turning state's witness. His former comrades invited him to a meal as a peace offering, but he was found dead the next morning with five stab wounds and cooking salt sprinkled in the wound at his throat. As Dickie's analysis and the court documentation roundly demonstrate, the real Maviglia was murdered at the hands of the earliest incarnation of the 'ndrangheta; this crime was committed by members of a criminal sect, not by the misguided, well-intentioned brigands of Criaco's fictionalised version.

Criaco's fictional retelling and 're-claiming' of this episode of Calabrian history recalls a similar practice employed by Alvaro.[92] Just as Alvaro adapted elements from history and hearsay to add depth to his own fictional representations of the 'ndrangheta's past, so Criaco utilises the past to reimagine organised crime in Calabria, representing it in a more sympathetic light by removing its mafia associations and casting the murderers as victims. This process of borrowing and distorting collective history and the collective imagination is strikingly cyclical and actively embodies the processes of remediation observed by Erll.

Conclusions

I argue that the image of the 'ndrangheta in the public imagination has historically been tied inextricably to the image of Calabria itself, characterised by backwardness and 'otherness'. Within Calabrian cultural production, one can observe a deep awareness of this 'otherness', which is manifested in different ways in Calabrian representations of the 'ndrangheta. Some Calabrian authors seek to reclaim the narrative and reject the association between regional tradition and criminality, but adopt different strategies in order to do so. In Alvaro's work, the damage to Calabrian identity inflicted by its associations with organised criminality is reconciled through recourse to the 'traditional vs modern' model of 'ndrangheta history. In this model, a benign traditional iteration of the phenomenon is contrasted with a mafia that has been subject to corrupt external influences, firmly separated from traditional culture (or anything that can be identified as specifically Calabrian). Alvaro's insistence on the specificity and, to an extent, the superiority of the Calabrian context is an example of what I have defined as *calabresismo*.[93] By presenting a benign construction of the 'ndrangheta's past in his 1955 writings on the organisation, Alvaro creates an example of Neumann's 'fictions of memory';[94] disseminating an idealised construction of the past in response to the stimulus of perceived attacks on his home region in the national

91 Dickie (n 55) 178–95.
92 Phillips (n 9).
93 Ibid.
94 Neumann (n 17) 334.

press. This is done by designating a malign outside influence – be that Sicily or America or modern consumer capitalism.

The tensions between the framing of Calabrian organised crime as region-specific phenomenon with unique characteristics and as the result of 'imported' influences are interesting because of their recurrence in cultural representations of the organisation: some national press representations have used them to reinforce the image of Calabria and its mafia as fundamentally backward and in need of external 'help' to modernise.[95]

In contrast, Criaco subverts this construction of the 'ndrangheta's relationship to traditional society by reclaiming the traditional values that are so often aligned with those of the honoured society or 'old mafia' (as Castagna[96] and many others have termed it). In *Anime nere*, Criaco identifies the 'ndrangheta instead as an entirely separate, almost colonising power, whose hypocritical values have always been incompatible with those of the host society. In doing so, he presents a unique representation of the mafia's role within traditional culture and society, grafting characteristics traditionally ascribed to the 'benign' early 'ndrangheta, such as mutual support, onto another group – the 'children of the forest', who are portrayed as the descendants of the region's original settlers, as well as the successors of the Robin Hood-like brigands.

These constructions of the 'ndrangheta's past are significant, as I have argued, because of the influence of fictional constructions of the past on both other spheres of cultural responses and on memory culture. As Neumann notes:

> The concepts of memory staged within the medium of fiction may influence the extra-literary memory culture [...] these concepts can influence the creation and reflection of individual as well as collective images of the past. As a medium of cultural self-reflection, literature – through its aesthetic structure – paves the way for cultural change.[97]

There is much work still to be done on the relationship between the 'ndrangheta and popular values and traditions in the public imaginary at both regional and national level. As Truzzolillo observes, and as I note in the introduction to this chapter, the implications of this conflation are substantial, 'in terms of disguise and legitimization, for the actual development of the criminal organization, irrespective of whether or not this is a mythical representation'.[98] I have demonstrated that this is perpetuated by cultural representations and that these representations are in turn capable of being absorbed into academic narratives – but there is much more to be learned.

95 See, for example, Adriaco Luise, 'Una ventata di contestazione scuote la feroce mafia calabrese', *La Stampa Sera* (29 October 1969) 3.

96 Castagna (n 27) 31.

97 Neumann (n 17) 341.

98 Truzzolillo (n 26) 369.

2 Italy's 'circle of legality'

The confiscation and social use of assets in the fight against the mafia

Stefania di Buccio[1] *and Amber Phillips*[2]

Introduction

In Italy, the term 'mafia' is used to refer to a number of different criminal organisations, including (but not limited to): Sicily's Cosa Nostra; the Camorra (from the region of Campania); the Calabrian 'ndrangheta; and Puglia's Sacra Corona Unita, as well as a number of foreign mafias operating on Italian territory.[3] While these groups differ in terms of their structure and organisation, they share certain key characteristics: they are all secret criminal organisations seeking to control territory and accumulate economic resources for the benefit of their members, operating across illegal and legal markets at national and international level. Financial and social prestige are two key sources of mafia power, and the economic impact of mafia activities is substantial, persisting in the economic and social fabric and negatively impacting free competition long after individual offenders have served their time. Recognising the distinct nature of mafia criminality, Italy has developed a specific regulatory framework in response to this economic threat.

In this chapter, we explore the Italian legal system's response to the economic infiltration of the mafias via the so-called 'circle of legality', which acts as an instrument of social justice, depriving the mafias of the economic resources on which they structure their power and handing back wealth and opportunities to affected communities. A key weapon in Italy's anti-mafia arsenal is its innovative freezing and confiscation measures (including non-conviction-based 'preventive' measures) targeting mafia assets, which we outline at length below.

The chapter will first explain the specificity of mafia-type crime, helping to illustrate the necessity of a targeted and sophisticated legislative response. It then applies the concept of social capital to highlight the connectivity of the mafias and illustrate the nature of their links with the 'legal' economy, before moving on to address Italy's legislative response to the mafia's economic infiltration, focusing

1 Judicial Administrator and PhD in Organised Crime Studies, University of Milan.

2 Senior Lecturer in Criminology, University of the West of England. NB All translations from Italian are by the authors, unless otherwise specified.

3 Nando Dalla Chiesa, *Mafia globale. Le organizzazioni criminali nel mondo* (Laurana Editore 2018).

DOI: 10.4324/9781003020813-3

on two landmark laws: the Rognoni-La Torre Law of 1982 and the 'Libera' Law of 1996. Finally, the chapter introduces the concept of the 'circle of legality', outlining some successful case studies and identifying key challenges.

The specificity of mafia-type crime

In order to understand the specificity of mafia-type organised crime in Italy, it is helpful to briefly examine the history and origins of the mafias, dividing our focus into five key areas: social, political, ideological, institutional, and economic.[4] With regard to the social element, it should be noted that mafia behaviours are acknowledged and to an extent accepted by the society surrounding the mafia group. This can take the form of the so-called 'grey zone' of enablers and facilitators who do not actively join the mafia organisation, but tolerate and accept its existence.[5] The interclass nature of the mafia phenomenon[6] allows it to impact all levels of society, affecting politics, business, professions, and the surrounding community.

At a political level, historians agree that mafia-type organised criminal groups can ensure their continued existence and expansion if they are able to secure privileged relationships with government and public officials.[7] Indeed, the origins of Italy's mafias can be viewed as part of the 'concrete process of the formation and functioning of the [Italian] state'.[8] The mafias emerged around the time of Italy's unification in the mid-19th century, a period in which the boundary between legal and illegal – the establishment of which is a fundamental requirement for the constitution of a legitimate social and public order – was structurally blurred. Crucially, the mafias developed *within* and not *against* the formal and informal systems of public order management that were active at the time. Social scientists have suggested that this should be understood through the framework of the state carrying out a 'transaction with the mafia';[9] i.e. that the early state utilised mafia-type groups to impose order, and these groups remained a part of the social fabric thereafter. The legacy of the 'transaction' is that the mafias have established

4 Isaia Sales, *Storia dell'Italia mafiosa* (Rubettino 2015) 207.

5 Felia Allum, Rossella Merlino and Alessandro Colletti, 'Facilitating the Italian Mafia: The grey zone of complicity and collusion' (2019) 24 (1) *South European Society and Politics*, https://www.tandfonline.com/doi/abs/10.1080/13608746.2019.1575563, accessed 7 July 2021.

6 Umberto Santino, 'La mafia come soggetto politico. Ovvero: la produzione mafiosa della politica e la produzione politica della mafia' in Giovanni Fiandaca and E. S. Costantino (eds.), *La mafia, le mafie* (Laterza 1994) 122. According to the author, the mafia phenomenon involves 'the most disadvantaged in society [...] and the most advantaged: politicians and administrators linked in one way or another to the mafia, professionals (lawyers, financial consultants, doctors, technicians) who work in the service of the mafia, entrepreneurs and merchants, associates and nominees.'

7 Sales (n 4) 208.

8 Santino (n 6) 128.

9 Rocco Sciarrone and Luca Storti 'Complicità trasversali fra mafia ed economia. Servizi, garanzie, regolazione' (2016) *Stato e mercato*, 3, 357.

themselves as interlocutors capable of neutralising the actions of law enforcement agencies on a regulatory, judicial, symbolic and cultural level.[10] Simply put, they are able to evade justice, further consolidating their own power and 'legitimising' themselves.[11]

Third, mafia-type crime is often labelled 'ideological criminality', in that it is an entity that vocationally seeks to transform its interests into cultural values,[12] with a view to asserting its legitimacy within a territory. As Lupo has observed, 'the mafia organisation appropriates cultural codes, instrumentalises them, modifies them'[13] in such a way as to project an ideology that enhances consensus in the host community.[14] The social consensus developed through this appropriation of cultural codes also has the function of increasing the tolerance of illegal activities, including those for which mafias are most notorious: extortion racketeering.[15] Such activities, which require a level of compliance from the victims, can be read as the systemic affirmation of the mafia's power within a territory. The collection of protection money, or *pizzo*, represents a level of active cooperation with the victim, who, by paying, accepts a de facto legal system. In paying the mafia, the individual tacitly accepts the duopoly of power (state and mafia); the community that pays the *pizzo* simultaneously acknowledges the mafia's territorial control.

The 'institutional' characteristic of the mafia[16] is connected to the latter point; the mafia cannot be defined as an 'ordinary' criminal organisation, precisely because it poses as a 'criminal institution'[17] and is recognised as such by both its victims and those institutions and individuals who seek to repress it. The mafia's use of violence (which, of course, breaches the monopoly of the state) is carefully controlled so as to remain below the threshold of alarm. The purely predatory dimension is accompanied by a systematic vision, aimed at the affirmation of power.[18] Mafia-type organisations must therefore strike a careful balance; on one side, they operate as secret organisations operating within a given territory in a stable manner; on the other, however, in order to successfully intimidate the inhabitants of the territory, they must also cultivate awareness of their existence.

The final historical feature of mafia-type organisations is economic: in addition to their predatory activities (extortion) and involvement in illicit trades (e.g. drugs and weapons), mafias also reinvest the capital accumulated through the use

10 Henner Hess, *Mafia. Le origini e la struttura* (Laterza 1993) 19–20.
11 Ibid.
12 Sales (n 4) 209.
13 Salvatore Lupo, *History of the Mafia* (Columbia University Press 2004) 32.
14 This might be achieved, for example, through the co-opting of religious ceremonies.
15 Tano Grasso and Aldo Varano, *'U Pizzu. L'italia del racket e dell'usura* (Baldini & Castoldi 2002).
16 Santino Romano, *L'ordinamento giuridico*, ed. M. Croce (Quodlibet 2018).
17 Sales (n 15) 211.
18 Monica Massari and Vittorio Martone (eds.), *Mafia Violence. Political, Symbolic, and Economic Forms of Violence in Camorra Clans* (Routledge 2019).

of violence back into the legal economy.[19] Indeed, the growth and expansion of this form of crime occurs precisely when it is not limited to the professionalised use of violence, but is geared at the accumulation and reinvestment of assets. In economic terms, this reinvestment activity effectively transforms the mafia into an economic 'producer', engaging not only in the movement of wealth but also in its production.[20] All these behavioural variations only have real impact if they are interconnected and supported by the ability to draw on additional resources, which can be described by the concept of social capital,[21] which will be discussed in more detail below. When combined, the above characteristics are what form the intrinsic difference between mafia-type crime and other organised crime. The distinction is not a difference of degree, but a difference in kind,[22] and this requires a particular intervention by the state.

The mafia's social capital in the legal economy

Mafia organisations operate as actors *within* society, which can be understood as an organisational, cognitive, and normative structure that exercises a direct or indirect influence in codifying processes of adherence to value schemes, conditioning and regulating social action.[23] The power that a subject is able to wield within a society is determined by the social capital, both actual and potential, that it is able to exercise, with social capital being understood as the set of relational resources that an actor can employ for the achievement of its own ends, based on its placement within social networks.[24] According to Bourdieu,[25] there is an equivalence between capital and power (i.e. the capacity to act and produce effects or advantages for the agent); power manifests in the form of capital, and capital is a form of power. Following the definition proposed by Coleman,[26]

19 Francesca Calamunci, Marco De Benedetto and Damiano Silipo, 'Anti-Mafia Law Enforcement and Lending in Mafia Lands. Evidence from judicial administration in Italy' (2021) *The B.E. Journal of Economic Analysis & Policy* 21 (3) 1067–106, https://doi.org/10.1515/bejeap-2020-0353, accessed 30 July 2021.

20 Isaia Sales and Simona Melorio, 'Le mafie nel Pil', in Enzo Ciconte, Francesco Forgione and Isaia Sales (eds.), *Atlante delle mafie. Storia, economia, società, cultura*, vol. 4 (Rubettino Editore 2016) 20.

21 Rocco Sciarrone, 'Il capitale sociale della mafia' (1998) 18 *Quaderni di Sociologia* 51, http://journals.openedition.org/qds/1476, accessed 30 July 2021.

22 Antonio La Spina, *Mafia, legalità debole e sviluppo del Mezzogiorno* (Il Mulino 2005) 47.

23 Rocco Sciarrone and Luca Storti, *Le mafie nell'economia legale. Scambi, collusioni, azioni di contrasto* (Il Mulino 2019) 11–12 and 34; W. W. Powell and P. J. Di Maggio (eds.), *The New Institutionalism in Organizational Analysis* (University of Chicago 1991).

24 Pierre Bourdieu, 'The Forms of Capital' in J. Richardson, *Handbook of Theory and Research for the Sociology of Education* (Greenwood 1986) 241.

25 Ibid. James Coleman 'Social Capital in the Creation of Human Capital' (1998) 94 *American Journal of Sociology* 95.

26 James Coleman, *Foundations of Social Theory* (Harvard University Press 1990).

social capital represents a stock of resources that can be activated to achieve the objectives of the individual or the collective.[27]

As noted above, a key distinguishing feature of mafia organisations is their networked relationships with the society and territory within which they operate. Without this connective tissue represented by the network of contacts, complicity, and connivance, the very nature of the organisation would change, reducing it to a 'purely criminal' phenomenon.[28] The ability to reproduce in distant and distinct spatial and temporal contexts is explained by the capacity to build and manage networks of relationships across a range of sectors (e.g. economic, political), including in international contexts. This allows the organisation to establish relationships of cooperation, interaction, hybridisation, and exchange with subjects external to the organisation, by virtue of variously cohesive interests.[29]

The amount of social capital possessed by an agent depends on the size of the network of connections that they are able to mobilise, as well as the volume of capital – economic, cultural, or symbolic – possessed by those with whom they are connected.[30] In this regard, Sciarrone has applied Granovetter's concept of 'weak ties',[31] which, in contrast with the 'strong ties' that exist between the associates (*mafiosi*), are characterised by their functional nature and relative indifference to the criminal organisation's ethos and goals. Nevertheless, they represent significant potential for the expansion of the mafia organisation's network. Morphologically, the mafia is a densely interconnected network, with the density reducing progressively towards the periphery. However, it is precisely these 'weak' outer ties that lend the organisation greater strength, allowing it to connect to the surrounding social structures. Indeed, diffusion and expansion processes have a greater chance of success if they pass through 'weak' links, which might arguably be better defined as 'loose'[32] given the potential for elasticity, which makes them suitable for building networks and strengthening local ties,[33] including with public authorities. The mafia uses its extensive network of loose ties and highly interdependent networks to act as an efficient mediator, with the power to guide and condition the behaviour of other actors. In creating these flexible networks, mafia groups are able to connect with the 'outside world'

27 Ibid. 98.

28 Umberto Santino, *Dalla mafia alle mafie. Scienze sociali e crimine organizzato* (Soveria Mannelli 2006) 252.

29 Vincenzo Ruggiero, *Economie sporche. L'impresa criminale in Europa* (Bollati Boringhieri Editore 1996) 60.

30 Pierre Bourdieu (n 26) 187.

31 See Rocco Sciarrone, *Mafie vecchie Mafie nuove* (Donzelli 2009) 49; M. Granovetter, 'The Strength of Weak Ties' (1973) *American Journal of Sociology* 78, 6 1360–80. According to Granovetter, 'the strength of a tie is a (probably linear) combination of the amount of time, the emotional intensity, the intimacy (mutual confiding), and the reciprocal services which characterize the tie' (1361).

32 G. Bonazzi, *Storia del pensiero organizzativo*, (Franco Angeli, 1995) 392.

33 Mark Granovetter (n 31) 127.

and exploit its resources, absorbing its skills and converting them into increased strength for the organisation itself. This is the basis for the aphorism that 'the mafia's strength lies outside the mafia'.[34]

The mafia's mechanisms of reproduction concern both the processes of expansion and the relationship with the legal economy. In positive law, there is a dichotomous relationship between 'legal' and 'illegal', whereas the social sciences require us to consider them as two poles on a continuum,[35] capable of blurring into one another.[36] The success of a mafia depends not only on its capacity to adapt to the environment in which it operates, but also on its ability to interact and interfere with other actors,[37] actively changing the society around it.[38] It should be stressed that the mafias diminish the economies of their home regions, harming economic growth and development. They effectively represent an 'enterprise-state', an analytical category that finds its theoretical premise in the legal definition of the crime of mafia-type criminal association in the Italian Criminal Code.[39] According to Dalla Chiesa, this definition emphasises the Weberian dimension of mafia action,[40] which is able to impose its decisions even against the will of the interested parties through the use of violence, imposing a jurisdiction and a tax system parallel to that of the state.[41]

Block identifies two different manifestations of the criminal organisation: the 'power syndicate' (which aims to control territory) and the 'enterprise syndicate' (which is geared at illicit profits).[42] Over time, these manifestations developed an increasingly reciprocal relationship, due to their structural and functional interconnectedness.[43] Over the last 50 years in Italy and internationally there has been a shift from the control of illicit markets to licit market activities, so much so as to create a substantial fusion between the power syndicate and enterprise syndicate

34 Nando Dalla Chiesa, *La convergenza. Mafie e politica nella Seconda Repubblica* (Malatempo Editore, 2010) 17.

35 Rocco Sciarrone and Luca Storti (n 9) 363.

36 Umberto Santino (n 6) 24. According to Santino, 'polarisations are always wrong, but even more so when applied to complex phenomena'. On the critical distinction between licit and illicit, see also R. Sciarrone, *All'ombra delle mafie* (Il Mulino 2011), 404.

37 Erhard Friedburg, *Il potere e la regola* (Etas 1993) 67.

38 Nando Dalla Chiesa (n 34) 42.

39 Article 416-*bis* of the Italian Criminal Code.

40 Nando Dalla Chiesa (n 34) 39–41; Max Weber, *Economia e società, I. Teoria delle categorie sociologiche* (Edizioni di Comunità 1995) 23.

41 Nando Dalla Chiesa (n 34) 39–41.

42 Alan Block *East Side West Side: Organizing Crime in New York 1930–1950* (University College Cardiff Press 1980).

43 Rocco Sciarrone, 'Il capitale sociale della mafia. Relazioni esterne e controllo del territorio', in *Quaderni di Sociologia* (n 18) 1998, 61–69.

model.[44] The two dimensions now combine in the concept of 'controlling territory through the economy'.[45]

In essence, social capital can take on different forms, including information[46] and cultural or symbolic capital,[47] as well as economic capital.[48] For this reason, mafia-type organisations must weave a consensual relationship with the economic system, understood as a dense social space, within which operate the other actors and their cultural and social institutions and their relevant policies.[49] The mafia's predatory activities have always been accompanied by a level of mediation with the political and economic system, and the threat of violence represents a force that must interact with the market, affecting and manipulating its laws. Cooperation in the economic sphere depends on norms and values that must be established and pre-existing before the dialogue begins; a foundation on which new rules and conventions produced by the interaction between the different actors can be constructed.[50] In other words, for a mafia to become part of the legal economy, it must first be welcomed in by the pre-existing, 'legal' actors. It is then able to consolidate its position and strengthen and reproduce itself, with implications not only for the illicit economy, but for the licit economy too. From this position of strength, it is able to take an active role within the economy as a whole, in the markets, and in the systems that govern entrepreneurship.

From criminal entrepreneurship to entrepreneurial crime and illegally accumulated assets

Given that the strength of the mafia also lies in its capacity to convert social capital into economic capital and vice versa, doing so in a mutually reinforcing relationship, it follows that the economic system is a key target for the mafia, both in terms of illegal and legal markets. Indeed, the involvement in both is part of what defines it as a mafia in the first place. The mafia is a social as well as a criminal

44 This aligns with the position of Stefania Pellegrini, *L'impresa grigia. Le infiltrazioni mafiose nell'economia legale. Un'indagine sociologico-giuridica* (Ediesse 2019) 32. According to Pellegrini: 'The distinction between groups engaged in illicit trafficking and groups that politically control a territory, according to Alan Block's well-known distinction between enterprise syndicate and power syndicate, can have an analytical-conceptual value, but not an empirical relevance. For example, subjects belonging to a political-territorial power group can organize illicit trafficking, and, conversely, drug traffickers can constitute themselves as political-territorial power groups. In fact, the two types of group intertwine and overlap, both partially and fully.'

45 Stefania Pellegrini (n 44) 4.

46 James Coleman (n 25) 104.

47 Rocco Sciarrone, 'Mafia e potere: processi di legittimazione e costruzione del consenso' (2006) *Stato e Mercato* 374–5. According to Sciarrone, symbolic capital 'legitimises power, constructing a vision which is accepted and recognised by the social order'.

48 Bourdieu (n 24) 63.

49 Sciarrone and Storti (n 9) 8.

50 Erhard Friedberg (n 37) 67.

phenomenon that interacts with the economy on multiple levels; not only in the movement of financial capital (through, for example, theft or extortion), but also in the production of financial capital via the legal economy, as confirmed by historical and sociological studies.[51]

Economic activities are classified as 'criminal' when either goods or services themselves are illegal or when legal goods or services are provided without the required lawful authorisations. In both cases, the economic activities are responding to a market demand.[52]At this stage it is helpful to clarify the difference between the criminal economy – composed of illegal activities – and the 'shadow' or 'underground' economy, which, to use the IMF's definition, in addition to illegal activities also includes 'unreported income from the production of legal goods and services, either from monetary or barter transactions'.[53] This includes activities that are voluntarily hidden from the tax authorities (e.g. tax evasion, tax avoidance, and unreported income from self-employment). It is generated by false declarations concerning both the turnover and costs of production units (in order to under-declare added value) and the actual use of labour inputs, i.e. irregular employment. This includes production activities carried out in informal contexts, based on employment relationships not regulated by formal contracts, i.e. through personal or family relationships. Mafias operate across all these areas; in the criminal economy, through the trafficking of illegal goods, in the shadow economy, and in the legal economy, either through criminal methods or the reinvestment of capital of illicit origin.

Increased erosion of the line between legal and illegal leads to increased mafia contamination of the economy, as a situation is created whereby actors are able to expand their networks across different social spheres via 'linking' or 'bridging'.[54] Another way in which it is possible to achieve this is through the interpenetration of diversified 'licit' economic activities, for example in the catering, construction, or transport sectors.[55] This process represents a major challenge to the market system;[56] the huge availability of resources of illicit origin gives the mafias an intrinsic ability to influence the rules of behaviour and to escape charges of

51 Isaia Sales and Simona Melorio (n 20) 20–21.

52 Commission of the European Communities, International Monetary Fund, Organisation for Economic Cooperation and Development, United Nations and World Bank, *System of National Accounts* 2008 (2009), 100, https://unstats.un.org/unsd/nationalaccount/docs/SNA2008.pdf, accessed 31 July 2021.

53 Friedrich Schneider and Dominik Enste 'Hiding in the Shadows: The growth of the underground economy' (2002) *Economic Issues* 30, https://www.imf.org/external/pubs/ft/issues/issues30/, accessed 31 July 2021.

54 For more on the concept of 'bridging' social capital with relation to Camorra clans, see Giacomo Di Gennaro, 'Mercati illegali e struttura di classe: perché si parla poco di borghesia camorristica' in Giacomo Di Gennaro and Domenico Pizzuti (eds.) *Dire camorra oggi* (Guida 2009) 107.

55 Mark Granovetter, 'Economic Action and Social Structure: The problem of embeddedness' *American Journal of Sociology* 91 (3) 1985, 481–510.

56 Isaia Sales and Simona Melorio, *Le mafie nell'economia globale* (Guida Editori 2017) 21.

deviance, leading to normalisation, justification, and even denial of the mafia's existence.[57] For example, a mafia organisation might invest the proceeds of drug trafficking into a large hotel complex in order to launder illicit profits. In doing so, jobs will be created in the community, helping to strengthen social consensus. This leads to tolerance of the presence of mafia investments in the market, on the basis that they provide wealth to the community. However, the true effects of this presence soon emerge, often in the form of labour exploitation and the erosion of competition.

A capitalist economic system based on predatory behaviours,[58] where all the actors move in contexts of widespread or tolerated illegality, generates environmental characteristics that allow mafia-type criminal gangs to expand their activities and to insert themselves into the legal economy. Mafia actors take on increasingly chameleonic forms to adapt to different environments and aid their penetration of the economic system, blending in seamlessly with their surroundings and concealing the illicit source of their investment capital. The mafia economy rests on a domination of the system underpinned by a wide range of characteristics and structures linking it to legal entrepreneurship, with which it shares the same economic space, but without having to abide by the same rules and regulations.[59] This process leads to the accumulation of wealth: the profits that come from criminal activities are reinvested in legal activities, but always in illicit ways, which, in turn, bolster the shadow economy. These assets allow the mafia to further assert its power and consolidate social consensus in a given territory, making it vital to target measures at these forms of wealth, to attack the means through which the mafia has moved from criminal to legal markets, creating new social capital.

Italy's novel response and the circle of legality

Two landmark laws stand out in Italy's response to mafia infiltration of the economy, each complementing the other. The first is the Rognoni-La Torre Law of 1982,[60] named for Pio La Torre, an Italian politician who was assassinated by the mafia in the same year after presenting the draft bill to parliament. The law saw the introduction of a new strategy for state intervention against illicitly acquired property, which today represents a crucial tool in the fight against the mafias'

57 Alessandra Dino (ed.), *Criminalità dei potenti e metodo mafioso* (Mimesi 2009).

58 P. Asso and C. Trigilia, 'Mafie ed economie locali' in R. Sciarrone (ed.) *Alleanze nell'ombra* (Donzelli Editore 2011) 21.

59 S. Clementi 'Dimensione economia criminale. Problematiche legale alle misurazioni' in Guido Rey (ed.) *La mafia come impresa. Analisi del sistema economico criminale e delle politiche di contrasto* (Franco Angeli 2017) 264.

60 Law no. 646 of 13 September 1982, http://legislature.camera.it/_dati/leg08/lavori/stenografici/sed0122/ sed0122.pdf, accessed 10 May 2021.

economic activities thanks to its focus on the confiscation of financial assets.[61] The Rognoni-La Torre law introduced the application of asset tracing, freezing and confiscation measures to individuals suspected of being involved with the mafia. Crucially, it amended Article 416 of the Italian Criminal Code to create a new offence; that of 'association of a mafia type'. Under the legal definition, such associations consist of three or more members, who 'make use of the power of intimidation afforded by the associative bond and the state of subjugation and criminal silence which derives from it to commit crimes'.[62]

Indeed, the starting point for understanding Italy's anti-mafia legislation is its 'non-neutral' approach to *mafioso* proprietors;[63] actors that represent a tangible (and increasingly well concealed) criminal presence in the legal economy. The incarceration of individual *mafiosi* is not sufficient to eliminate the medium- and long-term effects of mafia activity on the economy, including the enduring impact on free competition.[64] These effects persist in the fabric of society and the economy well beyond the lifespan of any individual perpetrator. There is therefore a need for regulatory interventions geared at breaking the vicious cycle that has contaminated the socioeconomic fabric.[65] Under the Rognoni-La Torre Law, confiscation measures have proved an innovative and effective weapon in tackling the link between mafia-type groups and the economy. These measures are implemented in two different proceedings: criminal proceedings, which allow for the adoption of *post delictum* measures (i.e. after liability has been determined);[66] and non-conviction-based proceedings, which allow for the application of confiscation measures *praeter delictum* (i.e. before or regardless of the ascertainment of the criminal responsibility of a subject and based on various requirements). The general category of non-conviction-based proceedings covers a wide range of modern forms of confiscation, applied following an asset-related trial, which does not need a conviction as a prerequisite. The prototype of this model is constituted

61 Stefania Di Buccio, 'L'aggressione dei patrimoni illecitamente accumulati: esigenza comune. Diversi strumenti. Sequestri e confische nel procedimento penale e nel procedimento di prevenzione' in Stefania Pellegrini (ed.), *Il Circolo della Legalità* (Bologna University Press 2019) 9.

62 Article 416-*bis* of the Italian Criminal Code.

63 Clotilde Champeyrache, 'La non neutralità dell'identità del proprietario: elementi di teoria dell'impresa legale mafiosa', in Guido Rey, 2017, 67.

64 R. Alfonso, 'La confisca nel procedimento di prevenzione' in Alberto Cisterna and Alfredo Bargi (eds.), *La giustizia patrimoniale penale* (Utet 2011) 783; L. Fornari, *Criminalità del profitto e tecniche sanzionatorie* (Cedam 1997) 39.

65 Francesco Menditto, 'Le confische nella prevenzione e nel contrasto alla criminalità da profitto (mafie, corruzione, evasione fiscale)' (2015) *Diritto Penale Contemporaneo*, https://archiviodpc.dirittopenaleuomo.org/ d/3627-le-confische-nella-prevenzione-e-nel-contrasto-alla-criminalita--da-profitto--mafie-corruzione-evas, accessed 31 July 2021; S. Di Buccio, 'Gli strumenti di aggressione patrimoniale: dall'ablazione al riutilizzo' in S. Pellegrini (ed.) *L'aggressione dei patrimoni mafiosi e il riutilizzo dei beni confiscati* (Aracne Editore 2015) 43–4.

66 Traditionally, 'post-conviction confiscation' recovers the proceeds of crime, via court order, after the crime itself has been proved in a criminal court to the criminal standard.

by civil forfeiture, which is increasingly widespread in common law countries (e.g. Part 5 of the 2002 Proceeds of Crime Act in England and Wales). In Italy, these measures are called 'preventive' measures and they are imposed in preventive proceedings.

La Torre's foresight lay precisely in this two-pronged approach to asset measures, which, alongside the normal criminal proceedings, introduced an alternative, faster, more effective path: a preventive confiscation order can be issued by a judge should an individual is considered to pose a 'social danger' and there is found to be an imbalance between the assets held and the declared income or activity carried out. The concept of 'social danger' (*pericolosità sociale*)[67] refers to individuals categorised as 'dangerous persons', e.g. due to their potential affiliation with a criminal organisation or involvement in certain serious crimes or for having a lifestyle funded by the proceeds of crime. Although a conviction is not required, for confiscation, it is sufficient that it be proved that the subject has a discrepancy between their assets and their declared income that they are unable to justify.

The second landmark piece of anti-mafia legislation is Law no. 109 of 1996, also known as the 'Libera Law' for the *Libera* non-profit anti-mafia association, itself founded in 1995.[68] It was introduced following a *Libera*-backed citizens' initiative which saw 1.5 million Italians sign their support for a law to allocate assets confiscated from *mafiosi* to civil society projects.[69] Prior to 1996, assets confiscated from the mafia were simply sold off, which carried the obvious risk that the same individuals would eventually be able to reacquire the assets via a nominated third party. Selling off the assets also lacked any symbolic impact in the fight against mafia infiltration into the economy.

These new confiscation and allocation measures created new risks for organised criminals operating in the legal economy, leading to the emergence of forms of adaptation aimed at further camouflaging criminal property in the legal economy. The mafias have adopted various adaptive strategies in their entrepreneurial activities, which can be summarised as follows:

1 the transition from mafia mediation in markets to mafia ownership of productive activities;
2 the camouflaging of ownership through straw buyers and through *mafiosi* buying companies and shares;
3 businesses in the 'grey zone', characterised by the symbiosis of mafia and non-mafia entrepreneurs.

67 Articles 1 and 4 of the Anti-Mafia Code.

68 Since its foundation in 1995, *Libera* has grown into a large network of anti-mafia cooperatives, associations, schools, trade unions, church dioceses, scout groups and more, with a presence in all 20 Italian regions and 278 local offices, as well as the Libera International network, which brings together 35 countries around the world.

69 N. Dalla Chiesa, *La scelta di Libera* (Edizioni Gruppo Abele 2014) 60.

In the case of the last, as demonstrated by Pellegrini,[70] the 'legal' businesses initiate a dialogue with the *mafioso* in order to access the illicit competitive advantages that the mafia can guarantee in terms of investment capital, reduction of competition and suppression of trade unions.

There is, therefore, a clear need for legal intervention capable of breaking the vicious circle that has contaminated the socioeconomic fabric, through regulatory provision of remediation and decontamination activities.[71] This is the goal of Legislative Decree 159/2011, which is often referred to as the 'Anti-Mafia Code'[72] and combines the La Torre Law and the Libera Law. The aim is to separate the individual business unit from the network that has been infiltrated by the mafia and return the market to a state of healthy competition through asset recovery procedures.

Freezing and confiscations in criminal proceedings and in preventive proceedings

The mechanism through which the state is able to acquire mafia assets is confiscation, which can be preceded by freezing as a provisional measure. The owner of the property signs it over to a public official (the judicial administrator) who manages and administers the property on behalf of the Court pending the assessment proceedings.[73] Freezing is a precautionary measure that renders the property temporarily inaccessible to the owner and carries a resultant suppression of their civil liberties, pending the completion of checks carried out by a court. Confiscation, meanwhile, consists in the expropriation of the property by the state, following an assessment of the property's connection to a crime or to a fact representative of danger to society. Assets that can be frozen or confiscated include: movable property such as cash, vehicles, and animals; real estate such as land or houses; and businesses of any type, from catering to manufacturing to services. Freezing and confiscation operate in different ways depending on the type of proceedings. In all cases, the common goal is to target resources accumulated through criminal dynamics, applying a specific regulatory discipline, with different probative and procedural instruments.[74]

The innovation of the Italian approach is that there are two different procedures to achieve the goal of confiscation of illicit assets accumulated by criminal organisations: criminal proceedings (regulated by the code of criminal procedure), and preventive (non-conviction- based) proceedings. In criminal proceedings (defined

70 Pellegrini (n 44).

71 Menditto (n 65).

72 Giovanni Fiandaca and Costantino Visconti, 'Il "codice delle leggi antimafia": risultati, omissioni e prospettive' (2012) *Legisl. pen.* 182. It should be noted that the name 'Anti-Mafia Code' is somewhat misleading, as a range of other measures targeting the mafia are contained in (inter alia) the Criminal Code and the Criminal Procedure Code.

73 Di Buccio (n 65)

74 Di Buccio (n 65).

as the sequence of judicial activities aimed at ascertaining the criminal responsibility of the accused person), precautionary seizure (freezing) of assets can be ordered with the aim of preventing the commission of further crimes.[75] However, confiscation is only ordered at the end of the proceedings (a process that can take from five to seven years) and only includes the 'proceeds of crime', in addition to any property derived from or obtained, directly or indirectly, through the commission of an offence. Preventive proceedings, meanwhile, are regulated by the 2011 Anti-Mafia Code,[76] and were introduced under the Rognoni-La Torre law. These proceedings provide a fast and direct method for targeting dubious assets and apply not only to the proceeds of crime, but to any assets which cannot be proved to be of legitimate origin. Under Articles 1 and 4 of the Anti-Mafia Code, prosecutors do not need to prove that the suspect has committed a specific offence, only that they are dangerous because their lifestyle is disproportionate to their declared income. Suspected *mafiosi* have their income assessed in terms of lifestyle, economic activities, financial means, and property, and investigations also extend to their associates and family members. Individuals can also be subject to preventive measures if they are suspected of belonging to a mafia organisation or if they are accused of having committed other specific crimes or living off illicit proceeds. A wide range of financial crimes can be pursued by these measures, such as theft, robbery, extortion, fraud, usury, laundering or self-laundering, and tax offences.

The public prosecutor and the chief of police with authority for requesting the application of preventive measures, conduct investigations into the person's standard of living, financial resources and assets, in order to determine their origin. Such investigations are extended to the family members of the person suspected of belonging to the mafia-type organisation. In order to obtain the preventive confiscation order, the assets attributable to the suspect must appear to be disproportionate compared to their declared income or to their declared economic activity. The main benefit of this preventive confiscation is the shifting of the burden of proof: proving the discrepancy between the value of the assets available to the suspect and their legal income falls to the public prosecutor, while the burden of proof of the legal origin of such funds falls to the suspect. If there is insufficient evidence of the legitimate origin of the assets, the judge orders the preventive confiscation. Preventive confiscation may also be applied in instances where the suspect is deceased and the proceedings continue against their beneficiaries.

These confiscation measures are geared at preventing capital of illicit origin from being introduced into the legal economy. The two procedures – criminal and non-conviction-based – share certain characteristics imposed by the need to

75 Di Buccio (n 61).

76 Legislative Decree no. 159 of 6 September 2011. See A. Balsamo, 'Codice antimafia' *Digesto discipline penalistiche*, VIII, (Utet 2014) 41. A. Balsamo and P. Mattarella, 'Codice antimafia (riforma del)', *Digesto discipline penalistiche*. X, (Utet 2018) 41.

comply with due process, as set out in constitutional legislation, European legislation and international conventions.[77] Both procedures occur before a judge, respecting the rights of the defence and the right to be heard. Following the introduction of the Anti-Mafia Code, as well as interventions by the Constitutional Court and the European Court of Human Rights,[78] the case law of the Italian Court of Cassation has specified the need to respect the accountability principle in preventive measures.[79]

The difference in content and procedure between the two proceedings is simple: in criminal proceedings, criminal responsibility is proved beyond all reasonable doubt by the prosecution. The end result is the confiscation of the assets and production units considered as proceeds of the crime. By contrast, in preventive proceedings, a judgment of the 'social danger' posed by the subject is required, which consists of the Court carrying out a broad assessment of the individual's personality, behaviours, and activities and the effects that these have produced in terms of illicit asset accumulation.[80]

The Italian legal system, through these asset-based measures, has laid the foundations for the modern 'trial of assets',[81] juridical and flexible, capable of affecting the economic physiognomy of the mafia phenomenon.

Returning confiscated assets to the community: the circle of legality

Together, the elements of confiscation (represented by the Rognoni-La Torre Law) and restitution (represented by the Libera Law) form what has been described as the 'circle of legality' today embodied in the Anti-Mafia Code,[82] an instrument of social justice that deprives the mafia of the economic resources that reinforce its power and restores to the community what organised crime has stolen in terms of opportunities and wealth. The Anti-Mafia Code governs the path that allows assets to be restored to communities impacted by the mafia's infiltration of the economy. In this way, an asset that had been exploited by a few individuals becomes a source of wealth for all. The path can be divided into three phases, the first of which, removal, has been outlined in the section above: removal occurs either through non-conviction-based freezing or confisca-

77 European Convention on Human Rights, Palermo Convention.

78 *De Tommaso v Italy* (2017) 65 EHRR 19. See F. Basile, 'Quale futuro per le misure di prevenzione dopo le sentenze De Tommaso e Paternò?', in *Giurisprudenza italiana*, ISSN 0017-0623, No 2, 2018, 455.

79 Fabio Basile, 'Tassatività delle norme ricognitive della pericolosità nelle misure di prevenzione: Strasburgo chiama, Roma risponde', presented at the conference 'Tassatività della legge penale e mediazioni interpretative: vizio o necessità?' Catanzaro 22 June 2018, https://archiviodpc.dirittopenaleuomo.org/d/6186-tassativita-delle-norme-ricognitive-della-pericolosita-nelle-misure-di-prevenzione-strasburgo-chiam, accessed 29 July 2021.

80 M. Francesca Cortesi and Leonardo Filippi, 'Il processo di prevenzione' in Spangher (ed.) *Trattato di Procedura penale* VII (Nel diritto editore 2011) 576.

81 A. Balsamo (n 76) 3.

82 Stefania Pellegrini (ed.), *Il Circolo della Legalità* (Bononia University Press 2019).

tion or through freezing or confiscation ordered as a result of a conviction for mafia-related crimes pursuant to Article 240-*bis* of the Italian Criminal Code. Below, we outline phase two (judicial administration) and phase three (allocation), in which assets can be allocated either to the public sector, to a municipal authority, or to non-profit associations or foundations.

Phase two, which follows the seizure of the asset, requires the appointment of a judicial administrator, a public official with specific skills and qualifications who works closely with the appointed judge who ordered the measure. Administrators are usually chartered accountants or publicly registered lawyers[83] and are responsible for managing the asset and, in the event that the asset is a business or economic activity, continuing its activities, increasing the profits where possible. The administrator must, of course, be aware that the asset may be returned to the defendant in the event that the specified conditions are not met. A good administrator is able to manage the asset dynamically in view of its potential destination, in such a way as to maximise its benefit to its potential community recipients.[84]

Increasingly, the assets being frozen or confiscated take the form of businesses, which require the judicial administrator to work carefully in order to protect employees and support the costs of shifting the operation from illegal to legal. Administrators are faced with a complex balancing act in order to protect the various interests involved, while at the same time maximising the value of the assets wherever possible. It should be noted that in the specific case of companies or businesses, the aim is to stem the expansion of the mafia phenomenon and to drain the channels of economic accumulation.[85] The activity of the judicial administrator is monitored by the appointed judge, and the two operate in a functionally interdependent relationship determined by the obligations set down by law.[86] Third parties whose rights in relation to the property are directly prejudiced by the order must, in order to exercise said rights, demonstrate that they are acting in good faith, i.e. that their credit was not instrumental to the alleged illegal activity. This must arise as a result of proper judicial process and be decided on by an appointed judge.

When confiscation reaches the appeal stage, the asset is transferred to the National Agency for the Administration and Allocation of Assets Frozen and Confiscated from Organised Crime (ANBSC),[87] which deals with phase three;

83 Decree no. 160 of 19 September 2013, Ministry of Justice, regulations setting forth provisions concerning registration in the register of judicial adminstrators under Legislative Decree no. 14 of 4 February 2010, in force since 8 February 2014.

84 Paolo Florio, Gianmichele Bosco and Luca D'amore, *Amministratore giudiziario: sequestro, confisca, gestione dei beni, coadiutore dell'ANBSC* (Wolters Kluver Italia 2014) 154.

85 Francesco Menditto, *Le misure di prevenzione patrimoniali e personali* (Giuffrè Editore 2013) 634.

86 Ordine dei Dottori Commercialisti e degli Esperti contabili di Roma 'd.lgs. 159/2011 – Codice Antimafia- Linee Guida in tema di amministrazione e custodia giudiziaria dei beni sequestrati alla criminalità' 2012.

87 Full Italian title: *l'Agenzia Nazionale per l'amministrazione e la destinazione dei beni sequestrati e confiscati alla criminalità organizzata.*

the allocation of the asset for institutional purposes (i.e. for the benefit of government agencies) or for social purposes. The agency nominates an assistant who will be tasked with managing the asset (generally this will be the judicial administrator). The final stage of the circle of legality (which applies equally to preventive proceedings and criminal proceedings related to mafia crimes) is to allow civil society that has suffered the presence of the mafias to benefit from the confiscated assets. Before the Libera Law, the assets were turned over to the state before being sold off which, as noted above, presented a significant risk in that mafia groups could simply repurchase the assets by using straw buyers. In contrast, making the assets available for social purposes means that they can be given to non-profit organisations and associations, which are able to use them for the benefit of the community.

Allocation must take place according to the criteria indicated in Article 48 of the Anti-Mafia Code. All sums of money that are not used for the management of other confiscated assets or to compensate victims of mafia-type crimes are donated to the *Fondo Unico Giustizia* (FUG),[88] along with the profits from the sale of any movable property. Movable property such as cars, motorcycles, or boats can be used by government bodies such as police departments. Real estate, meanwhile, can be used for institutional or social purposes, in recognition of the need to compensate the community that has suffered from the presence of the mafia. If the ANBSC allocates the real estate to the state for the purposes of justice, public order, and civil protection,[89] it is often converted into police barracks or public property. However, it should be noted that converting residential buildings into public facilities poses a number of practical difficulties, particularly with regard to safety and capacity regulations.

If the assets are transferred by the ANBSC to the municipality where the property is located or to the provincial or regional authority, the local body receives the asset and must assign it, by public tender, to associations, foundations, or cooperatives that provide free community services. Local authorities can also utilise the assets to generate rental income, but the proceeds must be used to fund services for the community. Direct allocation to non-profit organisations was introduced in 2017 with a reform of the Anti-Mafia Code.[90] Assets are only put up for sale by the ANBSC in the event that all attempts to use or assign them for institutional or social purposes should fail (for example if they are in a dilapidated condition, or if the cost of any remedial works required to render them usable should prove excessively high).

Businesses that have been managed by a judicial administrator prior to final confiscation can be rented or sold by the ANBSC under the following conditions.

88 This fund was set up in 2008 with the goal of centralising the management of confiscated resources and is managed by Equitalia Giustizia S.p.A., which reports to the state.

89 Such assets, if suitable, can also be allocated to the state for other public uses connected to the performance of the institutional activities of state administrations, tax agencies, state universities, public bodies, and cultural institutions.

90 Law no. 161 of 17 October 2017.

The rental of production units is permitted where there are good prospects and the units are provided for a consideration, if contracted with public or private companies, or free of charge, without charges to be borne by the state, if contracted with worker cooperatives made up of employees of the confiscated company. When selecting the tenant, priority is given to solutions that retain existing employment levels; a particularly gratifying solution to this is the preponderance of cooperatives built by employees who have organised and emancipated themselves from precarious and irregular employment under the mafia to create a legal source of work and wealth for the benefit of the community. Evidently, immovable assets cannot be rented out if a member of the cooperative is a spouse, relative, or cohabitant of the previous owner or if they have been the subject of any confiscation orders.

As noted above, in exceptional circumstances a business may be sold. To select the transferee or tenant of the company assets, the ANBSC proceeds either by public tender or, if necessity or convenience demands it, by private negotiation. In extreme cases, a company can be liquidated, if this course of action best represents the public interest or if the liquidation is targeted to compensate the victims of mafia-type crimes. In all cases, the proceeds deriving from the rental, sale, or liquidation of the assets, net of expenses incurred, go to the FUG to be paid to the appropriate income chapter of the state budget aimed at supporting of the victims of mafia. On the closure of the phase, should assets return, even via a third party, to the availability or control of the person subject to the confiscation order, the allocation can be revoked by the same body that awarded it by virtue of a provision known as a *Clausola di Salvezza* or 'salvation clause'.

The circle of legality: successes and challenges

This section will first sketch out some successful case studies of the circle of legality, before moving on to addressing some key ongoing challenges. There are many cases in Italy of confiscated assets being turned into shared community resources. These resources can be split into two categories: real estate (buildings and land), and companies. A study conducted by *Libera* in 2021[91] surveyed 867 different third-sector subjects engaged in the management of real estate confiscated from organised crime, across 17 Italian regions. Of these, 468 were associations of various types, while 189 were social cooperatives (including worker cooperatives of confiscated companies and consortia). There were also 11 amateur sports associations, 23 third-sector subjects who manage subsidiary welfare services in agreement with public bodies, 36 joint ventures, 60 religious associations, 26 foundations, 14 scout groups, and finally six schools. The region with the most active projects managing confiscated assets is Sicily with 218, followed by Calabria with 147, Campania with 135, and Lombardy with 133.

91 'Fattiperbene', *Libera* (2021), https://www.libera.it/schede-1573-fattiperbene, accessed 31 July 2021.

One of the numerous examples from Sicily is the *Al Reves* social cooperative, which runs a clothing business in a property confiscated from the mafia in the city of Palermo. A social enterprise project, it brings together stylists, tailors, and sewing enthusiasts from a diverse range of backgrounds to work together in the recycling and reuse of used clothing. The project also includes opportunities for offender rehabilitation. In Campania, meanwhile, the *Aldilà dei Sogni* [Beyond Dreams] cooperative manages a property confiscated from a Camorra clan in Maiano di Sessa Aurunca. The cooperative provides services and training opportunities for vulnerable individuals (for example people suffering from addiction or mental health problems). These individuals become members of the cooperative and are supported on a path to autonomy, moving away from the state welfare system to become integrated, where possible, into the world of work. *Aldilà dei Sogni* has worked to develop a social micro-economy through networking with other local organisations providing a range of activities and services, from sport to education. These two cases form just a tiny part of the picture, of course; there are multiple instances of confiscated real estate being used to support shelters, youth centres, ethical manufacturing, or housing solutions for victims of trafficking. Farming cooperatives have been established on confiscated land, generating legal employment opportunities and offering produce for sale at a price to value ratio that maintains a legal, healthy economy.[92]

Shifting the focus from real estate to companies, a key symbolic success story is that of Calcestruzzi Ericina Libera, a company that manages three concrete production plants in Sicily, confiscated from a Cosa Nostra boss. In this case, the company assets were entrusted to a cooperative set up by the company's own workers. The cooperative faced substantial difficulties; potential customers were initially hesitant to use the company's services, fearing reprisals from its former owners. Today, however, the company is profitable and Calcestruzzi Ericina is the first example in Italy of a confiscated asset that has returned to a legal production entity, in the form of a pioneering facility that uses the recovery of aggregates to protect the environment.[93]

Another successful example of a confiscated business is Geotrans, a Sicilian transport company confiscated from the mafia in 2014. Thanks to the work of judicial administrator Luciano Modica and the commitment of the company's employees, Geotrans was able to break the illegal mafia market monopoly on the fruit and vegetable transport sector. There were difficulties, including the alleged interference of the previous owners with regard to the company's customer base,[94] but the workers (who are now running the cooperative) ultimately

92 Libera Terra Mediterraneo is a consortium that coordinates the production activities of its member cooperatives, united under the ethos of Libera.

93 Elena Ciccarello, 'Lo strano caso della Calcestruzzi Ericina' (*Unilibera,* 30 May 2007), http://unilibera.liberapiemonte.it/2010/10/14/lo-strano-caso-della-calcestruzzi-ericina/, accessed 1 July 2021.

94 'Aziende confiscate e mortalità: Geotrans, coraggio di ripartire' (*Live Sicilia,* 26 June 2020), https://livesicilia.it/2020/06/26/aziende-confiscate-e-mortalita-geotrans-coraggio-di-ripartire/?refresh_ce, accessed 1 July 2021.

prevailed, with support from the Sicilian AddioPizzo movement.[95] As a further measure of its success, the company has obtained European Social Accountability certification (SA8000) in recognition of its ethical practices.[96]

The history of the social reuse of assets confiscated from the mafia is characterised by many individual triumphs such as these, but also by missed opportunities, which are indicative of the difficulties still encountered in the application of pioneering legislation. Such difficulties include slow-moving bureaucracy, the frequent changes of institutional interlocutors, and the fact that any employees or directors with links to the *mafioso* former proprietor(s) must be let go, potentially leading to staffing issues. A key challenge faced by judicial administrators in managing companies prior to definitive confiscation is the fact that once the company begins to operate legally, it is burdened with numerous costs that it previously avoided (particularly in terms of taxes); this is referred to as the 'price of legality',[97] and it represents the starkest challenge to the success of an allocation process. According to ANBSC data from 2013, regarding companies confiscated up to 2012: out of a total of 1,707 confiscated companies, 497 were no longer under ANBSC management due to liquidation or bankruptcy.[98] Another recent study[99] examined the impact of preventive measures on bank–firm relationships in the four Italian regions with the highest concentration of mafia activity over the period 2004–2016. It found that after entering judicial administration, mafia-infiltrated companies experienced a 19% reduction in bank credit and had a higher probability of being credit rationed than other comparable firms. These companies also tend to be disadvantaged when it comes to loan applications.

Italy has made some targeted efforts to tackle these challenges. For example, to offer financial support to companies in judicial administration, a 2017 reform of the Anti-Mafia Code[100] increased funding for the enhancement of businesses and job protection, in order to fight the mafia's social consensus and prevent the community from perceiving that the mafia provides work, while the state takes it away.[101] To access these funds, an application must be presented by the

95 AddioPizzo (which can be loosely translated as 'goodbye extortion') is a grassroots anti-mafia movement originally established in Sicily. It brings together businesses and consumers who refuse to pay protection money to the mafia.

96 Ornella Sgroi, 'La Geotrans riparte: confiscata alla mafia, è salva con AddioPizzo Rinascita di un'azienda catanese sottratta alla mafia e in amministrazione giudiziaria' *Corriere della Sera,* 11 May 2020, https://www.corriere.it/buone-notizie/20_maggio_11/geotrans-riparte-confiscata-mafia-salva-addiopizzo-3aaae472-92a9-11ea-88e1-10b8fb89502c.shtml, accessed 1 July 2021.

97 Stefania Pellegrini (n 4) 62.

98 See https://benisequestraticonfiscati.it/sala-stampa/dati-e-statistiche/aziende/, accessed 31 July 2021.

99 (n 19).

100 Law no. 161 of 17 October 2017.

101 Laura Miani, Luigi Lusentini and Stefania Balzarotti. 'Modello integrato per la gestione e il risanamento delle aziende sequestrate e confiscate alla criminalità organizzata: linee guida', (27). https://www.cgil.lombardia.it/sito_icaro/index.html, accessed 31 August 2021.

judicial administrator and approved by the judge, to ensure that only companies that have a concrete possibility of maintaining profitability, and saving jobs, are financed. Meanwhile, in order to combat the hostile operating environment post-confiscation, with clients and suppliers intimidated by potential mafia reprisals, opportunities for government-facilitated networking were also introduced with the 2017 reform. A government official (prefect) can invite key stakeholders from the relevant sector to facilitate business contacts and connections for the seized or confiscated company. These provisions also seek to encourage the sharing of experience and resources between confiscated companies, for example regarding maximising employee retention. Through these measures and targeted funding support, Italian legislation is aiming to develop 'networks of legality', in the form of relationships between confiscated companies, which in this way are able to build a self-sustaining legal market.

As yet, it is still too early to effectively measure the success of these recent measures. Monitoring of the management of asset-based measures paints a complex picture of challenges; for example, on 5 August 2021, the Parliamentary Inquiry Committee on the Mafias published a long report analysing the management of seized and confiscated assets, suggesting a number of improvements.[102] The report, which is the result of two years of research, investigates the concrete application of asset-based measures, based on interviews with judges, judicial administrators, local authorities, and representatives from the banking sector, charities, and the ANBSC. The report identified a number of criticisms: first, in terms of judicial administration, the most significant and frequently faced challenge relates to confiscated businesses and their relationship with banking institutions. The report found that, in line with the findings of the study mentioned above,[103] confiscated businesses often struggle financially and fail to retain employees. Second, the report found that with regard to the allocation phase, interviewees criticised the lack of effective communication between the ANBSC and local authorities, with the result that the latter is often unaware of the presence of confiscated assets available for reuse in their area. Other key criticisms of the ANBSC concerned a lack of sufficient trained staff to manage assets; a lack of communication between the ANBSC and courts; and a failure to provide effective tools for monitoring assets and assessing their social impact when allocated.

Conclusion

This chapter has set out that the nature of mafia organisations – groups that exploit social capital and economic capital to acquire positions of power within

102 Commissione Parlamentare di inchiesta sul fenomeno delle mafie e sulle altre associazioni criminali, anche straniere, 'Relazione sull'analisi delle procedure di gestione dei beni sequestrati e confiscati' (Approved at the hearing of 5 August 2021), https://www.senato.it/service/PDF/PDFServer/DF/363848.pdf, accessed 31 August 2021.

103 (n 99).

society – presents a need for tailored and specific legislative response that is capable of weakening the mafias' grip on economic resources. Separating *mafiosi* from their assets undermines their ability to mobilise and capitalise on the assets within the wider socioeconomic landscape and effectively limits their ability to grow and expand. Italy's innovative, asset-focused anti-mafia legislation recognises the economic and symbolic power of the confiscation and reuse of mafia-owned assets. The goal of the measures is admirable; the model of the circle of legality seeks to return assets back to the community, fostering new networks grounded in social cohesion and respect for the rule of law; thus simultaneously undermining mafia consensus.

As outlined above, these admirable intentions are met with significant logistical challenges, particularly when it comes to businesses; dynamic entities that must remain competitive and profitable post-freezing or confiscation, despite significant changes in circumstances. The complex bureaucracy of moving between judicial administration and the ANBSC, and the difficulties linked to accessing financial support, also represent key challenges, alongside the threat of being undermined by *mafiosi* former owners.

Despite these significant challenges, the number of reallocated confiscated assets is growing, and the significant potential of Italy's legislative approach has been recognised at international level. At the 12th Conference of the Parties to the Palermo Convention against Transnational Organised Crime held in Vienna in October 2020,[104] the Conference adopted the 'Falcone' resolution,[105] presented by Italy and named for the pioneering anti-mafia prosecutor who was murdered in 1992. The resolution, which reflects on the implementation of the Palermo Convention after 20 years, specifically identifies the importance of asset recovery measures in the fight against organised crime, with Paragraph 9 citing 'the social reuse of assets for the benefit of communities' as a model that the states parties are encouraged to consider.

In order to be effective, efforts to counter mafia-type crime must work across a range of different fronts. The fight against mafia-type crime can never be won by focusing all resources and efforts on just one facet of a highly complex, deeply rooted phenomenon; responses must be as dynamic and complex as the organisations themselves to have any hope of success. The circle of legality recognises not just the economic power of the mafias, but also their social capital, striking an important symbolic blow.

104 A. Balsamo, 'Twenty Years Later: The new perspectives of the Palermo Convention' (2020) 6 (3) *Rivista di studi e ricerche sulla criminalita organizzata*, http://dx.doi.org/10.13130/cross-14727, accessed 1 November 2021.

105 UN Resolution 10/4, Celebrating the twentieth anniversary of the adoption of the United Nations Convention against Transnational Organized Crime and promoting its effective implementation, United Nations, Treaty Series, vol. 2225, No. 39574.

3 Unexplained wealth orders and the right not to self-incriminate

Marnie Lovejoy[1]

Introduction

In April 2016, shortly after the Panama Papers exposed the dubious dealings of the offshore finance industry and its links to the UK,[2] the government released the Action Plan for anti-money laundering and counterterrorist finance.[3] The Action Plan announced the need to create 'aggressive new legal powers [...] to enable the relentless disruption of criminals and terrorists'.[4] These aggressive legal powers include unexplained wealth orders (UWOs), which were introduced to the Proceeds of Crime Act 2002 through the Criminal Finances Act 2017.[5] The aim of UWOs is to facilitate the recovery of illicit assets, where the authorities are unable to use other freezing or recovery tools because of their inability to obtain evidence.[6] UWOs are an instrument of compulsion. They compel a person to provide information about the origin of targeted assets, in cases where the court suspects the value of the assets to be disproportionate to the person's known legitimate income.[7] To lie or to give misleading statements under this compulsion is a criminal offence[8] and non-compliance results in the legal presumption that the assets are recoverable in civil proceedings.[9] The design of this

1 Principal Lecturer, Associate Head, Portsmouth Law School, University of Portsmouth.
2 International Consortium of Investigative Journalists, 'The Panama Papers: Exposing the Rogue Offshore Finance Industry', https://www.icij.org/investigations/panama-papers/, accessed 17 August 2020.
3 Home Office and HM Treasury, 'Action Plan for anti-money laundering and counter-terrorist finance' (Home Office/HM Treasury 2016).
4 Ibid. 3.
5 Proceeds of Crime Act 2002, ss 362A–3262I (England, Wales and Northern Ireland); Proceeds of Crime Act 2002 (investigations: Scotland), ss 396A–396I (Scotland).
6 Explanatory Notes to the Criminal Finances Act 2017, paras 12–13.
7 Proceeds of Crime Act 2002, s 362B(3).
8 Ibid. s 362E.
9 Ibid. s 362C(2); civil recovery proceedings are covered in Part 5 of the Proceeds of Crime Act 2002 and are based on the fact that assets originate from unlawful conduct.

DOI: 10.4324/9781003020813-4

new legal instrument follows an international trend to target criminal assets *in rem* rather than prosecute criminal conduct *in personam*.[10]

However, such instruments are controversial. They are intrusive and circumvent procedural safeguards commonly applicable in criminal proceedings.[11] The common argument that such safeguards should not apply to these modern instruments because they are tools of administrative or civil law is not entirely convincing considering the criminal law connotation of the issue as well as the severe potential consequences for the affected person.[12] The design and application of UWOs appears, at least *prima facie*, to infringe several fair trial guarantees: the presumption of innocence, the principle of legality, the principle of equality of arms and as an instrument of coercive compulsion certainly the right not to self-incriminate.[13]

This chapter will focus on the last principle of the above. The right not to self-incriminate, if indeed applicable in UWO proceedings, could be violated at various stages. First, the fact that a person is compelled under threat of a fine or imprisonment to provide potentially incriminating information is per se problematic. Second, questions will arise in relation to the use of information obtained in this manner, either in criminal[14] or civil proceedings, but also in relation to potential negative inferences drawn from a refusal to answer a UWO.[15] Because of the limited scope of a single chapter in a book, the following analysis will focus mainly on problems regarding the right not to self-incriminate at the investigation stage and will not discuss the problems in relation to the use of coercively obtained information or negative inferences drawn from non-compliance to such an order at a later trial stage.

In the UK courts, the application of the privilege against self-incrimination[16] in UWO proceedings has been discussed to a limited extent in the *Hajiyeva*

10 For example: 'Open-ended Intergovernmental Working Group on Asset Recovery, "Model provisions on in rem forfeiture"' (24 August 2011); Swiss Federal Law on freezing and recovering illicit assets of politically exposed persons, SR 161.1.; European Commission, 'Commission Staff Working Document:

Analysis of non-conviction based confiscation measures in the European Union' (12 April 2019).

11 Jennifer Hendry and Colin King, 'How Far Is Too Far? Theorising non-conviction-based asset forfeiture' 11 (2015) IJLC 396, 406; C. King, 'Using Civil Processes in Pursuit of Criminal Law Objectives: A case study of non-conviction-based asset forfeiture' 16 (2012) IJEP 337 f.

12 Home Office and HM Treasury (n 3), 22.

13 Hugo Daniel Lodge, *Criminal Finances Act 2017, A Guide to the New Law* (Law Society 2017), 55.

14 S 362F Proceeds of Crime Act 2002 offers a 'use immunity', e.g. statements gathered through a UWO cannot be used in criminal proceedings. The value of this provision in relation to the right not to self-incriminate is discussed below.

15 For problems relating to negative inferences see *Murray v United Kingdom* (1996) 22 EHRR 29.

16 The discussion was, however, limited to the civil procedure privilege under s 14 of the Civil Evidence Act 1968. Although there are overlaps between s 14 Civil Evidence Act

case.[17] However, the judicial assessment in this case did not extend to a detailed analysis of Strasbourg case law on the principle deriving from Article 6 of the European Convention on Human Rights. In order to evaluate the future success of UWOs as a truly innovative legal tool, such an analysis is crucial. Only if the use of UWOs can withstand legal challenges before the European Court of Human Rights will these new investigatory powers ultimately be able to serve their purpose of facilitating the fight against financial crime.

Functioning of unexplained wealth orders under sections 396A to 396I Proceeds of Crime Act 2002

The Criminal Finances Act 2017 introduced UWOs as new investigatory powers by amending Chapter 2 of Part 8 of the Proceeds of Crime Act 2002. In an *ex parte* hearing,[18] without notice to the respondent, the High Court can issue a UWO on application of a law enforcement authority[19] if the following requirements are met:[20] First, the person holding the targeted assets is either a politically exposed person (PEP) from a non-EEA country[21] or there are reasonable grounds for suspecting that the person is or was involved in serious crime.[22] Second, the value of the targeted assets is above the threshold of £50,000[23] and the court is satisfied that there are reasonable grounds for suspecting that the known sources of the respondent's lawfully obtained income would have been insufficient for the purpose of enabling the respondent to obtain the property.[24] This is a surprisingly low evidential threshold, particularly since the respondent does not have the opportunity to challenge the evidence prior to the issuing of the UWO.[25] The person targeted by a UWO will receive notice that a UWO was issued only *ex post* and will be given a period to respond to the request.[26] The order will request the respondent to set out the nature and extent of their interest in the property, how they obtained the property, details of the settlement, if

1968 and the principle under Article 6 European Convention of Human Rights, the guarantees are not identical; see *Gold Nuts Ltd v Revenue and Customs Commissioner* [2016] UKFTT 82 (TC), [2016] S.T.I 1342.

17 *National Crime Agency v Hajiyeva* [2018] EWHC 2534 (Admin), 1 WLR 5887; *Hajiyeva v National Crime Agency* [2020] EWCA Civ 108, 1 WLR 3209.

18 Lodge submits that the fact that UWOs are issued in *ex parte* hearings might to be challenged in the future; see Lodge (n 13), 45 and 55.

19 The National Crime Agency; Her Majesty's Revenue and Customs; The Financial Conduct Authority; the Director of the Serious Fraud Office; the Director of Public Prosecutions, see Proceeds of Crime Act 2002, s 362A(7).

20 Proceeds of Crime Act 2002, s 362B.

21 Ibid. ss 362B(4)(a) and 396B(7).

22 Ibid. s 362B(4)(b); serious crime is defined under s 362B(9).

23 Ibid. s 362B(1)(b).

24 Ibid. ss 326(3) and 326(6); criticism to this central test in Lodge (n 13), 46–8.

25 Lodge (n 13), 46–7.

26 Proceeds of Crime Act 2002, s 362A(6).

property is held by the trustees of a settlement and any other information in connection with the property.[27]

To give false or misleading statements to a UWO, either knowingly or recklessly, is a criminal offence.[28] Non-compliance to a UWO has the effect that the targeted property is presumed to be recoverable under Part 5 of the Proceeds of Crime Act 2002.[29] What heightens the concerns in relation to the right not to self-incriminate at the investigation stage is that the first UWO was issued with a penal warning attached to it. Although such a consequence is not set out in the statutory provisions covering UWOs, under the current use of this legal instrument, a compelled person can be held in contempt of court for disobeying a UWO and can face a fine or imprisonment. The following penal notice was attached to the UWO against Zamira Hajiyeva: 'If you disobey this order you may be held to be in contempt of court and may be imprisoned, fined or have your assets seized.'[30]

This warning is further specified under the important notes to the order:

> Further or alternatively, any person who disobeys the Unexplained Wealth Order, or knows of either order and does anything which helps or permits another to breach the terms of the same, may be held to be in contempt of court and may be imprisoned, fined or have their assets seized.[31]

The consequences set out in the statutory provisions together with the practice of attaching a penal notice to a UWO have therefore a twofold impact on a respondent who refuses to provide information about the targeted assets because it might be incriminatory. First, they can be held in contempt of court and face a fine or imprisonment in committal proceedings and, second, their targeted assets are presumed be recoverable in civil proceedings. Especially the threat of penal sanctions for disobedience to a UWO seems to encroach on the right not to self-incriminate. It allows authorities to obtain potentially incriminating evidence from a suspect through coercion, while they themselves are either unwilling or unable to obtain the evidence in a different way.[32] It could be argued that the purpose of UWOs is not to gather evidence for future criminal or civil actions against a person, but to start purely *in rem* recovery proceedings of specific assets.[33] However, the following analysis will show that this argument might

27 Ibid. s 362A(3).

28 Ibid. s 362E.

29 Ibid. s 362C.

30 *National Crime Agency v Hajiyeva* (n 17) 89.

31 Ibid. 90.

32 Explanatory Notes to the Criminal Finances Act, para 12; the right not to self-incriminate might also be engaged if information obtained through a UWO is later used in criminal proceedings or if negative inference is drawn from the refusal to answer a UWO, but this is outside the scope of this chapter.

33 Home Office and HM Treasury (n 3), 22.

be flawed. It fails to take into consideration the strong criminal law connotation of UWOs and it could lead to a situation where high profile criminals are being offered a *de facto* immunity for their crimes.

Zamira Hajiyeva: the woman who spent £16.3 million in Harrods

On 27 February 2018, the National Crime Agency (NCA) obtained the first ever UWO, which targeted, among other assets, a Knightsbridge property that was bought for £11.5 million by Vicksburg Global Inc., a British Virgin Island company, controlled by Zamira Hajiyeva.[34] Hajiyeva, who infamously spent £16.3 million in the department store Harrods in 10 years,[35] is the wife of Jahangir Hajiyev.[36] He is the former chairman of the state-owned International Bank of Azerbaijan and was sentenced to 15 years in prison in Azerbaijan in 2016 for charges of fraud, embezzlementb and misappropriation of public funds. In 2016, Hajiyeva herself was apparently arrested *in absentia* by Azeri authorities and, in 2018, was briefly detained in the UK, based on a request for extradition.[37] In September 2019, the Magistrates' Court blocked her extradition on the grounds that she would not receive a fair trial in Azerbaijan.[38]

The UWO against Hajiyeva was based on the assumption that her husband is a PEP within the definition of the law and that there are reasonable grounds for suspecting that Hajiyev's lawful income from his role as chairman of the bank would have been insufficient to obtain the targeted property. According to the NCA, Hajiyeva herself did not have any independent income either and mainly relied on her husband's provision.[39] An interesting fact that was not mentioned in the judgment is that the Home Office granted Zamira Hajiyeva a Tier 1 investor visa in return for a seven-figure investment in UK bonds and shares in 2010.[40] Apparently, the origin of the funds available to this couple wase not suspicious to the authorities at that time, even though Hajiyev was the chairman of the International Bank of Azerbaijan and therefore a PEP.

In July 2018, Hajiyeva applied to the High Court to have the UWO against her discharged on eight grounds: According to Hajiyeva's submissions, Mr Hajiyev was not a PEP within the meaning of the law; the NCA had mischaracterised the respondent's role when persuading the court that the income requirement in the

34 *National Crime Agency v Hajiyeva* (n 17) [10-20]; see also J. Brassey and R. Burns, 'Guilty until Proven Innocent! Unexplained Wealth Orders: what are they and could they affect you and your clients?' (2020) 26 T&T 468.

35 Ibid. 83.

36 Ibid. 11.

37 Ibid. 17–20; *Hajiyeva v National Crime Agency* (n 17) 9.

38 *Hajiyeva v National Crime Agency* (n 17) 9.

39 Ibid. 57.

40 Sean O'Neill, 'Attracting the Megarich While Keeping Out Illicit Money' *The Times* (London, 11 October 2018).

act was met; the NCA had been wrong to place reliance on Mr Hajiyev's conviction in a non-EEA country; the NCA had not established the income requirement to the relevant standard; the order ought to be discharged by virtue of the penal warning wrongly attached to it; the order offended the respondent's right to peaceful enjoyment of her possessions under Article 1 of the First Protocol to the Convention for the Protection of Human Rights and Fundamental Freedoms; the order offended the privilege against self-incrimination and spousal privilege under s 14 Civil Evidence Act 1968; and, given all the circumstances of the case, the court ought not to have exercised its discretion to make the order.[41]

Of particular interest here is Hajiyeva's argument that the order violated her privilege against self-incrimination under s 14 Civil Evidence Act 1968.[42] The High Court, as well as the Court of Appeal, dismissed this ground firmly, but their arguments were limited to the civil guarantee under this provision and did not take into account Strasbourg case law on Article 6 of the European Convention on Human Rights. The High Court held that the UWO did not violate the privilege against self-incrimination,[43] because this privilege only applies as regards to criminal offences under the law of any part of the UK.[44] According to Supperstone J, there was no real and appreciable risk in the present case that Hajiyeva or her husband would be prosecuted for such offences in the UK.[45] The court further submitted that if they were prosecuted in the UK, the offences would comprise qualifying offences under the Fraud Act 2006 for which the privilege against self-incrimination has been excluded by s 13(1) Fraud Act 2006.[46] The court also stated that with the creation of UWOs, parliament effectively abrogated the privilege against self-incrimination to that extent.[47] In December 2019, the Court of Appeal dismissed an appeal by Hajiyeva and reiterated Supperstone J's submissions in relation to the privilege under s 14 CEA 1968.[48]

Hajiyeva has not been granted leave to bring the case to the Supreme Court and at the time of writing it is not known if Hajiyeva intends to bring this case to the Human Rights Court in Strasbourg.[49] Since the issuing of this first UWO, this new legal instrument has been used a number of times again with variable success.[50] The legal issue of a potential infringement of the right not to self-

41 *Hajiyeva v National Crime Agency* (n 17).
42 Ibid. (n 17) 45–56; the following discussion is limited to the right not to self-incriminate and does not take into consideration potential spousal privileges.
43 Civil Evidence Act 1968, s 14.
44 *National Crime Agency v Hajiyeva* (n 17) 107.
45 Ibid. 108.
46 Ibid. 113; this argument is flawed, as *Hajiyeva* is more likely to be prosecuted for money laundering offences in the UK than for fraud offence; see below.
47 Ibid. 110–12.
48 *Hajiyeva v National Crime Agency* (n 17) 45–56.
49 Jonathan Ames, 'Zamira Hajiyeva: McMafia banker's wife could lose her £15m home after court defeat' *The Times* (London, 6 February 2020).
50 *National Crime Agency v Hussain et al* [2020] EWHC 432 (Admin), [2020] 1 W.L.R. 2145; *National Crime Agency v Baker* [2020] EWHC 822 (Admin), [2020] 4 WLUK 113;

incriminate has, however, not yet been raised again. The following analysis is therefore a first attempt to examine whether UWOs at the investigation stage are reconcilable with the guarantees under the criminal limb of Article 6 of the European Convention on Human Rights.

The right not to self-incriminate under Strasbourg case law

The right not to self-incriminate, although generally acknowledged to lie at the heart of the notion of a fair trial, is not expressly set out in the European Convention on Human Rights.[51] The Court describes the principle and its rationale in the case of *Saunders v UK* as follows:

> Their rationale lies, inter alia, in the protection of the accused against improper compulsion by the authorities thereby contributing to the avoidance of miscarriages of justice and to the fulfilment of the aims of Article 6 [...]. The right not to incriminate oneself, in particular, presupposes that the prosecution in a criminal case seek to prove their case against the accused without resort to evidence obtained through methods of coercion or oppression in defiance of the will of the accused. In this sense the right is closely linked to the presumption of innocence contained in Article 6 para. 2 of the Convention.[52]

It is clear from this statement that the right not to self-incriminate applies within the realm of criminal law only and it seems to be the view of the domestic courts that UWO proceedings are located outside criminal law territory and therefore outside of the scope of this principle.[53] However, the extent of the application of the criminal limb of Article 6 of the Convention depends on the existence of a criminal charge in the autonomous sense of this term,[54] not its formal domestic classification.[55] A review of Strasbourg case law on this issue is therefore pivotal and the following analysis shows that the High Court and the Court of Appeal might have set aside concerns in relation to the right not to self-incriminate too

on the *Baker* case, see also A. Clancy, 'Proving the Dough: National Crime Agency v Baker & Ors' (2021) MLR 84(1) 168.

51 European Court of Human Rights, 'Guide on Article 6 of the European Convention on Human Rights' (updated 30 April 2020), https://www.echr.coe.int/Documents/Guide_Art_6_criminal_ENG.pdf, accessed 25 August 2020, para 184.

52 *Saunders v United Kingdom* (1997) 23 EHRR 313 68.

53 *National Crime Agency v Hajiyeva* (n 17) [108].

54 The ECtHR assesses the existence of a criminal charge according to the 'Engel criteria': the classification in domestic law, the nature of the offence and the severity of the penalty that the person concerned risks incurring, see *Engel et al v the Netherlands* (1979–80) EHRR 706.

55 Although the classification in domestic law is the starting point, this criterion is not decisive unless an offence is classified as criminal; see European Court of Human Rights (n 51) para 19.

prematurely in the *Hajiyeva* case.[56] *Funke v France*[57] is one of the key Strasbourg cases on the question whether a conviction for refusing to provide potentially incriminating information violates the right not to self-incriminate under the criminal limb of Article 6. It therefore offers a good starting point for this study.

The key case of Funke v France

Funke was suspected of tax offences, but was never formally charged and tax proceedings against him were never opened. He was, however, compelled by French custom officers, under threat of fines and imprisonment, to produce statements of overseas bank accounts that they suspected existed.[58] Funke refused to comply with this request and was later convicted in proceedings for disclosure of documents. Funke claimed that his criminal conviction for the refusal to comply with the compulsion violated his right to a fair trial.[59] The French government objected to this using the argument that no criminal proceedings had ever been opened against Funke and the criminal limb of Article 6 should therefore not apply.[60] The court dismissed this objection because Funke did not complain about the actual tax proceedings, but the disclosure of information proceedings in which he had been convicted for a refusal to produce potentially incriminating bank statements on compulsion by custom officers. The court concluded the question of a potential infringement of Funke's right to remain silent as follows:

> The Court notes that the customs secured Mr Funke's conviction in order to obtain certain documents which they believed must exist, although they were not certain of the fact. Being unable or unwilling to procure them by some other means, they attempted to compel the applicant himself to provide the evidence of offences he had allegedly committed. The special features of customs law [...] cannot justify such an infringement of the right of anyone 'charged with a criminal offence', within the autonomous meaning of this expression in Article 6 (art. 6), to remain silent and not to contribute to incriminating himself. There has accordingly been a breach of Article 6 para. 1 (art. 6-1).[61]

A comparison of the situation in *Funke* to the UWO proceedings reveals interesting parallels. As mentioned above, a respondent to a UWO who disobeys the order, e.g. remains silent, faces a fine or imprisonment in committal proceedings

56 *National Crime Agency v Hajiyeva* (n 17) [104-116]; *Hajiyeva v National Crime Agency* (n 17) [45-56].
57 *Funke v France* (1993) 16 EHRR 297.
58 Ibid.
59 Ibid. 38.
60 Ibid. 39.
61 Ibid. 44.

because UWOs are issued with a penal warning attached to them.[62] A person targeted by a UWO is, therefore, compelled under the threat of penal sanctions to provide potentially incriminating evidence.[63] The crucial point, however, is that *Funke* was deemed to be charged with a criminal offence in the autonomous meaning of the expression, while, at least in the case of *Hajiyeva*, the domestic courts did not consider that criminal proceedings in the UK were anticipated. Supperstone J clearly stated that:

> [...] I do not consider that the evidence discloses a real and appreciable risk that Mrs Hajiyeva or her husband will be prosecuted for offences in the UK. [...] Accordingly the threshold test for the privileges to apply has not been satisfied.[64]

According to the Convention jurisprudence, the existence of a criminal charge is assessed autonomously and can be defined as the official notification given to an individual by the competent authority of an allegation that the affected person has committed a criminal offence. This is the case if the situation of the suspect has been substantially affected by actions taken by the authorities as a result of a suspicion against them.[65] The European Court of Human Rights has held in previous cases that a charge exists in the autonomous sense, not only when a person is arrested or formally charged with an offence, but already when a person is questioned about their involvement in a criminal offence, even if they are treated as a mere witness.[66]

In the *Hajiyeva* case, the High Court used the threshold test for the application of the privilege in civil procedures,[67] e.g. whether there was a real and appreciable risk that Hajiyeva or her husband would be prosecuted for offences in the UK and concluded that this threshold had not been reached. In other words, the court implied that Hajiyeva was, at the time of issue of the UWO, not charged with an offence because criminal proceedings were at that time neither pending nor anticipated.[68] This argument might be formally correct because no criminal proceedings had ever been opened against Hajiyeva in the UK. However, substantially, this situation does not seem to be as clear. The strong criminal law connotation of UWOs has to be taken into consideration when assessing this issue.[69] It cannot be ignored that UWOs are based on the suspicion that the known lawful sources of the respondent's income have been insufficient to acquire the

62 *National Crime Agency v Hajiyeva* (n 17) 89–90.
63 Either statements or documents can be requested through UWOs.
64 Ibid. 115.
65 *Deweer v Belgium* App no 6903/75 (ECtHR, 27 February 1980) 42–6.
66 *Heaney and McGuinness v Ireland* (2000) 22 EHRR 12; *Kalēja v Latvia* App no 22059/08 (ECtHR, 5 October 2017).
67 *National Crime Agency v Hajiyeva* (n 17) 108.
68 Ibid.
69 E.g. *Bendenoun v France* App no 12547/86 (ECtHR, 24 February 1994) 4.

targeted property. In other words, the authorities suspect that the targeted property has been acquired unlawfully.

A respondent to a UWO is, therefore, suspected of holding criminal property. What seems to have been overlooked is that this constitutes in itself a criminal offence in the UK. Under s 329 of the Proceeds of Crime Act 2002 a person commits an offence if they acquire, use or possess criminal property. It would therefore not be fanciful to describe UWO proceedings as proceedings in which a person is questioned about their suspected involvement in a criminal offence – namely money laundering, even though the questioning does not take place in the usual criminal justice setting, but in proceedings that are at least formally classified to be civil in nature. Faced with this background, it would not be surprising either if the European Court of Human Rights were to come to the conclusion that a person affected by a UWO could, in certain circumstances, at least substantially, be considered as charged with a criminal offence.

The argument against such a conclusion would be that UWOs are purely *in rem* instruments; they are intended to target property and not persons and they were not designed to imply guilt. This argument is sustainable in situations where UWOs are used to target 'abandoned' illicit assets, acquired or held by criminals that are not currently within the jurisdiction of the UK and that are for whatever reason not available for prosecution in the UK.[70] However, the design of UWOs is much broader. UWOs can be used if the holder of the targeted property is in the UK. It is even possible that UWOs are issued against illicit assets that stem from crimes that were committed entirely in the UK.[71] It is difficult to support the view that UWOs only target property and not the holder of property in situations where a respondent to a UWO effectively holds criminal property in the UK and is physically 'available' to prosecution authorities. This person is under suspicion of having committed a criminal offence as described above, otherwise a UWO would be baseless. It is not realistic in such a scenario to treat the respondent to a UWO as a mere third party as they themselves will have likely committed an offence.[72]

The High Court submitted in the *Hajiyeva* case that neither Hajiyeva nor her husband was facing criminal proceedings in the UK,[73] but it cannot be argued that a respondent to a UWO would never face criminal prosecution in the UK. Such an assumption would indeed lead to highly undesirable consequences. It would mean that a respondent to a UWO enjoys *de facto* immunity from criminal prosecution for money laundering offences committed in the UK because they

70 For example because the person is in a country with which mutual legal assistance or extradition is doomed to fail or the person is dead.

71 E.g. in relation to a respondent who has been involved in serious crime; Proceeds of Crime Act 2002, s 362B(4)(b)(i): '*the respondent is, or has been, involved in serious crime (whether in a part of the United Kingdom or elsewhere)*'.

72 E.g. acquiring, using or possessing criminal property under s 329 Proceeds of Crime Act 2002.

73 *National Crime Agency v Hajiyeva* (n 17) 108.

were targeted by a UWO before proceedings were opened. The use of UWO proceedings would allow them to relinquish their property to the authorities and therewith buy themselves out of criminal responsibility. Surely, this cannot be within the spirit this new legal instrument and it is surely not within the public interest that large scale financial crimes are not being prosecuted and criminals are not being held criminally accountable. UWOs should be a measure of last resort where orthodox prosecution would fail, but not an alternative settlement that allows high profile criminals to escape justice.

For these reasons, there seems to be a realistic prospect that the European Court of Human Rights could rely on its findings in *Funke v France*[74] and conclude that under certain circumstances a person affected by a UWO has to be considered charged with a criminal offence even though no formal prosecution has yet been opened. In certain circumstances, criminal proceedings must be anticipated. Otherwise, UWOs would offer a blank *de facto* immunity to all respondents. This means that UWOs could fall under the scope of the criminal limb of Article 6 of the European Convention on Human Rights and the right not to self-incriminate would apply.

*Post-*Funke *cases*

There are several other cases that followed the *Funke* judgment[75] and concluded that respondent states have violated the applicant's right not to self-incriminate in prosecutions for failure to provide information, even though the applicant was not formally charged with a criminal offence and it seems reasonable to assume that the *Funke* judgment[76] would influence a judicial assessment of UWO proceedings as well. In *Heaney and McGuinness v Ireland*,[77] the applicants were arrested in relation to terrorist offences and compelled under threat of penal sanctions to provide a full account of their movements. Even though they were not formally charged with a criminal offence, the fact that they were arrested and questioned in relation to an IRA bombing meant for the Strasbourg Court that they were at least suspected of having been involved in a criminal offence and therefore substantially charged in the autonomous sense of the term.[78] In *Marttinen v Finland*,[79] the applicant refused to provide information about his assets in a debt enforcement enquiry relying on his right not to self-incriminate. The applicant was subject to correlating pre-trial investigations for debtor's fraud, which were frozen at the time of the compulsion. The Finnish Supreme Court argued in this case that:

74 *Funke v France* (n 57).
75 Ibid.
76 Ibid.
77 *Heaney and McGuinness v Ireland* (n 66).
78 Ibid. 41–59.
79 *Marttinen v Finland* App no 19235/03 (ECtHR, 21 July 2009).

> The purpose of the powers of enforcement authorities to oblige the debtor to provide an account of his property, and of the coercive means available to ensure compliance with this obligation, is to make enforcement more efficient. Although it is possible to impose a threat of a fine to secure compliance with the obligation to give the information requested in connection with the enforcement inquiry, and a sentence may be ordered on a person concealing information or giving false information, the debtor is not, when complying with his or her obligation to give information on his or her property for the purposes of enforcement, a person charged with a criminal offence within the meaning of Article 6 of the Convention, to whom the rights of the accused would apply.[80]

The European Court of Human Rights did not agree with this submission and held that Marttinen should be considered charged in the autonomous sense of the expression. According to the Strasbourg Court it is not a requirement for the application of the principle that the allegedly incriminating evidence obtained through coercion was actually used in a criminal trial.[81]

There are, however, cases with a similar set of facts in which the Strasbourg Court has denied the application of the right not to self-incriminate in investigation procedures because it considered the applicant not to be charged with a criminal offence. Although these cases seem to contradict *Funke prima facie*, they can be distinguished based on their facts. In *Weh v Austria*,[82] Weh's car was caught by a speed camera exceeding the speed limit and proceedings against an unknown driver were opened. Weh was required by the state authorities to provide the identity of the driver at the time of the speeding incident. Weh inaccurately stated that the driver was a person living in Texas in the USA. He was later fined for providing inaccurate information.[83] The Strasbourg Court held in this case that the right not to self-incriminate had not been violated. The case was, according to the Court, distinguishable from cases such as *Funke*[84] or *Heaney and McGuinness*[85] because the criminal proceedings against the applicant were less likely:

> In Funke and in Heaney and McGuinness [...] criminal proceedings were anticipated, though they had not been formally opened, at the time the respective applicants were required to give potentially incriminating information. In Funke the customs authorities had a specific suspicion against the applicant, in Heaney and McGuinness the applicants had been arrested on suspicion of terrorist offences. In the present case the proceedings for

80 Ibid. 21.
81 Ibid. 58–66.
82 *Weh v Austria* (2005) 40 EHRR 37.
83 Ibid. 11–23.
84 *Funke v France* (n 57).
85 *Heaney and McGuinness v Ireland* (n 66).

> speeding were conducted against unknown offenders, when the authorities requested the applicant under section 103 § 2 of the Motor Vehicles Act to disclose who had been driving his car on 5 March 1995. There were clearly no proceedings for speeding pending against the applicant and it cannot even be said that they were anticipated as the authorities did not have any element of suspicion against him.[86]

Later cases in relation to the procurement of a driver's identity by compulsion show that the distinguishing characteristics from *Funke v France*[87] in these cases are not so much, as suggested in *Weh*,[88] the degree of likelihood of the criminal proceedings, but the degree of the compulsion used. In *O'Halloran and Francis v UK*,[89] the Strasbourg Court set out, citing *Brown v Stott*,[90] that the compulsion in such cases flowed from the fact that all who own or drive motor cars know that by doing so they subject themselves to a regulatory regime to protect public safety and they therefore accept certain responsibilities including the present compulsion.[91] The court further set out that the compulsion in this case was narrow, because it only required the affected person to provide the authorities with the identity of the driver. Interesting for the assessment of UWOs is the following statement of the court in this case:

> The information is thus markedly more restricted than in previous cases, in which applicants have been subjected to statutory powers requiring production of 'papers and documents of any kind relating to operations of interest to [the] department' [see *Funke*, cited above, § 30], or of 'documents, etc., which might be relevant for the assessment of taxes' [see *JB v Switzerland*, cited above, § 39].[92]

It seems likely from this statement that the Strasbourg Court would consider the compulsion used in UWO proceedings to be less restricted than the one in *Weh* or *O'Halloran and Francis*.[93] As mentioned above, UWOs require the respondent to provide extensive information about the targeted assets: namely, to set out the nature and extent of their interest in the property, how they obtained the property, details of the settlement, if property is held by the trustees of a settlement and any other information in connection with the property.[94] This is not comparable with the procurement of the identity of the driver of one's car

86 *Weh v Austria* (n 83) 52–3.
87 *Funke v France* (n 57).
88 *Weh v Austria* (n 83).
89 *O'Halloran and Francis v United Kingdom* (2008) 46 EHRR 21.
90 *Brown v Stott* [2001] 2 WLR 817.
91 *O'Halloran and Francis v United Kingdom* (n 90) 57.
92 Ibid. 58.
93 *O'Halloran and Francis v United Kingdom* (n 90).
94 Proceeds of Crime Act 2002, s 362A(3).

at a specific moment in time and the compulsion does not derive from a regulatory framework that supports public safety, but from a suspicion that money laundering offences have been committed.

In the case of *Fayed v UK*,[95] administrative investigation proceedings by inspectors of the Department for Trade and Industry (DTI)[96] were considered to be outside the application of the criminal limb of Article 6. The Court described these proceedings as follows:

> [Their] purpose [...] was to ascertain and record facts which might subsequently be used as the basis for action by other competent authorities – prosecuting, regulatory, disciplinary or even legislative [...].[97]
>
> Acceptance of the applicants' argument would entail that a body carrying out preparatory investigations at the instance of regulatory or other authorities should always be subject to the guarantees of a judicial procedure set forth in Article 6(1) by reason of the fact that publication of its findings is liable to damage the reputation of the individuals whose conduct is being investigated. Such an interpretation of Article 6(1) would in practice unduly hamper the effective regulation in the public interest of complex financial and commercial activities. In the Court's view, investigative proceedings of the kind in issue in the present case fall outside the ambit and intendment of Article 6(1) [...].[98]

This raises the question as to whether the Strasbourg Court could *per analogiam* consider that UWO proceedings are also fact-finding procedures or preparatory proceedings outside the scope of the criminal procedure guarantees of Article 6. However, some characteristics of UWOs make such an analogy difficult. UWOs are not used to investigate complex corporate or financial issues. In fact, they do not require any investigatory work as such. UWOs simply compel the respondent, under threat of a fine or imprisonment, to explain how they have obtained the targeted property.[99] It is not because of the complexity of the issue that UWOs are used, but because enforcement agencies are unwilling or unable to obtain this information, or evidence relating to this information, themselves.[100] A second point that cannot be neglected is that DTI investigations are used to establish a set of facts. These facts might well be just descriptive and neutral in value. This

95 *Fayed v United Kingdom* (1994) 18 EHRR 393; the same reasoning was later followed in *Saunders v United Kingdom* (n 52).
96 Based on s 432(2) Companies Act 1985.
97 *Fayed v United Kingdom* (n 96) 61.
98 Ibid. 62.
99 Proceeds of Crime Act 2002, s362A(3).
100 Explanatory Notes to the Criminal Finances Act, paras 12.

is different with UWOs – if a respondent does not have the right to remain silent to a UWO, their answer will inevitably be either exculpatory or incriminating.[101]

The above shows that it is reasonable to believe that because of the strong criminal law connotation of UWOs and the degree and nature of the compulsion used, the Strasbourg Court could find that under certain circumstances a respondent to a UWO should be considered charged with a criminal offence in the autonomous meaning of the term. This would mean that UWOs, if they are issued with a penal warning attached to them, might violate the right not to self-incriminate under the criminal limb of Article 6 of the Convention. This would not, however, be the case if parliament lawfully abrogated the right not to self-incriminate, as the High Court submitted in the *Hajiyeva* case.[102]

Valid abrogation of the right not to self-incriminate in UWO proceedings

According to the High Court, parliament abrogated the privilege against self-incrimination by creating the legal instrument of UWOs.[103] Whether such an abrogation is compatible with the European Convention, depends, first, on whether the right not to self-incriminate is an absolute or a qualified right and, second, if the right is qualified, whether the infringement is justified. The Strasbourg Court did not find it necessary in the case of *Saunders v United Kingdom* to decide whether the right not to self-incriminate was absolute or not.[104] However, the Court stated that it did not accept the respondent state's argument that the public interest in the investigation and punishment of corporate fraud could justify a marked departure of the basic principle of fair procedure.[105] Post-*Saunders*, the Court's position seems to have shifted not only in terms of the definition of the right not to self-incriminate, but also on the issue as to whether it can be balanced against public interest grounds. In other words, the Court seems to accept that in certain circumstances the legislator can validly abrogate the right not to self-incriminate.[106]

The case of *Jalloh v Germany* was concerned with a person being forced to produce real evidence. Through forceful administration of an emetic substance, the applicant regurgitated a small bag of cocaine.[107] The Court clearly distinguished

101 Because the compulsion through UWOs is not used to assess a person's tax liability, it can also not be compared to the case of *Allen v United Kingdom* (2002) 35 EHRR CD289.

102 *National Crime Agency v Hajiyeva* (n 17) 110–12.

103 Ibid. 110–12.

104 *Saunders v United Kingdom* (n 52) 74.

105 Ibid.

106 For a detailed discussion of this shift, see Andrew L.-T. Choo, *The Privilege Against Self-Incrimination and Criminal Justice* (Hart 2013), 62 f.

107 *Jalloh v Germany* (2007) 44 EHRR 32.

this case from cases such as *Funke v France*[108] or *JB v Switzerland*,[109] where the right not to self-incriminate was violated in the sense that a suspect was compelled to produce potentially incriminating documents rather than other forms of real evidence that are usually not covered by the principle.[110] However, the Court also set out to what extent an infringement could be considered lawful. Interestingly, and in an apparent departure from its statement in *Saunders*,[111] the Court engaged in a balancing test between public interest factors and the violated right:

> In order to determine whether the applicant's right not to incriminate himself has been violated, the Court will have regard, in turn, to the following factors: the nature and degree of compulsion used to obtain the evidence; the weight of the public interest in the investigation and punishment of the offence in issue; the existence of any relevant safeguards in the procedure; and the use to which any material so obtained is put.[112]

In the following case of *O'Halloran and Francis v the United Kingdom*,[113] in which the applicants were compelled to reveal the identity of the driver of their car, the Court reiterated these factors, but dropped the public interest element once again:

> In the light of the principles contained in its Jalloh judgment, and in order to determine whether the essence of the applicants' right to remain silent and privilege against self-incrimination was infringed, the Court will focus on the nature and degree of compulsion used to obtain the evidence, the existence of any relevant safeguards in the procedure, and the use to which any material so obtained was put.[114]

In light of these cases, it seems evident that the right not to self-incriminate is not an absolute right. However the Court's assessment of when an infringement is justified and whether public interest factors are decisive is inconsistent. It is therefore difficult to assess at this point whether the Strasbourg Court would accept that parliament has lawfully abrogated the right not to self-incriminate by creating UWOs. Clearly the investigation of financial crimes and the recovery of illicit funds are in the public interest. However, the degree of compulsion exercised through UWOs is, as discussed above, undeniably high.[115]

108 *Funke v France* (n 57).
109 *JB v Switzerland* App no 31827/96 (ECtHR, 3 May 2001).
110 *Jalloh v Germany* (n 108) 113.
111 *Saunders v United Kingdom* (n 52).
112 *Jalloh v Germany* (n 108) 117.
113 *O'Halloran and Francis v UK* (n 90).
114 Ibid. 55.
115 See above, discussion of UWO in light of *Funke v France* (n 57).

Statutory 'use immunity' and potential infringements of the right not to self-incriminate

UWOs can only be used under the statutory safeguard that statements in response to such order cannot be used in evidence against the respondent in criminal proceedings.[116] This 'use immunity' is a feature that the legislator has often attached to statutory compulsion powers after the Strasbourg decision of *Saunders v UK*[117] and it will clearly give some weight in the Court's assessment whether UWOs infringe on the very essence of the right not to self-incriminate.[118] However, whether this 'use immunity' is capable of curing all the discussed concerns in relation to the right not to self-incriminate is doubtful. It should not be overlooked that the European Court of Human Rights made it clear that it is not a requirement for a violation of the right not to self-incriminate that the evidence obtained has actually been used in criminal proceedings:

> The Court points out that in previous cases it has expressly found that there is no requirement for allegedly incriminating evidence obtained by coercion to be actually used in criminal proceedings before the right not to incriminate oneself applies. In particular, in the case of Heaney and McGuinness v. Ireland (no. 34720/97, §§ 43-46, ECHR 2000–XII) it found that the applicants could rely on Article 6 §§ 1 and 2 in respect of their conviction and imprisonment for failing to reply to questions, even though they were subsequently acquitted of the underlying offence. Indeed, in the case of Funke v. France [cited above, §§ 39–40], the Court found a violation of the right not to incriminate oneself even though no underlying proceedings were brought, and by the time of the Strasbourg proceedings none could be.[119]

Academics have also raised concerns to what extent 'use immunity' could cure potential problems that compulsion powers create in relation to the right not to self-incriminate. Choo concluded that the availability of 'use immunity' would protect the privilege against self-incrimination at least to the extent of the immunity granted, but he seems sceptical about whether 'use immunity' will dissipate concerns deriving from the actual use of compulsion powers rather than the use of evidence obtain by compulsion:

> The availability of 'use immunity' to a person would mean [...] that, to the extent to which immunity is guaranteed, the provision of information by him or her can no longer 'reasonably lead to, or increase the likelihood of, the prosecution of that person for a criminal offence'. Thus the privilege against self-incrimination would, by definition, be protected to that extent. It would

116 Proceeds of Crime Act 2002, s 362F.
117 *Saunders v United Kingdom* (n 52).
118 Choo (n 106), 34 f.
119 *Marttinen v Finland* (n 80) 64.

> be naïve, however, to believe that any concerns generated by legal compulsion to provide potentially self-incriminatory information will dissipate to the extent to which 'use immunity' is available to protect the privilege. After all, it might be considered undignified for a person to be compelled, on pain of a criminal sanction, to provide information revealing criminal wrongdoing even though there is no possibility of this being used against him or her in a subsequent trial. Such compulsion might be regarded as objectionable in itself and, as a practical matter, might well produce information that proves to be of indirect assistance to the authorities.[120]

The discussion above has shown that UWOs might potentially violate the right not to-self incriminate at the investigation stage, if the Strasbourg Court comes to the conclusion that a respondent to a UWO is charged in the autonomous sense of the expression. The concern raised in this chapter relates to the compulsion itself rather than the use of evidence obtained through it. It is not unreasonable to think that the Strasbourg Court could draw on the parallels to the *Funke*[121] case and conclude that UWOs, independent of the use of the gathered evidence, violate the right not to self-incriminate in its very essence. This violation would not be cured by the availability of a use immunity.

Concluding thoughts and recommendations

According to the above analysis, there is a reasonable possibility that the European Court of Human Rights could find that UWOs in their investigation stage do violate the right not to self-incriminate because a person affected by such an order could, in certain circumstances, be considered charged with a criminal offence under the autonomous meaning of the expression. It is difficult to predict whether the Court would accept that parliament has abrogated the right not to self-incriminate to a lawful extent by creating UWOs or whether the available 'use immunity' granted is a sufficient safeguard to dissipate concerns in relation to this right.

The two main problems of UWOs are the following: first, they are issued with a penal warning attached to them, which means that a respondent could face criminal sanctions for a refusal to provide potentially incriminating information and, second, because of their design, their scope is broad and seems to overshoot the original target. UWOs should be measures of *ultima ratio* that step in where orthodox prosecution fails, but they cannot be used as an alternative settlement for high profile money laundering cases. Otherwise, authorities would grant a *de facto* immunity to respondents to UWOs, which cannot be in the public interest. The following recommendations would limit the scope of UWOs to more reasonable range and would not only address the issues mentioned in relation to

120 Choo (n 106), 35.
121 *Funke v France* (n 57).

the right not to self-incriminate but bring the legal instrument back in line with its initial rationale.

First, the concerns in relation to the right not to self-incriminate are heightened by the fact that the order, in practice, is issued with a penal warning. It seems that parliament did not intend such a consequence. According to the statutory provisions, the only consequence for non-compliance to a UWO is that the targeted property is presumed to be recoverable in civil recovery proceedings.[122] To extend the consequences for non-compliance not only seems unnecessary, but it potentially undermines the future success of this innovative legal instrument by creating potentially defeating issues in relation to the right not to self-incriminate.

Second, UWOs were designed to step in where orthodox prosecution fails, not for the mere convenience of enforcement agencies. Their use is justified, for example, where criminal property is in the UK, but the holders are outside of the jurisdiction, potentially in a country with which mutual legal assistance proceedings are doomed to fail due to political or other reasons. However, the statutory provisions do not include such a caveat. UWOs can be issued if the respondent is in the UK. There is no reason why, in these circumstances, criminals should not face orthodox prosecution. UWOs should not have the perverted effect of allowing criminals to avoid criminal responsibility simply by relinquishing property targeted by UWOs. This cannot be within the spirit of this legal tool. The legislator should therefore add as a legal requirement for issuing UWOs that the holder of the targeted property is outside the jurisdiction of the UK and that mutual legal assistance and extradition will not be successful because of political or factual reasons or that the respondent is not available for prosecution for other reasons.

Finally, there seems to be a desperate need for a cultural change in relation to illicitly acquired assets of high net worth individuals that are invested in UK property. What is frankly disturbing in the case of Zamira Hajiyeva is that 10 years ago, she was granted a Tier 1 investor visa by the Home Office in return for a seven-figure investment in UK bonds and shares. How is it possible that politically exposed persons with extraordinary wealth are being courted by government in this way? How is it possible that the legal professionals involved in the conveyance of the property, later targeted by a UWO, did not suspect that the funds used were illicit? How is it possible that the bank granting a mortgage to the Hajiyevas had no reservations about doing so? It seems that draconian measures, such as unexplained wealth orders, would not be necessary if there was a genuine commitment not to allow the UK to become a safe haven for illicit funds.

122 Proceeds of Crime Act 2002, s 362C.

4 The introduction of anti-money laundering legislation in the Vatican City State

Susan Clark Garnett[1]

Introduction

Since its establishment, the Vatican Bank has been shrouded in secrecy and viewed by the outside world with suspicion.[2] It stands accused, at best, of being involved in shady dealings, and, at worst, of being involved in illegal activity throughout its history. However, in 2011, the Vatican introduced legislation[3] governing its financial institutions with the aim of establishing an anti-money laundering and counterterrorism financing (AML/CTF) system in line with established international practices.

This initiative is significant because it is the first time the Vatican has adopted international standards and the recommendations set out in European Union (EU) law. The aim here is to, first, explore the reasons for this new found receptiveness, to both international standards and EU law and, second, to provide some evaluation of the extent to which these sources of law, both hard and soft law, have brought Vatican practices in line with the accepted anti-money laundering standards of the international community.

Money laundering – a problem of global concern

The International Monetary Fund (IMF) described money laundering as a 'problem of global concern'[4] that 'poses a threat to financial system integrity, and may undermine the sound functioning of financial systems, good governance

1 Associate Lecturer in Criminology, Bath Spa University.

2 Paul Vallely, 'Can Pope Francis clean up God's Bank?' *The Guardian* (13 August 2015), https://www.theguardian.com/world/2015/aug/13/can-pope-francis-clean-up-gods-bank , accessed 21 January 2020.

3 Law N. CXXVII On the Prevention and Countering of the Laundering of Proceeds of Criminal Activities and of the Financing of Terrorism 30 December 2010, http://www.ior.va/content/dam/ior/documenti/media/documenti/DecretodelPresidentedelGovernatorato.pdf, accessed 20 December 2020.

4 International Monetary Fund, Public Information Notice 01/41, IMF Executive Board Discusses Money Laundering (29 April 2001), https://www.imf.org/en/News/Articles/2015/09/28/04/53/pn0141, accessed 20 November 2020.

DOI: 10.4324/9781003020813-5

and the fight against corruption'.[5] It is also the case that money laundering in one jurisdiction can have negative spillover effects on the economies of other jurisdictions.[6]

In simple terms, the negative economic implications of money laundering on a particular nation can be broadly grouped into three categories. First, money laundering goes hand-in-hand with tax evasion and the non-payment of import and export duties by smuggling goods in and out of a country. Such activities deprive governments of important sources of revenue. Second, money launderers have a tendency to direct and redirect their money from one asset to another with the objective of creating a complex web of financial transactions to hide the illegal origin of the money. The money is hidden where it is least conspicuous, rather than being used to make more money. These counterintuitive investments can potentially destabilise the overall financial system by increasing market volatility, which weakens investor confidence.[7] Third, money laundering activities involving irregular and unpredictable capital flows tend to increase interest and foreign exchange rates, both of which are potentially problematic for governments.[8]

Definition of money laundering

It has been claimed that most countries[9] subscribe to the definitions adopted by the United Nations in the Vienna Convention[10] and Palermo Convention[11] where money laundering is defined as:

> The conversion or transfer of property, knowing that such property is derived from any [drug trafficking] offence or offences or from an act of participation in such offence or offences, for the purpose of concealing or disguising the illicit origin of the property or of assisting any person who is involved in the

5 Ibid.

6 Kern Alexander, Rahul Dhumale and John Eatwell, *Global Governance of Financial Systems: The International Regulation of Systemic Risk* (Oxford University Press 2006) 67.

7 John McDowell and Gary Novis, 'The Consequences of Money Laundering and Financial Crime' (2001) US Dept of State, Bureau of International Narcotics and Law Enforcement and Affairs 6, https://www.hsdl.org/?view&did=3549, accessed 20 November 2020. [6–8]

8 Ibid. 8.

9 Paul Schott, 'Reference Guide to Anti-Money Laundering and Combating the Financing of Terrorism' (2006) The World Bank, http://documents1.worldbank.org/curated/en/558401468134391014/pdf/350520Referenc1Money01OFFICIAL0USE1.pdf, accessed 20 January 2021.

10 UN Economic and Social Council (ECOSOC), *United Nations Convention Against Illicit Traffic in Narcotic Drugs and Psychotropic Substances*, 19 December 1988, https://www.refworld.org/docid/ 49997af90.html, accessed 8 January 2021. [Vienna Convention]

11 UN General Assembly, *Protocol to Prevent, Suppress and Punish Trafficking in Persons, Especially Women and Children, Supplementing the United Nations Convention against Transnational Organised Crime*, 15 November 2000, https://www.refworld.org/docid/4720706c0.html, accessed 8 January 2021. [Palermo Convention]

> commission of such an offence or offences to evade the legal consequences of his actions; [12]
>
> The concealment or disguise of the true nature, source, location, disposition, movement, rights with respect to, or ownership of property, knowing that such property is derived from an offence or offences or from an act of participation in such an offence or offences, and; [13]
>
> The acquisition, possession or use of property, knowing at the time of receipt that such property was derived from an offence or offences or from an act of participation in such offence [...] or offences.[14]

These definitions identify the underlying objective of money laundering as allowing criminals to access the profits of their illegal activities by distancing themselves from it.

The amount of criminal proceeds that enter the international financial system annually is unknown but estimates suggest the amount is in excess of hundreds of billions of dollars. In 2018 the United Nations estimated that amount of money laundered globally per year is 2–5% of global GDP, or $1.6 to $4 trillion a year.[15] Even the lower estimate underlines the seriousness of the problem.[16]

The process of money laundering

The process of money laundering can be broken down into three discrete steps. First, the illicit funds are 'placed' into the financial system. The second step, known as 'layering', involves funnelling the money into the economy through various financial transactions designed to hide the origins of the illicit funds. Finally, the funds are 'integrated' into the system when the illicit funds re-enter the mainstream economy, taking on the appearance of a legal transaction.

Placement is the most difficult part of money laundering in the sense that it is the point at which criminals are most vulnerable to detection.[17] The US General Accounting Office has defined placement as:

> [...] the concealing of illicit proceeds by (1) converting cash to another medium that is more convenient or less suspicious for purposes of exchange,

12 Vienna Convention (n 10) Article 3(b).
13 Vienna Convention (n 10) Article 3(c)(i).
14 Palermo Convention (n 11) Article 6(b)(i).
15 United Nations Office of Drugs and Crime 'Money Laundering and Globalisation', https://www.unodc.org/unodc/en/money-laundering/globalisation.html, accessed 20 November 2020.
16 Ibid.
17 US General Accounting Office, 'Money Laundering: The volume of currency transaction reports filed could and should be reduced' (15 March 1994) 3, https://www.gao.gov/assets/110/105432.pdf, accessed 5 October 2020.

such as property, cashier's checks, or money orders, or (2) depositing funds into financial institutions accounts for subsequent disbursement.[18]

The international financial framework to combat money laundering

Initiatives to combat money laundering have generally prioritised making placement more difficult. In 1980, the Council of Europe produced a Recommendation[19] highlighting the role banks can play in combating money laundering. It stressed the importance of banks introducing customer identity checks or customer due diligence (CDD) measures,[20] which were a cornerstone of a preventive AML/CFT regime.[21]

The Basel Committee on Banking Supervision is a forum for agreeing international regulation on banking conduct and sets guidelines for worldwide regulation of banks. In 1981, it adopted a Statement of Principles on Money Laundering[22] focusing attention on the problem of money laundering through financial institutions. The Statement of Principles included the obligation for banks to make reasonable efforts to determine the true identity of all their customers and advised banks to take appropriate steps when they became aware that the deposits were proceeds of crime by denying assistance, severing ties, closing or freezing accounts. This was followed by the European Council Directive on Money Laundering,[23] which, again, focused primarily on the role of financial institutions in preventing and detecting money laundering. The Directive made it a priority for the banks to know the true identity of their customers. What is distinctive about the Directive is that it sets out institutional obligations to inform the relevant authorities of suspicious activity in mandatory terms.

In 1988, the United Nations also turned its attention to the problem of money laundering. Article 3 of the Vienna Convention[24] required each participating

18 Ibid.

19 Council of Europe Committee of Ministers Recommendation No. R (80)10 of the Committee of Ministers to Member States on Measures Against the Transfer and Safekeeping of Funds from Criminal Origin (27 June 1980), https://search.coe.int/cm/Pages/result_details.aspx?ObjectID=09000016804f6231, accessed 20 November 2020.

20 Council of Europe, 'Anti-Money Laundering and Combating the Financing of Terrorism: The Holy See (including the Vatican City State)' Mutual Evaluation Report-Executive Summary (4 July 2012) 8, https://rm.coe.int/mutual-evaluation-report-anti-money-laundering-and-combating-the-finan/16807160fa, accessed 20 January 2020. [Moneyval Evaluation Report HS 2012]

21 Ibid.

22 Committee on Banking Regulation and Supervisory Practices, Concordat on Supervision of Banks' Foreign Establishments, in IMF, 'International Capital Markets: Recent Developments and Short-Term Prospects' (1981, Occasional Paper No. 7) 29–32. The original Concordat was not released to the public until March 1981.

23 Council Directive 91/308/EEC on the Prevention of the Use of the Financial System for the Purpose of Money Laundering, O.J. L 166, 28 June 1991.

24 The Vienna Convention (n 10).

country to criminalise drug-related money laundering. It required each participating country to establish a criminal offence for conspiring, aiding and abetting, and facilitating the commission of a drug trafficking offence, including money laundering.

However, the Financial Action Task Force (FATF) is the only international body dedicated to the prevention and detection of financial crime. FATF was established in 1989 by the leaders of the G7 states in response to the threat posed by money laundering to the systemic stability of the financial system. The Task Force was responsible for examining money laundering techniques and trends, reviewing the action that had already been taken at national and international levels and setting out measures that were still required to combat money laundering.In April 1990, FATF issued a report containing a set of *Forty Recommendations*, which constituted international minimum standards in the fight against money laundering. In 2001, the mandate of FATF was expanded to include the development of standards in the fight against terrorist financing (TF).In October 2001, FATF issued *Eight Special Recommendations* to deal with the issue of terrorist financing and a *Ninth Special Recommendation* was published in October 2004.[25] The result is a stronger and clearer set of standards.

Although the FATF recommendations are stated as voluntary codes of good practice they have, in effect, become mandatory for all countries. In other words, they have become 'soft law'. Although there is no universally accepted definition of soft law,[26] Guzman and Meyer have provided the following useful definition. Soft law 'includes non-binding rules or instrumentals that interpret or inform our understanding of binding rules or represent promises that in turn create expecta tions about future conduct.'[27] The FATF recommendations are best understood as promises that, although not binding, create an expectation of future compliance. Sixteen of the FATF recommendations are considered priorities. These are divided into essential and key recommendations. The four essential recommendations related to money laundering are the criminalising of money laundering, customer identification, conservation of information and the reporting of suspicious activity.[28]

25 FATF (2012–2020), International Standards on Combating Money Laundering and the Financing of Terrorism & Proliferation, FATF, Paris, France, www.fatf-gafi.org/recommendations.html, accessed 20 January 2021.

26 Andrew Guzman, Timothy Meyer, 'International Soft Law' 2010 2(1) *Journal of Legal Analysis* 171. [171–225]

27 Ibid. 74.

28 Alessio Sarais, 'Moneyval and the Santa Sede: Some notes on the recent regulatory provisions for financial transparency in Santa Sede in the Vatican City State' [2014] Iura Orientalia X 135, 136. [135–47], http://www.iuraorientalia.net/IO/IO_010_2014/III_06_Sarais.pdf, accessed 12 January 2021.

The Vatican City State

Before looking at the recent reforms of the Vatican financial system it is worth providing some context in relation the Vatican City State (VCS) as it is such a unique jurisdiction. The Vatican is a territory of 108.7 acres (1.2 square miles) situated within the City of Rome. As such, it is the smallest state in the world. It has a population of around 800, made up of Holy See (HS) officials, the Swiss Guard and members of religious orders.[29] It is comprised of a palace with museums, a basilica and a large garden. It is a unique jurisdiction not just because of its size but also because its sovereign leader, the pope, is the spiritual leader of 1.3 billion followers.

Historical context

The VCS was given special status in Italian law in 1929 under the Lateran Treaty[30] negotiated between the Holy See (HS) and Benito Mussolini, founder of the National Fascist Party and Prime Minister of Italy from 1922–1943. Under the Lateran Treaty,[31] the Italian government gave the pope the Vatican Palace, its gardens and provided financial compensation for the loss in 1870 of the papal states. The Lateran Treaty[32] also acknowledged the legal personality of the HS and recognised the territorial boundaries between Italy, on the one hand, and the VCS, on the other.[33] In terms of organisational structure, the pope is the supreme commander or absolute monarch and he is head of his court, the HS and his territory, the VCS.[34] As head of state, he holds full legislative, executive and judicial powers.[35]

The settlement under the Lateran Treaty left the church with more cash than it had had since it lost its empire in 1870.[36] Hence the claim that '[t]he modern wealth of the Vatican is based on the generosity of Benito Mussolini.'[37] In order

29 The Vatican City (Holy See) Risk and Compliance Report (January 2017) 5, http://knowyourcountry.info/files/vaticancityamlreportaug2014_1.pdf, accessed 20 January 2021.
30 Treaty between the Holy See and Italy in the name of the Most Holy Trinity, 1929. [The Lateran Treaty]
31 The classification of the Lateran Treaty as a treaty is not universally accepted. See Geoffrey Robertson, *The Case Against the Pope* (Penguin Books 2010) 63–78 for a useful discussion on the criteria of a treaty.
32 The Lateran Treaty (n 30).
33 The status of the VCS as a sovereign nation state is contested. See Geoffrey Robertson, *The Case Against the Pope* (Penguin Books 2010) 79 for a useful discussion on whether the VCS meets the criteria of a state set out in the Montevideo Convention on Rights and Duties of States 1933.
34 Geoffrey Robertson, *The Case Against the Pope* (Penguin Books 2010) 12.
35 Art. 1 of *Fundamental Law of Vatican City State of 26 November 2000* Article 1 'The Supreme Pontiff, Sovereign of Vatican City State, has the Fullness of Legislative, Executive and Judicial Powers', https://Vatican_Fundamental_law_2000_en.pdf, accessed 20 January 2021.
36 Gerald Posner, *God's Banker* (Simon & Schuster 2015) 50.
37 David Yallop, *In God's Name* (Constable & Robinson 2007) 82.

to manage this income the Instituto per le Opere di Religione (IOR), known as the Vatican Bank, was established in 1942. The purpose of the IOR was the management and custody of personal and real property intended for religious work or charity. In 1990, the purpose of the IOR was restated as follows: 'The purpose of the Institute is to provide for the custody and administration of moveable and immovable property transferred or entrusted to the Institute by natural or legal persons and designed for religious works or charity.'[38]

The ongoing child sex abuse scandal dominates the headlines relating to the Roman Catholic Church. However, in the past it was always the church's financial activities that brought it notoriety. It is claimed that the IOR became the 'world's best offshore bank in the 20th century, where members of Italy's upper class, the mafia, and the freemasons allegedly laundered their money'.[39] 'The administration of the Vatican Bank has been so unbelievably sordid and incompetent that it defies a rational presentation.'[40] 'The bank's history has been defined by scandal, secrecy, and noncompliance with the West's standard anti-fraud measures.'[41]

It has been suggested that the real purpose of the IOR should be determined not by looking at the originating legal documents, but rather, by examining the IOR's activities. By 1945, communism was viewed as a dangerous enemy by the church and 'fear of the world-wide spread of communism dominated the policies of Pope Pius XII'.[42] It has been argued that the ulterior purpose of the IOR was to channel money to help fight communism.[43]

There is evidence that the Vatican was involved in the relocation of Germans and Croatian war criminals 'on the run' between 1944 until 1950.[44] The Vatican used the ratlines[45] to get war criminals to South America where they could help

38 IOR Instituto per le Opere di Religione, Chirograph of John Paul II for the Works of Religion is given a new structure 1 March 1990 para 1, http://www.ior.va/content/dam/ior/documenti/media/documenti/IOR-Statutes_English%20translation.pdf, accessed 12 October 2020

39 Maya Perry, 'With New Rules, Pope Aims to Reform Scandal-Ridden Vatican Bank' (13 August 2019) Organised Crime and Corruption Reporting Project, https://www.occrp.org/en/daily/10465-with-new-rules-pope-aims-to-reform-scandal-ridden-vatican-bank, accessed 20 November 2020.

40 Nick Patricca, 'The Vatican Bank Follies' *Windy City Times* (2013) 29(1) 4, *Gale One-File: News*, link.gale.com/apps/doc/A348647342/STND?u=uniaber&sid=STND&xid=ff161c34, accessed 24 January 2021.

41 Andrew Wiener, 'Why Does the Vatican Need a Bank and What is With the History of Scandal?' (10 July 2014) Foreign Policy FT, https://foreignpolicy.com/2014/07/10/why-does-the-vatican-need-a-bank-and-whats-with-the-history-of-scandal/, accessed 20 November 2020.

42 Michael Phayer, 'Pope Pius XII, the Holocaust, and the Cold War' (1998) 12(2) *Holocaust and Genocide Studies* 233. [233–56]

43 Patricca (n 40).

44 Leon Cohen, 'Scholar: Fear of communism led Vatican to help Nazis criminals' *Wisconsin Jewish Chronicle* (30 April 2008), https://www.jewishchronicle.org/2008/04/30/scholar-fear-of-communism-led-vatican-to-help-nazi-criminals/, accessed 20 November 2020.

45 The 'ratlines' were Vatican-run escape routes for war criminals trying to avoid prosecution.

fight communism.[46] It is claimed that the Vatican helped relocate Krunoslav Draganović, Ante Pavelić, Franz Stangle,[47] Gustav Wagner,[48] Adolph Eichmann,[49] Claus Barbie (the 'Butcher of Lyon')[50] and Dr Joseph Mengele.[51] In 1947, a US State Department memorandum entitled 'Illegal Emigration Movements in and through Italy' identified the Vatican as 'the largest single organisation involved in the illegal movement of emigrants including many wanted war criminals'.[52] The numbers of war criminals that the Vatican paid to relocate is unknown, but figures from Argentina alone suggests it runs to many thousands.[53]

This practice of using the IOR to fund illegal activity was not limited to the immediate post-war years. In 1980, with the pope's blessing, the IOR illegally sent money to Solidarity in Poland.[54] John Paul II has since widely been credited with helping to undermine communist rule in Poland.[55] However, it is claimed that the practice did not stop there. Former and current Vatican officials have confirmed that the bank has been used to channel cash, often secretly or with limited information given to correspondent banks, to vulnerable Christian groups in Cuba and Egypt.[56]

The most notorious scandal was in 1982, when the IOR was directly linked to criminal activity through its ties with the Banco Ambrosiano, the largest private banking group in Italy. The Banco Ambrosiano 'played a leading role on the international financial crime scene'.[57] Its President, Roberto Calvi, was a financial advisor to the Vatican and also a member of Propaganda Due or P-2, an illegal Masonic lodge. Under Calvi, the Banco Ambrosiano set up extensive networks of subsidiaries and shell companies for the Vatican Bank. Money was borrowed

46 Cohen (n 44).
47 Posner (n 36) 147.
48 Ibid. 148.
49 Ibid. 149.
50 Ibid. 152.
51 Ibid. xiii.
52 Alan Levy, *The Wiesenthal File* (Constable & Co. Ltd 1993) 301 quoted in Dianne Kirby, 'History, Memory and the Living Witness: The Vatican, the Holocaust and the Cold War' (2011) 26(1) *Intelligence and National Security* 106, 108. [106–13]
53 European Jewish Congress, 'Wiesenthal Centre reveals names of 12,000 Nazis in Argentina' (4 March 2020), https://eurojewcong.org/news/news-and-views/wiesenthal-centre-reveals-names-of-12000-nazis-in-argentine/, accessed 20 November 2020.
54 Yallop (n 37) 88.
55 Timothy Garton Ash is quoted as saying: '[T]he remarkable thing is that all participants on all sides of the issue in Poland attribute a major role to the Pope' in Richard Bernstein, 'Pope helped Bring Poland Freedom' *New York Times* (6 April 2005), https://www.nytimes.com/2005/04/06/world/europe/pope-helped-bring-poland-its-freedom.html, accessed 20 November 2020.
56 Rachel Sanderson, 'The Scandal at the Vatican Bank' *Financial Times Newspaper* (6 December 2013), https://www.ft.com/content/3029390a-5c68-11e3-931e-00144feabdc0, accessed 12 October 2020.
57 Letizia Paoli, 'The Banco Ambrosiano Case: An investigation into the underestimation of the relations between organised and economic crime' (1995) 23 *Crime, Law & Social Change* 345, 346.

using letters of credit signed by Bishop Paul Markincus, President at the IOR. In 1982, the Banco Ambrosiano collapsed under $1.4 billion in unsecured loans. The collapse was said to be the largest in Western banking history.[58] Forensic investigators for Italy's central bank confirmed that the Banco Ambrosiano's biggest debtor was the IOR. Eventually, the IOR paid $244 million to the Ambrosiano's creditors in a voluntary contribution while simultaneously denying any wrongdoing.[59]

What this potted history suggests is that since its establishment, the IOR has been involved in illegal activity. The allegations range from buying illegal travel documents for Nazis and Croatian war criminals through to money laundering and collaborating with the mafia and the illegal Masonic lodge, Propaganda Due. One possible explanation for why the IOR did not feel obliged to abide by the rule of law is that it viewed manmade rules and laws as unimportant and, as such, did not apply to the church and its institutions. The point is eloquently made in a quote by a manager at a large European bank who said: 'We would say, [to the IOR] we need to answer the regulator on this matter.' The [IOR] would say: 'We answer to God.'[60] In spite of being linked to the largest banking collapse in Western history, the IOR did not introduce an anti-money laundering system at the time and instead continued to prioritise secrecy.

The Vatican financial institutions

In spite of having a small population, minimal crime and no market economy,[61] the Vatican needs a financial system to pursue its mission, which is to 'govern, protect, control and extend the Church'.[62] The Vatican's financial system is made up of two major institutions, the IOR and the Administration of the Patrimony of the Apostolic See (Amministrazione del Patrimonio della Sede Apostolica (APSA)). The APSA is a department of the HS that was established in 1967 by Pope Paul VI. It is governed by articles 172–175 of the Apostolic Constitution

58 Tribunal di Milano, 'Ordinanza-sentenza di rinvio a giudizio per la bancoratta del Banco Ambrosiano emessa dai giudici istruttori Antonio Pizzi e Renato Bricchetti' (7 April 1989) quoted in Letizia Paoli, 'The Banco Ambrosiano Case: An investigation into the underestimation of the relations between organised and economic crime' (1995) 23 *Crime, Law & Social Change* 345.

59 Victor Simpson and Nicole Wakefield, 'Vatican Bank Hit by Financial Scandal … Again' *The Independent* (19 December 2010), https://www.independent.co.uk/news/world/europe/vatican-bank-hit-by-financial-scandal-again-2164321.html, accessed 20 November 2020.

60 Sanderson (n 56).

61 Moneyval Evaluation Report HS 2012 (n 20) 3.

62 Cannon 331 of the Code of Cannon Law of 1983 quoted in Francesco De Pascalis, 'Financial Crime Prevention and Control: The reforms of a "unique' jurisdiction under EU law and international standards' (2015) 17(4) *European Journal of Law Reform* 528, 532.

Pastor Bonus[63] and was modified by Pope Francis in 2014.[64] It is an entity of the Roman Curia and its competency under article 172 of *Pastor Bonus* is to 'administer the properties owned by the Holy See in order to provide the funds necessary for the Roman Curia to function'. [65]

The IOR is not a division of the VCS neither is it an office of the church's organisational and curial structures. It is an independent autonomous 'charitable institute', run by a board of supervisors (usually laymen), overseen by a committee of cardinals under papal direction. In effect, the institution has one shareholder and that is the pope.[66] The only branch of the bank is located inside the VCS and it currently oversees over US$5.5 billion.[67] The IOR is the larger of the financial institutions with a distribution network in more than 100 countries and approximately 19,000 accounts.[68]

Reform of the Vatican financial services system

Having resisted mounting pressure to introduce anti-money laundering systems during the latter half of the last century, the IOR began the introduction of AML/CTF standards in the mid-2000s.[69] This process did not reform an existing system, but rather created an AML/CTF system from scratch. There are various theories as to why the IOR decided to introduce these changes. Interestingly, there are very few suggestions by academics, journalists or commentators that the Vatican decided to introduce these legislative reforms in 2011 because it was the right thing to do. Instead, it is claimed that other factors informed the Vatican's decision to comply with AML international standards.

The terrorist attacks of 11 September 2001 prompted a crackdown on money laundering by the world's financial authorities.[70] Money laundering suddenly went from being understood as merely a criminal matter to being an issue of national security because of its role in hiding the financing of terrorism. Consequently, international authorities increased the pressure on private banks to comply with international AML standards.

63 Pope John Paul II, Apostolic Constitution Pastor Bonus, 172, Rome, 1988, http://www.vatican.va/content/john-paul-ii/en/apost_constitutions/documents/hf_jp-ii_apc_19880628_pastor-bonus-index.html, accessed 20 December 2020. [Pastor Bonus]

64 Apostolic letter issued motu proprio of the Supreme Pontiff Francis 'Transferral of the Ordinary Section of the Administration of the Patrimony of the Apostolic See to the Secretariat for the Economy' (8 July 2014), http://www.vatican.va/content/francesco/en/motu_proprio/documents/papa-francesco-motu-proprio_20140708_trasferimento-apsa.html, accessed 20 November 2020.

65 Pastor Bonus (n 63).

66 Posner (n 36) 118.

67 Perry (n 39).

68 Wiener (n 41).

69 Ibid.

70 Vallely (n 2).

The IOR uses the services of more than 40 correspondent banks in Europe, the USA, Australia and Japan to transfer funds around the world.[71] Therefore, it is financially connected to almost every country in the world. Unsurprisingly, the international community was keen to see the Vatican financial regulatory system aligned with international standards. As a result, the Vatican came under increasing pressure from partner institutions demanding compliance with the FATF recommendations.[72] In fact, FATF warns its members not to have business relationships with those countries that do not comply with the FATF recommendations.[73]

Some have speculated that Vatican compliance with the FATF recommendations was inevitable in the long term because any other course of action would almost certainly have limited Vatican access to the global banking system.[74] This would, in turn, have impacted on how the Vatican did business and potentially undermined both its financial stability and its moral authority.[75] Others have pointed out that the Vatican could have decided to outsource part of its financial activities to external service providers.[76] However, in doing so the Vatican would have become dependent on the economic system of a foreign country and lost some of its financial independence. Alternatively, the Vatican could have created its own currency but it would still have been obliged to adopt equivalent standards in relation to AML/CTF, in order to continue to do business with other EU financial institutions.

It has also been suggested that the euro crisis of 2008 increased the pressure on the IOR to adopt international AML/CTF standards; Sanderson, for example, observes that 'Pressure from the Organisation for Economic Co-operation and Development, Europe's Financial Stability Board [...] led to a crackdown on states that failed to comply with international rules.'[77] It is alleged that senior officials in the EU persuaded the Bank of Italy to launch investigations into the dealings of the IOR.[78] The result was that in 2009 and 2010 Italian magistrates conducted a series of investigations into AML/CTF rule violations at the IOR. In September 2010, the Italian government froze nearly 23 million euros in IOR assets in connection with money laundering investigations. The money was being sent from an IOR bank account in Credito Artigianato to a German branch of

71 Moneyval Evaluation Report HS 2012 (n 20) 32.
72 Wiener (n 35).
73 Alexander et al. (n 6) 73.
74 Mads Adenas and Isabella Cortesi, 'The Creation of a Vatican Financial Regulatory Rramework' (2017) 6(2) Law and Economics Yearly Review 242, 251 [242–64], http://www.laweconomicsyearlyreview.org.uk/Law_and_Economics_Yearly_Review_LEYR_Journal_vol_6_part_2_2017.pdf, accessed 20 November 2020.
75 Deborah Caldwell, 'How the Vatican's Finances Work'(19 March 2013) NBC News, https://www.nbcnews.com/business/business-news/how-vaticans-finances-work-flna1C8930020, accessed 20 January 2021
76 Adenas and Cortesi (n 74) 242.
77 Sanderson (n 56).
78 Ibid.

JP Morgan Chase and to an Italian bank, Banca del Fucino. The IOR did not disclose the origin or destination of the money, in violation of the AML/CTF European and Italian laws.

Court documents illustrate that prosecutors believed the IOR deliberately flouted anti-laundering laws 'with the aim of hiding the ownership, destination and origin of the capital'.[79] The prosecutors also believed that while the bank has expressed a 'generic and stated will' to conform to international standards, 'there is no sign that the institutions of the Catholic Church are moving in that direction'.[80] In fact, the prosecutor found 'exactly the opposite'.[81] Ultimately, the bank denied wrongdoing and the funds were eventually released in June 2011.[82] However, while accepting that there was mounting pressure on the Vatican to comply with international AML standards from various sources, Francesco De Pascalis has suggested that the IOR's decision to reform flowed directly from the bilateral Monetary Agreement (the Monetary Agreement)[83] between the EU and the HS/VCS, which entered into force 1 January 2011. The Monetary Agreement provided that the euro was to be the official currency of the VCS, in spite of its not being a member of the European Union and 'having little chance of becoming one'.[84] The importance of the Monetary Agreement was that it provided for the mandatory implementation of the EU AML/CTF framework. For example, Article 8 of the Monetary Agreement required compliance with the European Directive 2005/60/EC on the Prevention of the Financial System for the Purpose of Money Laundering and Terrorist Financing (3rd EU AML Directive).[85] 'The adoption of the euro as its official currency determined – over time – the obligation [by the Vatican] to implement the EU legislation against financial fraud.'[86]

Although the adoption of the euro as its national currency may have meant that the incorporation of EU AML/CTF measures at the IOR were inevitable, the timing of the introduction of that system may have been influenced by the continuing pressure from the Bank of Italy. In 2011, the Bank of Italy warned Italian credit institutions that the IOR was a non-member state and had an inadequate AML/CTF regime in place and therefore, enhanced CDD measures would need to be applied. The HS could either issue new anti-money laundering laws

79 Simpson and Wakefield (n 59).

80 Ibid.

81 Ibid.

82 Philip Pullella and Lisa Jucca, 'Vatican Image Hurt as JP Morgan Closes Account' (19 March 2012) Reuters, https://uk.reuters.com/article/uk-vatican-bank/vatican-bank-image-hurt-as-jp-morgan-closes-account-idUKBRE82I0P820120319, accessed 20 November 2020.

83 Monetary Agreement between the European Union and the Vatican City State (2010/C28/05) 2009.

84 Adenas and Cortesi (n 74) 244.

85 Directive 2005/60/EC of the European Parliament and of the Council of 26 October 2005 on the prevention of the use of the financial system for the purpose of money laundering and terrorist financing, OJ L 309, 25.11.2005.

86 Adenas and Cortesi (n 74) 251.

to conform to EU and international norms or face immediate increased scrutiny. The IOR chose to adopt new standards.

Law N. CXXVII, On the Prevention and Countering of the Laundering of Proceeds of Criminal Activities and of the Financing of Terrorism,[87] was finalised on 30 December 2010 and came into effect on 1 April 2011. This legislation was introduced by Pope Benedict XVI and it required compliance from all Vatican institutions around the world. Importantly, the legislation also criminalised money laundering and introduced identification and verification procedures. It also created an independent Financial Information Authority, the Autorità di Informazione Finanziaria (AIF),[88] known by its Italian acronym, which some have suggested is perhaps the most significant provision in this initial AML legislation.[89] The AIF was the equivalent to a financial intelligence unit (FIU) required under the FATF recommendations. The AIF was to be a watchdog over all Vatican finances and responsible for ensuring that transactions complied with the new transparency laws. The AIF was the unit responsible for detecting suspicious activities by overseeing the records and reports of financial institutions and by sharing this information with other financial intelligence units around the world.

The Vatican and Moneyval evaluation

This new AML regime needed to be judged against the standards in the 3rd EU AML Directive and the FATF recommendations. The HS is not part of the Council of Europe but it does have observer status. In February 2011, the secretary general of the Council of Europe received a request from secretary of state for the HS to become subject to the evaluation and follow-up procedures of Moneyval.[90] The Committee of Ministers accepted the application on 6 April 2011 and Moneyval made two on-site visits to the VCS between November 2011 and March 2012.[91] Following the November 2011 on-site visit, the new law was rapidly revised to take into account the evaluators' emerging findings. A revised decree, Law N. CLIX,[92] was issued in January 2012 and came into force

87 Law N. CXXVII (n 3).

88 Renamed in late 2020 as the Supervisory and Financial Information Authority or ASIF.

89 Francesco De Pascalis, 'Financial Crime Prevention and Control: The reforms of a "unique" jurisdiction under EU law and international standards', *European Journal of Law Reform* 2015 17(4) 544.

90 Moneyval Evaluation Report 2012 HS (n 19) 3.

91 Ibid.

92 Law N. CLIX – Decree of the President of the Governorate of the Vatican City State promulgating amendments and additions to Law n. CXXVII, *On the Prevention and Countering of the Laundering of the Proceeds of Criminal Activities and the Financing of Terrorism*, of 30 December 2010, 25 January 2012, at https://www.aif.va/ENG/pdf/Decreto_del_Presidente_del_Governatorato_n_CLXVI.pdf, accessed 20 November 2020 [Law N. CLIX].

as Law N. CLXVI in April 2012[93] introducing substantial modifications. One of the new measures removed, in part, the independence of the AIF, compelling it to cooperate with the Secretariat of State, in relation to prevention and intervention duties. Article 2 quinquies[94] of Decree N. CLIX states that the 'Secretariat of State is responsible for the definition of the policies for the prevention and countering of money laundering and the financing of terrorism.' Article 2 septies[95] of Decree N. CLIX states that the 'President of the AIF shall submit to the Secretariat of State a report on the activities pursued by the Authority during the previous year.'[96] The Moneyval mutual evaluation report focused on the revised legislation but pointed out the difficulty in evaluating the application of the new legislation given that it had been in operation for such a short period of time.

The Moneyval report was published in July 2012[97] and concluded that the new regulator, the AIF, lacked the legal powers and independence needed to monitor and sanction the Vatican's financial institutions, the IOR and the APSA. In a press release, the Council of Europe stated:

> The legislative base for supervision needs strengthening. The evaluators considered that there was a lack of clarity about the role, responsibility, authority, powers and independence of the Financial Information Authority (AIF), as the AML/CFT supervisor [...][98]

It recommended that the powers of the AIF be extended to give exclusive supervisory powers in all aspects of AML/CTF. It also recommended that the AIF should be given powers to sanction officials in all Vatican financial institutions and have the power to restrict or suspend a financial institution from trading. In addition, the report recommended the adoption of provisions that identify the categories of people authorised to open accounts at the IOR. The report concluded that the Vatican Bank was compliant or largely compliant in only nine out of 16 core standards.[99] The Council of Europe's press release stated that of the 45 relevant recommendations 23 (51%) were partially compliant (PC) or non-compliant (NC) and 22 (49%) were compliant (C) or largely compliant (LC).[100]

Following the Moneyval on-site visits between November 2011 and March 2012 but prior to the publication of the report in July 2012, other difficulties

93 Law N. CLXVI – Pontifical Commission for the Vatican City State, Prevention and Countering of the Laundering of the Proceeds of Criminal Activities and the Financing of Terrorism, 25 April 2012 [Law N. CLXVI].

94 Quinquies refers to subsection 5.

95 Septies refers to subsection 7.

96 Ibid.

97 Moneyval Evaluation Report 2012 HS (n 20).

98 Council of Europe Communications, Council of Europe report calls for Holy See to strengthen supervisory regime, https://rm.coe.int/1680721478, accessed 20 November 2020. [CoE report summary]

99 Wiener (n 41).

100 CoE report summary (n 98).

befell the Vatican Bank. In March 2012, the US State Department named the HS as a jurisdiction of concern in relation to money laundering.[101] In mid-March 2012, Italian newspapers reported that JPMorgan Chase had closed the Vatican Bank's account with an Italian branch of the US banking giant due to concerns about a lack of transparency. Under pressure from the US Treasury Department, JPMorgan Chase closed the account because the IOR had failed to provide sufficient data on money transfers after requesting the information for a year and half.[102] JPMorgan Chase claimed that €1.8 billion passed through the account over an 18-month period[103] and described the IOR account as a 'sweeping facility', meaning it was emptied out at the end of each day with funds transferred to another IOR account in Frankfurt.[104] According to German newspaper *Der Spiegel*, investigators suspected that the account was used to launder funds from 'dubious sources'.[105]

The Vatican again came under pressure in 2012 from the Bank of Italy. Vatican City's 80 cash machines and credit card payment services were managed by Deutsche Bank and in the summer of 2012, the Bank of Italy began questioning Deutsche Bank about whether it possessed a licence to operate cash machines for the Vatican state. The Bank of Italy pointed out that the Vatican was not compliant with international rules on money laundering and sent a letter ordering Deutsche Bank to close its accounts with the Vatican Bank by the end of the year.[106] This it did; and as Sanderson writes: 'On 1 January 2013, at peak holiday time, there were no ATMs functioning anywhere inside Vatican City.' A senior banker commented that: 'The message sent was simple: if you want to participate in the modern world, you have to adopt modern rules.'[107]

What followed was a number of legislative changes. On 11 July 2013, Pope Francis published an apostolic letter in the form of a *motu proprio*: 'On the Jurisdiction of the Judicial bodies of the Vatican City State in Criminal Matters.'[108] This extended the jurisdiction of the VCS in specific criminal matters to organs

101 US State Department, Bureau of International Narcotics and Law Enforcement Affairs, International Narcotics Control Strategy Report, Volume II Money Laundering and Financial Crime (7 March 2012) 33, https://2009-2017.state.gov/documents/organisation/185866.pdf, accessed 20 November 2020.

102 Wiener (n 41).

103 Ibid.

104 Pullella and Jucca (n 82).

105 Andreas Wassermann and Peter Wansierski, 'Transparency v Money Laundering: Catholic Church fears growing Vatican Bank Scandal', *Spiegel International* (2 July 2012), https://www.spiegel.de/international/europe/a-growing-vatican-bank-scandal-threatens-catholic-church-image-a-842140.html, accessed 20 November 2020.

106 Sanderson (n 56).

107 Ibid.

108 Pope Francis, apostolic letter in the form of a motu proprio 'On the Jurisdiction of the Judicial bodies of the Vatican City State in Criminal Matters'11 July 2013, http://www.vatican.va/content/francesco/en/motu_proprio/documents/papa-francesco-motu-proprio_20130711_organi-giudiziari.html, accessed 20 January 2021.

of the HS and outside Vatican City. On 8 October 2013, the Vatican further refined the AML/CTF system through the introduction of Law N. XV111 on Transparency, Supervision and Financial Intelligence.[109] This legislation made a number of significant changes to the AML/CTF regime. Article 71 provided for the creation of a national list of those organisations that are regarded as a threat to international peace and security.[110] Article 41 introduced a suspicious transaction reporting regime, and the AIF has issued guidance on indicators of anomalous transactions.[111] Article 46 strengthened the supervisory powers of the AIF in line with recommendations made in the Moneyval report of 2012. Between them, Articles 65 and 66 established the AIF as the prudential supervisor and regulator responsible for the supervision of all Vatican financial institutions and provided for a full set of administrative sanctions. In parallel with the legislative reforms, the IOR created an internal verification process for its customer database and clarified categories of customers that could hold accounts at the IOR and published those details on its website.

Since issuing its first on-site report in July 2012, Moneyval has conducted three desk-based progress reports on the HS and VCS. The first desk-based review published in December 2013[112] acknowledged that 'considerable efforts have been made by the authorities of the HS and of the VCS to implement the recommendations made by the [previous] evaluation team'.[113] The report also expressed satisfaction with the adaptation of a confiscation regime from Article 13 of the Palermo Convention.[114] Further reforms in 2014 established both the Council for the Economy and the Secretariat for the Economy[115] with the aim of enhancing the supervision and oversight of the financial institutions of the Vatican.

In 2015, the second desk-based review again made various positive comments on the effective working of the AIF and the fact that the HS had established a functioning reporting system and was responding well to international

109 Sarais (n 28) 136.

110 Law N. XV111 On Transparency, Supervision and Financial Intelligence, 8 October 2013, Art 71, https://www.aif.va/eng/pdf/legge_n_XVIII_20131008.pdf, accessed 20 January 2021.

111 Moneyval Evaluation Report 2012 HS (n 20).

112 Council of Europe, Committee of Experts on the Evaluation of Anti-Money Laundering Measures and the Financing of Terrorism, The Holy See (including the Vatican City State), Progress Report and written analysis by the Secretariat of Core and Key Recommendations, 9 December 2013, published in English, http://www.coe.int/t/dghl/monitoring/moneyval, accessed 20 November 2020. [Progress Report 2013]

113 Ibid. point 8.

114 The Palermo Convention (n 11).

115 Motu Proprio Fidelis Dispensator et Prudens of His Holiness Pope Francis Establishing a New Coordinating Agency for the Economic and Administrative Affairs of the Holy See and the Vatican City State, 24 February 2014, https://w2.vatican.va/content/francesco/en/motu_proprío/documents/papa- francesco-motu-proprío_20140224_fidelis-dispensator-et-prudens.html, accessed 20 November 2020.

cooperation requests. However, the Moneyval review noted that the HS had frozen considerable amounts of money and yet no criminal prosecutions had taken place. Moneyval therefore recommended that the HS proactively pursue all outstanding investigations in financial crime cases. Importantly, the Moneyval Committee stressed that the overall effectiveness of the HS's engagement with combatting money laundering depended on the results that were achieved by the courts.[116]

In 2017, the third desk-based review welcomed the results of the continued efforts made by the HS and the VCS to further strengthen its institutional, legal and operational frameworks in the fight against money laundering and the financing of terrorism. However, the 2017 review noted again that 'the results on the law enforcement/prosecutorial/judicial side, two years after the last review, remain modest.'[117] Nevertheless, Moneyval concluded that the IOR had made substantial progress in establishing a 'functional and sustainable anti-money laundering system'.[118]

By October 2020, it appeared that the Vatican might have achieved an appropriate level of financial transparency 'after decades in which it's secretive bank, the IOR, was seen as a money-laundering haven'.[119] The three desk-based reviews had been mainly positive in spite of the fact that the 2015 and 2017 evaluation reports had sounded a note of caution, both stating that the overall effectiveness of the HS's engagement with combatting money laundering depended on the results that were achieved by the prosecution and the courts. The second on-site visit by evaluators from Moneyval took place between 30 September and 12 October 2020. This review focused on the number of successful prosecutions that have been achieved.[120] However, the figures prior to 2016 were less than encouraging.[121] The first conviction for money laundering, since the introduction of anti-money laundering legislation in 2011, was in December 2018.

The timing of the second on-site review was unfortunate because the Moneyval inspectors arrived amid another financial controversy. The emerging scandal involves the purchase of a London property for £180 million. The allegation implicates the former deputy of the Secretariat of State in the purchase of

116 Council of Europe, 'Moneyval Publishes Report on the Holy See' Newsroom, 8 December 2017, para 65, https://www.coe.int/en/web/moneyval/-/moneyval-publishes-a-report-on-the-holy-seeCouncil of Europe, accessed 20 January 2021.[Progress Report 2017]

117 Andrea Gagliarducci, 'Vatican Finances: How the institutional crisis can harm the Holy See's international credibility' (21 October 2019) Catholic News Agency, https://www.catholicnewsagency.com/column/vatican-finances-how-this-institutional-crisis-can-harm-the-holy-sees-international-credibility-4077, accessed 20 January 2021

118 Progress Report 2017 (n 116).

119 'Council of Europe to Inspect Vatican's Financial Records in September' (3 July 2020) Daily Sabah, https://www.dailysabah.com/world/europe/council-of-europe-to-inspect-vaticans-financial-records-in-september, accessed 20 January 2020.

120 Ibid.

121 Gagliarducci (n 117).

the property using church funds through offshore companies.[122] The offices of the Secretariat of State were raided by police in October 2020 and documents and computers were seized. The scandal will do little to boost the financial community's confidence in the effectiveness of the Vatican's AML measures. The Moneyval inspectors will arrive at a delicate moment for another reason. Starting in the spring of 2021, the European Union 'plans to pour about €209bn into Italy in order to help it recover from the covid-19 pandemic. Even allowing for inflation and economic growth, that is more than was invested in the country through the post-war Marshall Plan'.[123]

It is anticipated that much of the EU cash will be directed towards the poorer regions of Italy in the south. Unfortunately, that is where Italy's mafias have their power base and can most easily steer aid and contracts their way; as *The Economist* points out: 'Having an inadequately regulated mini-state on their doorstep would offer them an easy way to launder their gains.'[124] Italy's anti-mafia investigators have already warned that the mafias have their eyes on the EU economic package.[125] The Vatican will almost certainly come under more pressure to comply with accepted international AML standards. Market forces will ultimately determine whether the Vatican can continue to do business on the global stage, but the immediate question for the EU is how long can or should it be patient with the Vatican in these circumstances?

Conclusion

Moneyval's second on-site report is yet to be published. It was scheduled for discussion and adoption at Moneyval's 61st plenary meeting, held between 26–30 April 2021. It seems clear that in the long-term implementation of an adequate, transparent, anti-money laundering system by the Vatican will determine whether the Vatican's financial system will remain central to the mission of the Roman Catholic Church.

If the Vatican AML system is judged inadequate, market forces will eventually reduce the relevance of its activities, potentially compromising the economic independence of the HS. Given the scale and number of financial scandals that have engulfed the Vatican since World War II, this might arguably be a good thing. After all, perhaps cleaning up the VCS is simply not possible given the vested interests at stake and rivalries at play. More time may not be the answer.

122 Raven Saunt, 'Vatican Cardinal Resigns from his Post amid £180m Financial Scandal Following Purchase of London Apartment Block using Church Funds' (25 September 2020) Mail Online, https://www.dailymail.co.uk/news/article-8772407/Vatican-cardinal-resigns-post-amid-180m-financial-scandal.html, accessed 20 November 2020.

123 'A Holy Mess: Has the Vatican cleaned up its finances?' (26 September 2020) The Economist, https://www.economist.com/finance-and-economics/2020/09/26/has-the-vatican-cleaned-up-its-finances, accessed 20 November 2020.

124 Ibid.

125 Ibid.

In any case, it is easy to make the argument that the EU and the global financial community have been tolerant for long enough. This is especially the case since, although generally there is a direct relationship between countries having weak anti-money laundering regulations and the prevalence of criminal activities within that country, this is not the case for the VCS. The negative effects of an inadequate anti-money laundering system in the VCS will only be felt in other countries. The economic threat from money laundering has arguably never been greater, given the planned 2021 EU COVID-19 rescue package. That rescue package will inevitably draw attention to jurisdictions with weak AML regimes and bring into sharp relief the fact that the financial stability and integrity of the EU and the wider global financial system is only as strong as that of its weakest neighbour.

5 How and to what extent has public-private financial information sharing improved the UK's counterterrorist financing reporting regime?

Charlie Robson and Nicholas Ryder[1]

Introduction

The current system for reporting suspicions of money laundering and terrorist financing is not effective. For too long, reporting entities in the private sector have been asked to form the front line of a poorly functioning counterterrorism financing (CTF)[2] reporting regime, without adequate information flow from public sector agencies that could improve their reporting decisions.[3] In order to address this problem, more than 20 countries, including the United Kingdom, have committed to the development of public-private financial information sharing partnerships (FISPs) that bring law enforcement agencies and other public agencies together with financial institutions to tackle money laundering and terrorist financing.[4] These partnerships have contributed to improvements in the quantity and quality of reports of suspicion related to particular economic crime threats; the timeliness and relevance of such reporting to active investigations or live incidents; arrests, asset recovery or other disruption of criminal networks; and heightened understanding of risk in both the public and private sectors.[5] Therefore, the aim of this chapter is to assess whether and to what extent public-private information sharing has improved the UK's CTF reporting regime. The chapter is split into three parts. First, a detailed overview of the UK's CTF

1 Charlie Robson is an Associate Lecturer in Law at the University of the West of England, Bristol, UK. Nicholas Ryder is Professor of Law at Cardiff University, School of Law and Politics, UK.

2 For an early discussion of this, see Joan Wadsley, 'Money Laundering: Professionals as policemen', *Conveyancer and Property Lawyer*, 1994, July/August 275–88.

3 Nick Maxwell and David Artingstall, 'The Role of Financial Information-Sharing Partnerships in the Disruption of Crime' (2017) RUSI Occasional Paper (24).

4 Nick Maxwell, 'Expanding the Capability of Financial Information-Sharing Partnerships' (2019) RUSI Occasional Paper, 7.

5 Ibid. 8.

DOI: 10.4324/9781003020813-6

suspicious activity reporting (SAR)[6] regime is provided. This is followed by an in-depth critical analysis of the regime, whereby several weaknesses are identified, including the low threshold adopted by regulated entities when reporting suspicion, defensive reporting and the low quality of submitted terrorism financing SARs, the threat posed by cheap acts of terrorism and the financing of terrorism through legitimate means. According to the Law Commission, these weaknesses hinder the effectiveness of the UK CTF SARs regime and raise significant risks of harm that could subsequently be an immediate threat to UK public safety.[7] The third part of the chapter discusses attempts made by the UK to develop a more effective, intelligence-led response to terrorist financing through the development of the Joint Money Laundering Intelligence Taskforce (JMLIT). This part provides an overview of the structure and functioning of JMLIT and comments on the partnership's ability to enhance the UK's fight against terrorism financing. The chapter concludes that if JMLIT continues at its current rate of performance, it has the potential to become a key part of the UK's CTF strategy. However, this is subject to several weaknesses of the partnership being addressed.

The UK CTF SARs regime: an overview

Before this chapter can give an in-depth analysis of the UK CTF SARs regime, it is essential that an overview of the laws pertaining to the regime is provided. Offences relating to the UK's CTF SARs regime are contained within the Terrorism Act (TA) 2000, which has been described as the cornerstone of the UK's CTF strategy.[8] Its introduction represented an overhaul of the UK's anti-terrorism legislation, which had previously been principally directed at terrorism in, or related to, Northern Ireland.[9] Section 15–21A of the TA 2000 contain a number of principal offences relating to terrorist financing. These will now be discussed in further detail. Section 15 creates offences in respect of terrorist fundraising.[10] Under this section, it is a criminal offence for a person to provide,[11] receive[12] or invite[13] another to provide money or property, knowing or having reasonable cause to suspect that it may be used for the purposes of terrorism. Section 16 contains offences in respect of the use and possession of money or other property for the purposes of terrorism.[14] Under this section, it is a crimi-

6 These are also referred to as Defence Against Terrorism Financing Suspicious Activity Reports.
7 Law Commission Anti-Money Laundering: The SAR's Regime Consultation Paper (Law Com No. 236, 2018) 12.
8 Karen Harrison and Nicholas Ryder, The Law Relating to Financial Crime in the United Kingdom (Routledge 2016) 48.
9 R.E. Bell, 'The Confiscation, Forfeiture and Disruption of Terrorist Finances' (2004) Journal of Money Laundering Control, 7(2), 105–125.
10 Terrorism Act 2000, s 15.
11 Ibid. s15 (1).
12 Ibid. s15 (2).
13 Ibid. s15 (3).
14 Ibid. s 16.

nal offence to possess or use money or other property while knowing or having reasonable cause to suspect that it may be used for the purposes of terrorism.[15] Section 17 contains an offence in relation to funding arrangements. Under this section, a person commits an offence if he enters into or becomes concerned in an arrangement, as a result of which money or other property is made available, or is to be made available, to another while knowing or having reasonable grounds to suspect that it will, or may be, used for the purposes of terrorism.[16] Section 18 contains the offence of entering into or becoming concerned in an arrangement, which facilitates in any way the retention or control by or on behalf of another person or terrorist property.[17] Section 19 places a duty of disclosure on an individual who, during the course of their employment 'believes' or 'suspects' another person has committed an offence under sections 15–18 of the Act to disclose the information to a 'constable' as soon as possible.[18] Failure to disclose to a constable such a belief or suspicion, and the information on which it is based, is a criminal offence.[19] However, of most importance to this chapter is section 21A, which places the duty to disclose on the 'regulated sector'. The 'regulated sector' is defined in schedule 3A of the TA 2000[20] as 'businesses consisting of the acceptance by a credit institution of deposits or other repayable funds from the public, or the granting by a credit institution of credits for its own account'.[21] An offence is committed under section 21A if three conditions are met. The first condition is that the accused knows or suspects, or has reasonable grounds for knowing or suspecting, that another person has attempted[22] or committed an offence under sections 15–18 of the TA 2000.[23] The second condition is that the information or other matter on which the accused has based his knowledge or suspicion, or which gives reasonable grounds for such knowledge of suspicion, came to him in the course of a business that operates within the regulated sector.[24] The final condition is that the accused does not disclose the information or other matter to a constable or nominated officer, normally a money laundering reporting officer (MLRO), as soon as practicable after he received the information.[25]

15 Ibid. s16 (2).
16 Ibid. ss 17 (a) and (b).
17 Ibid. s 18.
18 Ibid. s 19(1).
19 Ibid. s 9 (2).
20 Ibid. Sch 3A, as substituted by Terrorism Act 2000 (Business in the Regulated Sector and Supervisory Authorities) Order 2007, SI 2007/3288; Terrorism Act 2000 and Proceeds of Crime Act 2002 (Amendment) Regulations 2007, SI 2007/3398. The duty required by 2005/60/EC, Art 22, and is defined by types of person rather than by activity.
21 Ibid.
22 The elements of attempt were added by the Terrorism Act 2000 and Proceeds of Crime Act 2002 (Amendment) Regulations 2007, SI 2007/3398, Sch 1, paras 3,4 as required by 2005/60/EC, art 22.1.
23 Terrorism Act 2000, s 21A(2).
24 Ibid. s 21A(3).
25 Ibid. s 21A(4).

There are two forms of disclosure that a reporting entity may make.[26] First, they can make a required disclosure that provides intelligence to law enforcement agencies in relation to terrorism financing. The failure to lodge a SAR where the conditions for reporting are met is criminal unless one of the exemptions applies. Second, they can make an authorised disclosure, these are 'arrangements with prior consent'.[27] This is when a bank official or an employee may intend to complete a financial transaction[28] but before completion, becomes suspicious or forms the belief that the transaction involves terrorist property. If they disclose their suspicion to the National Crime Agency (NCA) and obtain consent to proceed, they will be protected from criminal liability in relation to a terrorism financing offence.[29] The NCA refer to this as a 'Defence against Terrorism Financing' (DATF) SAR. This chapter will take into account both types of disclosure when analysing the effectiveness of the UK CTF reporting regime.

Is the UK CTF reporting regime effective?

The effectiveness of SARs in relation to terrorist financing was previously highlighted by the Serious Organised Crime Agency, which took the view that 'although the numbers continue to be small in proportion to the total numbers of SARs, their value can be significant, as has been demonstrated in previous years in which major terrorist incidents have taken place.'[30] This is a view echoed by the Law Commission, which states that 'intelligence provided by SARs can assist with the building of a comprehensive financial profile of known individuals.'[31] Such profiles provide an essential piece of the investigate jigsaw puzzle and can, in turn, be instrumental in understanding whether there will be a secondary attack.[32] However, several studies have questioned the effectiveness of the SARs regime.[33] Specifically, this section of the chapter focuses on one of the most recent studies published by the Law Commission in July 2018.[34] The Law Commission

26 Law Commission (n 6) 51.
27 Ibid.
28 Or entering into a financial arrangement. Terrorism Act 2000, s 21ZA.
29 Terrorism Act 2000, s 21ZA and offences in ss 15 to 18.
30 Serious Organised Crime Agency 'The Suspicious Activity Reports Regime Annual Report 2009' (2010 London: Serious Organised Crime Agency) at 11. SOCA was replaced by the NCA in 2013 by virtue of the Crime and Courts Act 2013 as part of a wide range of financial crime reforms introduced by the then Coalition Government. For a more detailed discussion and reflection on the performance of the SOCA and its predecessor the Asset Recovery Agency, see Law Commission (2020 London: Law Commission) 47–56.
31 Law Commission (n 6) 50.
32 Ibid.
33 See, for example, Mathew H. Fleming, *UK Law Enforcement Agency Use and Management of Suspicious Activity Reports: Towards Determining the Value of the Regime* (Home Office 2005).
34 Law Commission, *Anti-Money Laundering: The SARS Regime Consultation Paper* (Law Com No 236, 2018).

made a series of recommendations for the reform of some aspects of the anti-money laundering (AML) regime in Part 7 of the Proceeds of Crime Act 2002 (POCA) and of the CTF regime in Part 3 of the Terrorism Act 2000. In particular, the chapter identifies several issues with terrorist financing SARs, including; the inconsistent application of suspicion in terrorism financing cases, the low quality and value of terrorist financing SARs received by the National Terrorism Financing Intelligence Unit (NTFIU) and defensive reporting.

Weaknesses of terrorism financing SARs

Adoption of a low threshold for suspicion

In the absence of a statutory definition or guidance, it has been left to the courts to determine what 'suspicion' means. There is no case law guidance on the definition of the term 'suspicion' from a terrorist financing perspective. However, the courts have offered sparse guidance on the term as it relates to the money laundering reporting obligations imposed by the POCA 2002. In the context of money laundering, the leading authority on the interpretation of suspicion is *R v Da Silva*.[35] In this case, the court stated: '[I]t seems to us that the essential element of the word suspect and its affiliates, in this context, is that the defendant must think that there is a possibility, which is more than fanciful, that the relevant facts exist. A vague feeling of unease would not suffice.'[36] There is thus no requirement for the suspicion to be 'clear' or 'firmly grounded and targeted on specific facts' or based on 'reasonable grounds'.[37] Marshall criticises the test and argues that the boundary between unease and suspicion is unrealistic and difficult to identify. He states that 'the problem presented by the test adumbrated by the Court of Appeal is that the boundary between a real but "vague feeling of unease" and the thought that there is "a more than fanciful possibility" that a transaction might constitute a money laundering offence or that someone is engaged in money laundering, is easy to articulate but in practice likely to be near impossible to identify'.[38] The dilemma facing any person considering making a report seems to be the question of at what point misgivings become suspicion.[39] The test in *R v Da Silva* was applied in the Civil Division of the Court of Appeal in *K v National Westminster Bank*.[40] Here, Longmore LJ stated: '[T]here is, moreover, no mechanism whereby any officer of the bank can be required to attend for cross-examination since there is no provision enabling the relevant

35 *R v Da Silva* [2006] EWCA Crim 1654.
36 Ibid.
37 Ibid.
38 Paul Marshall, 'Does Shah v HSBC Private Bank Ltd make the anti-money laundering consent regime unworkable?' (2010) *Butterworths Journal of International Banking and Financial Law*, 8(9), 287.
39 Ibid.
40 *K v National Westminster Bank* [2007] 1 WLR 311, [2006] EWCA Civ 1039.

person to give evidence of his suspicion.'[41] However, this statement is not easy to reconcile with Longmore LJ's more recent position in *Shah v HSBC*, in which he stated: '[T]here is no reason as to why the bank should not be required to prove the important fact of suspicion.'[42] The conflicting nature of these two statements by Longmore LJ has caused widespread consternation surrounding the meaning of the term from both a money laundering and terrorism financing point of view.

The overall lack of clarity surrounding the test set out in *R v Da Silva* has resulted in the inconsistent application of suspicion by reporters, with many frequently adopting a very low threshold for suspicion.[43] In many cases, a low threshold for suspicion led to the intelligence provided in SARs not being useful. For example, this can be seen in the aftermath of the terrorist attacks in London in 2017, whereby numerous banks were submitting SARs to close accounts and pay back customers because they had some fleeting transactional relationship with one of the attackers or had lived on the same street.[44]

Defensive reporting and low quality terrorism financing SARs

The concern about the lack of clarity in the definition of the concept of suspicion has resulted in unnecessary SARs being submitted that provide low value intelligence or defensive SARs in the absence of any real suspicion being submitted. The Law Commission found that reporting agencies often tend to submit terrorism financing SARs on the basis of a police inquiry or simply because money is being transferred to a country associated with terrorism.[45] The NTFIU notes that such SARs are often defensive rather than articulating any independent ground for suspicion.[46] As a result, these types of SAR are unlikely to provide any useful information to the NTFIU.[47]

Defensive reporting can also be triggered by concerns in the reporting sector about difficulties of compliance and the serious consequences that may flow from this.[48] A person guilty of an offence under section 21A of the TA 2000 could receive a maximum prison sentence of five years, a fine or both.[49] Large penalties imposed in the UK by the Financial Conduct Authority (FCA) for non-compliance with AML regulations, even when there is no evidence of any crime being committed, have created a 'fear factor' among the regulated sector.[50] This

41 Ibid.
42 *Shah v HSBC* [2010] EWCA Civ 31.
43 Law Commission (n 6) 57.
44 Ibid.
45 Law Commission (n 6) 58.
46 Ibid.
47 Ibid. 59.
48 Home Office, *Report on the Operation in 2004 of the Terrorism Act 2000* (Home Office, 2004, 19–20).
49 Terrorism Act 2000, s 21A (12).
50 See N. Ryder, 'A False Sense of Security? An analysis of legislative approaches towards the prevention of terrorist finance in the United States and the United Kingdom', (2007) *Journal of Business Law*, November, 821–50.

fear factor has in turn resulted in a dramatic increase in the number of terrorism financing SARs submitted to NTFIU. To illustrate, between 2013 and 2015 the total number of terrorism financing SARs submitted directly to the NTFIU increased by 240% from 318 to 1,082.[51] In addition, the total number of terrorism financing SARs disseminated to NTFIU by the NCA during the same period increased by 121% from 856 to 1,899.[52] The number of terrorism financing SARs disseminated to NTFIU continued to increase with 2,026 terrorism financing SARs being disseminated in 2017,[53] with a further 2,688 being disseminated in 2018,[54] a 33% increase from the previous year. This overall volume of SARs can be problematic in isolating essential intelligence. For example, in relation to the 9/11 attacks on the World Trade Center in New York, one of the terrorists had been the subject of a SAR in 2000. The 9/11 Commission was critical of the US SAR regime: the SAR relating to one of the suicide terrorists was one of over 1.2 million such reports filed with the US authorities between 1996 and 2003.[55] The terrorist attacks were funded by al-Qaeda through several wire transfers and cash provided by Khalid Sheikh Mohammed. The wire transfers ranged between $5,000 to $70,000 and Khalid Sheikh Mohammed 'delivered [...] $120,000, to the plot facilitator Abdul Aziz Ali'.[56] Ali sent several bank-to-bank transfers ($10,000, $20,000 and $70,000) to bank accounts (SunTrust Bank in Florida) belonging to two of the terrorists: Marwan al Shehhi and Muhamad Atta. SunTrust Bank were required to comply with the Financial Recordkeeping and Reporting of Currency and Foreign Transactions Act (Bank Secrecy Act 1970) which imposes a legal obligation on US deposit taking institutions to complete and submit a currency transaction report to the Financial Crime Enforcement Network for all financial transactions of $10,000 or more. It is important to note that the Bank Secrecy Act 1970 was not meant to tackle terrorism financing; it was aimed at tackling organised crime, white collar crime and deterring and preventing the use of secret foreign bank accounts for tax fraud.

Another issue identified in the report is concerns expressed by the NTFIU as to the quality of SARs it is receiving. According to the NCA, on average, less than 35% of terrorism financing SARs disseminated to the NTFIU are considered to be of good quality and either lead to a longer term investigation or add substantially

51 FATF 'Anti-money Laundering and Counter-terrorist Financing Measures – United Kingdom, Fourth Round Mutual Evaluation Report' (FATF, Paris, 2018) 51, http://www.fatf-gafi.org/publications/ mutualevaluations/documents/mer-united-kingdom2018.html, accessed 13 February 2019.

52 Serious Organised Crime Agency, *The Suspicious Activity Reports Regime Annual Report 2012* (2013) 7.

53 National Crime Agency, *The Suspicious Activity Reports Regime Annual Report 2017* (2018) 9.

54 Ibid. 4.

55 Ryder (n 49) 825.

56 National Commission on Terrorist Attacks Upon the United States *Monograph on Terrorist Financing* (National Commission on Terrorist Attacks Upon the United States 2004) 26.

to an existing investigation.[57] The poor quality of many SARs negatively impacts the quality and usefulness of the financial intelligence available to the competent authorities.[58] This issue is somewhat mitigated by the Joint Money Laundering Taskforce, which has significantly increased the quality of SARs in some areas but is limited to the largest financial institutions.[59]

Legitimate and low cost terrorism

Additionally, it is important to discuss both the funding of terrorism through legitimate means and the increasing threat posed by inexpensive acts of terrorism and how this exploits loopholes in the SARS regime. The threat posed by inexpensive acts of terrorism was identified by HM Treasury in 2002 who stated that the 'UK experience bears out the relatively low costs required for an effective terrorist attack'.[60] More recently, the 2017 UK National Risk Assessment established that 'the UK's terrorist financing threat largely involves low levels of funds being raised by UK individuals to send overseas, fund travel or fund attack planning'.[61] Similarly, the FATF confirmed that 'terrorist financing activity in the UK is usually low-level, involving small amounts of funds raised by UK based individuals to fund their own travel to join terrorist groups, to send to terrorist associates, or to finance their own terrorist attack plans.'[62] Therefore, terrorism is a cheap enterprise[63] as, although the sums raised may be large, the amounts of money needed to finance individual terrorist operations may be small and concealed. For example, the Bishopsgate bomb in 1993 caused over £1bn worth of damage to property yet cost only £3,000 to mount.[64] Notably, there was no evidence of a SAR being submitted. This is also the case for several other attacks, including the 7 July London bombings, which cost an estimated £8,000

57 National Crime Agency, 'Financial Intelligence: The impact of SAR's in in reducing financial crime' (NCA website), https://www.ukciu.gov.uk/(bmhlcii2veploumtsv2ixted)/Information/Info.aspx, accessed 12 January 2020.

58 FATF (n 50) 51.

59 Ibid. JMLIT was established in 2015 as a private/public partnership with the NCA and the financial sector to improve the sharing of information between reporting entities and law enforcement agencies. This approach aims to increase the understanding of how the financial services sector has been exploited by money launderers and other financial criminals, thus enabling law enforcement agencies to obstruct the flow of the proceeds of crime.

60 HM Treasury, *Combating the Financing of Terrorism. A Report on UK Action* (HM Treasury 2002) 11.

61 HM Treasury, *National Risk Assessment of Money Laundering and Terrorist Financing* (HM Treasury 2017) 6.

62 FATF (n 50) 10.

63 Joshua Prober, 'Accounting for Terror: Debunking the paradigm of inexpensive terrorism', 1 November 2005, http://www.washingtoninstitute.org/policy-analysis/view/ accounting-for-terror-debunking-the-paradigm-of-inexpensive-terrorism, accessed 24 May 2020.

64 Nicholas Ryder, *The Financial War on Terrorism: A Review of Counter-Terrorist Financing Strategies Since 2001* (Routledge Research in Terrorism and the Law 2015) 49.

to execute;[65] the Finsbury Park Mosque attack on 19 June 2017 which cost an estimated £225 to carry out;[66] the Parsons Green tube bombing on 15 September 2017 in which Ahmed Hassan manufactured an improvised explosive device using a £20 Amazon gift voucher;[67] and the London Bridge and Borough Market attacks in June 2017. For the last, the terrorists rented a vehicle that can be hired for £30 per day, and the knives cost approximately £3.[68] Furthermore, the explosives used by the terrorists to carry out the 2017 Manchester Arena attacks can be purchased on Amazon for just £95, and the knife used by the terrorist of the February 2020 Streatham Common attack was stolen from a Low Price store and cost approximately £4.[69]According to the head of Scotland Yard's terrorism financing unit, the five terrorist attacks in UK in 2017, which killed a total of 36 people, cost just £5,000 to execute.[70] Overall, the Global Terrorism Index estimates that three-quarters of terror attacks in Europe between 1994 and 2013 cost less than US$10,000.[71] This estimate includes all costs associated with the attack such as travel, communication, storage, acquiring of weapons and bomb making materials.[72] Interestingly, the same study found that most plots during this time period, including the 2016 Paris and Brussels terrorist (2016), were self-funded through legitimate sources such as wages or income, savings or credit cards.[73] A recent investigation into the Paris and Brussels attacks revealed that salaries, savings, profits from commercial enterprises, social welfare benefits,

65 House of Commons, Report of the Official Account of the Bombings in London on 7 July 2005 (London 2005).

66 See *R v Darren Osborne*, Woolwich Crown Court, 2 February 2018, sentencing remarks Mrs Justice Cheema-Grubb, https://www.judiciary.uk/wp-content/uploads/2018/02/r-v-osborne-sentencing-remarks.pdf, accessed 10 July 2020.

67 Ibid.

68 V. Dodd, 'London Bridge Attackers Bought Knives from Lidl for £4 Each, Say Police' (*The Guardian*, 11 June 2017), https://www.theguardian.com/uk-news/2017/jun/11/london-bridge-attackers-bought-knives-from-lidl-for-4-each-say-police, accessed 21 December 2019.

69 David Brown, 'Streatham Attack: He grabbed knife near till then ran out and began stabbing' (*The Times*, 3 February 2020), https://www.thetimes.co.uk/article/streatham-attack-he-grabbed-a-knife-near-the-till-then-ran-out-and-began-stabbing-b0wtt7tv6, accessed 4 February 2020.

70 Tom Harper, 'From London Bridge to Ariana Grande, UK Terror Attacks Cost just £5000 to Execute' (*The Times*, 9 September 2018), https://www.thetimes.co.uk/article/from-london-bridge-to-ariana-grande-uk-terror-attacks-in-2017-cost-just-5-000-vck5tdttg, accessed 10 September 2018.

71 Institute of Economics and Peace 'Global Terrorism Index 2017: Measuring and understanding the impact of terrorism' (2017) 5, http://visionofhumanity.org/app/uploads/2017/11/Global-Terrorism-Index2017.pdf, accessed 23 November 2018.

72 Ibid.

73 Institute of Economics and Peace 'Global Terrorism Index 2017: Measuring and understanding the impact of terrorism' (2017) 5, http://visionofhumanity.org/app/uploads/2017/11/Global-Terrorism-Index2017.pdf, accessed 23 November 2018.

selling of personal assets or donations were among the techniques used to raise money for the attacks.[74]

These examples illustrate that the CTF reporting obligations have done very little to prevent acts of terrorism from being financed. If the terrorist or terrorist cell is largely self-sufficient, there is no need for them to be involved in funding activities that could lead to the submission of a SAR.[75] Furthermore, if the terrorist attack is carried out using a small amount of money, there is no reason why suspicion would be raised and lead to the submission of a SAR.

This section has illustrated how intelligence that the regulated sector provides to law enforcement via SARs and DATF SARS can be useful. However, further analysis reveals that the current system for reporting suspicions of terrorism financing through the UK financial system is not working effectively. The section has identified several weaknesses in the UK's CTF reporting regime, including the low threshold adopted by reporting entities when reporting suspicions of terrorism financing, low quality reporting, defensive reporting and the threat posed by cheap acts of terrorism and terrorism financed through legitimate sources. In order to improve the intelligence that law enforcement receives, a new model has emerged: the public/private-partnership information-exchange model. Such partnerships bring together key stakeholders from law enforcement, the government and financial institutions and allow the exchange of information about specific typologies of money-laundering and terrorist-financing risks. The next section of this chapter will provide some background information on the public/private-partnership information exchange model and discuss attempts made by the UK to develop a more effective, intelligence-led response to terrorist financing through the development of JMLIT.

Public-private partnerships: an intelligence-driven reporting model

Public-private information sharing partnerships represent another way in which financial intelligence can be exploited, ensuring that law enforcement agencies benefit from the information held by regulated entities and, conversely, that regulated entities are attuned to the priorities of law enforcement agencies and appraised of relevant typologies.[76] This is a view shared by the FATF, which stated 'effective information-sharing is [a] cornerstone of a well-functioning AML/

74 Thomas Renard, 'Counter Terrorism in Belgium: Key challenges and policy options' (Egmont Paper 89, October 2016) 35.

75 Nicholas Ryder, 'Is it Time to Reform the Counter-terrorist Financing Reporting Obligations? A critical and comparative assessment of the counter-terrorist financing reporting obligations in the European Union and the United Kingdom.' (2018) *German Law Review*, 19 (5) 7.

76 Maxwell (n 2) 24.

CTF framework'.[77] Historically, however, reporting entities in the private sector have been asked to be the front line of the AML/CTF process without adequate information flow from public sector agencies that could inform their reporting decisions.[78] Poor information sharing has hindered the ability of the UK regime to adequately detect suspicions of terrorist financing. In a bid to counteract the fragmentation in the flow of information, the UK, along with several other jurisdictions, has committed to the development of financial information sharing partnerships (FISPs). FISPs are defined by Maxwell and Artingstall as 'a new kind of information sharing exchange which aim to provide for more dynamic information sharing on financial crime risks between public and private sectors'.[79]

The partnership models in each jurisdiction are constituted and operate in different ways. Furthermore, each partnership prioritises certain typology topics. For example, Canada's Project Protect focuses on money laundering risks arising from human trafficking in the sex trade,[80] Australia's Fintel Alliance focuses on the analysis of Panama Paper-related offences[81] and Hong Kong's Fraud and Money Laundering Intelligence Taskforce focuses on trade-based money laundering and fraud.[82] However, this section focuses on JMLIT, which has four priority areas of focus: tackling the laundering of the proceeds of bribery and corruption, tackling trade-based money laundering, tackling the laundering of the proceeds of human trafficking and organised immigration crime and tackling terrorist financing, which includes a focus on foreign terrorist fighters and international money flows that support terrorist funding.[83]

77 FATF, 'FATF Guidance on the Risk-Based Approach to Combating Money Laundering and Terrorist Financing: High Level Principles and Procedures' (FATF, Paris June 2007), https://www.fatf-gafi.org/publications/fatfrecommendations/documents/fatfguidanceontherisk-basedapproachtocombatingmoneylaunderingandterroristfinancing-highlevelprinciplesandprocedures.html, accessed 10 March 2017.
Prober (n 62).

78 Maxwell (n 2) 25.

79 Maxwell (n 2) 47.

80 Tavia Grant, 'Canadian Banks, Police Following Money Trail to Target Human Trafficking' (The Globe and Mail, 21 February 2017), https://www.theglobeandmail.com/news/national/canadian-banks-police-following-money-trail-to-target-human-trafficking/article34093888/#:~:text= Canadian%20banks%2C%20police%20following%20money%20trail%20to%20target%20human%20trafficking,-Open%20this%20photo&text=Project%20Protect%20is%20a% 20partnership, to%20detect%20and% 20investigate%20traffickers, accessed 28 January 2020.

81 Australian Transaction Reports and Analysis Centre 'About the Fintel Alliance' (AUSTRAC, 3 March 2017), https://www.austrac.gov.au/about-us/fintel-alliance, accessed 20 January 2020.

82 Hong Kong Monetary Authority 'Fraud and Money Laundering Intelligence Taskforce Launched' (HKMA, 26 May 2017), https://www.hkma.gov.hk/eng/news-and-media/press-releases/2017/05/20170526-3/, accessed 29 July 2020.

83 JMLIT, 'Introduction to the Joint Money Laundering Intelligence Taskforce (JMLIT Toolkit)', http://www.nationalcrimeagency.gov.uk/publications/623-jmlit-toolkit-presentation/file, accessed 13 February 2019.

The Joint Money Laundering Intelligence Taskforce

Due to the very small amounts of funds involved in most acts of terrorism in the UK coupled with the challenge that, in terrorism financing cases, a regulated entity must focus not only on the origin of the funds but also the destination, it has proved challenging for regulated entities to identify terrorist financing proactively, without the benefit of investigative and contextual information from public authorities.[84] JMLIT aims to counteract this problem by offering a distinct approach to identifying suspicions of terrorist financing, by enabling information sharing and collaboration across public and private partnership members to identify terrorist financing risks.[85]

According to Royal United Services Institute (RUSI), FISPs typically support two major types of output: 'knowledge and insight sharing to support strategic analysis' and 'tactical information sharing'.[86] When sharing insight knowledge to support strategic analysis, public and private members of the partnership co-develop typologies or knowledge products covering financial crime threats and highlight relevant behavioural indicators.[87] Typically, these products do not contain confidential identifying information about specific suspects or entities or individual clients or customers of financial institutions and, as such, do not require enabling legislation. These knowledge products are made available to non-members of partnerships and are either published and accessible online (such as in the USA or Singapore) or are released through non-public distribution channels to regulated entities (such as in the UK or Hong Kong).[88] By the same token, where legislation allows, partnerships have facilitated tactical information sharing of sensitive information relevant to law enforcement or national intelligence investigations to be shared with regulated entities.[89] This information might include the names of specific individuals, legal entities or other identifying information relevant to a case. Member-regulated entities can then use this awareness of priority threats, from the perspective of law enforcement or other public agencies, to search their systems in response to that identified suspicion or indicator.[90] Depending on the legal gateway and format of the partnership, regulated entities can share sensitive information with law enforcement either through formal reports or dynamically within the partnership.[91] JMLIT makes use of both

84 Tom Keatinge and Florence Keen 'A Sharper Image: Advancing a risk-based response to terrorist financing' (2020) RUSI Occasional Paper, March 2020, 9.

85 Ibid.

86 Keatinge and Keen (n 83).

87 Clare Ellis and Ines Sofia de Oliveira, 'Tackling Money Laundering, Towards a New Model for Information Sharing', RUSI Occasional Papers (September 2015).

88 Keatinge and Keen (n 83) 72.

89 Ibid. 73.

90 Institute of International Finance 'IIF Financial Crime Information Sharing Report' (IFF 31 March 2017), /Publications/ID/952/IIF-Financial-Crime-Information-Sharing-Report, accessed 12 January 2020.

91 Maxwell (n 2) 49.

outputs by operating a 'public-private taskforce format for tactical information sharing linked to several typology co-development groups'.[92]

Structure

The JMLIT is structured around three key components: an operational group, a strategic group (which includes experts groups aligned to the four priority areas) and an alerts service.[93] A management board oversees the overall direction and performance of the JMLIT and promotes collective ownership of the priorities.[94] The operations group, which focuses on tactical intelligence sharing among public and private sector participants, is at the centre of the JMLIT model. The operations group aims 'to fill intelligence gaps where suspected money laundering crosses multiple financial institutions'.[95] Its membership includes the NCA – which houses the UK's Financial Intelligence Unit – HM Revenue and Customs, the City of London Police and other law enforcement bodies as well as 10 of the UK's largest financial institutions.[96] The NCA acts as the focal point for sharing intelligence among the operations group's participants[97] and is able to share information derived from a variety of sources – including law enforcement information, intelligence derived from SARs and other methods – related to specific investigative targets of law enforcement concern.[98] The banks can use this information regarding suspected individuals and entities to search their internal systems for relevant information, which they can then bring back to the operations group to build a more complete picture of financial activity than can be achieved through traditional SAR processes.[99] This enables JMLIT to function as a 'two-way street' and expedites the information sharing process relating to specific,

92 Keatinge and Keen (n 83) 56.

93 JMLIT 'Public-private Information Sharing Partnerships to Tackle Money Laundering in the Finance Sector' (JMLIT), https://thecommonwealth.org/sites/default/files/inline/4%20UK%20approach%20to%20public-private%20partnerships.pdf, accessed 20 March 2020.

94 Ibid.

95 JMLIT, 'Introduction to the Joint Money Laundering Intelligence Taskforce (JMLIT Toolkit)', http://www.nationalcrimeagency.gov.uk/publications/623-jmlit-toolkit-presentation/file, accessed 13 February 2019.

96 Ibid. Specifically, the operations group's membership includes the NCA's Economic Crime Command and National Intelligence Hub; FCA; HMRC; City of London Police; Cifas; UBS; Barclays; Santander; Standard Chartered; RBS; HSBC; BNP Paribas; Citigroup; Nationwide; Lloyds Bank; JP Morgan; Western Union; Nationwide; Deutsche Bank; Metro Bank and the Post Office.

97 JMLIT, 'Introduction to the Joint Money Laundering Intelligence Taskforce (JMLIT Toolkit)', http://www.nationalcrimeagency.gov.uk/publications/623-jmlit-toolkit-presentation/file, accessed 13 February 2019.

98 Nick Kochan, 'How Law Enforcement is Partnering Up with Banks in AML Fight' (Wolters Kluwer, 9 March 2016), https://www.wolterskluwer.com/en/solutions/banking-finance-risk-reporting-compliance, accessed 16 March 2020.

99 P. Horlick, 'Countering the Financing of Terrorism and Depriving Terrorist Groups, Particularly Al-Qaida, ISIL (Da'esh) and their Affiliates, from Their Sources of Funding', UN

high priority threats. Both law enforcement agencies and financial institutions can use the intelligence derived to dedicate resources to addressing these operational targets.

The Crime and Courts Act 2013 provides a clear legal underpinning to JMLIT's activities. Section 7 of the 2013 Act provides that a 'person may disclose information to the NCA if the disclosure is made for the purposes of the exercise of any NCA function'.[100] Furthermore, an NCA officer may disclose information obtained by the NCA in connection with the exercise of any NCA function if the disclosure is for any permitted purpose,[101] with some limited restrictions. Section 7 creates a legal gateway by which the NCA and the financial sector can communicate to the extent that the communication helps the NCA fulfil its role. The result is that the NCA can harness capabilities across the financial sector in order to fill intelligence gaps where suspected terrorism financing crosses multiple financial institutions. JMLIT is one of only two public private partnerships that benefit from specifically designated legislation; the other is the Netherlands Taskforce on Terrorism Financing, which relies on Article 20 of the Netherlands Police Information Act 1993.

The strategic group is run by an industry group, UK Finance. Its participants include several law enforcement agencies and 25 financial institutions.[102] Whereas the operations group focuses on the targeted sharing of sensitive intelligence, the strategic group shares non-sensitive information in order to develop typologies, threat trend assessments and other strategic products. The broader public and private sectors can draw on this information to understand four high priority threat areas: bribery and corruption; trade-based money laundering; immigration crime and human trafficking; and terrorist financing.[103] The aim of the strategic group is to enable the public and private sectors to 'horizon scan' for threats to the UK financial system related to these criminal activities.[104]

Barriers to information sharing under JMLIT

JMLIT assists in CTF efforts on both the strategic and tactical level. On the strategic side, there is a terrorist financing expert group. This group is chaired by the National Terrorist Financing Investigation Unit and the Office for Security

joint open briefing of the Counter-Terrorism Committee and the 1267/1989/2253 ISIL (Da'esh) and Al-Qaida Sanctions Committee, New York, 14 April 2016.

100 Crime and Courts Act 2013, s 7.

101 Ibid.

102 JMLIT, 'Introduction to the Joint Money Laundering Intelligence Taskforce (JMLIT Toolkit)', http://www.nationalcrimeagency.gov.uk/publications/623-jmlit-toolkit-presentation/file, accessed 12 January 2019.

103 Matt Allen, 'Uniting to Tackle Financial Crime' (BBA, 27 February 2015), https://www.bba.org.uk/news/bba-voice/uniting-to-tackle-financial-crime/#.XyvQWhNKhQI, accessed 1 May 2020.

104 Ibid.

and Counter Terrorism in the Home Office. It acts as a regular forum (approximately every six weeks) at which experts from the public and private sectors can share emerging/newly identified CFT threats and typologies and coordinate project activity designed to combat the threat more effectively. According to the Law Commission, this has allowed firms to better understand the risks they face and, as a result, has led to a significant increase in quality of submitted SARs.[105] Examples of projects that are currently in process include the development of typologies on financial indicators associated to home grown/lone wolf terrorists, the review of financial indicators common to individuals convicted of counterterrorism offences and a project aimed at developing a better understanding of terrorist financing risks affecting corporate and investment banks.[106]

On the tactical side, the operations group is available to the NTFIU and counterterrorism network to support proactive or reactive enquiries into CFT investigations including through an out of hours 'critical incident' function. JMLIT has been utilised on a number of occasions by the NTFIU and has provided a quick and efficient means through which a wide range of tactical information can be requested and obtained. In a number of instances, the information provided has proved highly significant to the successful development of the investigation.[107] For example, in the aftermath of the London Borough Market terrorist attack, numerous financial institutions proactively reached out to the head of the NTFIU to offer assistance in identifying the terrorist networks involved, allowing the NTFIU to more rapidly obtain a full financial picture.[108] Furthermore, after the London Bridge attack the NTFIU, together with support from the UKFIU, initiated a 24/7 response and the case was brought to JMLIT within 12 hours of the attack. Within a few hours of the briefing, financial institutions were able to provide assistance to identify the payments for van hire and establish spending patterns, allowing further investigative strategies to be identified.[109] According to FATF, this assistance was 'crucial in allowing investigators to conclude that the attack involved only three attackers with no broader network'.[110]

Overall, since its inception, JMLIT has supported and developed over 600 law enforcement investigations that have directly contributed to over 150 arrests and the seizure or restraint of over £34 million.[111] Although JMLIT is in its infancy, it has already added a valuable extra dimension to the UK's effort to tackle the financing of terrorism by facilitating more effective information sharing and collaboration. The taskforce is seen as a successful programme for public and private sector engagement and has been cited by FATF as an example of best practice in

105 FATF (n 76) 48.

106 Ibid. 9.

107 HM Treasury, *National Risk Assessment of Money Laundering and Terrorist Financing* (HM Treasury 2017) 6.

108 NCA, 'Joint Money Laundering Intelligence Taskforce' NCA (London 2018) 4.

109 Ibid. 11.

110 FATF (n 76) 92.

111 NCA, 'Joint Money Laundering Intelligence Taskforce' NCA (London 2018) 4.

this area.[112] However, several barriers to effective information sharing exist within JMLIT's framework. Limitations regarding JMLIT's scope and lack of investment in technology are widely evident in several critiques of the partnership.[113] This section will now discuss these barriers to information sharing in more detail.

Lack of investment in technology

JMLIT's low technology format, which as previously illustrated, at the operational level, revolves around in-person case briefings by NCA staff, has proved valuable and effective at the current rate of activity. However, to expand the number of participants receiving information, the rate of information flow, the capacity for handling a larger number of cases and to support shared analytics capabilities, technology solutions and larger scale distributions of information will likely need to supplement JMLIT's in-person briefing format. Real time access to the different stakeholders' information allows for greater responsiveness and, from the FIUs' perspective, to advise partner departments on financial intelligence relating to terrorism financing.[114] It also gives capacity for supervisory authorities, law enforcement agencies and financial institutions to take required action, better understanding what, whom and where to search.[115] According to the EU 'setting up a framework for real-time information exchange and analysis between all relevant national stakeholders is a prerequisite towards an enhanced CFT framework.'[116] An example of how real time information exchange can assist in the detection and prevention of financial flows linked to terrorism can be seen in the USA whereby the TFOS, through conducting near real time financial tracking of a terrorist cell and providing specific and identifiable information to a foreign intelligence agency, were able to prevent six potentially terrorist attacks.[117] The lack of investment by HM Government has not only limited the ability of JMLIT, but also the NCA. For example, in 2019 the NCA stated that its annual budget needed to be increased from £424m to £.1bn to tackle serious

112 FATF (n 76) 47.

113 Maxwell (n 3).

114 Egmont Group 'Enhancing Public-Public Cooperation to Better Disrupt Money Laundering and Terrorism Financing' (EGMONT, 2019), https://egmontgroup.org/sites/default/files/filedepot/external/2019%20-%20HoFIU%20-%20Enhancing%20Public-Public%20Cooperation%20from%20the%20FIU%20Perspective.pdf, accessed 12 July 2020.

115 FATF 'Guidance for a Risk Based Approach: Effective supervision and enforcement by AML/CTF supervisors of the financial sector and law enforcement' (FATF, October 2015), https://www.fatf-gafi.org/media/fatf/documents/reports/RBA-Effective-supervision-and-enforcement.pdf, accessed 13 February 2020.

116 Egmont Group (n 113) 47.

117 US Congress House of Representatives, 'Identify, Disrupt and Dismantle: Coordinating the Government's Attack on Terrorist Financing' (House Hearing, 108 Congress) December 15 2003, https://www.govinfo.gov/content/pkg/CHRG-108hhrg93428/html/CHRG-108hhrg93428.htm, accessed 12 January 2017.

and organised crime. An important part of this funding was in response to how criminal enterprises continued to exploit new forms of technology.[118] In 2015, HM Inspectorate of Constabulary and Fire & Rescue Services were heavily critical of the lack of investment afforded to the NCA to improve its use of new forms of technology.[119]

Limited scope and membership

Another cited weakness of JMLIT is the limited scope of its membership. This is a view supported by FATF, which in its recent mutual evaluation report (MER) of the UK's anti-money laundering and counterterrorist financing measures, determined that 'while the JMLIT provides an excellent resource to competent authorities in accessing information held by the largest institutions in relation to high priority cases, it is not an appropriate avenue for the majority of cases and only provides access to a limited number of the biggest financial institutions'.[120] The number of JMLIT members is small relative to the number of entities that are regulated for AML/CTF purposes in the UK. According to RUSI, out of the 19,600 FCA regulated entities subject to AML/CTF reporting obligations in the UK, only 15 are currently involved in the partnership and all of them are banks.[121] However, it should be noted that in total, these entities represent 93% of UK retail banking by market share.[122] The exact proportions of total SAR filings by partnership members in the UK is not public information. However, given the fact that, in the UK, banking as a sector contributes almost 85% of the total SAR fillings, with four banks (all JMLIT members) contributing 80% of that reporting, the figure is likely to be a high proportion of the total.[123] As such, the partnership may reasonably be seen to represent the vast majority of producers of suspicious reporting.

However, it is important to note that the scope of JMLIT's membership does not currently extend to several other sectors that are particularly vulnerable to abuse from terrorism financiers. For example, there is no evidence of the partnership engaging with money transfer companies, building societies or electronic payment companies. This lack of engagement is concerning when taking into account the fact that over 26% of terrorism financing SARs disseminated to NTFIU in 2019 were from these industries alone.[124] According to the Law Commission, the current relatively small size of the taskforce was a feature of its design because it ensured adequate security and instilled trust and confidence

118 NCA 'Annual Plan 2020–2021' (London 2020) 4.
119 HMICFRS 'An Inspection of the NCA' (London 2015).
120 FATF (n 76) 51.
121 Maxwell (n 3) 12.
122 Ibid.
123 FATF I(n 76) 122.
124 National Crime Agency, 'The Suspicious Activity Reports Regime Annual Report 2019' (2019) 4.

among JMLIT members.[125] However, the limited membership of JMLIT, which does not include at high risk areas from money laundering (such as estate agents and the legal profession), limits JMLIT to receiving information from just 0.07% of the total regulated entities subject to CTF reporting obligations in the UK. This, in turn, hinders the ability of the partnership to share and access potentially crucial intelligence relating to terrorism financing across the reporting sector.

The expansion of JMLIT was included in the UK's 2019–2022 Economic Crime Plan. As part of the plan, the National Economic Crime Centre is currently leading the enhancement of JMLIT and aims to expand the partnership 'to include additional sectors, geographical areas and additional organisations within sectors currently included in JMLIT' by July 2020.[126] Furthermore, UK policymakers have described an intention to include accountancy and professional perspectives in JMLIT information sharing[127] allowing for more opportunities to share financial intelligence relating to terrorism financing.[128] However, in a recent paper by the Law Commission, concerns were raised by several consultees, including the NCA and the City of London Police, that JMLIT operations may be hampered by expansion in practice. The NCA state that 'we do not believe that the simple expansion of the current JMLIT would be the most effective mechanism for wider engagement'.[129] Other consultees doubt whether expansion could be achieved without placing strain on the effectiveness of operations. They note that 'JMLIT may become bureaucratic, unwieldy and, in turn, less effective.'[130] Furthermore, no clear consensus has emerged about which entities ought to be included in the JMLIT membership. According to the Law Commission, there is some support for expansion to the regulated sector generally.[131] However, other consultees expressed concerns about the logistics of taskforce operations that would apply with greater force to that option.[132] The City of London Police share many of the concerns above and suggest that an alternative to expansion could be to have 'sub-sets of JMLIT concentrating on different sectors thereby allowing full access or the ability for JMLIT to co-opt additional members on a short-term basis to allow for their resources/expertise in connection with a particular piece of work'.[133] However, although this may be a cheaper alternative to expansion, it does not fully account for the benefits that could be brought from expanding the scope of the membership. As a result of the conflicting views between consultees,

125 HM Treasury 'Economic Crime Plan 2019–2022' (London 2019).
126 Ibid. 20.
127 Maxwell (n 3) 7.
128 Ibid.
129 Law Commission, *Anti-Money Laundering: The SAR's Regime Report* (Law Com No 384, 2019) 166.
130 Ibid. 165.
131 Ibid.
132 Ibid.
133 Ibid. 168.

the Law Commission has refrained from making any specific recommendations about changes to the membership of JMLIT.[134]

This section has highlighted how JMLIT has achieved significant impact in the fight against terrorism financing in the UK. Emerging data provides evidence that the JMLIT has provided crucial assistance in terrorism financing investigations resulting in improved law enforcement outcomes. Furthermore, JMLIT has provided private sector entities in the UK with significant value in contributing to their terrorism financing risk awareness and has led to increased understanding in the public sector agencies about complex financial issues and services, and corresponding vulnerabilities to abuse. This, in turn, has led to a significant increase in the quality of submitted terrorism financing SARs. However, this section has highlighted several barriers to information present within the partnership, namely the limited scope of the partnership and its lack of investment in technology. In order to ensure that JMLIT is operating at its full capacity, the partnership must achieve the ambition of real time information exchange and move beyond its existing model characterised by manual and slow information transfer, low technology, limited visibility of the financial sector outside retail banking and limited bandwidth to process operational cases.

Conclusion

Intelligence that the regulated sector provides to law enforcement via terrorism financing SARs can be useful. However, further analysis reveals that the current system for reporting suspicions of terrorism financing through the UK financial system is not working effectively. The low threshold adopted by reporting entities when reporting suspicions of terrorism financing continues to lower the quality of financial intelligence provided to the NTFIU. Furthermore, harsh penalties imposed by the FCA due to non-compliance, coupled with a lack of awareness in private sector agencies regarding terrorism financing risks, has resulted in an excessive number of terrorism financing reports being filed.

Intelligence provided to law enforcement can be improved through adequate financial information sharing between the public and private sector. The UK has become a world leader in promoting the appropriate sharing and use of information on economic crime. The establishment of the JMLIT as an operational pilot in 2015 has led to a paradigm shift in how financial intelligence can be exchanged and analysed and several other countries have now established their own public-private FISPs. Indeed, FATF refers to JMLIT as 'an innovative model for public/private information sharing that has generated very positive results since its inception in 2015 and is considered to be an example of best practice'.[135]

134 Ibid. 167.
135 FATF (n 66) 47.

JMLIT has 'made very quick progress in aiding voluntary information sharing [...] and has quickly demonstrated the benefits of this kind of working'.[136] The partnership has 'significantly improved' the quality of terrorism financing SARs by providing private sector entities in the UK with significant value in contributing to their terrorism financing risk awareness in addition to increasing understanding in the public sector agencies about complex financial issues and services, and corresponding vulnerabilities to abuse. According to the Law Commission, terrorism financing SARs submitted through JMLIT are considered to be 'of a very high standard'.[137] JMLIT has also providing 'crucial assistance' in several terrorism financing investigations resulting in improved law enforcement outcomes.[138]

However, the chapter has highlighted several barriers to effective information sharing that exist within the partnership, including the limited scope of JMLIT membership and the lack of investment in technology. Due to low levels of public funding, JMLIT has suffered from a lack of investment in technology to support the 'real time' exchange of information. Therefore, it is of paramount importance that HM Government redresses the budgetary imbalance of both JMLIT and the NCA if the UK is to maintain its reputation of having a robust stance towards financial crime. Real time access to the different stakeholders' information will allow for greater responsiveness and, from the FIU's perspective, the ability to disseminate financial intelligence to partners relating to terrorism financing.[139] It would also give capacity for supervisory authorities, law enforcement agencies and financial institutions to take required action, better understanding what, whom, and where to search.[140] Furthermore, at the time of writing, JMLIT is limited to receiving information from just 0.07% of the total regulated entities subject to CTF reporting obligations in the UK. This, in turn, hinders the ability of the partnership to share and access potentially crucial intelligence relating to terrorism financing across the reporting sector. Whether or not JMLIT's membership will be expanded in the future remains unclear. Plans to expand the partnership have been included in the UK's 2019–2022 Economic Crime Plan,[141] however, several law enforcement agencies, including the NCA and the City of London Police, have expressed concerns that JMLIT operations may be hampered by expansion in practice. As a result, the Law Commission has refrained

136 Financial Conduct Authority 'Effectiveness and Proportionality: Our financial crime priorities – speech by Rob Gruppetta, Head of Financial Crime Department', 10 November 2016, https://www.fca.org.uk/news/speeches/effectiveness-proportionality-financial-crime-priorities, accessed 14 February 2019.

137 FATF (n 76) 51.

138 Ibid.

139 Egmont Group (n 113) 47.

140 FATF 'Guidance for a Risk Based Approach: Effective supervision and enforcement by AML/CTF supervisors of the financial sector and law enforcement', October 2015, https://www.fatf-gafi.org/media/fatf/documents/reports/RBA-Effective-supervision-and-enforcement.pdf, accessed 13 July 2020.

141 HM Treasury (n 124).

from making any specific recommendations about changes to the membership of JMLIT.[142]

Overall, JMLIT is a great step in the fight against terrorism financing. If the partnership continues at its current rate of performance, it has the potential to become a key part of the UK CTF strategy. However, this heavily depends on the willingness of stakeholders to work at addressing several barriers to effective information sharing that exist within the partnership.

142 Law Commission (n 128) 168.

6 The future of criminal finance

'bin Ladens' and the cashless society

Rikard Jalkebro[1] *and William Vlcek*[2]

Introduction

The pursuit of criminal money as a distinct law enforcement activity is often attributed to the US Bank Secrecy Act 1970 and the subsequent creation of money laundering as a distinct criminal activity in 1986. The practice of money laundering is the process of transforming the proceeds of crime into a form that appears to have a legitimate origin, helping to conceal the other criminal activities of those in possession of this money. The criminalisation of money laundering provided law enforcement agencies with a means to target 'drug lords' in the US 'war on drugs' initiated in the 1980s.[3] The scope of anti-money laundering (AML) was internationalised with the establishment of the Financial Action Task Force (FATF) in 1989, which sits at the centre of a network of FATF-style regional bodies (FSRBs) bringing global coverage to AML activities. At the same time, the scope of anti-money laundering legislation extended from the proceeds of illegal drugs trafficking to include all forms of criminal conduct, terrorist finance and financing the proliferation of weapons of mass destruction.[4] In parallel, the form of criminal proceeds evolved from cash and bank accounts to be anything of economic value – precious stones and metals, real estate, stocks, bonds and essentially any form of moveable property with value. Yet cash remains a concern because it is anonymous, it is hard to trace and it is portable. All of these make cash largely invisible to the measures created to monitor and track the economy to prevent money laundering. On the surface, then, the predicted shift from the widespread use of cash to a cashless society, for example using electronic payment methods through bank cards and mobile payment apps, could significantly reduce the quantity of criminal money in the economy. This shift, in turn, raises a number of questions about its unintended consequences, the enthusiasm

1 Associate Professor, Anwar Gargash Diplomatic Academy.

2 Senior Lecturer in Global Political Economy, University of St Andrews.

3 J. C. Sharman, *The Money Laundry: Regulating Criminal Finance in the Global Economy* (Cornell University Press 2011) 20.

4 Mark T. Nance, 'The Regime that FATF Built: An introduction to the Financial Action Task Force' (2018) 69 Crime, Law and Social Change 109.

DOI: 10.4324/9781003020813-7

for its intended consequences notwithstanding. Several of these questions are explored in this chapter.

Economists attribute three primary functions to money in society: that it represents a medium of exchange, a store of value and a unit of account. At the same time, sociologists investigate the function of money as a social construction and its pivotal role in the credit–debt relations that underpin the political economy of society.[5] For the purposes of this chapter, money serves all of the above functions and more. Indeed, the transition from money-as-cash in society to a 'cashless' society has implications for both how people think of money as well as the cultural practices that involve the use of money in any particular society. Both features, the political economic and the sociological, will be present in the following discussion and analysis.

Recognising the role of cash in the criminal economy and the anti-money laundering measures developed to counter and eliminate this role, one may ask how it was reflected in the creation of a major new international currency at the beginning of the 21st century? The introduction of the euro currency, coins and banknotes, for the member states of the Eurozone within the European Union occurred on 1 January 2002, including the high value €500 note. The risk of criminal misuse attached to this high value note was recognised, but as explained below, its social benefits were deemed to outweigh that risk. In time, it came to be called the 'bin Laden' note by some commentators with intimations of criminal misuse and accompanied by increasing calls to withdraw it from circulation.[6] On 4 May 2016, the European Central Bank (ECB) announced that it would cease production of the €500 note and no longer issue it after 2018. This announcement further stated: 'In view of the international role of the euro and the widespread trust in its banknotes, the €500 will remain legal tender and can therefore continue to be used as a means of payment and store of value.'[7] Clearly, the ECB continued to privilege the social benefits attributed to high value notes, its partial acquiescence to calls for the elimination of such notes notwithstanding.

In spite of these developments, Sweden provides a useful and interesting case for the cashless society. Not only is it on track to become the world's first cashless society, but it also has a fascinating history with cash and banking in general. Among other things, Sweden had the first modern-style European banknote and established the first central bank. A Swedish economist, Knut Wicksell, was also the first to theorise in depth a model for a cashless economy.[8] Furthermore, Sweden represents a stable democracy with high levels of trust in state institutions; in spite of this, Sweden has faced significant difficulties in detecting and

5 Geoffrey Ingham, *The Nature of Money* (Polity 2004) 69.

6 e.g. Peter Sands, *Making it Harder for the Bad Guys: The Case for Eliminating High Denomination Notes* (M-RCBG Associate Working Paper Series, 2016).

7 European Central Bank, *ECB Ends Production and Issuance of €500 Banknote* (European Central Bank 2016).

8 As cited in Lars Jonung, 'Afterword to "It Will Soon Be 1984 ..."' (2020) 17 *Econ Journal Watch* 251 252.

preventing complex money laundering schemes. Serious crime has been prevalent and the response has been a critical part of the move toward a cashless society. Before exploring the case of Sweden, the chapter provides a brief discussion on the origins of the term 'bin Laden' for the €500 note, followed by an explanation of the argument promoting the benefits for a cashless society.

€500 – the 'bin Laden' note

The creation of the euro currency in both coins and notes was the culmination of a multi-year project to establish a common currency under the obligations of the Maastricht Treaty of the European Union, signed in 1992. There was a transition period in 2002 during which national currencies continued to circulate alongside the new euro currency, a period particularly fruitful for the conversion of high denomination banknotes where those existed in the national currency, e.g. Austria, Germany and the Netherlands.[9] In particular, the €500 note was in line with the 1,000 Deutschemark note it replaced, which included these notes' function as a store of value in Eastern Europe.[10] These authors highlight the widespread use of high denomination notes as a store of value for individuals hoarding them to avoid taxation, due to the fear of a banking failure and the privacy engendered by the use of cash in any transaction, but they also point to the use of high value notes in the underground economy.[11] The use of the €500 note as a store of value was recognised by the European Central Bank and continued to be identified as one of its benefits as recently as 2014.[12] In the latter report on money laundering through bulk cash transfer, the FATF observed that possessing cash 'for store of value purposes, and the cross-border transportation of cash in order to facilitate' the store of value function is not *necessarily* [emphasis added] illegal.[13] Nonetheless, the report's focus is on the illegal usage of cash and the ease that high denomination notes offer for facilitating these illegal activities.

It must be acknowledged that the probable application of a high value euro note to illegal purposes was recognised when the range of denominations to be offered in the new currency was established.[14] A history of the introduction of the euro currency explains that the decision to include the €500 note 'was made after careful evaluation'.[15] This ECB publication went on to explain, as already

9 Jef Vuchelen and Leo Van Hove, 'An Early Evaluation of the Introduction of Euro Banknotes and Coins' (2002) 29 *Journal of Economic Studies* 370, 375.

10 Brendan Brown, *What Drives Global Capital Flows? Myth, Speculation and Currency Diplomacy* (Palgrave Macmillan 2006) 63.

11 Vuchelen and Van Hove, 374; Brown, 63.

12 Financial Action Task Force and Middle East & North Africa Financial Action Task Force, *Money Laundering Through the Physical Transportation of Cash* (2015) 44.

13 Ibid.

14 Antti Heinonen, *The First Euros: The Creation and Issue of the First Euro Banknotes and the Road to the Europa Series* (European Central Bank and Suomen Pankki 2015) 42.

15 European Central Bank, *How the Euro Became Our Money: A Short History of the Euro Banknotes and Coins* (European Central Bank 2007) 12.

indicated, that the €500 note served to replace already existing high denomination banknotes in several national currencies, most prominently the 1,000 Deutschemark note, because it also circulated outside Germany. Consequently, the risk from criminal misuse was not a new one with the introduction of the euro. Rather, in serving to replace these existing high denomination notes, the €500 note served to continue their function as a store of value and for high value transactions in those national political economies where such large payments in cash remain standard practice. Equally, the ECB and other European Union monetary authorities did not use the introduction of the euro currency as an opportunity to reduce the use of high value notes in criminal activity.[16]

The application of the nickname 'bin Laden' to the €500 note is frequently cited to Kenneth Rogoff in recent publications. The text in his footnote is offered without attribution, stating simply that: 'The 500-euro notes are sometimes referred to as "Bin Ladens," because most people have heard of them, but few have seen one.'[17] There is also the unreferenced claim offered by Peter Sands: 'It should be no surprise that in the underworld the €500 note is known as a "Bin Laden".'[18] Other authors cite an op-ed contribution to the *New York Times* in 2010.[19] An alternative origin story was offered in the online magazine *Slate* at the time of the withdrawal of the €500 note from production in 2019. This writer declared: 'Because of its illicit reputation—and because "many know what it looks like" but "few have ever seen one"—the European media ominously dubbed the note "the Bin Laden".'[20] We were unable to identify a specific reference to the usage of 'bin Laden' among money laundering professionals, which would indicate an everyday usage of this nickname for the €500 note, for example, with Europol or the Financial Action Task Force.[21] In the years after 2001 and prior to his assassination, the sobriquet of 'bin Laden' for a currency note that was in circulation but largely unseen is very believable. At the same time, it plays to the underlying assumption that these high value notes served the needs of criminals and terrorists far more than serving the mundane purposes of

16 Vuchelen and Van Hove, 383.

17 Kenneth S. Rogoff, *The Curse of Cash* (Princeton University Press 2016) 200, n 1.

18 Sands, 12.

19 Jonathan Lipow, 'Turn In Your Bin Ladens' *New York Times* (New York, 17 December 2010) op-ed, https://www.nytimes.com/2010/12/18/opinion/18lipow.html, accessed 13 December 2019; e.g. Bill Maurer, 'Afterword – Mobile Money, Money Magic, Purse Limits and Pins: Tracing monetary pragmatics' (2011) 4 *Journal of Cultural Economy* 349.

20 Amos Barshad, 'The Life and Death of the Bin Laden' Slate, https://slate.com/news-and-politics/2019/08/euros-500-bin-ladens.html, accessed 25 February 2020; citing Jon Henley, '€500 "Bin Laden" Banknotes to be Axed' *The Guardian* (London, 4 May 2016), https://www.theguardian.com/business/2016/may/04/500-euro-banknote-could-be-scrapped-crime , accessed 12 December 2019.

21 see, e.g., EUROPOL Financial Intelligence Group, *Why Is Cash Still King? A Strategic Report on the Use of Cash by Criminal Groups as a Facilitator for Money Laundering* (2015); Financial Action Task Force and Middle East & North Africa Financial Action Task Force, *Money Laundering Through the Physical Transportation of Cash*.

the ordinary citizen. Moreover, calling these notes 'bin Ladens' does make for a more eye-catching media headline, as shown by these referenced articles.[22]

The conflation of high denomination currency with a globally recognised terrorist provides a security dimension supporting the argument made against the continued use of cash in society. This language reinforces measures to combat the financing of terrorism; it also underpins the public safety line of argument that cash has mainly become the province of criminals as the necessary mechanism to support the laundering of criminal income into legal assets. This argument is often supported by reference to the quantity of high value notes in circulation outside of the place of origin, thus the US$100 note outside the United States and the €500 note outside the Eurozone.[23] While there is evidence for criminal use of these notes in this fashion, we must not forget the desire of people to hold currency they are confident will retain its value and liquidity, in contrast, perhaps, to their local domestic currency. In other words, these ordinary citizens also prize the utility of these high denomination notes as a store of value, not a victim to the inflation-induced decline in value their domestic currency might experience, such as seen in the Venezuelan bolivar and the Zimbabwean dollar in the 21st century.

The case for a cashless society

In 2015, the University of Zurich and the Liberales Institut, Zurich, hosted the European Money and Finance Forum conference, 'Cash on Trial'. The conference was organised in the format of a trial, with statements for the 'prosecution' and the 'defence', with additional 'expert witness' presentations for the court.[24] The starting point for the conference was that cash is guilty of three problems with consequences for society. First, it is a costly and outmoded medium of exchange. Second, it is the facilitator for criminal conduct. Third, cash represents a constraint on government monetary policy, specifically, the imposition of negative interest rates on retail bank customers, because cash provides an alternative to bank deposits for individuals and small firms.[25] The last charge is of interest to monetary economists but not relevant to our discussion beyond the fact that high denomination banknotes make the hoarding of cash to maintain the store of value of one's money easier. The first charge was critiqued by one contribution

22 Lipow, 'Turn In Your Bin Ladens'; Henley, '€500 "Bin Laden" Banknotes to be Axed'; Ben Clatworthy, 'Don't Get Stuck with a "Bin Laden" €500 Note', *The Times* (London, 18 August 2018) 57; Barshad, 'The Life and Death of the Bin Laden'.

23 Melinda Weir, 'The Boom in Benjamins' (2019) 56 *Finance and Development* 60; Deutsche Bundesbank, *The Demand for Euro Banknotes at the Bundesbank* (Monthly Report, March, 2018) 50.

24 Christian Beer, Ernest Gnan and Urs W. Birchler (eds.), *Cash on Trial, SUERF Conference Proceedings 2016/1* (SUERF – The European Money and Finance Forum 2016).

25 Christian Beer, Ernest Gnan and Urs W. Birchler, 'Introduction – Cash on trial' in Christian Beer, Ernest Gnan and Urs W. Birchler (eds.), *Cash on Trial, SUERF Conference Proceedings 2016/1* (SUERF – The European Money and Finance Forum 2016) 5.

to the conference proceedings with a basic, market-oriented observation. While cash may be costly for some economic actors (shops and banks that handle, sort and transport it), if its continued use was inefficient and costly for society at large, then better alternatives would arise to replace cash.[26] The increased use of electronic payment methods (debit cards, credit cards, mobile phone apps) in a number of national economies has been observed, yet without the universal acceptance given to cash. The COVID-19 pandemic further encouraged non-cash payment methods due to the fear that cash may represent a viral transmission mechanism.[27] Nonetheless, cash continued to be accepted during lockdown, for example, at our local Aldi store.[28] This highlights the fact that non-cash payment methods are not universally available or desired for everyone, a point that we return to below.

As suggested above, the main claim for eliminating cash is its role in criminal activities. Here again, one short critique offered for this charge in the 'trial against cash' was the observation that crime has been around for much longer than cash 'and it is therefore naïve to believe that cash is the cause of these problems'.[29] In and of itself, this is an accurate statement. Yet our argument is not that cash 'causes' crime; rather, it is that the anonymity of cash renders criminal activity harder to track and trace. Additionally, this short critique does not address the full scope of attention given to the proposition that the elimination of cash could have a significant impact on criminal activity. The logic of this proposition is, in part, a natural evolution of the campaign against criminal money since at least the 1970s. Moreover, that campaign points to the story of Al Capone, convicted of tax evasion (for failing to pay income tax on his illegal income) rather than any of the other crimes attributed to him.[30] This tale of 'follow the money' to bring down the organised crime leader is often related in the story for the origins of AML, although, as explained at the opening of this chapter, AML activity concerns more than just cash. Cash, however, remains a prominent element of large-scale criminal activity, demonstrated at the time of writing by European police operations using data collected from a hacked messaging app. News reports of the arrests prominently displayed images of piles of bundled cash confiscated alongside weapons and drugs.[31]

26 Aleksander Berentsen and Fabian Schär, 'The Fallacy of a Cashless Society' in Christian Beer, Ernest Gnan and Urs W. Birchler (eds.), *Cash on Trial, SUERF Conference Proceedings 2016/1* (SUERF – The European Money and Finance Forum 2016) 14. This point is demonstrated in the Sweden case study.

27 Martin Arnold and Arthur Beesley, 'Cash Demand Surges in Europe Despite Coronavirus Lockdown' *Financial Times* (London, 15 April 2020), www.ft.com, accessed 16 April 2020.

28 Brendan Greeley, 'The Comfort of Cash in a Time of Coronavirus' *Financial Times* (London, 16 July 2020), https://www.ft.com/, accessed 16 July 2020.

29 Berentsen and Schär, 14.

30 Sharman (n 3) 16.

31 Joseph Cox, 'How Police Secretly Took Over a Global Phone Network for Organized Crime' (*Vice* 2020), https://www.vice.com/en_us/article/3aza95/how-police-took-over-encrochat-hacked, accessed 7 July 2020; BBC News, 'Operation Venetic: More than 50

A fuller development of the charge that cash facilitates crime is made by the economist Kenneth S. Rogoff, first made in 1998 and subsequently revisited in other publications, including his monograph on the topic, *The Curse of Cash*.[32] Rogoff also addresses the main points identified at the 'Cash on Trial' conference, the role of cash in the underground economy and the inability of central banks to impose negative interest rates due to cash hoarding. In addition, because his focus is on the US$100 bill, Rogoff also considers the international dimension for withdrawing this high value note from international circulation along with the potential of digital money and gold as alternatives for the functions served by high value notes. These last aspects are not relevant for this discussion and while the argument that high value notes represent a barrier to negative interest rates is not a concern here, Rogoff feels that the issue is intertwined with the elimination of cash from the modern economy.[33] To be clear, *The Curse of Cash* is not an argument for the complete elimination of cash (at least not in the near term), rather, it is one for the elimination of the high value denominations in circulation. 'The idea is to reduce wholesale use of cash in tax evasion or illegal activities' over a long time period (10–15 years) with explicit government support for the unbanked and financially excluded members of society.[34]

Support for his argument includes data on the average size of transactions and the fact that most cash transactions are actually small and do not require the high value notes in question.[35] The case made is that the elimination of high value currency notes will substantially reduce the incidence of criminal activity with no impact on citizens' everyday transactions. High value notes not only make the movement of large quantities of illegal cash easier than if it consists of small denomination bills, but they also ease practices of tax evasion and other criminal conduct. The book briefly outlines a number of these activities in which cash is an important mechanism – corruption, counterfeiting, human trafficking and terrorism. More emphasis is placed, however, on tax evasion and paying workers in cash because these activities distort the economy. Tax evasion shifts the burden of paying for public goods to those law-abiding citizens who pay their taxes.[36] Similarly, using cash to pay workers under the table reduces tax revenue while suppressing the wages of lawful employment. Rogoff focuses on cash payments

arrests in "unprecedented" crime raids' (*BBC News* 2020), https://www.bbc.co.uk/news/uk-scotland-53263211, accessed 7 July 2020; BBC News, 'Hundreds Arrested as Crime Chat Network Cracked' (*BBC News* 2020), https://www.bbc.co.uk/news/uk-53263310, accessed 7 July 2020.

32 Kenneth Rogoff, 'Blessing or Curse? Foreign and underground demand for euro notes' (1998) 13 *Economic Policy* 262; Rogoff, *The Curse of Cash*.

33 Rogoff (n 32) 1.

34 Ibid. 92.

35 Rogoff, *The Curse of Cash* 49.

36 Ibid. 59.

to illegal immigrants, but it is equally true for any firm paying employees in cash without reporting those employees to the government.[37]

While *The Curse of Cash* provides the most extensive development of his argument, there are relevant points raised in connection with some of his earlier work on this topic. Rogoff (1998), for example, also highlighted a relationship between domestic holdings of high value currency with tax evasion.[38] It was a point he referred to in his acknowledgements in 2016: 'I cannot count how many people over the years have given me anecdotal evidence from personal experience of cash hoarding to avoid taxes.'[39] It is an observation that fails to include the individual choices of citizens based on historical experiences with high inflation and bank failure that fuel this desire to retain cash as a store of value. For the discussants of the 1998 paper, this view represented 'a somewhat parochial American perspective' that was oblivious to significant societal differences between his American experience and that of Europe, which offer alternative explanations for large cash hoardings by law-abiding Europeans.[40] This criticism is reflected in the discussion on the use of high value notes in the ECB's 2017 occasional paper on 'The Use of Cash by Households in the Euro Area'.[41] The report summarised the results of a survey on the use of cash and other payment methods by Eurozone citizens in 2016. To better understand the basis for the statement that high value notes are not used in everyday transactions, the survey specifically asked about the possession and use of €200 and €500 notes by individuals. The results regarding cash as a store of value and emergency reserve found in this survey are different from the US data used by Rogoff regarding the US$100 bill:

> However, since on average almost one out of five respondents responded having had high denomination banknotes in their possession, the survey results do at least refute the claims that ordinary citizens do not use these banknotes or that they hardly ever come into people's hands via regular channels such as banks' counters.[42]

This figure for 'nearly 20 per cent' is consistent, however, with the observation that approximately 70% of all €500 notes printed in Germany circulate outside Germany (20% in the Eurozone and 50% beyond the Eurozone).[43] Clearly, this

37 Ibid. 74.
38 Rogoff (n 32).
39 Rogoff (n 17) 222.
40 Rogoff (n 32) 95.
41 Henk Esselink and Lola Hernández, *The Use of Cash by Households in the Euro Area* (Occasional paper series, 2017).
42 Ibid. 45.
43 Deutsche Bundesbank, *The Demand for Euro Banknotes at the Bundesbank* 50. The printing of Euro notes is shared among the national central banks of the Eurozone. Between 2004 and 2014, the €500 note was printed by Austria, Germany and Luxembourg. See https://www.ecb.europa.eu/stats/policy_and_exchange_ rates/ banknotes+coins/production/html/index.en.html.

last point is consistent with the claim that these 'bin Ladens' facilitate cash hoarding and criminal conduct on a global scale.

A lengthy review of *The Curse of Cash* considered all aspects, emphasising the points where Rogoff moves away from being an economist to being a public policy proponent, often setting aside the economic aspects of the proposal to highlight societal impacts. In other words, identifying where Rogoff highlighted the illicit nature of underground economic activities without addressing the economic demand for those activities or the extent to which for some countries the 'underground' economy was a significant portion of the total economy.[44] More generally, on the topic of eliminating the €500 note, Christopher Murphy argued that the decision to discontinue it focused on its use by criminals and terrorists without regard to any consequences for law-abiding citizens. The cash hoarding aspect is more than simply a barrier to negative interest rates; it is a defence against a run on the bank during a financial crisis such as experienced in the Eurozone.[45] In addition to that experience, Cypriot citizens had their bank deposits in excess of €100,000 subjected to a 15.6% levy as part of the bail-in imposed by the Eurogroup to stabilise the Cypriot banking sector in 2013.[46] Finally, as Hummel (2017) emphasised, Rogoff's monograph is as much a public policy proposal as it is an analysis from an economist on the elimination of high value currency denominations.[47]

Our proposition is that reducing the use of cash to the point of achieving a 'cashless' society might achieve the desired goal for a reduction in criminal activity. The claims made for the role of cash in the underground economy appear substantial until set alongside the amount of criminal money to be laundered, that some studies suggest is circulating in the global economy.[48] A cashless future, in fact, may not reduce the demand for laundering criminal money when one newspaper headline reads, 'Cryptocurrency Scams Took in More Than $4 Billion in 2019' and another 'Email Scammers Are Savvier, and More Successful, Than Ever'.[49] The absence of cash from these criminal activities demonstrates that the

44 Jeffrey Rogers Hummel, 'The War on Cash: A review of Kenneth Rogoff's *The Curse of Cash*' (2017) 14 *Econ Journal Watch* 138, 139; for a global analysis of underground economies, see Leandro Medina and Friedrich Schneider, *Shadow Economies Around the World: What Did We Learn Over the Last 20 Years?* (International Monetary Fund 2018).

45 Christopher Murphy, 'Pecunia Non Olet: The case for the €500 banknote' (2016) 24 *European Journal of Crime, Criminal Law and Criminal Justice* 340, 351.

46 Ibid. 347; Panicos O. Demetriades, 'Political Economy of a Euro Area Banking Crisis' (2017) 41 *Cambridge Journal of Economics* 1249.

47 Hummel (n 44).

48 Sharman (n 3) 20.

49 Corinne Ramey, 'Email Scammers Are Savvier, and More Successful, Than Ever' *Wall Street Journal* (27 February 2020) U.S., https://www.wsj.com/articles/email-scammers-are-savvier-and-more-successful-than-ever-11582808400, accessed 29 February 2020; Paul Vigna and Eun-Young Jeong, 'Cryptocurrency Scams Took in More Than $4 Billion in 2019' *Wall Street Journal* (8 February 2020) Markets, https://www.wsj.com/articles/cryptocurrency-scams-took-in-more-than-4-billion-in-2019-11581184800, accessed 26 February 2020.

anonymity provided by cash is not a necessary prerequisite for the successful execution of highly profitable crime. Nonetheless, the journey from the widespread use of cash to a cashless society need not be described without an illustration. We now turn to the experience of Sweden, where an article in *The Economist* in 2016 observed: 'Only tourists pay in cash.'[50]

Sweden leads the way

Sweden has been highlighted as the poster child for the cashless society and is predicted to become the first cashless country by 2030 or as soon (and specific) as 24 March 2023.[51] Ingemar Ståhl eerily predicted this in his satirical spin on an Orwellian future Sweden already in 1979: '[A]s a result of the steady expansion of electronic surveillance systems, it can be expected that cashless transactions will increasingly become the norm.'[52] Sweden's move to a cashless society has been a two-pronged approach; on the one hand, it is a technology and market-driven one, but, on the other hand, it has been about responding to crime. Arguably, the long-term effects have been unintended and less driven by direct policy interventions.[53] Public policy has rather responded to issues that have appeared in an event-driven fashion. Sweden is undoubtedly a stable liberal democracy and has since the interwar period been a mostly social-democratic country. The Social Democratic Party has dominated Swedish politics since 1932 and has been in a governing position for all but five mandate periods (17 years). The stable welfare state, as well as its history of 'neutrality', has characterised the Swedish self-image. These factors have led to high levels of societal trust.[54]

Arvidsson states that a starting point for analysing a service like cash is to understand the local context of the government and the law.[55] Unsurprisingly, the Swedish government states that access to basic payment services should be provided to everyone in society; however, only in such cases where the market fails to do so. This has made the cash market decentralised and market driven, which is yet another factor explaining the reduction of cash in Sweden. There is a legal foundation for Sweden to go cash free as its commercial law is unusual in the sense that it allows shops to overrule the law requiring companies to accept

50 'Emptying the Tills' *The Economist* (11 August 2016), https://www.economist.com/finance-and-economics/2016/08/11/emptying-the-tills, accessed 8 May 2017.

51 Rogoff (n 17) 109; Kyree Leary and Chelsea Gohd, 'Sweden Could Stop Using Cash by 2023' (*World Economic Forum*, 2017) 1, https://www.weforum.org/agenda/2017/10/sweden-could-stop-using-cash-by-2023/, accessed 26 February 2020; Niklas Arvidsson, Jonas Hedman and Björn Segendorf, *När slutar svenska handlare att ta emot kontanter? [When will Swedish merchants stop receiving cash?]* (Handelsrådets Forskningsrapport, 2018).

52 Ingemar Ståhl, 'It Will Soon Be 1984 …' (2020) 17 *Econ Journal Watch* 242.

53 Jonung, 'Afterword to "It Will Soon Be 1984 …"' 253.

54 Esteban Ortiz-Ospina, 'Trust' (*OurWorldInData.org* 2016), https://ourworldindata.org/trust, accessed 31 July 2020.

55 Niklas Arvidsson, *Building a Cashless Society: The Swedish Route to the Future of Cash Payments* (SpringerBriefs in Economics, Springer International Publishing 2019) 46.

the Swedish krona (SEK) as legal tender.[56] Simply put, if a shop has a sign saying that cash is not accepted, it is assumed that customers have entered into a legal agreement to essentially use electronic payments.[57] Now, we turn to a brief historical overview before highlighting recent developments on the route to making Sweden a 'cashless society'.

Banking and cash have a long and exciting history in Sweden; the first Swedish coins were minted during the Viking age, around the year 995, but only in the late 13th century did Sweden go through monetisation. The earliest sign of an actual monetary system was when coins began to be counted rather than weighed. The early monetary system was based on silver and the coins functioned as commodity money.[58] By 1624 Sweden introduced the copper standard to replace silver, but as Sweden's and the world's largest copper coin weighed in at 20 kilos, a well-needed change was in place. Europe's earliest modern-style banknotes were introduced in Sweden during 1661 by the bank Stockholm Banco.[59] A few years later, the bank's owner, Johan Palmstruch, was so enthralled with his bank's success that he kept printing more credit notes. This led to a financial bubble that burst when he could not repay his creditors and the bank collapsed. Hence, Sweden found itself in its first financial crisis. Palmstruch was found guilty of mismanaging the bank in 1668 and initially sentenced to death should he fail to repay all that he owed. However, he was reprieved and given a life sentence only to be released within two years of the initial conviction. Arguably, Palmstruch became Sweden's first white collar criminal, making Sweden's history of cash truly one that is interconnected with crime. The collapse of Stockholm Banco would also lead to stricter regulations and the establishment of what would become the world's first central bank (Riksbank).[60]

Sweden's 'modern' history of cash is, of course, more relevant for this chapter. We can, therefore, fast forward to the 1970s, which is the starting point of crime statistics in Sweden. Bank and postal robberies were on a stable level throughout the 1970s and 1980s, perhaps the most famous one being the Norrmalmstorg robbery and hostage crisis in 1973, which was the origin of the term 'Stockholm syndrome'.[61] Robberies of banks and post offices would spike in the 1990s, peaking in 1994 with 216 reported robberies.[62] Since the mid-1990s, these types of

56 Riksbank, *The Riksbank Proposes a Review of the Concept of Legal Tender* (Riksbank 2019).

57 Riksbank, *Så betalar svenskarna 2019 [This is how the Swedes will pay in 2019]* (Sveriges Riksbank, 2019) 12.

58 Rodney Edvinsson and Bo Franzén, 'Sveriges tidiga formella penningväsende' [Sweden's early formal monetary system] (2015) 135 *Historisk Tidskrift* 377.

59 Gunnar Wetterberg, *Money and Power: From Stockholms Banco 1656 to Sveriges Riksbank Today* (Sveriges Riksbank 2009) 25, 42.

60 The Riksbank was founded in 1668, while the Bank of England was founded in 1694.

61 Michael Adorjan et al., 'Stockholm Syndrome as Vernacular Resource' (2012) 53 *Sociological Quarterly* 454.

62 Robert Svensson, *Bank-, post- och värdetransportrån: En analys av rånen under 1990-talet [Bank, post and cash-in-transit robberies: An analysis of the robberies during the 1990s]* (The Swedish National Council for Crime Prevention, 2004).

robberies have decreased dramatically, thanks in large part to improved safety measures and the initiative to make bank branches cash free, thus offering fewer opportunities to those looking to rob banks and post offices.

By 2003, the number of bank and post office robberies had gone down to a level similar to the mid-1970s, but they would surge in the following two years. Swedish statistics record all reported events as crimes even if some are later found not to have constituted criminal offences.[63] In the Swedish context, one also needs to look at cash-focused crime transferring to other types of robberies, such as those linked to cash-in-transit vehicles that drastically increased during the early 2000s. One would be inclined to assume that a shift took place as banks became more secure and cash free to a larger extent, and therefore it was easier to hit the less secure transports and depots. However, according to a report by the Swedish National Council for Crime Prevention (Brå), there is little evidence for this.[64] By contrast, in 1998 and 1999, Sweden saw a doubling of cash-in-transit robberies and by the early and mid-2000s, robberies of cash-in-transit vehicles became a recurring theme, with at least a couple of robberies per month.[65] Fors and Hansén also note that in the first five years of the new millennium, the amount of stolen cash in Sweden made up 10% of the total value of that stolen in Europe. This would culminate with two particularly large-scale robberies within a couple of days in August 2005. These sparked outrage in society and the Swedish Transport Workers Union enforced a stop on the use of cash-in-transit vehicles in the major metropolitan areas in Sweden (amounting to half of the population), resulting in a mass shutdown of ATMs due to a cash shortage. Another negative consequence was that shops had to store more cash than usual, which naturally led to a higher risk to shop staff and security guards. The outcome of the pressure applied by the unions meant that two employees rather than one staffed the cash transports and technologies were implemented to ensure the destruction of stolen bills. This also prompted action from the Swedish Commercial Employees' Union, which lobbied for an overall reduction of cash in Swedish society.[66] Furthermore, a surge in public transport robberies had previously pushed for an end to cash handling for driver safety, whereby the government acted and stopped cash payments on public transport in favour of electronic travel passes or SMS or card payments. Another outcome of the improved security measures of cash-in-transit rendered them too challenging a

63 Brå, 'Crime in Sweden – The difficulties in making international comparisons' (The Swedish National Council for Crime Prevention n.d.), https://www.bra.se/bra-in-english/home/crime-and-statistics/international-comparisons.html, accessed 30 July 2020.

64 Svensson, *Bank-, post- och värdetransportrån: En analys av rånen under 1990-talet [Bank, post and cash-in-transit robberies: An analysis of the robberies during the 1990s]*.

65 Fredrik Fors and Dan Hansén, 'Pressured to Learn? Swedish police experiences of curbing organized crime' (2014) 15 *Journal of Scandinavian Studies in Criminology and Crime Prevention* 19, 6.

66 Arvidsson (n 55) 32.

target, which led to a brief increase, once again, in the number of bank robberies, but a more significant increase in robberies of shops and stores.[67]

By 2007, the measures mentioned above led to the lowest robbery statistics in 20 years.[68] That said, those engaged in criminal activity often adapt, meaning that they are one step ahead. Hence, the success would be short lived as armed bank robberies more than doubled during 2008.[69] A robber turned author cites the 'problem-solving challenge' as a reason for his career choice, which is confirmed by one of Sweden's foremost criminologists.[70] Another alternative explanation could be the relatively low penalties, so-called *straffrabatt* (lit. 'penalty discount') for young offenders, combined with the relative ease with which cash may be hidden, leading to a 'low-risk, high-reward'- type scenario. Sweden's general goal in the treatment of young offenders has been to avoid incarceration by promoting rehabilitation by placing young people in institutions. The modus operandi for cash-in-transit robberies included 'selling the concept' or outsourcing by hiring younger people without criminal records. Often, there was an insider with unique insight into transit schedules and other crucial information.

Nevertheless, it was easier to escape the scene of the crime when the robbery happened in-transit rather than at the bank or ATM. Dummy bombs, iron caltrops, burning vehicles, automatic weapons and explosives were often used during these robberies, which demonstrates the high level of preparation and skill used to execute them. Arguably, the most spectacular robbery in Sweden's history, where all the methods mentioned above were used, was the 2009 helicopter heist in Västberga, outside Stockholm, when the G4S cash distribution depot was broken into by perpetrators landing on its roof.[71] These types of robberies take planning and execution, and the robbers made bomb threats and placed dummy bombs at the hangar for the police helicopters. Caltrops were also deployed in order to inhibit the police response. Seven of the robbers were arrested and sentenced, but the money was never retrieved. This event further inspired Swedes to give up cash.

AML and terrorism financing measures are often cited as reasons for lower cash usage.[72] Brå's study of the money laundering offences as a follow-up to the application of the new law in 2014 shows that reported crimes have increased

67 Brå, *Brottsutvecklingen i Sverige fram till år 2007 [Crime trends in Sweden up to 2007]* (Swedish National Council for Crime Prevention, 2008) 147.

68 Ibid.

69 Fors and Hansén (n 65) 10.

70 Anders Adali and Theodor Lundgren, *Svenska Rånare [Swedish Robbers]* (Lind & Co 2017) 11.

71 Angelique Chrisafis, 'Gang Use Helicopter in Hollywood-style Raid on Swedish Cash Depot', *The Guardian* (London, 23 September), https://www.theguardian.com/world/2009/sep/23/swedish-cash-depot-helicopter-raid, accessed 24 July 2020; Jonas Bonnier, *The Helicopter Heist: A Novel Based on True Events* (Other Press 2017). *Time* magazine has listed it on its Top 10 Brazen Heists of all time.

72 Rogoff (n 17) 107.

significantly.[73] However, few organised crime individuals have been caught, which was one of the primary purposes of the legislation. Instead, most of the increase is due to fraud-related crimes. For example, 77% of the AML efforts are connected to transactions, cash withdrawals and turnover, while only 13% of the measures are connected to cash handling. The Swedish Anti-Money Laundering Act also makes it indirectly more difficult for handling cash as a private citizen. Arvidsson notes that: '[A]t the offices which do handle banknotes and coins, the customer must explain where the cash comes from, according to the regulations aimed at money laundering and terrorist financing.'[74] Hence, without a valid ID and a satisfactory explanation for the customer's various transactions, the origin of the money and what it is to be used for means that the bank or payment service provider is not allowed to perform it. As discussed above, a cashless future may not reduce the demand for laundering criminal money. Spectacular and organised robberies are nowadays rare; organised crime figures have moved on to other targets. One worrying tendency among criminal gangs and organised crime groups is to lure or threaten young people to act as money mules and withdraw or transfer money from their accounts or 'Swish'.[75] As reported, cash-related crimes are decreasing while there has been an increase in reported fraud cases; computer-related fraud where people's card details and CCV codes have been used. Identity theft is another form of fraud that is increasing; one such example is 'Operation Casino', where 108 people were convicted of laundering money in European casinos. The fraud was set up as a Ponzi scheme where recruiters would offer people a sum of money for 'lending' their *BankID* (bank data) or card reader to the fraudsters to take out loans whereby the 'victim' would later report identity theft. The money would be transferred to mules, who would launder the money in the casinos along the French Riviera.[76] A new law and a proposal for a state e-identification system have been proposed as a means to tackle the number of online card fraud cases.

Since 2000, Sweden has implemented several policies and changes that have aided the evolution towards becoming a cashless society, although as the discussion below will demonstrate, factors implemented many decades earlier also played a part in this. Starting in the early 2000s, some bank branches were made cash free. Cash management was privatised in 2002, which meant that private

73 Li Hammar, Karolina Hurve and Fredrik Marklund, *Money Laundering Offences: A Follow-up of the Application of the Law* (The Swedish National Council for Crime Prevention 2019).

74 Arvidsson, as quoted in Katarina Ahlfort, *Cashless future for Sweden?* (KTH 2015); Ibid.

75 SVT, 'Tusentals ungdomar används för att tvätta pengar åt kriminella' [Thousands of youths are used to launder money for criminals] (*SVT Nyheter* 2019), https://www.svt.se/nyheter/lokalt/skane/tusentals-ungdomar-anvands-for-att-tvatta-pengar-at-kriminella, accessed 31 July 2020.

76 SVT, '108 personer döms i Kasinomålet – huvudman får åtta års fängelse' [108 people sentenced in the Casino case – principal gets eight years in prison] (*SVT Nyheter,* 2020), https://www.svt.se/nyheter/lokalt/ uppsala/dom-meddelas-i-kasinomalet-folj-svt-direkt rapportering, accessed 2 March 2021.

contractors assumed responsibility for distributing cash, thereby forming private cash depots, resulting in the Riksbank only operating one depot to distribute banknotes today. This can, of course, be seen as an intentional top-down solution to the increased cost of cash management. As early as the 1960s, Swedish banks launched systems to automate tasks in the banking system leading to companies paying wages and salaries directly to employees' bank accounts rather than cash.[77] Another step towards electronic supremacy was taken in the 1980s and 1990s, where card companies and banks actively promoted electronic card payments in favour of cash and cheques. Sweden is among the leading countries in the distribution and use of digital technologies.[78] In addition to a robust digital infrastructure, this openness to new technologies serves to further explain Sweden's rapid journey to becoming cashless. There are various examples of the widespread nature of cash-free services, such as churches passing digital payment systems with collection plates, homeless people selling the Swedish version of the *Big Issue* taking digital payments and even people implanting microchips in their hands.[79]

Another significant policy change in 2007–2008 which affected the circulation of cash was the RUT (Rengöring Underhåll och Tvätt – Cleaning Maintenance and Laundry) and ROT (Renovering Ombyggnad Tillbyggnad – Renovation Reconstruction and Extension) tax reduction schemes. These incentivised people to hire 'white labour' as opposed to cash-in-hand (grey sector and black money), which is discussed by Rogoff as an essential part of the underground economy with significant costs to society.[80] Hence, this encouraged more transparency in this particular sector, which led to cash payments being replaced by invoicing. The Swedish Tax Agency (Skatteverket) had a substantial tax revenue deficit every year due to widespread facilitated tax fraud. The Cash Register Act 2010 attempted to curb fraud among retailers making it more difficult to handle money outside the register by enforcing receipts and installing a box downloading all sales data directly to the Skatteverket.[81] Skatteverket concluded that the reform resulted in evident reductions in tax evasion with additional estimated tax revenue of 3 billion SEK. It also inadvertently led to a reduction in the use of cash.[82]

77 Arvidsson (n 55) 29.

78 OECD, *OECD Reviews of Digital Transformation: Going Digital in Sweden* (OECD Publishing 2018).

79 Arvidsson (n 55) 57; Oscar Schwartz, 'The Rise of Microchipping: Are we ready for technology to get under the skin' *The Guardian* (London, 8 November 2019), https://www.theguardian.com/technology/ 2019/nov/08/the-rise-of-microchipping-are-we-ready-for-technology-to-get-under-the-skin, accessed 28 July 2020.

80 Rogoff (n 17).

81 Eurofund, 'Cash Register Legislation, Sweden' (*Eurofund*, 2013), https://www.eurofound.europa.eu/ data/tackling-undeclared-work-in-europe/database/cash-register-legislation-sweden, accessed 30 July 2020. This was remarkably predicted by Ingemar Ståhl in his satirical article from 1979; see Ståhl, 'It Will Soon Be 1984 …'.

82 Skatteverket, *Requirement of Cash Registers: Impact Evaluation* (English Summary of the Swedish Tax Agency Report 2013:2, 2013).

Furthermore, in 2012, Sweden's third largest cash transport company, Panaxia, was involved in a scandal stealing its customers' money, which led to a shortage of cash for retailers and customers as well as empty ATMs.[83] This event further contributed to the lack of trust in cash management providers in particular and of cash in general. Concurrently in 2012, Swish, a mobile payment service, was launched. The main benefit is real time person-to-person payments making it a suitable cash replacement. Currently, seven out of ten Swedes use it and in 2018, Swish represented 6% of all payments; debit and credit cards are still the main form of payment with 58%.[84]

While Sweden is rapidly moving towards cash-free services and a cashless society, the Riksbank introduced new banknotes and coins over the period 2014–2016. This change also worked as an incentive for many retailers to switch to the digital route. The decision, however, was made in 2007 at the peak of cash in circulation to improve the efficiency, security and also to improve the environmental sustainability of the new money.[85] In spite of being open to cash-free solutions, Swedes possess national pride and are protective of their currency. The krona's cultural importance was manifested in the excitement of selecting the people to be depicted on the new notes. Five criteria were established: (1) important cultural achievements; (2) mainly achieved during the 1900s; (3) connection to the people also with an international appeal; (4) represent different parts of Sweden; and, finally, (5) equality: three women and three men. The outcomes were seemingly successful, judging by the objectives of the exchange. Swedes were initially hesitant about the new coins and the necessity of the new money, which further spurred a public debate on the future of cash. Another interesting outcome is that much money was missing, a recent press release from the Riksbank states that there is still 5.5 billion SEK (8% of the total value) missing old currency notes and coins that were rendered obsolete with the introduction of new notes and coins during 2015–2017.[86] It is also likely that some of this missing money is linked to criminal activities such as robberies. Over 2,000 applications to exchange expired currency have been denied as it is difficult to prove the money is not linked to crime.[87]

83 Robin Teigland and others, *The Rise and Development of FinTech: Accounts of Disruption from Sweden and Beyond* (Routledge 2018).

84 Riksbank (n 57).

85 Riksbank, *Sedel – och myntutbytet i Sverige: Sammanfattning och utvärdering [Banknote and coin exchange in Sweden: Summary and evaluation]* (Sveriges Riksbank, 2018)

86 Riksbank, '5,5 miljarder kronor i ogiltiga sedlar – lös in dem innan avgiften höjs' [SEK 5.5 billion in invalid banknotes – redeem them before the fee is raised] (*Sveriges Riksbank,* 2020), https://www.riksbank.se/ sv/press-och-publicerat/nyheter-och-pressmeddelanden/pressmeddelanden/2020/55-miljarder-kronor-i-ogiltiga-sedlar---los-in-dem-innan-avgiften-hojs/, accessed 26 July 2020.

87 Patricia Hedelius, '5,9 miljarder kronor på drift efter sedelbyten' [SEK 5.9 billion adrift after banknote exchange] *Svenska Dagbladet* (Stockholm, 11 June 2018), https://www.svd.se/59-miljarder-kronor-pa-drift-efter-sedelbyten, accessed 26 July 2020.

Consequences and conclusions

The move toward a cashless society has been anticipated for a number of years and the Swedish experience demonstrates the many facets of the challenge this move represents. As Rogoff concludes: '[I]t will certainly be ironic if Sweden, the first country in Europe to issue a paper currency [...] became the first country to get rid of it.'[88] Yet Sweden has not followed his 'plan' as it kept the 1,000 SEK note (even though it is worth less than €100). Does this prove that Sweden going cashless is not a top-down plan? Sweden's digital journey towards a cashless society started decades ago. It has done so slowly in some respects and rapidly in others. The country's tradition of social welfare and concern for all will hopefully serve as a force to make the transition toward a cashless society positive in the sense that it will not create a group of people that live outside the system hurt by this transformation. For the unbanked segment of society, the move to a cashless economy remains a challenge.

More important, the efforts in Sweden sought to reduce the movement and storage of cash in quantities that attracted criminal activity. This aspect differs from the leading argument linking cash with crime, its acquisition as a marker of success followed by its laundering in order to live a comfortable, legitimate lifestyle. It is a situation that may have been unique to Sweden, yet it also highlights the role of characteristics unique to any national political economy that in turn shape its use of cash as an everyday practice. Sweden's long history of peace (its last war was in 1814) and lack of human or climate-induced disasters or threats are arguably reasons that the situation is the way it is. There are high levels of trust in the government in spite of dire consequences (something that is seen in Sweden's COVID-19 approach as well). Arvidsson reminds us that 'money is about trust' and points out that it is likelier that a smaller country with high trust in politicians and the banking system is more likely to decrease the use of cash in its national political economy.[89] Thus, in other national political economies where historical experience has reduced citizens' trust in banks, they may have good reason to possess a strong desire to hoard cash. In 2019, 70% of Swedish banks were cashless, 7 million out of 10 million Swedes were using Swish and more and more businesses stopped accepting cash. Arguably, Swedes' high level of trust in both institutions and new technologies has played a significant role in people embracing a more cash-free economy. Although there are relatively few fraudulent card purchases (second lowest in the EU after the Netherlands), concerns about fraud and data protection are now influencing the debate.[90]

The present situation, with various measures implemented to contain the spread of COVID-19, appears to have accelerated that move, from a concern that cash and coins represent a potential transmission vector for the virus. The grubby

88 Rogoff (n 17) 109.
89 Arvidsson (n 55).
90 Riksbank (n 57) 21.

nature of a medium that is handled and exchanged by many different people is recognised, an observation Rogoff included as yet another reason for the elimination of cash.[91] Yet contemporary reports suggest that while traces of cocaine may be found on the banknotes in your wallets, they are not a transmission vector. Speaking at a Bundesbank press conference, the head of the Frankfurt am Main Health Office, virologist René Gottschalk noted: 'If the virus were spread via banknotes or table surfaces, the number of cases would be higher.'[92] Contrasting these concerns, as already noted, was the increase in cash withdrawals in Europe and the USA, because most people have confidence in cash as a store of value and as a reliable medium of exchange in the absence of electricity to support card payment systems. As quoted in one article on the continued desire for cash, it is 'the recognition that in a pinch I can use cash and it will work with anybody.'[93]

The trend in Sweden since 2012 is a steady downwards spiral for cash withdrawals and a steady increase in 'Swish' payments, although the most common form of payment is still debit and credit cards.[94] Looking forward, the Riksbank is currently also reviewing the launch of a digital currency, e-krona.[95] Outrage over crime in Sweden was essential in pushing for today's cashless society. However, Sweden also demonstrates the point that a near cashless society cannot eradicate crime. Those involved in crime will learn and adapt and will find a way to exploit the current system, cash or no cash.

91 Rogoff (n 17) 78.

92 Deutsche Bundesbank, *Cash Poses no Particular Risk of Infection for Public* (Deutsche Bundesbank 2020).

93 Bill Maurer, as quoted in Greeley, 'The Comfort of Cash in a Time of Coronavirus'.

94 Riksbank (n 57).

95 Arvidsson (n 55) 78.

7 Crypto-assets and criminality

A critical review focusing on money laundering and terrorism financing

Ilias Kapsis[1]

Introduction

The crypto-asset ecosystem has continued to grow and by early 2023 there were over 22,476 such assets in circulation.[2] While bitcoin remains the most significant crypto-asset by market value and maintains a significant ecosystem linked to it, other types of digital asset have emerged, two originating from the crypto-assets ecosystem and one from the public sector: initial coin offerings (ICOs), 'stablecoins' and central bank issued digital currencies (CBDCs). ICOs are digital tokens based on cryptography and blockchain, which are issued by businesses and individuals in exchange for official currencies (fiat money) or other crypto-assets.[3] The tokens offer privileged access to goods, services or other financial instruments depending on the issuer's offer, while the issuer gains the capital needed to fund their project. ICOs have gained popularity since 2017 with an increasing number of companies and individuals issuing them.[4] 'Stablecoins' aim to address a number of challenges facing bitcoin-type crypto-assets such as price volatility, issuer anonymity and limited consumer protection. They offer more transparency and stability by using identifiable and therefore accountable, issuers, while offering a range of financial services.[5] They aim to reduce price volatility by backing the coin with assets (physical collateral or crypto-assets) or using algorithms

1 Associate Professor of Law, University of Bradford.

2 Robby Houben and Alexander Snyers, 'Crypto-assets- Key Developments, Regulatory Concerns and Responses' (Study for the Committee on Economic and Monetary Affairs, Policy Department for Economic, Scientific and Quality of Life Policies, European Parliament, Luxembourg, PE 648.779-April 2020), https://www.europarl.europa.eu/thinktank/en/document/IPOL_STU(2020)648779 accessed 26 March 2021.

3 European Securities and Markets Authority (ESMA), *Advice on Initial Coin Offerings and Crypto-Assets* (ESMA50-157-1391, 9 January 2019) para 17, www.esma.europa.eu/document/advice-initial-coin-offerings-and-crypto-assets, accessed 26 March 2021; Houben and Snyers (n 2) 23–4.

4 Ibid. 10.

5 Financial Stability Board, *Regulatory Issues of Stablecoins* (FSB 18 October 2019) 2–3, www.fsb.org/2019/10/regulatory-issues-of-stablecoins/, accessed 26 March 2021.

DOI: 10.4324/9781003020813-8

(algorithmic stablecoins).[6] Stablecoins gained growing international attention in 2019 following the announcement by Facebook of its intention to launch Libra, an, albeit now abandoned, stablecoin with global reach.[7] CDBCs constitute efforts of central banks to respond to the growing appearance of privately issued digital currencies and the increasing market demands for a digital equivalent to cash.[8] Various models of CBDCs are under consideration with several central bank research projects currently under way (Committee on Payments and Market Infrastructures and Markets Committee 2018). In April 2020, China started testing a CBDC in several Chinese cities (*South China Morning Post* 2020), and other central banks are prepared to follow. The potential appearance of CBDCs along with the entry of big technology companies[9] will expand and transform the market of digital currencies (DCs) and will influence the development of the crypto-asset ecosystem.

The association of crypto-assets with criminal activities from the early days of their existence is well documented. High profile incidents include the collapse in 2014 of Tokyo-based Mt Gox, the largest cryptocurrency exchange at the time, and the Silk Road, a dark web marketplace. Both scandals were particularly damaging to the ecosystem's reputation. In the case of Mt Gox 740,000 bitcoins were stolen from customer e-wallets, leading to the exchange's bankruptcy.[10] Most of the stolen bitcoins have not been recovered to date, while the legal efforts of 24,000 affected customers to be compensated for the losses are ongoing.[11] The Silk Road, established in 2011 as an online marketplace for drugs, used bitcoin for payments.[12] It had significant traffic until it was shut down in

6 *Financial Stability Board* Ibid. 2–3; European Banking Authority, *Report with Advice for the European Commission on Crypto-assets.* January (EBA 9 January 2019) 7, www.eba.europa.eu/eba-reports-on-crypto-assets, accessed 26 March 2021; European Central Bank Crypto-Assets Task Force, *Crypto-Assets: Implications for Financial Stability, Monetary Policy, and Payments and Market Infrastructures* (*ECB Occasional Papers*, No 223, May 2019) 24, www.ecb.europa.eu/pub/pdf/scpops/ecb.op223~3ce14e986c.en.pdf, accessed 6 March 2021.

7 For more details, see https://www.diem.com/en-us/.

8 Codruta Boar, Henry Holden and Amber Wadsworth, 'Impending Arrival – A sequel to the survey on Central Bank digital currency' (2020) BIS Paper No.107, 4–5, www.bis.org/publ/bppdf/bispap107.pdf, accessed 6 March 2021.

9 Facebook was the first big technology company to enter into the crypto-asset market with its own digital currency. If Facebook is successful other big technology companies are likely to follow.

10 Ann Baydakova, '$2 Billion Lost in Mt. Gox Bitcoin Hack Can Be Recovered, Lawyer Claims' (*coindesk.com,* 12 September 2919), www.coindesk.com/2-billion-lost-in-mt-gox-bitcoin-hack-can-be-recovered-lawyer-claims, accessed 29 March 2021.

11 Alexandra Harney and Steve Stecklow, 'Twice Burned – How Mt. Gox's bitcoin customers could lose again' (*Reuters,* 16 November 2017), www.reuters.com/investigates/special-report/bitcoin-gox/, accessed 26 March 2021.

12 David Adler, 'Silk Road: The dark side of cryptocurrency' (*Fordham Journal of Corporate and Financial Law*, 21 February 2018), https://news.law.fordham.edu/jcfl/2018/02/21/silk-road-the-dark-side-of-cryptocurrency/, accessed 26 March 2021.

2013 by the FBI and the site owner was arrested.[13] More recently, bitcoin and cryptocurrencies have been associated with ransomware attacks. These attacks involve hackers stealing personal data and other sensitive information from individual and companies, which they then encrypt and ask victims to pay a ransom (usually in bitcoins) for the release of the data.[14] According to market estimates,[15] during 2020, victims of ransomware attacks paid nearly 350 million US dollars' worth of cryptocurrency to the attackers, an increase of 311% over the previous year. Cryptocurrencies have also been linked to terrorism. In August 2020, the US Department of Justice announced that it dismantled three terror finance campaigns linked to al-Qassam Brigades, Hamas's military wing, al-Qaeda, and Islamic State of Iraq and the Levant (ISIS), which were using sophisticated cyber-tools, 'including the solicitation of cryptocurrency donations from around the world'.[16] The cryptocurrency assets seized were valued at more than 1 million US dollars, the highest ever seizure of crypto-assets linked to terrorism financing.[17] In regard to other types of crime, crypto thefts, hacks and frauds (including scams) make up the largest proportion.[18] In 2020, there was a record growth in cryptocurrencies but criminal activity involving them showed a significant decline compared to 2019.[19] This was in great part due to the fact that during 2019 a single major fraud incident, the PlusToken Ponzi scheme[20] in China, had caused more than 2.9 billion US dollar losses to its victims. In 2020, the most serious incident involved WoToken, a scheme with similar characteristics to PlusToken and involving some of the same people, costing its investors 1.1 billion US dollars in losses.[21]

13 Ross Ulbricht, the owner of Silk Road, was convicted in the trial that followed and was sentenced to a double life sentence plus 40 years.

14 Andrea Tinianow, 'Bitcoin Demand Drives $1.4 Billion Ransomware Industry in the U.S' (*Forbes*. 1 July 2020), www.forbes.com/sites/andreatinianow/2020/07/01/bitcoin-demand-drives-14-billion-ransomware-industry-in-the-us/#78e5c73a32d8, accessed 26 March 2021.

15 Chainalysis, 'The 2021 Crypto Crime Report' (*Chainalysis*, 16 February, 2021), https://go.chainalysis.com/rs/503-FAP-074/images/Chainalysis-Crypto-Crime-2021.pdf, accessed 26 March 2021.

16 Office of Public Affairs, 'Global Disruption of Three Terror Finance Cyber-Enabled Campaigns' (United States Department of Justice, 13 August 2020), https://www.justice.gov/opa/pr/global-disruption-three-terror-finance-cyber-enabled-campaigns, accessed 26 March 2021.

17 Chainalysis, 'Chainalysis in Action: Department of Justice announces takedown of two terrorism financing campaigns with help from blockchain analysis' (*Chainalysis*, 13 August, 2020), https://blog.chainalysis.com/reports/cryptocurrency-terrorism-financing-al-qaeda-al-qassam-brigades-bitcointransfer , accessed 26 March 2021.

18 CipherTrace, 'Cryptocurrency Crime and Anti-Money Laundering Report *(ChipherTrace*, February 2021) 7, https://ciphertrace.com/2020-year-end-cryptocurrency-crime-and-anti-money-laundering-report/, accessed 26 March 2021.

19 Chainalysis (n 15) 5; ChipherTrace (n 17) 6.

20 ChipherTrace (n 18) 6.

21 Ibid. 6.

A 2020 report to the European Parliament[22] described a range of criminal activities involving crypto-assets, including: their use in the online trade of illegal goods or services in the dark web; money laundering; evasion of capital controls; payments in ransomware attacks; and thefts. The report cited the findings of Australian researchers[23] that up to half of all yearly bitcoin transactions could be linked to illegal activities. In June 2020, Bloomberg[24] reported that Estonia, the most crypto-friendly country in the EU, withdrew 500 crypto-asset firm licenses, or one-third of the market. The authorities cited 'several cases' of suspected embezzlement of clients or unauthorised activities abroad. In 2019, the European Securities and Markets Authority (ESMA) referred to 'widespread reports and concerns' around fraudulent initial coin offerings (ICOs), products linked to crypto-assets.[25] ESMA also cited a market report showing that up to 30% of the ICOs sampled lost all their value, while the vast majority were valued at below their ICO price. A 2018 report for Bloomberg found that 78% of ICOs were identified scams.[26] Numerous cases of theft of coins or tokens by hackers who targeted e-wallet providers and crypto-trading platforms have also been reported.[27] A significant proportion of the criminal activities take place within the ecosystem and do not involve the regulated sector.[28] In a sign of improvement, market research reported a 47% drop on the global average of direct criminal funds received by exchanges during 2019,[29] a three-year low as a result of stronger know-your-customer (KYC), customer due diligence (CDD) and anti-money laundering (AML) protocols.[30]

22 Houben and Snyers (n 2).

23 Sean Foley, Jonathan R. Karlsen and Tālis J Putniņš, 'Sex, Drugs, and Bitcoin: How much illegal activity is financed through cryptocurrencies?', (2019) 32, *Review of Financial Studies*, 1798, 1798.

24 Ott Umellas, 'EU Nation at Center of Dirty-Cash Storm Cracks Down on Crypto' (Bloomberg, 11 June 2020), www.bloomberg.com/news/articles/2020-06-11/eu-nation-at-center-of-dirty-cash-storm-cracks-down-on-crypto?sref=l0bGdXEa, accessed 26 March 2021.

25 ESMA (n 3) para 49.

26 Satis Group, *Crypstoasset Market Coverage Initiation: Network Creation* (*Bloomberg*, 11 July 2018), https://research.bloomberg.com/pub/res/d2246jsnqusjYSeacPbQc2IjVIw, accessed 26 March 2021.

27 Cristina Cuervo, Anastasiia Morozova and Nobuyasu Sugimoto, 'Regulation of Crypto Assets' (*International Monetary Fund* , FinTech Notes No. 19/03, 10 January 2020) 16, www.imf.org/en/Publications/fintech-notes/Issues/2020/01/09/Regulation-of-Crypto-Assets-48810, accessed 26 March 2021.

28 Tom Robinson and Yaya Fanusie, 'Bitcoin Laundering: An analysis of illicit flows into digital currency services' (Elliptic Center on Sanctions and Illicit Finance, 12 January 2018), https://info.elliptic.co/whitepaper-fdd-bitcoin-laundering, accessed 26 March 2021.

29 CipherTrace, 'Cryptocurrency Crime and Anti-Money Laundering Report, Spring 2020 *(CipherTrace*, June 2020) 6, https://ciphertrace.com/spring-2020-cryptocurrency-anti-money-laundering-report/?submissionGuid=9c633339-6b58-43ae-bf15-6c44d3187989, accessed 26 March 2021.

30 Know-your-customer rules require obliged entities to collect information about their customers and monitor their behaviour; customer due diligence refers to the process of collect-

Measuring the overall criminality linked to crypto-assets is very difficult due to the increased anonymity, decentralisation and operation of the ecosystem outside the regulated financial sector. In spite of efforts to bring the ecosystem to existing legal frameworks by amending or broadly interpreting existing rules, many crypto-assets remain under-regulated or unregulated.[31] The number of novel features and the constant evolution of their typologies and technologies render the applicability of existing frameworks problematic. Adoption of tailor-made legal regimes has been proposed instead and relevant efforts are under way in many countries and in the European Union, which, on 24 September 2020, proposed a relevant regulation.[32]

Compared to the regulated financial sector, where the size of annual criminal activity on money laundering-related crimes alone has been estimated by the United Nations[33] at between 800 billion and 2 trillion US dollars, the scale of criminal activity involving cryptocurrencies appears to be insubstantial. The use of cash and the regulated financial system are the main means through which money is laundered and terrorists fund their operations, but crypto-assets continue to attract negative headlines in the press and on social media, as well as frequent statements by regulators.

This chapter will review the relationship between crypto-assets and criminality, focusing in particular on the area of money laundering and terrorism financing, two key areas of criminal activity, and, in this context, the legal framework of the Financial Action Task Force (FATF) – which was updated in 2019 to incorporate crypto-assets – will be considered.

The crypto-assets ecosystem

According to FATF,[34] crypto-assets are virtual assets in circulation on the internet, which are used for a variety of functions such as media of exchange, units of account or stores of value. They were originally referred to as 'cryptocurrencies' or 'virtual currencies',[35] but their ability to perform money functions, especially as media of exchange and stores of value, has been disputed and more recent

---

ing and confirming customer ID information. KYC and CDD rules apply to regulated banks and their application to virtual assets are discussed later in the chapter.

31 ESMA (n 1); EBA (n 5).

32 Regulation of the European Parliament and of the Council on Markets in Crypto-assets, and Amending Directive (EU) 2019/1937. Brussels, 24.9.2020, COM(2020) 593 final, 2020/0265(COD).

33 https://www.unodc.org/unodc/en/money-laundering/globalization.html.

34 Financial Action Task Force, *Virtual Currencies Key Definitions and Potential AML/CFT Risks* (*FATF* Report, June 2014) 4.

35 Ibid.

literature uses the term 'crypto-assets',[36] 'virtual assets'[37] or 'tokens'.[38] There is a significant variety of crypto-asset types, including inter alia non-asset-backed, anonymous, bitcoin-type assets; asset-backed 'stablecoins'; and initial coin offerings (ICOs). Crypto-assets exhibit a variety of financial functions including payments/exchange/currency functions, investment functions and utility functions.[39] All crypto-assets have in common their reliance on cryptography and distributed ledger technology (DLT) and that they are privately issued.[40] Some crypto-assets are convertible (meaning that they can be exchanged for real money back and forth), while others are not.[41] Some crypto-assets are centralised, issued and administered by a central private authority that also sets out the rules under which they operate, while others are decentralised, having no central authority to administer them and no central monitoring or oversight.[42] These are math-based, open-source, peer-to-peer crypto-assets, of which bitcoin is the group lead. Those crypto-assets that are not backed by assets have no intrinsic value and their price tends to be very volatile.[43] Those backed by assets are more stable but their stability depends on the quality of the backing assets and the credit standing of the issuer.[44] ICOs' value depends on the rights or interests to assets, products and services attached to them.[45]

The crypto-assets ecosystem, apart from issuers and users, who are often anonymous or pseudonymous, is comprised of mixers and tumblers who are used to provide enhanced anonymity; decentralised trading platforms and exchanges where crypto-assets are traded and exchanged for real currency or other crypto-assets; miners who are used in decentralised crypto-assets to generate ('mine') new ones and verify transactions; e-wallet providers who provide the virtual wallets, which are used for storing, holding and transferring crypto-assets, and who can also provide services to crypto-asset holders (custodian wallet service providers); and other products and services.[46] The ecosystem is constantly evolving being enriched with new types of asset and related products and services and new types of business, many in supportive roles.

36 Financial Stability Board (FSB), *Crypto-asset Markets, Potential Channels for Future Financial Stability Implications (FSB* 10 October 2018) 3, www.fsb.org/wp-content/uploads/P101018.pdf, accessed 26 March 2021.

37 Financial Action Task Force, *Guidance for a Risk-based Approach - Virtual Assets and Virtual Asset Service Providers* (*FATF* June 2019) para 5.

38 EBA (n 5) 7.

39 Ibid.

40 Ibid.

41 FATF (n 34) 4.

42 Ibid. 5.

43 Cuervo, Morozova and Sugimoto (n 27) 14–15.

44 Dirk Bullmann, Jonas Klemm and Andrea Pinna, 'In Search for Stability in Crypto-assets: Are stablecoins the solution?' (European Central Bank, Occasional Paper No. 230, August 2019) 4.

45 Houben and Snyder (n 2) 23–4.

46 FATF (n 37) para 33.

Potential causes of criminality

From an anti-money laundering (AML), counterterrorist financing (CFT) and tax evasion perspective, the broad anonymity and pseudonymity (including issuers and users) supporting the function of crypto-assets remain the most important sources of concern.[47] For bitcoin, users are able to enter into the system and transact using fake IDs, while mixers and tumblers can be used to provide online tools than can obscure the chain of transactions on the blockchain by mixing multiple transactions and creating series of complex, semi-random dummy transactions that make it impossible to link a specific transaction to a bitcoin address.[48] The exchanges, where crypto-assets are exchanged for real money (and vice versa) or for other crypto-assets, apply loose or no control regarding the source of the funds; as such, they are the main recipients of criminal funds.[49] FATF considers that the anonymity-enhanced crypto-assets and the businesses and services supporting them create an environment that allows for reduced transparency and increased obfuscation of financial flows.[50] The constant evolution of the ecosystem allows for the emergence of new illicit financing typologies including the increasing use of virtual-to-virtual layering schemes that can operate efficiently, securely and at low cost. Anonymity can offer criminals easy access to 'clean cash', while terrorists have been known to use bitcoin to mask transfers of funds for terrorist activities.

Further, the absence of regulated intermediaries, which in crypto-assets is replaced by a peer-to-peer function, creates a regulatory and supervisory loophole as intermediaries in the regulated sector (inter alia payment systems and currency exchanges) are critical components in the public authorities' regulatory and supervisory architecture, which aims to detect and prevent financial crime. Regulated intermediaries are required to conduct KYC and CDD processes, to monitor customer activities and to undertake risk assessments.[51] The absence of regulated intermediaries in the case of crypto-assets leads to the absence of a critical tool in the efforts of public authorities to exercise these key crime prevention

47 See e.g. European Commission (2017). *Report from the Commission to the European Parliament and the Council on the Assessment of the Risks of Money Laundering and Terrorist Financing Affecting the Internal Market and Relating to Cross-border Activities,* Brussels 24.7.2019 COM/2017/0340 final; Malcolm Campbell-Verduyn, 'Bitcoin, Cryptocoins, and Global Anti-money Laundering Governance' (2018) 69 *Crime, Law and Social Change* 283.

48 FATF (n 34) 6; Dennis B. Desmond, David Lacey and Paul Salmon, 'Evaluating Cryptocurrency Laundering as a Complex Socio-technical System: A systematic literature review' 22 *Journal of Money Laundering Control* 480, 484.

49 *ChipherTrace* (n 29) 6.

50 n 37 para 4.

51 Therese Chambers, 'Unstable Coins: Cryptoassets, financial regulation and preventing financial crime in the emerging market for digital assets' (FCA, Speech delivered at The Advancement of Digital Assets and Addressing Financial Crime Risk, New York University School of Law, 5 March 2020), https://www.fca.org.uk/news/speeches/unstable-coins, accessed 26 March 2020.

and control functions. An additional problem is that the various individuals and businesses supporting the crypto-assets ecosystem not only operate outside existing regulations and public oversight, but also work to enhance anonymity, further frustrating the efforts of the authorities to come closer to the criminals. Further, financial transactions in the traditional financial system are carried through networks of service providers (credit/debit card providers for card payments, SWIFT for money transfers etc.), which are closed and controlled centrally by identifiable entities.[52] These entities authenticate and record transactions and vet all those seeking use of the network/service. Their centralised records are easily accessible for regulatory audit, while these entities have a number of reporting obligations regarding suspicious activities.

Crypto-assets, instead, operate on a peer-to-per basis using decentralised synchronised public ledgers for record keeping, with transactions often being authenticated and verified by a network of users spread in multiple locations on the internet. 'Permissionless' models are open to all users, while 'permissioned' models are available to a smaller group of users who are able to read and write to the ledger.[53] Transaction validation and ledger maintenance require user consensus for which consensus algorithms (e.g. the 'proof-of-work' algorithm used in the bitcoin network) are used.[54] In permissionless models, there are no ID checks for those involved in transactions or verification of transactions and the use of pseudonymity is widespread, but in permissioned models – where fewer individuals or entities have access to the ledger – anonymity is more limited.[55] The transactions, once validated and added to the blockchain, become irreversible. This is a way to protect the system from double spending of the crypto-asset,[56] which is often pursued by criminals. However, the irreversibility of transactions could be reduced through hacking attacks resulting in ledger alterations. Some blockchains are more vulnerable to such attacks than others.[57]

52 European Central Bank, *The Payment System* (Tom Kokkola, ed.) 25 (ECB 2010).

53 Financial Stability Board, *Decentralised Financial Technologies* (FSB, 6 June 2019) para 2.2.

54 Xiaofan Li and Andrew B. Whinston, 'Analyzing Cryptocurrencies' 22 *Information Systems Frontiers*.17, 18.

55 Robby Houben and Alexander Snyers, 'Cryptocurrencies and Blockchain: Legal context and implications for financial crime, money laundering and tax evasion' (Policy Department for Economic, Scientific and Quality of Life Policies, Directorate-General for Internal Policies, Study Requested by the TAX3 Committee, European Parliament, PE 619.024 July 2018) 15, www.europarl.europa.eu/cmsdata/150761/ TAX3%20Study%20on%20cryptocurrencies%20and%20blockchain.pdf, accessed 25 March 2021.

56 Raphael Auer, 'Beyond the Doomsday Economics of "Proof-of- work" in Cryptocurrencies' (BIS Working Papers No. 765, January 2019) 3, https://www.bis.org/publ/work765.htm, accessed 25 March 2021.

57 An incident involving an attack on Ethereum classic, a crypto-asset, resulted in the 'reorganisation' of more than 100 blocks in the blockchain leading to 88,500 coins being double-spent (Richard Gendal Brown, 'When "Final" Isn't Actually Final: Cracking blockchain's consensus conundrum' (*Forbes*, 22 November 2019). www.forbes.com/sites/richardgendalbrown/2019/11/22/when-final-isnt-actually-final-cracking-blockchains-consensus-conundrum/#c87b74660400, accessed 2 March 2021.

But even where the system's resilience is confirmed and ledgers cannot be altered, this can still be viewed as a vulnerability by law enforcers, because in such a case it is not possible for them or validators to intercept or reverse unlawful transactions such as those based on ML/TF[58] or those that are the result of use of force, fear or fraud.[59] Transactions are cleared and settled near instantaneously, allowing rapid transfers of funds across the world, which is advantageous to criminals while creating difficulties for law enforcement. However, the use of consensus mechanisms in transaction validation may also on some occasions render the finality of transactions less certain compared to transactions in the regulated system.[60] Uncertainty about transaction finality could leave room for exploitation by criminals.

The cross-border nature of crypto-assets allows parts of the ecosystem to be based on countries with loose or no AML/CFT or regulatory controls and oversight, which further complicates the efforts to detect and prosecute criminals. Tax evasion can also be the resulting outcome.[61]

Finally, the role of encryption should be highlighted. Strong encryption is used to protect private data and identities, address cybersecurity threats and prevent fraud and other unauthorised disclosures.[62] However, the high level of anonymity offered by encryption can also be used to hide criminal activities and therefore hinder the ability of public authorities to detect and prevent crime. The extensive use of encryption in the crypto-assets ecosystem is a source of concern for regulators.

Beyond AML/CFT and tax evasion, the swallow markets where most crypto-assets operate and their operation largely outside the regulatory perimeter, expose investors and consumers to numerous other risks such as mis-selling, market manipulation, fraud, theft, market bankruptcies and other offences.[63] The rules for the operation of the currencies and the rights of the parties are drawn by the private creators of these currencies and as such the extent of consumer and investor rights and protections varies considerably across the various crypto-assets, which adds to the legal uncertainty and confusion that can be subject to exploitation.

58 Christopher P. Buttigieg, Christos Efthymiopoulos, Abigail Attard and Samantha Cuyle, 'Anti-money Laundering Regulation of Crypto Assets in Europe's Smallest Member State' (2019) 13 *Law and Financial Markets Review* 221, 224.

59 Simon Longstaff, 'Blockchain: Some ethical considerations' (The Ethics Centre, 16 March 2019), https://ethics.org.au/blockchain-some-considerations/, accessed 25 March 2021.

60 Committee on Payments and Market Infrastructures, *Distributed Ledger Technology in Payment, Clearing and Settlement* (CPMI, February 2017) 16, https://www.bis.org/cpmi/publ/d157.pdf, accessed 15 March 2021.

61 Houben and Snyder (n 55) 70.

62 Ibid. 55; World Bank Group, *Distributed Ledger Technology (DLT) and Blockchain,* (FinTech Note, No. 1, 2017) 1, http://documents1.worldbank.org/curated/en/177911513714062215/pdf/122140-WP-PUBLIC-Distributed-Ledger-Technology-and-Blockchain-Fintech-Notes.pdf, accessed 25 March 2021.

63 Cuervo, Morozova and Sugimoto (n 27) 19.

The ease of market access (a simple internet connection and an email account are normally enough for a user to join), their high portability and the rapid execution and settlement of transactions, which evade regulatory scrutiny, add to the attractiveness of crypto-assets to criminals.

Law response: the revised FATF framework

The Financial Action Task Force (FATF) has taken the lead in international efforts to address crypto-asset criminality, focusing in particular on AML and counterterrorist financing (CTF). FATF issued its first document containing the definition of 'virtual currencies' (VCs) and the potential AML/CTF risks in 2014[64] and a year later it issued its first Guidance for a Risk-Based Approach to Virtual Currencies,[65] which included risk assessments to identify, evaluate and address ML/FT risks arising from the ecosystem. In 2018, FATF updated its terminology replacing VCs with 'virtual assets' (VAs) and adopted the concept of 'virtual asset service provider' (VASP) reflecting on the significant expansion of the ecosystem which demonstrated 'a range of new "assets" and services, business models, and activities and interactions'.[66] FATF also updated Recommendation 15 to reinforce the risk-based approach and related obligations of the countries. In June 2019, FATF adopted an Interpretive Note to Recommendation 15 to further clarify its application in regard to VAs and VASPs.[67] Furthermore, FATF also updated its 2015 VC Guidance and viewed the 2019 guidance as establishing 'the first global standards to address the money laundering and terrorist financing risks of virtual assets'.[68] In October 2019, FATF called for the inclusion of global 'stablecoins'[69] and their service providers into the scope of FATF standards either as VAs and VASPs or as traditional financial assets and service providers. In June 2020, FATF issued further analysis on stablecoins[70] (FATF 2020) and a 12-month review of the implementation of the 2019 guidance.[71] The analysis of stablecoins aimed to bring regulators up to speed with market developments and to ensure that all crypto-assets are subject to adequate AML/CFT checks, while the 12-month review aimed to identify issues in the implementation of existing standards. It was to be followed by a further review in June 2021.

64 n 34.

65 Financial Action Task Force, *Guidance for a Risk-based Approach - Virtual Currencies* (FATF June 2015).

66 n 37, para 3.

67 Ibid. 55.

68 Financial Action Task Force, 'Money Laundering Risks from 'Stablecoins' and other Emerging Assets' (FATF, Paris, 18 October 2019), https://www.fatf-gafi.org/publications/fatfgeneral/documents/statement-virtual-assets-global-stablecoins.html, accessed 20 March 2021.

69 Ibid.

70 Financial Action Task Force, *FATF Report to the G20 Finance Ministers and Central Bank Governors on So-called Stablecoins* (FATF, June 2020).

71 Financial Action Task Force, *12-month Review Virtual Assets and VASPs* (FATF, June 2020).

The FATF virtual assets framework does not predetermine any sector as higher risk; rather, FATF assessments identify sectors that may be vulnerable to ML/TF. More detailed assessments will have to take place at national level focusing not only on the sectors but also on individual entities within the sectors. The level of risk exhibited by each entity could vary. FATF's own assessments for VAs, VA-related activities and VASPs concluded that they can exhibit ML/TF risks and called countries to act by carrying out domestic risk assessments and creating domestic frameworks and processes to mitigate the identified risks. The responsibility for risk identification, management and mitigation extends also to local VASPs that have their own part to play in controlling risks and assisting regulators.

In order to be able to capture the broad range of VA types, products, services and business models linked to them, FATF adopts broad interpretations of VAs and VASPs. The updated guidance defines VAs as 'a digital representation of value that can be digitally traded, or transferred, and can be used for payment or investment purposes'[72] and asks to include crypto-assets (VAs) under all funds or valued-based terms in FATF recommendations, such as 'property,' 'proceeds,' 'funds', 'funds or other assets' and other 'corresponding value'.[73] The guidance calls for flexibility when dealing with VAs and VA activities because they involve a range of products and services in a rapidly evolving space. Some VAs that do not initially appear to be so may actually be VAs that enable the transfer or exchange of value or facilitate ML/TF.[74]

Virtual asset service providers (VASPs) are subject to relevant FATF recommendations based on the type of activity involved. The guidance targets VASP virtual-to-virtual and virtual-to-fiat transactions or financial activities or operations,[75] while leaving any VASP fiat-only or fiat-to-fiat activities to the traditional guidance.[76] VASPs include 'VA exchanges and transfer services; some VA wallet providers, such as those that host wallets or maintain custody or control over another natural or legal person's VAs, wallet(s), and/or private key(s); providers of financial services relating to the issuance, offer, or sale of a VA (such as in an ICO); and other possible business models'.[77] Countries are encouraged to apply 'a wide range of various VA services or business models' factors focusing in particular on their 'functionality or the financial activities that they facilitate'.[78]

Whether a person (natural or legal) is a VASP depends on how it uses the VA and for whose benefit.[79] If the individual or firm is engaged in the FATF-covered activities as a business, then they are VASPs. The type of technology used or

72 n 37, 57.
73 Ibid. para 65.
74 Ibid. para 50.
75 Ibid. para 34.
76 Ibid. para 24.
77 Ibid. para 35.
78 Ibid. para 36.
79 Ibid. para 46.

the use of decentralised or centralised platforms, smart contracts, or some other mechanisms are irrelevant. If individuals are not engaged as a business, then they are excluded by FATF. VA users may still be subject to national measures. Also, the FATF guidance does not cover 'closed-loop items that are non-transferable, non-exchangeable, and non-fungible'.[80] Airline miles, credit card awards or similar loyalty programme rewards or points are examples of that group. Similarly, creators and sellers of the technology and software used to support the regulated activities and providers of ancillary services are not included unless they are engaged in the regulated activities as a business.

Regarding the application of a risk-based approach, the guidance states that countries should take measures to prevent or mitigate ML/TF risks that are commensurate with the risks identified. Risk assessments should be undertaken within countries to assess the risks posed by VAs and VASPs. The risk-based approach will determine a number of factors, including the AML/CFT compliance requirements; the methods of supervision and compliance monitoring; and issues of engagement in customer relationships by those covered by the regime.[81] FATF calls national authorities to focus their efforts on the high risk VAs and VASPs, especially those demonstrating increased anonymity or obfuscation of VA financial flows[82] and to identify appropriate national agencies responsible for carrying out the regulation and supervision of VAs and VASPs. The guidance highlights that multiagency co-operation and coordination may be required for effective supervision and monitoring.[83]

FATF requires that a licensing or registration regime with conditions attached to allow effective supervision should be established for VASPs. Licensing should take place in the jurisdiction(s) where the place of business of the VASP is located,[84] while measures should be put in place to crack down on unlicensed or unregistered VASPs. FATF guidance calls for international cooperation between the supervisors and information sharing.[85]

In light of the features of VAs that make them susceptible to exploitation by criminals, the guidance emphasises the need to strengthen CDD processes for VAs. Depending on the outcome of risk assessments, countries are also encouraged to go beyond FATF recommendations, which establish minimum transaction thresholds and other conditions and require full CDD for all transactions involving VAs or performed by VASPs.[86] VASPs must be required to regularly review and update information, data and records collected under CDD. These transaction records should be kept for at least five years.[87] Given the constant

80 Ibid. para 47.
81 Ibid. para 26.
82 Ibid. para 58.
83 Ibid. para 64.
84 Ibid. para 79.
85 Ibid. paras 86–8.
86 Ibid. para 95.
87 Ibid. paras 101–102.

development and market launches of new VAs and released products and technologies, countries are expected to identify and assess the ML/TF risks relating to these developments and to require regulated entities to take appropriate measures to manage and mitigate the associated ML/TF risks before the launch of the new products or the adoption of the new technologies.[88] VAs should be particularly focused on taking steps to manage and mitigate the risks from 'anonymity-enhancing technologies or mechanisms, including but not limited to AECs, mixers, tumblers, and other technologies that obfuscate the identity of the sender, recipient, holder, or beneficial owner of a VA'.[89]

FATF guidance also covers fund transfers ('wire transfers'), both domestic and cross-border. Cross-border transactions and fund transfers are key features of the crypto-asset industry. According to market research,[90] in 2019, 74% of the bitcoin moved in exchange-to-exchange transactions was moved across borders. According to FATF Recommendation 16, VASPs or other obliged entities (including financial institutions) involved in VA transfers, are obliged to obtain, hold and exchange required originator and beneficiary information for the purpose of identifying and reporting suspicious transactions, monitoring the availability of information, taking freezing actions and prohibiting transactions with designated persons and entities.[91] The VASPs and obliged entities should be ready to provide the relevant information to competent authorities on request.[92] The information must be collected by the ordering institution during the customer due diligence stage and there is a minimum threshold of USD/EUR 1,000. The rule for collection and exchange of information is known as the travel rule.

FATF recommendations do not apply only to national authorities but also to VASPs and 'other obliged entities' including banks, securities broker-dealers, and other FIs when they engage in VA-related activities.[93] VASPs and the other regulated entities have the responsibility to identify, assess and take effective action to mitigate their ML/TF risks,[94] while also assisting regulators and supervisors to achieve the AML/CFT policy goals.

In October 2019, FATF turned its attention to emerging assets such as stablecoins, an implicit reference to Libra, later renamed as Diem, Facebook's planned global stablecoin.[95] FATF claimed that these assets and their associated networks and platforms could cause a shift to the VA ecosystem, which could have ML/TF implications. FATF identified two main concerns relating to stablecoins:[96] mass-market adoption of VAs and person-to-person transfers without using a regu-

88 Ibid. paras 108–9.
89 Ibid. para 110.
90 CipherTrace (n 29) 5.
91 n 36 para 115.
92 Ibid. para 116.
93 Ibid. para 170.
94 Ibid. para 26.
95 https://www.diem.com/en-us/ accessed 21 November 2021.
96 n 68.

lated intermediary. FATF called for stablecoins and their VASPs to be subject to the FATF standards. In June 2020, FATF issued a more detailed assessment of stablecoins.[97] In this assessment, stablecoins are more likely to be centralised with an identifiable developer of governance body. These could be classed as either financial institutions or VASPs. In both cases, they fall under the revised FATF framework. FATF considers that due to the centralisation and existence of identifiable issuers, stablecoins could raise fewer ML/TF concerns compared to decentralised stablecoins and crypto-assets.

Commentary on the updated FATF crypto-asset guidance

The incorporation of crypto-assets into the existing FATF AML/CFT framework is a decisive step towards legitimacy for the ecosystem. The implementation of the framework will reduce the use of the crypto-assets by criminals and help to build public trust in crypto-assets. Further, the risk-based approach, if based on realistic risk assessments, will help to prevent wholesale exclusions or excessive actions against the ecosystem, while the VASPs licensing and registration requirements, customer data collection and sharing and transaction recording will help to address the regulators' concerns about the increased anonymity and absence of transparency and accountability. VASPs, especially exchanges, are elevated to the forefront of the new FATF framework, in roles similar to those imposed on equivalent entities of the regulated financial sector. FATF hopes that as in the latter sector, exchanges can assist regulators with crime detection and prevention. VASPs could be held accountable in the case in which the policy goals fail to be achieved.

However, in spite of these positive aspects, there are also many challenges for effectively implementing the new FATF framework, while there are concerns that the regulation could become excessive and costly undermining crypto-asset future potential.

First, the FATF framework has been created with the regulated sector in mind, which may complicate the implementation of the rules to crypto-assets, an ecosystem with many innovative features. For example, the use of peer-to-peer, decentralised and anonymised networks in crypto-asset markets makes it much harder to identify the individuals or entities to which the FATF registration and licensing requirements for VASPs apply.

Compliance could also be a problem, as members of the ecosystem, most of them individuals or small entities, lack the knowledge, experience and resources necessary for compliance. There is also the 'cultural' factor, as enhanced anonymity, decentralisation and peer-to-peer functions are the core features of crypto-assets, which make them attractive to their users. The FATF framework requires the weakening of these features, which could spark resistance. A combination of

97 n 70.

these factors could indicate that compliance may be low, at least in the short/medium term.

By way of example, a rule similar to the FATF travel rule, requiring VASPs involved in VA fund transfers to collect information including the originator's name, account and ID number, physical address, date and place of birth and beneficiary's name and account number, already exists in the USA through the Bank Secrecy Act and has applied to crypto-assets since 2013.[98] Information from the crypto-asset industry indicates a low level of compliance with the US rule, with one industry participant asserting that '[n]ot a single major crypto business has actually been compliant on the travel rule despite the applicability of the rule since 2013'.[99] The Director of FinCEN has admitted that record keeping violations are the most commonly cited violations. US authorities seem to be applying the requirements leniently, which has been attributed[100] to the regulator's inclination to support innovation. However, following the FATF adoption of the rule, US authorities are moving towards a tougher stance.

Implementing the travel rule may face additional challenges, because the transition and storing of originator and beneficiary information raises concerns about customers' privacy and could also be in conflict with data protection laws in certain countries such as the GDPR in the EU. Although FATF emphasises the need for coordination by national authorities to ensure confidentiality and compliance with data protection, some concerns remain.[101] For example, an additional issue concerns the timeline for the implementation of the travel rule which was June 2020, one year after the adoption of the travel rule by FATF. Based on available evidence from the 12-month review of the 2019 standards by FATF, only 12 out of 32 jurisdictions that implemented the new standards also introduced the travel rule.[102] This was due, inter alia, to the absence of a 'holistic and scalable technological solution'. Apart from the absence of technology the crypto-assets ecosystem is highly fragmented and reaching a consensus on the standardisation of services that is required to facilitate compliance is not a simple process.

Second, there are further compliance issues and costs, which will be significant for VASPs. Regulated financial institutions have considerable knowledge and experience of dealing with regulatory requirements and audits. They deploy compliance departments with hundreds and even thousands of employees tasked with

98 Financial Crimes Enforcement Network, *Application of FinCEN's Regulations to Persons Administering, Exchanging, or Using Virtual Currencies (FinCEN,* FIN-2013-G001, 18 March 2013).

99 Will Heasman, 'Governments Begin to Roll Out FATF's Travel Rule Around the Globe' (*Cointelegraph* 14 February 2020), https://cointelegraph.com/news/governments-begin-to-roll-out-fatfs-travel-rule-around-the-globe, accessed 20 March 2021.

100 Ibid.

101 CipherTrace (n 29) 10.

102 n 70 para 43; Ian Allison, 'Inside the Standards Race for Implementing FATF's Travel Rule' (*Coindesk* 4 February 2020), https://www.coindesk.com/inside-the-standards-race-for-implementing-fatfs-travel-rule, accessed 3 March 2021.

the sole duty of ensuring the institution's compliance with an ever-increasing web of regulatory duties, including AML/CFT norms.[103] The cost of compliance is significant[104] and it is partly passed to consumers through higher transaction or service fees. The rest is absorbed by banks, thus squeezing their profit margins. Targeting VASPs will not fully address the AML/CFT risks because a significant part of criminal funds is transferred through over-the-counter, off-chain transactions.[105]

The crypto-assets ecosystem remains largely unregulated[106] with most VASPs being individuals or small companies that lack knowledge and experience of regulatory compliance. The absence of regulation and intermediation and the use of peer-to-peer function are viewed as advantages for crypto-assets against the regulated sector.[107] The FATF requirements along with steps taken to subject the ecosystem to proper regulatory controls will gradually reduce or even eliminate these advantages. In spite of FATF's technology-neutral approach to compliance, which gives VASPs flexibility in meeting the regulatory requirements, it is clear that new technologies will have to be installed and compliance staff will have to be hired. These will have considerable economic costs for VASPs. Regulators encourage industry collaboration to develop solutions. One of these collaborations is the Travel Rule Information Sharing Architecture (TRISA) Working Group, which involves global crypto-experts and aims to develop the solutions mentioned above, but also to develop a governance body.[108]

A major industry consolidation which will force smaller players to exit the market and transfer market control to larger players will likely follow. Expectations are that the vast majority of VASPs will go out of business,[109] which apparently is also the aim of regulators as fewer and larger VASPs are harder to manipulate by criminals who will also face fewer market entry options. A more consolidated industry is also easier to regulate and supervise.

103 Peter Farley, 'Spotlight on Compliance Costs as Banks Get Down to Business with AI' (*International Banker* 4 July 2017), https://internationalbanker.com/technology/spotlight-compliance-costs-banks-get-business-ai/, accessed 20 March 2021.

104 Deloitte has estimated that the increase in compliance costs after the financial crisis reached 60% for retail and corporate banks (Deloitte, 'The Future of Regulatory Productivity, Powered by RegTech.' (2017), www2.deloitte.com/us/en/pages/regulatory/articles/cost-of-compliance-regulatory-productivity.html, accessed 3 March 2021.

105 CipherTrace (n 29) 14.

106 EBA (n 6) 10.

107 Marek Dabrowski and Lukasz Janikowski, 'Virtual Currencies and Central Banks Monetary Policy: Challenges ahead' (Policy Department for Economic, Scientific and Quality of Life Policies, Directorate-General for Internal Policies, PE 619.009 – June 2018) 26, www.researchgate.net/profile/Marek-Dabrowski/publication/326069854_Virtual_currencies_and_central_banks_monetary_policy_challenges_ahead/links/5b36954d0f7e9b0df5dc6bd8/Virtual-currencies-and-central-banks-monetary-policy-challenges-ahead.pdf, accessed 20 March 2021.

108 CipherTrace (n 29) 16.

109 Ibid. 10.

However, the larger VASPs, which will survive the consolidation, may end up being companies such as Facebook, Google or other big tech companies. This poses its own set of challenges for regulators and facilitating through regulation such as FATF recommendations the taking over of crypto-asset markets by these groups may not necessarily be a wise choice. Money laundering activities carried out through the regulated sector continue to rise, despite tight AML/CTF regulations and it is through the regulated sector that the vast majority of criminal activities take place.

Fourth, the risk-based approach, may be hard to implement effectively and could end up overregulating the industry. FATF expects new crypto-assets to be subject to its extensive regulatory framework from the moment they appear on the market. The big question here is whether the risk assessments carried out for that purpose will be accurate or even meaningful. The FATF guidance provides a broad list of factors to be considered in the risk assessments, drawn from a wide range of sources. Also, the national authorities should be reflective of the broader policy objectives for the financial sector pursued by their country, in areas such as financial inclusion, financial stability, financial integrity and financial consumer protection goals.[110] Market competition issues should be considered as well along with the features of VASPs and VA products in the specific country. These criteria apply to the regulated sector as well, but the crypto-assets ecosystem is much smaller and reliable market evidence is scarcer. In such conditions, reliable risk assessments could be harder to achieve. As a result, the risk of regulatory undershooting or overshooting is a very likely outcome of underestimation or overestimation of the risks which the regulation will seek to address.

The small size of the industry also raises questions as to whether the benefits justify the potential costs of intervention for both industry and regulators. Several countries have refrained from adopting regulatory frameworks for crypto-assets on those grounds,[111] but FATF appears to be thinking otherwise. FATF appears to believe that crypto-assets are mature enough (or risky enough) to receive equal regulatory treatment like the massive regulated sector. Given that the costs of compliance of VASPs with the FATF updated guidance will be high, there is an obvious question as to whether this largely pre-emptive FATF action is aimed at imposing reasonable and proportional regulatory controls on crypto-assets or whether it will produce an unnecessarily restrictive and harmful framework that will undermine their future.

Fifth, with crypto-assets being a global market and with national authorities moving towards the adoption of FATF recommendations at different speeds, many VASPs could seek to establish their legal base in countries with more relaxed regulatory rules and weaker enforcement mechanisms. This is a problem well known to FATF from its experience of the regulated financial sector and

110 n 37 para 143.
111 See e.g. ESMA n 2.

highlighted also in its guidance on VASPs. FATF asks[112] countries and national authorities to treat all VASPs on an equal footing from a regulatory and supervisory perspective in order to avoid jurisdictional arbitrage. However, in the first 12-month review of the revised VASP standards published in June 2020, FATF reported that 35 out of 54 reporting jurisdictions adopted the new framework for VASPs, three opted for prohibiting the operation of VASPs, while 19 others had not yet adopted the new framework nationally.[113] The review already indicates an unequal pace of implementation while further divergence between states may emerge if the national risk assessments reveal inconsistencies between states in the treatment of VASPs.

Crypto-assets, criminality and the law: some further points

One of the reasons crypto-assets have been exploited by criminals has been the ambivalent position of law on their legal status and regulatory controls. AML/CFT is only one area where such ambivalence existed until FATF decided to take action. There are other areas linked to specific types of activity (e.g. payments, investments, money functions) where similar issues exist. In all these areas, crypto-assets have been divided by regulators between those falling within the regulatory perimeter and others falling outside it, while a third group sits on both sides (depending on how their variety of functions are allocated).[114] But even for those falling within the perimeter, which brings them within the scope of existing laws, problems still exist as crypto-assets' novel features and business models complicate the application of these laws.

Making an effort to offer legal clarity has significant advantages compared to the current situation where the absence of legal clarity is combined with repeated public warnings by regulators to consumers about the risks of involvement in crypto-asset markets.[115] These markets are not treated as illicit, but neither are they treated as compliant with the law, which spreads market confusion.

Absence of regulation offers advantages for innovations as innovators enjoy more freedom in the development of their products unrestricted by legal requirements and conditions, but the prolonged absence of any regulatory context becomes harmful. Crypto-assets have been in the markets since 2009 when bitcoin appeared. The technology is still improving but the public is joining the market in growing numbers. The latter development leaves no space for regulatory inaction. Participants in the ecosystem would welcome regulation and there is

112 n 37 para 19.
113 n 71 para 2.
114 ESMA (n 3); EBA (n 6).
115 Regulatory authorities around the world have routinely issued several public statements warning the public about the risks involved in crypto-asset markets and discourage public from joining these markets. See e.g. 'Joint ESAs Warning on Virtual Currencies' (12 February 2018); European Banking Authority, 'Opinion on "Virtual Currencies"' (EBA/Op/2014/08, 4 July 2014).

market evidence supporting this view.[116] Regulation could offer the required legal certainty and legitimacy while also increasing the depth of the market, helping to reduce the high price volatility which attracts speculators and shady investors.[117]

Through this prism, the revised FATF framework is a positive step as it adds the required legal clarity in the area of ML/TF. However, once the regulation has been adopted, the attention turns to its suitability for achieving the declared goals in a proportionate way. In the case of crypto-assets the proportionate way is to ensure that crime prevention rules will not end up unnecessarily hurting these useful innovations. As the new framework has not yet been fully implemented it is premature to make a judgment but the fact that the new framework treats crypto-assets in the same way as the regulated sector raises concerns that it may not be proportionate.

FATF is already facing significant criticism about its effectiveness on ML/TF prevention.[118] With money laundering activities growing globally and with the bulk of those activities going through the regulated sector which has been applying FATF Recommendations for decades, it is not surprising that scepticism towards FATF has been growing. The adopted approach for crypto-assets may add to that criticism.

Furthermore, when considering the treatment of crypto-assets, it is important to highlight that certain countries may have facilitated criminal behaviour in their efforts to exploit the market opportunities created by crypto-assets to support the ecosystem's growth locally. For example, Estonia, which was among the first EU countries to issue crypto-asset licenses to firms in 2017, provided these licenses under very loose conditions. Crypto-asset businesses could obtain licenses within 30 days for €300.[119] It is also important to stress that while crypto-assets have been frequently vilified by the press and regulators as facilitators of crime, the reality is that the traditional financial sector, due to its size, global reach and entrenchment in society, is still more likely to be used for illegal activities. The Danske Bank scandal in 2018, in which Denmark's largest bank was implicated in the laundering of an alleged 220 billion US dollars, came from a regulated lender.[120] Interestingly, at the centre of the scandal was a branch in Estonia, which has been

116 Raphael Auer and Stijn Claessens, 'Regulating Cryptocurrencies: Assessing Market Reactions' (*BIS Quarterly Review* September 2018) 52, https://www.bis.org/publ/qtrpdf/r_qt1809f.pdf, accessed 29 March 2021.

117 House of Commons, Treasury Select Committee, *Crypto-assets* (Twenty-Second Report of Session 2017–19, 12 September 2018) 22.

118 See, for example, Ronald F. Pol, 'Anti-money Laundering: The world's least effective policy experiment? Together, we can fix it' (2020) 3 *Policy Design and Practice* 73.

119 Jeffrey Gogo, 'Estonia Revokes 500 Crypto Firms' Licenses After $220 Billion Money Laundering Scandal' (*bitcoin.com* 13 June 2020), https://news.bitcoin.com/estonia-revokes-500-crypto-firms-licenses-after-220-billion-money-laundering-scandal/, accessed 20 March 2021.

120 Ibid.; Jamie Redman, 'Danske Bank Caught Using Gold Bullion to Launder Illicit Funds' (*bitcoin.com* 17 November 2020), https://news.bitcoin.com/danske-bank-caught-using-gold-bullion-to-launder-illicit-funds/, accessed 20 March 2021.

described as the 'safe haven' of cryptos. The cases of Danske and Estonia illustrate that financial crime prevention and detection, whether it concerns crypto-assets or the regulated sector, is not only a matter of having adequate legal frameworks in place, but also of having governments willing to exercise effective supervision and implementation of the agreed frameworks.

Finally, for the years to come the role of regulatory technology ('regtech') and CBDCs could contribute to efforts to contain crime within the crypto-asset ecosystem. Regtech concerns the use of the latest technologies (e.g. based on artificial intelligence and automation), which are being developed to support the financial sector's compliance with regulatory obligations, while also assisting regulators to monitor the markets.[121] The advantage of regtech is that it can support more targeted and near real-time market interventions by offering near real-time market intelligence. If used in crypto-asset markets, this could help in the early detection and prevention of crime. CBDCs offer the central banks alternatives to crypto-assets. They are expected to offer all state guarantees to users while relying on more robust technologies to prevent hack attacks and other crimes. ML/TF scrutiny will be also be closer and more effective. Although CBDCs are competitors to crypto-assets,[122] their appearance could push the crypto-asset ecosystem to take crime more seriously in order to maintain its market position.

121 Ioannis Anagnostopoulos 'Fintech and Regtech: Impact on regulators and banks' (2018) *Journal of Economics and Business* 7.

122 Raphael Auer and Rainer Boehme, 'The Technology of Retail Central Bank Digital Currency' (*BIS Quarterly Review* March 2020) 85.

8 Setting the conditions of competition

Repositioning the neoliberal state in the fraud debate

Kate Tudor[1]

Introduction

Beginning in the late 1970s, the neoliberal period has witnessed the revival of many of the philosophies, policies and practices of classical liberalism. In their attempts to protect the sovereignty of the individual and economic enterprise vis-à-vis what they perceived as unjustified and destructive regulation, the main proponents of the neoliberal shift – principally those comprising the Mont Pelerin Society[2] – were heavily influenced by these earlier ideas. In response to the forces of 'creeping socialism',[3] neoliberals sought to erect greater protections around individual economic freedoms by returning to the policies and practices of extreme economic liberalisation seen during the classical liberal period. However, under neoliberalism, the role of the state was reconstituted from liberalism's minimalist night-watchman – which was restricted to 'the maintenance of order and the enforcement of contracts'[4] – to one actively involved in the creation and maintenance of free market competition.[5] Consequently, a significant rupture exists between the popular interpretation of neoliberalism as state retraction and retreat and the reality of the active role played by the neoliberal state in the economy in order to further the interests of capital.[6] Within criminology, it is widely recognised that the conditions created by the neoliberal state have led to

1 Senior Lecturer in Criminology, Northumbria University.
2 The Mont Pelerin Society was formed in 1947 and was named after the location in Switzerland where the society first met. The group comprised of like-minded people drawn from numerous fields such as politics, philosophy, economics, business, education etc., who were united in their ambition to re-establish policies of extreme economic liberalisation. For an overview, see David Harvey *A Brief History of Neo-Liberalism* (Oxford University Press 2007).
3 Friedrich Hayek *The Road to Serfdom* (Routledge & Kegan Paul 1976).
4 Milton Friedman 'Neo-Liberalism and its Prospects' (*Farmand* 1951 February no page), https://miltonfriedman.hoover.org/friedman_images/Collections/2016c21/Farmand_02_17_1951.pdf, accessed 9 December 2021.
5 Ibid.
6 Kate Burdis and Steve Tombs 'After the Crisis: New directions in theorizing corporate and white-collar crime' in Steve Hall and Simon Winlow (eds.) *New Directions in Criminological Theory* (Routledge 2012).

DOI: 10.4324/9781003020813-9

a significant 'blurring of the boundaries' between licit and illicit practice, leading to the proliferation of harmful and criminal corporate practices now endemic throughout the neoliberal economy[7].

Drawing on data collected in interviews with those convicted for the perpetration of high yield fraudulent investment (Ponzi) schemes, this chapter seeks to extend the analysis of the state's responsibility in the creation of harm and criminality by examining the way in which the conditions present within the formal economy also facilitate more individualistic acts of economic predation further down the social scale, primarily through their role in setting the conditions for competition. It will be argued that the conditions present within the mainstream economic landscape mean that the criminal, semi-licit and harmful but legal actions of the powerful are not only tolerated, but often rewarded. The criminogenic potential of these conditions is realised not only through the proliferation of opportunities and rewards for crime, but also indirectly by creating a situation in which economic actors come to perceive the impossibility of competing effectively while remaining wedded to moral and legal codes. More particularly, the chapter offers insight into the ways in which these criminogenic currents in our contemporary arrangements facilitate, incentivise and motivate criminality among powerful economic actors, but also those operating further down the economic food chain.

The neoliberal state

The ascendancy of neoliberal thought within the political and economic realm can, in part, be attributed to the careful planning of a particular group of economists and philosophers who comprised the Mont Pelerin Society. The members of this group lamented what they perceived as the creeping influence of socialism and collectivist politics and the demise of liberal ideas within post-World-War-I society. Hayek, for example, claimed that 'although we had been warned by some of the greatest political thinkers of the nineteenth century [...] that socialism means slavery, we have steadily moved in the direction of socialism.'[8] Consequently, Hayek suggested that 'we have progressively abandoned that freedom in economic affairs without which personal and political freedom has never existed in the past.'[9] In response, the Mont Pelerin Society sought to construct protections around individual economic freedoms principally through the pursuit of a free market economy using political lobbying and liberal think tanks. However, far from constituting a politically homogenous group, considerable disagreement existed between Mont Pelerin members over the most desirable means of achieving the goal of a free market-based competitive order. While some sought to maintain fidelity to liberalism's minimalist night-watchman state, oth-

7 Ibid.; Vincenzo Ruggiero 'Networks of Greed' (2017) 1 (1) *Justice, Power and Resistance*, 3.
8 Hayek (n 3) 10.
9 Ibid.

ers identified the need to reconfigure liberal philosophy and the role of the state within this.[10] Thus, Friedman, for example, understood the liberal position on the role of the state to be underpinned by a 'negative philosophy'.[11] He therefore questioned the role of laissez-faire, favouring instead a situation in which the state assumes a limited, but active role in order to 'police the system, establish conditions favourable to competition and prevent monopoly, provide a stable monetary framework, and relieve acute misery and distress'.[12] The neoliberal state came to be required to 'preserve law and order, to enforce private contracts, to foster competitive markets'[13] and to 'guarantee the quality and integrity of money'.[14] Ultimately, the function of the neoliberal state can be understood to be the creation and maintenance of the 'conditions for capital accumulation'.[15] From this perspective, neoliberal economies are understood to be self-regulating according to competitive, market principles with inefficiency and corruption being seen as the inevitable outcomes of *excessive* state intervention.[16] Consequently – in official terms, at least – the state's role is restricted to a few core activities that ensure the requisite conditions for market operations.

However, unlike classical liberalism's view of the market as a natural entity, neoliberalism understands the market to be a human creation that requires a certain level of human input in order to ensure its existence and order. Crucially, then, state intervention is justifiable only when creating the conditions for free competition and must not be allowed to intervene in, or alter, market outcomes.[17] In order to maximise the effects of competition, therefore, neoliberalism has sought to extend the reach and scope of market transactions and thus '[redefined] social and ethical life in accordance with economic criteria and expectations'.[18] Market transactions are of such centrality to the neoliberal perspective that they come to be seen 'as a guide for all human action'.[19] Operating within competitive free markets that provide protection from excessive state regulation, entrepreneurial,

10 Eamonn Butler 'Removing Obstacles on the Road to Economic Freedom: 1947–1980' in John B Taylor. (ed.) *A Special Meeting The Mont Pelerin Society 1980–2020. From the Past to the Future: Ideas and Actions for a Free Society* (Hoover Institution/Stanford University 2020).
11 Friedman (n 4).
12 Ibid.
13 Milton Friedman *Capitalism and Freedom* (40th anniversary edn. University of Chicago Press 2002) 2.
14 Harvey (n 2) 2.
15 Harvey (n 2) 7.
16 Ibid. 2.
17 Bruno Amable 'Morals and Politics in the Ideology of Neo-Liberalism' (2011) 9 (1) *Socio-Economic Review* 3 6.
18 Jodi Dean *Democracy and Other Neo-liberal Fantasies: Communicative Capitalism and Left Politics* (Duke University Press 2009) 51.
19 Ibid.

creative individuals drive economic progress in a competitive order sustained by state intervention.[20]

In spite of this somewhat complex reality, the establishment of neoliberal economics has been accompanied by the language of classic liberalism with a great deal of discussion around state contraction, deregulation, free markets and laissez-faire policy. However, rather than accurately depicting changes between state–market relations, a chasm appears to exist between neoliberal rhetoric and practice, leading some to suggest that the system itself is one based in fraud and deceit.[21] Thus, in spite of the centrality of the small state, free markets and free competition to neoliberal *philosophy*, in reality, these things have very little to do with the implementation of neoliberal *policy*.[22] The use of neoliberal philosophy within contemporary right-wing political rhetoric has, therefore, served to 'maintain the fiction of an ontological separation between state and market' while in reality there has been a significant 'interweaving of state and private capital'.[23] Many commentators have sought to draw attention to the persistence of the state within neoliberalism and suggest that, rather than indicating a failure, or incomplete development, of neoliberalism, a strong state is, in fact, essential to the neoliberal model. The ideas of state capture,[24] or state occupation by powerful interests,[25] are used to explain the state's role in the organised transfer of wealth that lies at the heart of the neoliberal movement. Thus, rather than diminishing the power of the state, neoliberalism seeks to utilise political power in order to further the interests of the powerful, as the following excerpt demonstrates:

> Since there is no possible moral difference between modes of government, it doesn't matter whether the beast is 'big' or 'small'; all that matters is whose interests it serves. The object of the political war is not to shrink the state or shut it down; it is to capture the thing and run it for your constituents' benefit. [26]

In practice, therefore, neoliberalism is heavily dependent on 'political alliances'[27] and on the 'use of bureaucratic, legal and security apparatuses of the state in ways that benefit corporate and financial interests'.[28] Central to this process has been the financial sector's 'capture' of government in order to 'enrich' and 'un-tax the

20 Friedman (n 4).

21 David Whyte and Jörg Wiegratz 'The Moral Economy of Neo-liberal Fraud' in David Whyte and Jörg Wiegratz (eds.) *Neo-liberalism and the Moral Economy of Fraud* (Routledge 2017).

22 Mike Davis and Daniel Bertrand Monk 'Introduction' in Mike Davis and Daniel Bertrand Monk (eds.) *Evil Paradises: Dreamworlds of Neo-liberalism* (New Press 2007) x.

23 Burdis and Tombs (n 6) 283.

24 George Monbiot *Captive State: The Corporate Takeover of Britain* (Pan Books 2001).

25 Thomas Frank *The Wrecking Crew: The American Right and the Lust for Power* (Random House 2008).

26 Ibid. 39.

27 Dean (n 18) 50.

28 Ibid. 49

banking sector and its major clients', allowing for the development of distinctly 'oligarchic' political arrangements.[29] Similarly, Davis and Bertrand Monk suggest that one of the defining features of neoliberal policy has been the 'naked application of state power to raise the rate of profit for crony groups, billionaire gangsters, and the rich in general'.[30] Consequently, Harvey draws attention to the way in which state power has been employed in a process of economic restructuring allowing the economy to be 'disembedded' from political and social restraints erected during the post-war social-democratic period.[31] On account of its role in the removal of obstacles to accumulation, both Harvey[32] and Badiou[33] identify the central role played by neoliberal economic policy in the restoration of unchecked inequalities of the past. Accordingly, Harvey describes neoliberalism as 'a *political* project to re-establish the conditions for capital accumulation and restore the power of the economic elites'.[34]

Within this process, he is keen to highlight the Janus-faced nature of the neoliberal project in which a severe disjuncture exists between the espoused ideologies of neoliberalism, on the one hand, and the reality of its implementation, on the other. On this subject, he states:

> Masked by a lot of rhetoric about individual freedom, liberty, personal responsibility and the virtue of privatisation, the free market and free trade, it [neoliberalism] legitimised draconian policies designed to restore and consolidate capitalist class power.[35]

Both Badiou[36] and Harvey[37] discuss the systematic and wholesale transfer of wealth to the capitalist classes that takes place under the neoliberal model. However, this unrestrained and deliberate upward transfer of wealth contrasts sharply with the neoliberal account of the political-economic system in which processes of liberalisation open up the prospect of enrichment to all. Key to this argument is that by liberating economic actors and markets 'everyone benefits, not just some, *all*',[38] because the rewards of productivity will filter through the various strata of society in a 'trickle-down' or 'horse and sparrow' effect. This 'rising tides raise all boats' argument posits that the genius and creativity of 'wealth creators' can come to benefit society as a whole but in order to be able to do so, 'the market has to be

29 Michael Hudson *The Bubble and Beyond: Fictitious Capital, Debt Deflation and Global Crisis* (ISLET, 2012) 408.
30 Davis and Bertrand Monk (n 22) x.
31 Harvey (n 2).
32 Ibid.
33 Alain Badiou *The Century* (Polity 2008).
34 Harvey (n 2) 19.
35 David Harvey *The Enigma of Capital: And the Crises of Capitalism* (Profile Books 2010) 10.
36 Badiou (n 33).
37 Harvey (n 35).
38 Dean (n 18) 55.

liberated, freed from constraints, unleashed to realize its and our full potential'.[39] In practice, however, this ideal remains at odds with the reality of the significant acceleration of inequality under neoliberalism.[40] Rather than representing the outcome of nuances and variations in the neoliberal movement, this disjunction is deeply functional in facilitating processes of selective enrichment while simultaneously masking the reality of these arrangements.[41] Liberal philosophy, in this sense, has 'functioned not as the real ends of neo-liberal policy, but as its guiding myth and ideological alibi'.[42]

Rather than being implemented for its own sake, Harvey[43] suggests that neoliberal ideology has been used as 'justification and legitimation' for the means required in order to achieve elite restoration. Many authors have therefore sought to highlight the selective manner in which neoclassical ideas are implemented within the neoliberal project. Harvey,[44] for example, suggests that 'when neo-liberal principles clash with the need to restore or sustain elite power, then the principles are either abandoned or become so twisted as to be unrecognizable.'[45] Amid the lived reality of late capitalism, therefore, many of the espoused defining principles of neoliberalism are considered disposable should they conflict with the overall trajectory of capitalism and elite accumulation. Neoliberal capitalism, therefore, reveals itself to have no allegiances. Rather, it aligns itself flexibly with whichever arrangements allow for capitalist expansion at a given moment. Crucially, for the criminological discipline, myriad arrangements come to include those that incubate, facilitate and sustain harmful and criminal behaviours of elite financial actors.

Thus, while the neoliberal project has ostensibly set out on a project to establish free markets by reducing and removing regulation, the reality is that the period has witnessed a significant amount of reregulation, aimed at promoting and protecting the interests of finance,[46] while surreptitious attempts have been made to undermine *particular* aspects of business regulation. Thus, no simple, overt dismantling of regulation has taken place. Instead, we have witnessed a 'material and ideological undermining of regulatory bodies, leading to their virtual emasculation, or at least significantly reduced capacity'.[47] While this clan-

39 Ibid.
40 Harvey (n 2).
41 Badiou (n 33); Dean (n 18); Harvey (n 35).
42 Mark Fisher 'How To Kill a Zombie: Strategizing the end of neo-liberalism' (Open Democracy 2013), https://www.opendemocracy.net/en/how-to-kill-zombie-strategizing-end-of-neoliberalism/, accessed 9 December 2021.
43 Harvey (n 2) (19).
44 Ibid.
45 Ibid.
46 Burdis and Tombs (n 6) 283.
47 Paddy Hillyard and Steve Tombs 'Towards a Political Economy of Harm: States, corporations and the production of inequality' in Paddy Hillyard et al. (eds.) *Beyond Criminology: Taking Harm Seriously* (Pluto 2004) 52; see also Vickie Cooper and David Whyte 'Introduction: The violence of austerity' in Vickie Cooper and David Whyte (eds.) *The Violence of Austerity* (Pluto 2017) 2.

destine attack on regulatory bodies has often involved the restriction of funding, Frank suggests the strategic appointment of personnel is also key to understanding the process. Thus, often, regulatory agencies appoint people who are 'distinctly hostile to those agencies' very purpose' and who, therefore, ensure their impotence.[48] Throughout the mainstream economy, therefore, neoliberalisation has systematically worked to create 'zones of exception',[49] spaces in which the 'intelligent deviation'[50] of financial actors can take place without the risk of criminalisation or at least the likelihood of detection. The creation of such environments is known to have grave consequences in the form of the proliferation of harmful and criminal acts perpetrated by powerful economic actors.[51] In recognition of the expansion of economic criminality that has accompanied the neoliberalisation of the West, Wiegratz[52] suggests that fraud and predation are now inscribed at the heart of mainstream culture to the extent that they have become the 'new normal'.[53] Similarly, for Ruggiero, the routinisation of criminality within the mainstream economy is such that he suggests that it 'constitute[s] neither exceptional [behaviour] nor social pathology[y]'.[54] Given, the quotidian nature of legal violations within mainstream business, Bakan suggests that 'corporate illegalities are rife throughout the economy' and that '[m]any major corporations engage in unlawful behaviour, and some are habitual offenders with records that would be the envy of even the most prolific human criminals.'[55] Consequently, neoliberal economies are not only characterised by harmful behaviours incorporated within the boundary of legality by processes of deregulation, but also by unimaginable levels of criminality.[56] Moreover, many of these practices have elicited almost no

48 Frank (n 25) 40.

49 Giorgio Agamben *State of Exception* (University of Chicago Press 2005); Steve Hall *Theorizing Crime and Deviance: A New Perspective* (Sage 2012); Rowland Atkinson and Thomas Rodgers 'Pleasure Zones and Murder Boxes: Online pornography and violent video games as cultural zones of exception' (2015) 56 (6) BJC, 1291.

50 John Stuart Mill *On Liberty and Other Writings* (Cambridge University Press 2006) 60.

51 See, for example, Charles Ferguson *Inside Job: The Financiers Who Pulled off the Heist of the Century* (One World 2012).

52 Jörg Wiegratz 'Fake Capitalism? The dynamics of neo-liberal moral restructuring and pseudo-development: The case of Uganda' (2010) 37 (124) *Review of African Political Economy* 123; Jörg Wiegratz 'The Neo-liberal Harvest: The proliferation and normalisation of economic fraud in a market society' in Simon Winlow and Rowland Atkinson (eds.) *New Directions in Crime and Deviancy* (Routledge 2012).

53 David Whyte and Jörg Wiegratz (2017) 'Neo-liberalism, Moral Economy and Fraud' in David Whyte and Jörg Wiegratz (eds.) *Neo-liberalism and the Moral Economy of Fraud* (Routledge 2017) 1.

54 Vincenzo Ruggiero *Organized and Corporate Crime in Europe: Offers that Can't Be Refused.* (Dartmouth 1996) 155.

55 Joel Bakan *The Corporation: The Pathological Pursuit of Profit and Power* (Constable, 2005) 75.

56 Ibid.; Ferguson (n 51); Nicholas Shaxson *Treasure Islands: Tax Havens and the Men Who Stole the World* (Random House 2011).

meaningful responses from regulatory bodies and law enforcement agencies,[57] often resulting instead in highly lucrative returns.[58] As a result, their presence in the mainstream economy has been able to exert a significant influence over conditions of competition in contemporary financial markets.

Dirty economies

Thus, under contemporary capitalism, both economic structures and cultures have been subject to extensive revision, and this has significantly altered the way in which late capitalist subjects interact with, and think about, economic activity. Criminologists have increasingly recognised the ways in which mainstream economic reforms have blurred the boundaries between licit, semi-licit and illicit practice[59] and have drawn attention to the way in which the boundary between these categories is not only blurred, but also arbitrary and subject to constant revision.[60] Rather than representing a judgement on the moral or ethical desirability of a particular form of economic activity, the boundary of legality in the spectrum of enterprise may often simply reflect particular interests which are totally divorced from any consideration of the harmful outcomes of the behaviour under scrutiny.[61] Thus, the period of late capitalism has witnessed the development of 'dirty economies'[62] in which the distinction between legal and illegal conduct is unclear. Neoliberal processes of financialisation and de- and reregulation have played a central role in the development of these distinctly 'grey' territories of economic practice.

The technical apparatus of financial capital – and, in particular, the development of offshore financial centres (OFCs) – are also deeply implicated in the 'greying' of the economy. Within these spaces, entrepreneurs and businesspeople from across the spectrum of enterprise[63] come to engage in a range of economic practices that include illicit, semi-licit and legal yet harmful behaviours.[64] Crucially, however, rather than requiring state withdrawal, active state involvement is necessary for the creation and maintenance of these anomic spaces distributed throughout the global economy.

57 See, for example, Ferguson (n 51).

58 Bakan (n 55); Burdis and Tombs (n 6); Ferguson (n 51).

59 Dwight C Smith 'Paragons, Pariahs, and Pirates: A spectrum-based theory of enterprise' (1980) 26 (3) *Crime and Delinquency* 358; Ruggiero (n 54); Vincenzo Ruggiero 'On Liberty and Crime: Adam Smith and John Stuart Mill' (2008) 51 *Crime, Law and Social Change* 435; Ruggiero (n 7); Dick Hobbs 'Criminal Collaboration: Youth gangs, subcultures, professional criminals and organized crime' in Mike Maguire et al. (eds.) *The Oxford Handbook of Criminology* (2nd edn Oxford University Press, 1997).

60 Smith (n 59); Ruggiero (n 7).

61 Ibid.

62 Ruggiero (n 7).

63 Smith (n 59.

64 Ruggiero (n 7) 16.

In establishing these zones of exception,[65] neoliberal restructuring has firmly established harm at the heart of mainstream economic practice. The competitive impulse towards deregulation and impenetrable secrecy which has driven the development of a global network of financial centres (and in the neoliberal period, the creation of a range of financial vehicles for ensuring anonymity) has offered economic actors countless opportunities for acts of regulatory arbitrage[66] leading to the profusion of practices such as tax avoidance and transfer pricing.[67] While harmful, many of the practices that take place here remain technically legal. However, the 'regulatory blind spots' on which they are dependent are also known to provide fertile ground for the perpetration of illicit financial activity.[68] Thus, within these regulatory black holes sustained by state power, dirty and clean financial revenues come to be entwined to the extent that they can no longer be distinguished from one another.[69] Moreover, the distinction between legal and illegal actors also becomes increasingly confused as illicit entrepreneurs often depend on those working in mainstream institutions to act as intermediaries, or gatekeepers, to financial institutions and products.[70] Within late capitalist economies then, access to financial networks and institutions comes to be dependent on assessments of a person's ability to uphold the cardinal value of secrecy, rather than on an appraisal of their legal or moral legitimacy. Shaxson suggests that within offshore networks:

> [L]egal frameworks that distinguish between the criminal and the legitimate have been eroded and replaced by networks of trust [...] Individuals with sums to launder or invest with minimal taxation want to know they are dealing with people who can be trusted not to have moral qualms.[71]

The toleration and facilitation of both harmful and criminal practice are, therefore, integral features of the late capitalist economy.[72] The 'dirty'[73] or 'gray'[74]

65 Agamben (n 49).

66 Ronen Palan 'Futurity, Offshore and the International Political Economy of Crime' in Jens Beckert and Matias Dewey (eds.) *The Architecture of Illegal Markets: Towards an Economic Sociology of Illegality in the Economy* (Oxford University Press 2017); Ruggiero (n 7) 3; Nicholas Lord et al. (2019) 'Other People's Dirty Money: Professional intermediaries, market dynamics and the finances of white-collar, corporate and organised crimes' (2019) 59 (5) BJC, 1217.

67 Shaxson (n 56).

68 R. T. Naylor *Wages of Crime: Black Markets, Illegal Finance and the Underworld Economy* (Cornell University Press 2002); Jeffrey Robinson *The Sink: Terror, Crime and Dirty Money in the Offshore World* (Constable 2003); Shaxson (n 56); Palan (n 66).

69 Palan (n 66); Ruggiero (n 7) 8.

70 Ruggiero (n 7); Lord (n 66).

71 Shaxson (n 56) 220.

72 Ruggiero (n 7) 12.

73 Ibid.

74 Naylor (n 68).

economic spaces that this creates are deeply related to the proliferation of fraud for a number of reasons. First, in severing the links between harm and illegality, neoliberal reforms have ensured that numerous practices that closely resemble fraud, and, in particular, Ponzi fraud, are able to develop outside the ambit of legal prohibition. Many features of the mainstream economy – including, for example, pension funds, the loan-to-deposit ratios of banks, the rampant use of rehypothecation using financial instruments such as credit default swaps and collateralised debt obligations – have been identified as following the Ponzi model.

Second, for those engaged in legally defined financial fraud, the structures and products of contemporary capitalism (created, maintained and supported by state apparatus) offer a means by which to legitimate or launder the proceeds of their crimes, significantly reduce the likelihood of detection and prosecution and, ultimately, considerably increase the profitability of fraud.[75] As a result, both the institutions and personnel of the mainstream economy interact with fraudsters and their criminal revenues on a daily basis.[76] For this reason, the blurring of legal and moral boundaries within late capitalist enterprise must be understood to affect actors operating at both ends of the spectrum of enterprise. Thus, just as criminal practices have come to resemble legitimate business more closely, so too have licit practices become analogous to criminality. Crucially, however, the overlap between the two spheres is not restricted to cultures and practices. Rather, the funds of licit and illicit enterprise have also become materially intertwined as they follow the same routes through mainstream financial institutions and actors to the extent that they become inseparable. In seeking to advance the interests of capital, therefore, contemporary economic arrangements not only enable the spread of fraudulent activity but also make its identification increasingly difficult and, ultimately, less relevant. Within late capitalist economies, the revenues of criminality and fraud, it seems, are welcomed equally with others should they offer the prospect of profitability.[77] In providing discretion and profitability, the financial apparatus of neoliberalism not only facilitates, but also motivates, the ongoing participation of economic elites and corporations in harmful economic practice. Under such circumstances, economic sharp practice and malpractice alike are not only tolerated but rewarded by mainstream economic institutions and increasingly come to be accepted as means of surviving within contemporary capitalism.

On competition and constrained choices: the experiences of Ponzi fraudsters

Within criminology, the anomic forces of mainstream economic culture are understood not only to alter the subjective and behavioural experiences of those

75 Palan (n 66); Lord (n 66).
76 Naylor (n 68); Robinson (n 68); Shaxson (n 56).
77 Shaxson (n 56).

occupying positions of power in the legitimate economy, but also those operating on, or well beyond, its margins.[78] Consequently, criminological analysis has begun to sketch the ways in which the cultural currents of dominant economic arrangements spill over to exert a direct influence over those further down the economic food chain.[79] Thus, dominant economic cultural norms around entrepreneurialism, pursuing profit at any cost, aggressive acquisitiveness, innovation and so on, are all found to be expressed through illegitimate economic practices, often by those who lack strong links to the formal economy.[80] However, the current chapter extends the analysis of the relationship between neoliberalism and criminality by examining the indirect influence of the neoliberal state's programme of economic restructuring over the behaviours of low level illicit economic actors. It will be argued that, in setting the conditions of competition, the outcomes of these reforms serve to constrain the decision making of those navigating the vicissitudes of economic enterprise and ultimately facilitate the transition across the boundary of legality in the pursuit of profit.

The data presented below originates from a project in which 14 men who had been convicted for their perpetration of high yield fraudulent investment (Ponzi) schemes were interviewed over the period of around 18 months. The research explored the subjective and motivational aspects of fraud and identified a strong relationship between fraudulent enterprise and many aspects of contemporary capitalism including the dynamics of consumer culture[81] and economic cultures of sovereignty.[82] The issue of competition was also of extreme importance to the men in the study, who repeatedly sought to return to the topic during interviews. Crucially, their preoccupation with the issue of competition extended beyond

78 Nikos Passas 'Anomie and Corporate Deviance'(1990) 14 *Contemporary Crises*157; S. Hallsworth *Street Crime* (Willan 2005); Steve Hall et al. *Criminal Identities and Consumer Culture: Crime, Exclusion and the New Culture of Narcissism* (Willan 2008); Hall (n 49); Kate Tudor 'Toxic Sovereignty: Understanding fraud as the expression of special liberty within late-capitalism' (2018) 2 (2) *Journal of Extreme Anthropology* 7; Kate Tudor 'Symbolic Survival and Harm: Serious fraud and consumer capitalism's perversion of the Causa Sui Project' (2019) 59 (5) BJC, 1237.

79 Kate Tudor (n 78) 8.

80 Dick Hobbs 'Professional and Organized Crime in Britain' in M. Maguire et al. (eds.) *The Oxford Handbook of Criminology* (Oxford University Press 1994); Dick Hobbs *Bad Business: Professional Criminals in Modern Britain* (Oxford University Press 1995); Dick Hobbs *Lush Life: Constructing Organized Crime in the UK* (Oxford University Press 2013); Ruggiero (n 54); Vincenzo Ruggiero 'It's the Economy, Stupid! Classifying power crimes' (2003) 35 *International Journal of the Sociology of Law*163; Vincenzo Ruggiero 'On Liberty and Crime: Adam Smith and John Stuart Mill' (2008) 51 *Crime, Law and Social Change* 435; R. T. Naylor 'Towards a General Theory of Profit-Driven Crimes' (2003) 43 BJC 81; Simon Hallsworth *Street Crime* (Willan 2005); Steve Hall et al. *Criminal Identities and Consumer Culture: Crime, Exclusion and the New Culture of Narcissism* (Willan 2008); Kate Tudor *Ponzi Schemes: Illicit Entrepreneurialism in Late-Capitalism* (Emerald forthcoming).

81 Kate Tudor 'Symbolic Survival and Harm: Serious fraud and consumer capitalism's perversion of the Causa Sui Project' (2019) 59 (5) BJC, 1237.

82 Tudor (n 78).

the immediacy of their own relationships and experiences; they also reflected on the way in which their interpretations of the wider economic landscape also influenced their decisions to engage in harmful conduct. Respondents regularly sought to draw comparisons between the behaviours for which they were convicted and those routinely taking place within legitimate business. The commonplace nature of fraud, malpractice and harm in the mainstream economy was something of which they were acutely aware and chose to discuss frequently. Richard, for example, worked in the investments industry and he described his revelations as he first entered the sector:

> When I first started out, I was quite simply astounded by the levels of deceit and downright fraud that went on within the world of finance. This was, and is, considered normal practice in that world. I found out what a total racket it was. Often it is a legal racket, but it is a racket nevertheless. Believe me.
>
> **Richard**

Similarly, Pete sought to draw attention to the inequality of treatment between different actors engaged in essentially the same types of behaviour. He was very keen to point out that while behaviours might be equally harmful, they might not be perceived as being equally problematic:

> Man, we were torn apart for things that happen in banks every day. You see, our government is so stupid. I'll tell you why they're stupid because it's okay if you avoid paying tax legally, yeah? But this person has done it illegally. But it's exactly the same thing. So if you know how to manipulate the law and get around the law, it's okay to not pay tax. But if you just straight up try to avoid it and you don't know how to do it properly, *ooooh* you're a criminal. You've done wrong, you have. That's the difference, but they've both done the same thing. One went via the M25, the other went via the M1. It's as simple as that. At the end of the day, they both ain't paid it.
>
> **Pete**

Working in high finance, Cornelius was well acquainted with the reality of day-to-day practice in this industry. Cornelius felt an extreme sense of injustice about his convictions as he believed that the crimes for which he been punished represented normal conduct in the environment in which he worked:

> The way the authorities came after me was unbelievable. It was disgraceful [...] the resources they wasted on my case. They simply had no understanding of business. None whatsoever. I mean the people who work in these [police] departments, they're just policemen, they're not businessmen. They have no knowledge of how finance works. How could they? And let me tell you that was *perfectly* plain when it came to discussing these issues with them. All they know is the law and they see it from a very black and white

> perspective. But black and white does not take account of the realities of business, of what is required to make things work.
>
> The things they arrested me for [...] they weren't unusual or outlandish, just everyday business practices and of course, if you intervene at the wrong moment, they constitute a technical violation of the law and, yes, some people lose out, but that's investing! People couldn't win if others didn't lose. It's simple. So, in reality, if they were able to charge me for what might be construed as 'sharp practice', but which essentially constitutes normal business, I mean they could arrest almost every financier on the planet! The whole thing is ridiculous.
>
> Anybody [...] anybody would have made the same decisions. The decisions I made represented nothing more than sensible business strategies in the context of [investments].
>
> **Cornelius**

For many, the excerpts detailed above might be interpreted as representing a form of 'neutralisation' insofar as they offer a 'condemnation of the condemners' and a claim of allegiance to the 'higher loyalties' of business.[83] In so doing, the respondents seek to highlight the normalisation of 'sharp practice', rule breaking and harm within wider economic culture, suggesting that because their conduct is aligned with 'normal' practice in the wider economy, it becomes less problematic. From Cornelius' perspective, it was unfair that he was being singled out and punished for implementing a business model that underpinned a significant number of mainstream practices. In suggesting that fraud and sharp practice were a quotidian element of the wider economic landscape, the respondents' accounts demonstrated the way in which the way in the broader landscape of neoliberal capitalism is characterised by a pervasive culture of moral and legal ambiguity[84] on which fraudsters can draw in order to frame their own criminality through a lens of normality.

Where participants had experience of working in mainstream business and finance, their work allowed them insight into the 'new normal' of neoliberal capitalism.[85] However, even when respondents didn't have direct experience of working in these sectors, they displayed an awareness of the increasing ruthlessness of conduct that characterises economic exchange.

While this wider culture in which fraud has become the 'new normal'[86] undoubtedly gave the respondents access to some of the rationalisations set out

83 Gresham M. Sykes and David Matza 'Techniques of Neutralization: A theory of delinquency' (1957) 22 (6) *American Sociological Review* 664; M. Benson 'Denying the Guilty Mind: Accounting for involvement in a white-collar crime' (1985) 23 (4) *Criminology* 583, 588.

84 Burdis and Tombs (n 6).

85 Whyte and Wiegratz (n 53).

86 Ibid.

above,[87] given the sapience of their observations, their reference to these wider cultures of immorality and criminality cannot merely be considered attempts to rationalise or excuse their own conduct. Rather, their discussion of these factors indicated that their own conduct decisions were heavily shaped by their assessment of the necessities of the economic landscape in which they operated. Importantly, however, the respondents did not seek to endorse the 'new normal' of neoliberalism that they observed, indicating that their engagement in criminal and harmful conduct was not driven by a new form of neoliberal morality as Whyte and Wiegratz[88] suggest.

On the contrary, once respondents became more comfortable in discussing the harm that resulted from their actions, they remained committed to the fact that they did not intentionally seek to harm others; neither was it something from which they derived satisfaction. Without exception, all respondents maintained a commitment to the position that the harmful effects of their crimes were something they found to be regrettable. Thus, their accounts were infused by a form of capitalist realism[89] as they suggested that wider economic cultures came to frame their own behaviours by necessity, rather than choice.[90] From this position, they were able to distance themselves from their actions by occupying a position of resigned cynicism about the nature of the world while expressing the belief that they would make different choices in another context.[91] in spite of their dissatisfaction with the situation, they continued to participate according to rules with which they disagreed, highlighting late capitalist subjects' limited capacity to withdraw their participation from systems they know to be harmful and that they deem to be undesirable.[92]

During interviews, the primary way in which these behaviours were explained was with recourse to notions of economic survival. Central to these understandings was the idea that if ruthlessness, harm and criminality were endemic features of the everyday landscape of business, then to remain wedded to moral codes was to put oneself at a competitive disadvantage. The issue of competition was thus central to the way in which they explained their willingness to harm others. No respondents positively endorsed the predatory conduct they identified in mainstream economic practice, neither did they express support for their own harmful acts. Rather, they appeared to view their engagement in harmful acts of economic predation as a means of avoiding being left behind, an eventuality they appeared

87 Michael Benson 'Denying the Guilty Mind: Accounting for involvement in a white-collar crime' (1985) 23 (4) *Criminology* 583, 588.
88 Whyte and Wiegratz (n 53); Whyte and Wiegratz (n 21).
89 Mark Fisher *Capitalist Realism: Is There No Alternative?* (Zero Books 2009).
90 Tudor (n 78).
91 See Terry Eagleton *On Evil* (Yale University Press 2010) 144.
92 Simon Winlow and Steve Hall 'Realist Criminology and its Discontents' (2016) 5 (3) *International Journal for Crime, Justice and Social Democracy* 80, 88.

unable to countenance.[93] Ultimately, it seemed that wider economic conduct norms had the effect of constraining their choices over their own conduct by setting the conditions for competition.

Therefore, while they acknowledged that they had harmed others in the course of their investment schemes, this was accepted as a necessary evil of being able to succeed in an environment in which the rules of engagement were considered to reduce one's capacity to act as an ethical subject. Thus, the respondents' moral choices need to be framed in the context of Adorno's[94] work, which reminds us that the realisation of man's moral capacity is dependent on the creation of conditions in which ethical decision making can flourish.[95] From this perspective, predation and harm might 'be traceable back not to any corruption of the will, but to the "ill" that society allows no viable course of action that would be moral'.[96] The logic of this position is discernible in the following extract from an interview with Victor:

> Look, okay. So you want to know why I did it?
>
> **Victor**
>
> Well, yes, but what I am asking is if it bothered you. Were you concerned about the fact that you made people lose money [...] about the fact that they lost out because of what you did?
>
> **Interviewer**
>
> Of course it was unfortunate what happened. I'm not a complete bastard. I'm not impervious to all of this [...] this mess. But let's be realistic here. What was I supposed to do? Do you think you can get anywhere in this world without being willing to stray into muddy waters? It's like the phrase, you know the one about omelettes and eggs? You can't make an omelette if you don't crack some eggs [...] Whilst I'm not saying that I wanted to 'crack' the investors, what I'm saying is business can't happen without someone losing out and if you aren't willing to take the risk of someone losing out then there is no way you can compete with others who take that risk every day.
>
> **Victor**

The logic of the necessity of evil which is present in Victor's account is also mirrored in Cornelius' interpretation of his situation:

> Really, I mean really, can you *imagine* the consequences of taking a moral stance in business?! The whole idea is just ludicrous. If you weren't able to

93 Kate Tudor 'Symbolic Survival and Harm: Serious fraud and consumer capitalism's perversion of the Causa Sui Project' (2019) 59 (5) BJC, 1237.

94 Theodor Adorno *Problems of Moral Philosophy* (Polity 2001).

95 See also Eagleton (n 91) 147–8.

96 Peter Dews *The Idea of Evil* (Blackwell 2008) 202.

take risks, to cut a few corners, to take chances with the money, well what would be the point? Someone else would and they would succeed and you wouldn't. It is quite straightforward.

Cornelius

The accounts presented above demonstrate the way in which the majority of respondents understood moral choices to be incompatible with economic survival and success. Their narratives were thus indicative of the way that the model of competitive capitalism, which is identified by Bonger[97] as the creative force behind Hobbes'[98] *homo homini lupus*, is fundamentally at odds with moral and ethical regulation:

> 'Every man for himself' is the principle of success in such an environment. It is evident that the social sentiments must be strongly opposed in their development if the maxim just given is that which dominates. To act morally implies sacrificing one's own advantage for the sake of the general good. He who is compelled always to have his own interests at heart can give very little thought to the interests of others[99]

Given competitive capitalism's basis in sublimated violence,[100] egoism, ruthlessness and predation are the inevitable outcomes of unrestrained acquisitive struggle. As the interests of individuals are placed in conflict with one another under this model, Bonger suggests that competitive capitalism serves to '[weaken] the social instincts of man' allowing fraudulent exchange to proliferate.[101] At the core of Bonger's argument is his assessment of the way in which capitalism institutionalises Hobbes' 'war of all against all'.[102] Indeed, Boukli and Kotzé[103] recognise the way in which capitalism has actively sought to abandon notions of distributive justice[104] (see also Muller 2003) meaning that Aristotelian notions of *zemia* (loss) and *kerdos* (gain) come to be inscribed at the heart of society. This internal logic of imbalance arising from the ubiquity of self-interest and the attendant profusion of insecurity in the capitalist system is something that is identified by Sombart as having a deregulatory effect on conduct norms:

97 Willem Bonger *Criminality and Economic Conditions* (William Heinemann 1916) 290, 395.
98 Thomas Hobbes *Leviathan* (Hackett 1994).
99 Bonger (n 97) 600 –601.
100 Ibid. 389; Steve Hall and Simon Winlow 'Barbarians at the Gate: Crime and violence in the breakdown of the pseudo-pacification process' in Jeff Ferrell et al. (eds.) *Cultural Criminology Unleashed* (Glasshouse Press 2004).
101 Bonger (n 97) 400.
102 Ibid.
103 Avi Boukli and Justin Kotzé 'Introduction' in Avi Boukli and Justin Kotzé (eds.) *Zemiology: Reconnecting Crime and Social Harm* (Routledge 2018).
104 See also Jerry Muller *The Mind and the Market: Capitalism in Western Thought* (Anchor Books 2003).

> If acquisition is the first consideration, unrestricted competition is a matter of course. You need no longer be bound by considerations of any kind, whether moral, aesthetic or social. Unscrupulous is the adjective for your actions[105]

The insecurity generated by competitive capitalism thus provides the energy on which ruthless, harmful and often criminal attempts to secure triumph feed. By intervening to provide guarantees between economic actors through the consistent and equitable regulation of economic activity and the enforcement of law, the state is able to reduce levels of insecurity and, by extension minimise the acts of predation to which they give rise. However, under neoliberalism, the state has not only retreated from its role in regulating conduct, it has actively sought to intervene and regulate in a way that routinely supports and rewards the criminal and harmful behaviours of the economic elite. The data outlined above demonstrates that the conditions created by the state under neoliberalism provide fertile terrain not only for the criminality of economic elites, but also of those further down the social scale.

Conclusion

The chapter has outlined data collected during interviews with those convicted for investment fraud and has explored the way in which the subjective experiences of fraudsters are influenced by the conditions present in the neoliberal economy. The participants in the study all demonstrated an acute awareness of the presence of fraud and sharp practice in the mainstream economy and this exerted significant influence over their perceptions of what was necessary to survive. Their observations of the way in the success of others was underpinned by fraud, malpractice or those behaviours that, while technically legal, are difficult to differentiate from other legally proscribed conduct, not only provided access to rationalisations for fraud, but also served to restrict their decision making. The fraudsters in the study therefore described feeling constrained by the rules of the game in which those stepping outside moral and legal boundaries are routinely rewarded for their deviations. In the conversations that I shared with them, the Ponzi scheme operators in the study demonstrated an awareness of the deregulatory effect this reality exerted over economic conduct norms and expressed the belief that this, in turn, influenced their decision to participate in fraud.

Their accounts were thus infused with the belief that to remain wedded to legal and moral codes was to consign oneself to failure in advance. The wider rules of neoliberal capitalism meant that the men in the study felt that they were unable to compete effectively without stepping outside of the boundaries of legality. It is the contention of this chapter, therefore, that the conditions of competition

105 Werner Sombart *The Quintessence of Capitalism: A Study of the History and Psychology of the Modern Business Man* (Routledge 1915) 183–5.

established by the neoliberal state's rampant programme of de- and reregulation in order to establish the freedom of capital have created a situation that not only facilitates normative diversification, but also necessitates it.

Under such conditions, acts of economic predation come to be understood as a necessary evil of doing business and fraudulent enterprise can be rationalised as a means of self-preservation in an increasingly ruthless and cutthroat marketplace. In creating and maintaining conditions in which fraud, malpractice and harmful conduct are tolerated and rewarded, neoliberal states systematically undermine the sustainability of ethical economic practice and facilitate the proliferation of economic predation.

9 Representations of white collar crime in the Caribbean

Lucy Evans[1]

Introduction

White collar crime was first defined by Edwin Sutherland as a 'crime committed by a person of respectability and of high social status in the course of his occupation' and has since come to be understood as an umbrella term encompassing areas such as financial crime – including fraud, tax evasion, money laundering, and insider trading – environmental crime, occupational crime, and state–corporate crime.[2] White collar crime is a serious and pervasive problem that far exceeds street crime in its social and economic impact.[3] It is also a rapidly growing problem, in a context where technological advances have opened up new opportunities for fraud and where multinational corporations are increasingly powerful and insufficiently regulated.[4] Yet the study of white collar crime remains marginalised within the academic field of criminology, and this reflects its relative invisibility in the media and popular culture.[5]

While white collar crime is far from victimless, victimisation is 'diffuse' in that many people are indirectly affected.[6] Its complexity and widespread effects mean that white collar crime does not easily translate into accessible media sound bites. In addition, most forms of white collar crime are not included in official crime

1 Associate Professor in Postcolonial Literature, University of Leicester.

2 Edwin H. Sutherland, *White Collar Crime: The Uncut Version* (Yale University Press 1983) 7.

3 Steve Tombs and Dave Whyte, 'Researching Corporate and White-Collar Crime in an Era of Neoliberalism' in Gilbert Geis and Henry N. Pontell (eds), *International Handbook of White-Collar and Corporate Crime* (Springer 2007) 125; Michael L. Benson, Shanna R. Van Slyke and Francis T. Cullen, 'Preface', in Van Slyke, Benson and Cullen (eds), *The Oxford Handbook of White Collar Crime* (OUP 2016) ix.

4 David O. Friedrichs, 'White Collar Crime in a Postmodern, Globalised World' in Gilbert Geis and Henry N. Pontell (eds), *International Handbook of White Collar and Corporate Crime* (Springer 2007) 164.

5 Dylan Kerrigan and Nirmala Sookoo, 'White Collar Crime in Trinidad', in Randy Seepersad and Ann Marie Bissessar (eds), *Gangs in the Caribbean* (Cambridge Scholars 2013) 155.

6 Henry N. Pontell, 'Theoretical, Empirical, and Policy Implications of Alternative Definitions of "White-Collar Crime": "Trivialising the lunatic crime rate"' in Michael L. Benson, Shanna R. Van Slyke, and Francis T. Cullen (eds), *The Oxford Handbook of White Collar Crime* (OUP 2016) 42.

DOI: 10.4324/9781003020813-10

statistics, and this limits the scope of both public debate and academic research on white collar crime.[7] All this has generated perceptions of white collar crime as less significant than 'conventional' crimes or even as a 'non-issue'.[8] This, in turn, has resulted in relatively light penalties for white collar crime.[9] Where white collar crime is portrayed in the media, the focus tends to be on high profile individuals rather than the wider institutional and corporate cultures that facilitate it.[10] This emphasis on newsworthy acts of individual deviance obscures the 'routine, everyday harm' committed by organisations over long periods of time, affecting large numbers of people.[11] In this chapter, I explore how various forms of white collar crime are made visible in contemporary fiction and film. Focusing on one film and two novels – all set in the Caribbean region – I consider how writers and filmmakers adopt the political thriller format in order to address the representational challenges associated with white collar crime.

In what follows, I start by outlining longstanding issues surrounding the definition and conceptualisation of white collar crime and reflect on how fiction and film – and specifically the political thriller – might contribute to how white collar crime is perceived and understood. I then examine David Hare's portrayal of the crimes of American and European businessmen in the second film in his Johnny Worricker trilogy, *Turks and Caicos* (2014), which reinforces colonial and touristic tropes of the Caribbean as a playground for the wealthy and powerful. Next, I comment on D. N. Wong Ken's novel *The Runnings* (2003), looking at the representation of financial crime within Jamaica's political and business elites against the background of a late 20th-century political culture marked by violence and corruption. Finally, I show how Esther Figueroa's novel *Limbo* (2014), set in present-day Jamaica, presents environmental crime as a form of white collar crime, raising questions about state and corporate responsibility. I assess the insights these texts offer into the social and organisational structures – local and global – that enable and normalise white collar crime. In doing so, I seek to open up larger questions regarding the possibilities of humanities-based approaches to the study of this phenomenon. Furthermore, bearing in mind that most existing research on white collar crime focuses on North America, Europe, and Australia,[12] I seek,

7 D. Nelken, 'White-Collar and Corporate Crime' in M. Maguire, R. Morgan and R. Reiner (eds), *The Oxford Handbook of Criminology* (5th edn,, OUP 2012) 623.

8 Pontell (n 5) 51.

9 Michael L. Benson, Shanna R. Van Slyke and Francis T. Cullen, 'Core Themes in the Study of White-Collar Crime' in Slyke, Benson and Cullen (eds), *The Oxford Handbook of White Collar Crime* (OUP 2016) 10.

10 Henry N. Pontell, William K. Black and Gilbert Geis 'Too Big to Fail, Too Powerful to Jail? On the absence of criminal prosecutions after the 2008 financial meltdown' (2014) 61(1) *Crime, Law and Social Change* 1, 1–2.

11 Steve Tombs and David Whyte, *The Corporate Criminal: Why Corporations Must be Abolished* (Routledge 2015) 37.

12 Judith van Erp, Wim Huisman, Gudrun Vande Walle and Joep Beckers, 'Criminology and White Collar Crime in Europe' in van Erp, Huisman and Vande Walle (eds), *The Routledge Handbook of White-Collar and Corporate Crime in Europe* (Routledge 2015) 1.

through my readings of fiction and film set in the Global South, to broaden the scope of research on white collar crime culturally and geographically.

Conceptualising white collar crime

Sutherland's definition, in 1949, of white collar crime as a crime committed by a person of 'high social status in the course of his occupation' challenged the focus of criminology on crimes committed by people of the 'lower socioeconomic class'.[13] In illustrating the high frequency of and significant damage caused by white collar crime, he aimed to demonstrate that a 'general theory' of crime as a result of 'poverty and its related pathologies' was invalid. His work continues to be a key reference point in contemporary white collar crime scholarship. In 1970, Herbert Edelherz offered an alternative definition of white collar crime as 'an illegal act or series of illegal acts committed by nonphysical means and by concealment or guile, to obtain money or property, to avoid the loss of money or property, or to obtain business or personal advantage'.[14] Unlike Sutherland's definition, which is based on the social status of the offender, Edelherz's definition focuses on the nature of the offence. These competing definitions have generated two divergent approaches to the study of white collar crime, known as offender-based and offence-based approaches. Defending an offence-based approach, Shapiro argues that Sutherland's definition confuses the crime with the criminal,[15] while Croall contends that limiting the definition to crimes committed by those of high socioeconomic status precludes exploration of similar crimes committed by people at all levels of an organisation.[16] Proponents of the offender-based approach argue that to focus on the offence rather than the offender broadens the definition of white collar crime to such an extent that it is no longer meaningful.[17] As Pontell points out, 'de-collaring' white collar crime – removing it from the context of socioeconomic privilege and institutional power in which Sutherland's work had placed it – 'leads to trivialising the structural elements that are basic to such crimes'.[18]

In this chapter, I take an offender-based approach to the definition of white collar crime, exploring how a film and two novels frame white collar crime as 'elite crime or crimes of the powerful'.[19] Most white collar crime researchers

13 Sutherland (n 1) 7.

14 Herbert Edelhertz, *The Nature, Impact, and Prosecution of White-Collar Crime* (US Government Printing Office 1970) 3.

15 Susan Shapiro, 'Collaring the Crime, Not the Criminal: Reconsidering the concept of white-collar crime' (1990) 55 *American Sociological Review* 346, 346–7.

16 Hazel Croall, *Understanding White Collar Crime* (Open University Press 2001) 7–8.

17 Neil Shover, 'Generative Worlds of White-Collar Crime', in Gilbert Geis and Henry N. Pontell (eds.), *International Handbook of White-Collar and Corporate Crime* (Springer 2007); Benson, Slyke and Cullen (n 8); Pontell (n 5).

18 Pontell (n 5) 49.

19 Nelken (n 6) 631.

working with offender-based definitions, following Sutherland, have emphasised the need to recognise how socioeconomic status and material privilege impact on both the nature and extent of white collar crime and its treatment by criminal justice systems.[20] However, Kerrigan and Sookoo identify the need to consider race and ethnicity alongside class in order to fully understand the phenomenon of white collar crime in Trinidad and Tobago, noting that the word 'white' in the label 'white-collar crime' reflects the racialised dimensions of power, wealth, and privilege in Caribbean societies.[21] The setting of *Turks and Caicos* is a British overseas territory in the Caribbean region. The majority of its inhabitants are of African descent. *The Runnings* and *Limbo* are set in Jamaica, a former British colony in the Caribbean that became politically independent in 1962 and similarly has a population of majority African descent. Caribbean islands' shared history of colonialism and transatlantic slavery has shaped not only their demographics but also their social structure; Caribbean societies' racialised class hierarchies reflect enduring associations between class status and skin colour. An offender-based approach to the study of white collar crime in the Caribbean therefore necessitates a focus on race and ethnicity as well as class. Bearing in mind that the colonial enterprise was deeply gendered,[22] I suggest further that the gender dimensions of power, wealth, and privilege need to be considered in the study of white collar crime in Caribbean societies.

In line with offender-based criminological studies of white collar crime, I aim in my readings of fiction and film to shift analytical focus from 'crimes on the streets' to 'crimes in the suites'; a shift that – as Levi and Lord observe – is important in its challenge to stereotypes about the nature of crime and the characteristics of criminals.[23] Kerrigan and Sookoo note that in Trinidad, the media, state, and criminal justice system 'create a distorted image of who is responsible for crime' and the 'young, poor and black are over represented'.[24] In Jamaica, journalistic reports over decades have 'served to stigmatise and criminalise African Jamaicans', and the image of young, Black Jamaican men as dangerous and threatening to the social fabric both in Jamaica and abroad has been reinforced in films featuring Jamaican gangsters and Jamaican popular music.[25] The texts I discuss here disrupt this discourse by putting a spotlight on elite crime and by

20 Shover (n 16) 83.

21 Kerrigan and Sookoo (n 4) 158.

22 See Paula Morgan and Valerie Youssef, *Writing Rage: Unmasking Violence through Caribbean Discourse* (University of the West Indies Press 2006); Faith Smith, 'Introduction: Sexing the citisen', in Faith Smith (ed), *Sex and the Citisen: Interrogating the Caribbean* (University of Virginia Press 2011).

23 Michael Levi and Nicholas Lord, 'White-Collar and Corporate Crime', in Alison Leibling, Maruna Shadd and Lesley McAra (eds), *Oxford Handbook of Criminology* (OUP 2017) 723.

24 Kerrigan and Sookoo (n 4) 161.

25 Rivke Jaffe, 'Crime Watch: Mediating belonging and the politics of place in inner-city Jamaica', in Hannah Jones and Emma Jackson (eds), *Stories of Cosmopolitan Belonging: Emotion and Location* (Routledge 2014) 163.

demonstrating its pervasiveness, its significant social and economic costs, and its overlaps with organised crime.

The political thriller and white collar crime

Key features of thrillers are that, first, they are structured around a conflict between 'hero' and 'conspiracy', wherein the 'plot – the story – is the process by which the hero averts the conspiracy';[26] second, through this structure, they 'thrill' by generating emotional intensity or 'overload' in readers or viewers;[27] third, they convey a 'world gone awry' and 'off-balance', which the protagonist must find a way to navigate.[28] According to Castrillo, political thrillers adhere to all these conventions, but what distinguishes the political thriller from other types of thriller is that the central conflict it dramatises pits an individual protagonist against 'political and/or corporate power'.[29] The political thriller subgenre therefore to some extent lends itself to the topic of white collar crime.

In other ways, the thriller mode seems incompatible with this subject matter. White collar crime is 'rarely dramatic', and the thriller narrative needs to be dramatic to fulfil its function of generating emotional intensity in readers or viewers.[30] Specifically, it relies on scenes of fast paced action and graphic violence to create drama. The harms resulting from white collar crime extend beyond physical violence, causing emotional as well as physiological trauma in victims and destabilising societies by impeding economic development, damaging social harmony, and undermining public trust in governments and corporations.[31] This raises the question of whether the thriller's formal requirements therefore render it unsuitable as a means of conveying the full complexity of white collar crime's characteristics and impact.

However, rather than focus on how far the political thriller subgenre is – in general – either aligned or at odds with the topic of white collar crime, my aim here is to emphasise its versatility, looking at various ways in which writers and filmmakers have adapted and remodelled the thriller format in order to accommodate this subject matter. In her analysis of three political thrillers set in Jamaica, Mordecai argues that popular fiction can 'interrupt, and potentially reformulate the discursive field surrounding critical conjunctures like the Jamaican 1970s'.[32]

26 Jerry Palmer, *Thrillers: Genesis and Structure of a Popular Genre* (Edward Arnold 1978) 53, 67.

27 Martin Rubin, *Thrillers* (Cambridge University Press 1999) 6.

28 Pablo Castrillo, 'Towards a Narrative Definition of the American Political Thriller Film' (2015) 28 (4) *Communication and Society* 109, 112.

29 Castrillo (n 27) 120.

30 Pontell (n 5) 42.

31 Dylan Kerrigan, 'White-Collar Crime is Violent Crime' *Trinidad and Tobago Guardian* (1 April 2013); Kerrigan and Sookoo (n 4) 156.

32 Rachel L. Mordecai, 'Reading the Jamaican 1970s as Political Thriller: Lessons from pop fiction' (2019) 23 (1) Small Axe 62, 63.

A similar case can be made, I suggest, for the capacity of popular fiction and film – and in particular the political thriller – to reframe white collar crime, opening up new ways of seeing and understanding this phenomenon both within and beyond the Caribbean.

David Hare's *Turks and Caicos*: the Caribbean as a 'home for dirty money'

Turks and Caicos is the second in a trilogy of films written and directed by David Hare, a white British playwright, screenwriter, and director. The film's protagonist, a white British man named Johnny Worricker, has moved to the Turks and Caicos Islands to elude his former employer, MI5. Focusing on the ethically and legally questionable activities of wealthy American and European business executives, the film reflects on the fallout of both the 9/11 terror attacks and the 2008 global financial meltdown. A company called Gladstone International is shown to be profiting from the escalating demand for security in the USA following 9/11 and is investing money made from building detention camps all over the world in exclusive hotels on Turks and Caicos Islands. In connection with this, a UK-based organisation called The Bridge, posing as a charitable foundation, has been set up as a holding account for the same funds, which will finance the British prime minister's future career when he steps down from office.

The global financial meltdown is a key reference point in *Turks and Caicos*, which was written, directed, and set in its wake. The financial crisis caused grave socioeconomic harm in many countries, triggering the worst economic recession since the Great Depression in the 1930s. The background to the crisis is that subprime mortgages were given to applicants without appropriate assets, and bankers subsequently turned them into securities that were marketed globally as low risk investments.[33] Criminologists writing on the causes and effects of the crisis contend that fraud committed in the mortgage and investment banking industries brought about the financial meltdown and that despite the unprecedented scale of its damage, it resulted in few criminal prosecutions.[34]

In *Turks and Caicos*, the keynote talk of Sterling Rogers, founder of The Bridge, at an international financial colloquium, makes a direct reference to the global recession: 'We meet at a dangerous time when a setback in the financial markets has been misrepresented as a crisis in the engine-room of capitalism itself.' In another scene, he shows a colleague a graph with an ascending curve

33 Mark Button and Martin Tunley, 'The 2008 Financial Crisis and Fraud: The roles of immoral phlegmatism, deviancy attenuation and de-labelling', in Nicholas Ryder, Jon Tucker and Umut Turksen (eds), *The Financial Crisis and White Collar Crime – Legislative and Policy Responses: A Critical Assessment* (Routledge 2017) 7.

34 Pontell, Black and Geis (n 9); Spencer Headworth and John L. Hagen 'White-Collar Crimes of the Financial Crisis', in Shanna R. Van Slyke, Michael L. Benson and Francis T. Cullen (eds), *The Oxford Handbook of White-Collar Crime* (OUP 2016); Button and Tunley (n 32).

and reflects that there is 'nothing more beautiful' than 'money going to work'. The film therefore indicates that the 2008 meltdown and subsequent recession has not put a stop to the culture of relentless profit making that preceded it. After Worricker works with Pellissier, an undercover CIA agent, to expose the illegality of the activities of Gladstone International and The Bridge, there is a swift financial settlement rather than any talk of legal investigation or prosecution. The film thus reflects on both the culpability of financial organisations and the failure of governments to hold them accountable for their actions.

Turks and Caicos engages directly and critically with the phenomenon of white collar crime, foregrounding its relative invisibility, its prevalence, and its extensive damage. Yet the question remains as to how well the political thriller format works in service of the film's sharp social commentary. In some ways, the film conforms to political thriller conventions: it is structured around a conflict between a lone 'hero' – a rogue MI5 agent – and a 'conspiracy', and the narrative charts that hero's exposure of the conspiracy.[35] In addition, the hero-protagonist confronts and challenges political and corporate power. The film also reinforces the thriller's reputation as grounded in the 'master-discourse' of 'masculinity';[36] the protagonist is male and heterosexual, and although there is an attempt at progressive gender politics in the film's critical presentation of business executives as sexual predators, this is undermined by Worricker's characterisation as charming and universally attractive to women. However, the film's slow pace and its prioritising of conversation over action limits its success as a thriller.[37] There is one murder, but it happens off screen. There are no acts of violence, no weapons, and no car chases. Instead of relying on depictions of violent crime as a means of stimulating anxiety and excitement in viewers, Hare attempts to generate dramatic tension through his portrayal of white collar crime. For example, in one scene an undercover agent walks through dark empty streets to meet covertly with another agent and show him the graph representing Sterling Rogers' profits, and dramatic music accompanies another scene where Worricker, alone in his house, circles numbers on a spreadsheet. Ultimately, the film's structure as a sequence of long and involved conversations, and its overt political agenda, give precedence to the cerebral over the visceral.

The status of some Caribbean islands as offshore tax havens is well known and has a long history.[38] This has been illuminated by the recent Paradise Papers

35 Palmer (n 25) 53, 67.

36 Tony Davies, 'The Divided Gaze: Reflections on the political thriller', in Derek Longhurst (ed.), *Gender, Genre, and Narrative Pleasure* (Unwin Hyman 1989) 133.

37 See John Grace, 'Turks and Caicos; Arena; Whatever happened to Spitting Image? TV review', *The Guardian* (21 March 2014), https://www.theguardian.com/tv-and-radio/2014/mar/21/turks-caicos-tv-review-bill-nighy#comment-33372159, accessed 18 June 2020. Multiple readers' comments on this review criticise *Turks and Caicos* for its lack of 'thrills', 'suspense', 'twists and turns', 'dramatic tension' and 'urgency'.

38 See Sean Patrick Griffin, 'Caribbean Islands', in Lawrence M. Salinger (ed), *Encyclopedia of White-Collar and Corporate Crime* (Volume 1, Sage 2005).

scandal, a leak in 2017 of 13.4 million files that exposed how multinational corporations and high profile individuals based all over the world have been making use of offshore tax havens in various Caribbean countries.[39] The secrecy surrounding offshore havens, enhanced by the development of new technologies, situates them on the boundary between legality and illegality. The Caribbean is presented in *Turks and Caicos* as a locale in which crime can be committed with impunity by Europeans and Americans. A local policeman explains to Worricker that Gladstone International is based in Turks and Caicos for 'tax purposes' and later tells him: 'Down on my level, I keep coming across people who think that murder is a minor crime.' As a British overseas territory, Turks and Caicos falls under British jurisdiction but uses American currency. As a result, it is a place in which British colonial governance and US neocolonial influence intersects. The policeman's comments – and particularly his words 'down on my level' – shed light on the racial and class hierarchies that structure society on these islands, where wealthy white foreigners have such a strong sense of entitlement that they believe they can literally get away with murder, among other things. Pelissier's later description of Turks and Caicos as 'a home for dirty money' reinforces this idea that the islands enable and conceal elite crimes. This perception of Caribbean islands as 'tropical playgrounds' for the rich – also seen in the contemporary marketing of them as tourist destinations – echoes the sense of licence experienced by European colonial planters, who similarly transgressed the social and moral codes of Victorian England (Sheller 2004).[40]

While the title *Turks and Caicos* might seem to suggest that the identity of Caribbean islands is central to the film, Turks and Caicos serves as little more than a scenic backdrop against which a post-9/11 and post-financial crisis drama focusing on the UK and the USA, and the relationship between them, plays out. The film's portrayal of the Caribbean never extends beyond the image of an island paradise offered in its opening scene, where Worricker sits relaxing in a deckchair, first gazing at a sparkling aquamarine sea and pure white sand and then smiling at passing (white) women in bikinis. This image would not be out of place on the website promoting Sandals, a chain of upmarket all-inclusive hotels that spans the archipelago.[41] Indeed, reviewers have commented on the film's input into the marketing of Caribbean tourist destinations, one noting that Turks and Caicos' 'tourism bureau should send the production a large fruit basket'.[42] Hare's film presents Turks and Caicos as a place where there is nothing happening of interest

39 Nick Hopkins and Helena Bengtsson, 'What Are the Paradise Papers and What Do they Tell Us?' *The Guardian* (5 November 2017), https://www.theguardian.com/news/2017/nov/05/what-are-the-paradise-papers-and-what-do-they-tell-us accessed, 13 June 2020.

40 Mimi Sheller 'Natural Hedonism: The invention of Caribbean islands as tropical playgrounds', in Sandra Courtman (ed), *Beyond the Blood, the Beach and the Banana: New Perspectives in Caribbean Studies* (Ian Randle 2004).

41 Sandals website https://www.sandals.co.uk/, accessed 13 June 2020.

42 Brian Lowry, 'TV Review: Worricker trilogy: Masterpiece's 'Turks & Caicos', 'Salting the Battlefield', Variety (6 November 2014), https://variety.com/2014/tv/reviews/tv-review

except the suspicious activities of foreign business executives. The film thus reinforces the erasure of Caribbean islands enacted by the tourism industry.

Turks and Caicos recognises the criminality of the tourism industry only in terms of its connection to money laundering. The hotel that owns 'a large chunk of the island' is financed by unsavoury enterprises such as the building of detention camps. The film's moral outrage is directed towards the profits made from the US-led war on terror that have been channelled into tourism, rather than towards the tourism industry in itself. With its focus how the US economy has been 'ripped off' by the finance sector, *Turks and Caicos* overlooks global tourism's longstanding and ongoing theft from Caribbean island economies. The film is incisive in its critique of the socioeconomic inequity generated by offshore tax havens, which the CIA agent Pelissier describes as 'vaults of private wealth' that could be used to 'write off the world's debt in a day, in an hour, in a minute'. Yet it fails to address the structural inequalities generated by colonial and neocolonial power relations. What is more, it perpetuates those inequalities by actively contributing to the branding of the Caribbean as paradise islands that has made the region so profitable for Europe and the USA.

D. N. Wong Ken's *The Runnings*: fraud in the construction and tourism industries

The Runnings is set in Jamaica's capital city, Kingston, in the early 21st century. Like its author, the novel's protagonist, Brandon Chong, is a Chinese Jamaican lawyer specialising in commercial law. It centres on the underhand and often illegal financial dealings of powerful political leaders and business executives. The book's title refers both to the mechanisms of Jamaican politics and to the workings of Jamaica's criminal underworld, while also hinting at the convergences between these. Although the characters and events in the novel are fictional, *The Runnings* offers insights into Jamaica's divisive political culture, and into the complicated relationship between government, law enforcement, and criminal organisations under neoliberalism. Political violence in Jamaica dates back to the formation of the two main political parties, the Jamaican Labour Party (JLP) and the People's National Party (PNP) in the 1940s. Following the 1962 election, party political antagonism was transformed through both parties' partisan distribution of benefits including housing, jobs (particularly in the construction of new housing schemes), and weapons. This was linked to the creation of 'garrisons', described by Meeks as 'militarised inner-city communities that held allegiance to one or other of the dominant parties and ensured almost monolithic single-party voting on election day'.[43] These garrisons were controlled by criminal leaders,

-worricker-trilogy-masterpieces-turks-caicos-salting-the-battlefield-1201342866/, accessed 13 June 2020.

43 Brian Meeks, *Envisioning Caribbean Futures: Jamaican Perspectives* (University of the West Indies Press 2007) 69.

known as dons, who distributed the benefits and guaranteed, through violence, that community members voted for the right party.[44]

This system of political clientelism, which continued through the 1960s and 1970s, generated close ties between the political machinery and organised crime. These ties continued into the 21st century but the relationship between politicians and dons changed. While Sives focuses in her analysis of these decades on the growing empowerment of criminal actors and the corresponding disempowerment of the state in the context of economic recession, neoliberal structural adjustment, and the expansion of transnational drug trafficking,[45] Jaffe identifies the emergence of a 'hybrid state', suggesting that the links between politicians and dons can be understood as an 'illicit form of public-private partnership that emerged in the context of neoliberalization'.[46] Most commentators agree that connections between criminal actors and state agents have undermined the capacity of governments to address crime and corruption and that this, in turn, places in question the integrity and legitimacy of the state and its political and legal institutions.[47]

In *The Runnings*, the positioning of the government on the boundary between legality and illegality is a central concern. The novel begins with an attempt on Chong's life arranged by a senior government minister, Brian Ebanks. Chong had been advising on a legal case against the Jamaican Housing Corporation (JHC). The JHC had awarded a low income housing project to the St Thomas Industrial Providence Society, which 'in turn sub-contracted out the work' to Confab Construction Company (54). A man called Nicholas Swaby had employed Chong to investigate after he had put in a bid for the contract and had it turned down because of 'wrong politics' (55). Swaby was later 'accidentally' killed in a car accident. Following Swaby's death, Chong goes to the construction site only to find out that no building work has been done for the past seven months and suspects that a lucrative contract has been given by Ebanks to Confab in exchange for securing votes for Ebanks and protecting his party's interests. It is later revealed that Ebanks has developed a 'blueprint' for funding the party's 2002 election campaign, which involves substantial government contracts being awarded to contractors loyal to the party and 15% of the contract being returned to the party as donations (334–5).

44 For a full account of the history of garrison politics in Jamaica, see Amanda Sives, *Elections, Violence and the Democratic Process in Jamaica 1944–2007* (Ian Randle 2010).

45 Amanda Sives 'A Calculated Assault on the Authority of the State? Crime, politics and extradition in 21st century Jamaica' (2012) 58 *Crime, Law and Social Change* 415, 425.

46 Jaffe (n 24) 736.

47 See Obika Gray, *Demeaned But Empowered: The Social Power of the Urban Poor in Jamaica* (University of the West Indies Press 2004) 7–8; Lloyd Waller and Anthony Harriott 'Political Corruption and Organised Crime', in Anthony Harriott, *Organised Crime and Politics in Jamaica: Breaking the Nexus* (University of the West Indies Press 2008) 117; Sives (n 44) 415–6.

The narrator situates this example of fraud in government and the construction industry in relation to a history of state–corporate corruption; Ebanks' scheme succeeds multiple similar schemes within the government's housing programme. The corruption does not end with Ebanks either, since Prime Minister Hugh Robertson and his inner circle set up another lucrative scheme relating to casino building. They buy land cheaply through the Financial Services Adjustment Company (FINSAC), which was 'established by the government to rescue the banking sector from collapse' after a financial crisis in the 1990s (256). Since the debt taken on by FINSAC was 'a loss that the taxpayer would ultimately have to repay' (256), Robertson's casino building scheme involves theft of taxpayers' money. Robertson and his associates rationalise their illegal actions – which include not only fraud but also the murder of Ebanks to prevent him exposing the scheme – in terms of cost efficiency.

In its illustration of financial crime at the top level of government, the novel comments on the problems ingrained in a parliamentary system inherited from Britain where every 'significant administrative and executive position […] could find their appointments rooted in the prime minister', leading to a situation where 'the Office of the Prime Minister had become accountable to no one' (146–7).[48] As in *Turks and Caicos*, the members of the political and business elite implicated in fraud, corruption, and even murder are not brought to trial. It is suggested, in fact, that their crimes may not even curtail their careers, when Robertson says to his inner circle: '[S]ome of you will want another shot at being elected into Government. The Jamaican people have short memories.' (367)

The Runnings locates both Ebanks' misuse of government contracts and Robertson's casino building enterprise in relation to a longer history of white collar crime dating back to colonial times. Wong Ken draws attention to parallels between the workings of government in colonial and postcolonial Jamaica, linking the 'nepotism and cronyism' of the colonial governors, which operated 'along class lines', to the partisan awarding of government contracts in the post-independence period (334–5). In this way, *The Runnings* demonstrates how in the Caribbean region, 'newly emergent nations are mostly left with the corrupt, white-collar apparatus of the colonial state as the foundation of the post-colonial state'.[49] The novel conveys how the race and class hierarchies of plantation society persist into the country's post-independence present. For example, when Ebanks summons Wappy, an influential don who has been working for him on attempts to assassinate Chong, they meet in a building that, although it 'would not qualify as a great house', was 'in former days the property of some well-to-do landed gentry' (238). When Ebanks greets him 'sitting at one end of an old, mahogany six-seated dining table' (238), the weight of the island's history of empire and

48 Waller and Harriott note that corruption in Jamaica emerges from the 'Westminster parliamentary system inherited from Britain, which operates as a form of "authoritarian-democratic rule"' (n 47) 128.

49 Kerrigan (n 30).

plantation slavery – embodied by the heavy mahogany table – underpins Ebanks' position of power. A common feature in plantation great houses, mahogany furniture was produced across the Caribbean at the cost of many enslaved people's blood and hardship.[50] This history is invoked again when, following their meeting, Ebanks gives orders for Wappy to be tortured and then killed.

The Runnings adheres closely to the conventions of the classic thriller. The narrative is fast paced and action packed. Reviewers' descriptions of the novel as 'riveting', 'electrifying', 'irresistable', 'thrilling', 'spellbinding', 'visceral', and 'gripping' suggest that it has fulfilled the thriller's basic function of generating emotional intensity in readers.[51] In contrast with Hare's sidelining of acts of violence in *Turks and Caicos*, physical violence – graphically portrayed – is central to Wong Ken's narrative. The many explicit sex scenes, always involving Chong and sometimes featuring two women, play a similar role to the scenes of violent conflict in reinforcing the protagonist's prowess and virility. In both, there is a focus on mental and physical power and control. Both sex and violence are unashamedly glamorised in the novel, and Chong features as a Bond-like figure, indomitable and indefatigable in both contexts. The novel therefore complies fully with the 'standard masculinism' of the thriller genre.[52] Furthermore, *The Runnings* adopts the thriller's familiar narrative structure, dramatising a tension between 'hero' and 'conspiracy';[53] Chong is presented as a lone figure faced with a conspiracy involving senior members of government, law enforcement, and industry.

However, the novel's thriller components are spliced with sociopolitical critique, and Wong Ken locates the narrative geographically, culturally, and historically. The first paragraph situates the novel's action within Jamaica's physical and cultural environment through reference to both the 'sweltering, mid-morning heat' and the 'distinctive thumping of reggae music float[ing] from somewhere' (1). *The Runnings* also incorporates long passages on, for example, the legacies of Michael Manley's vision of democratic socialism and its connection to Cold War politics in the 1970s (12), the history of the Chinese in Jamaica (11– 13), the origins of the Jamaican state's abuse of power (138–9), garrison politics in Jamaica (35–6, 150–1), and Jamaica's parliamentary system (146–7). As well as embedding Wong Ken's characters and plot within the specifics of Jamaican society, politics, and history, these passages slow the narrative down, working against thriller genre's characteristic 'urgent forward motion'.[54] The pace is slowed further by Wong Ken's frequent use of footnotes to provide readers with context and to translate Jamaican patois words into American English.

50 See Jennifer L. Anderson, *Mahogany: The Costs of Luxury in Early America* (Harvard University Press 2012).

51 Tony Robinson, Kevin O'Brien Chang and Alton Morgan, reviews of *The Runnings* quoted in D. N. Wong Ken *The Runnings: A Novel* (Alternative Energy Limited 2003) n.p.

52 Mordecai (n 31) 63.

53 Palmer (n 25) 53.

54 Mordecai (n 31) 67.

The Runnings draws attention to the pervasiveness of white collar crime, its invisibility, and its devastating impact on individuals and societies. Wong Ken also positions his portrayal of elite crime in relation to Jamaica's history of colonialism and slavery, its decades of partisan politics, and the neoliberal turn in the global political economy. His merging of the genres of political thriller and 'social document' is crucial in enabling him to work with the concept of white collar crime.[55] *The Runnings* distorts the thriller format to create space for detailed social and political commentary, but not so far as to render it unrecognisable as a political thriller. As a result, Wong Ken manages to engage with the complexity of white collar crime's contexts, causes and effects without losing momentum.

Esther Figueroa's *Limbo*: white collar crime and the environment

Esther Figueroa is a Jamaican activist, filmmaker, and novelist. Her novel *Limbo* highlights the harmful activities of the tourism and extraction industries. *Limbo*'s protagonist, Flora Smith, is an environmental activist positioned as an investigator figure. Environmental crime has been categorised by criminologists as a form of white collar crime.[56] Figueroa's novel similarly frames environmental harm as white collar crime, while reflecting on its close connections to other forms of white collar crime such as financial crime and state–corporate crime.

This can be seen in Flora's account of a public hearing about the building of an alumina refinery in St Ann, where she was told by 'a friend very highly placed in the Jamaican government' that she should 'be careful' since the bauxite company was 'owned by one of Russia's most dangerous oligarchs'.[57] It is clear from this exchange that the interests of the bauxite mining company are protected by both (Jamaican) state and (Russian) corporate actors. Bauxite mining generates environmental harm through its disposal of toxic waste and resulting air, land, and water pollution. There is an 'absence of adequate legal and regulatory frameworks and enforcement mechanisms' for water and air pollution and waste mishandling in the Caribbean region as compared to in the Global North; a situation that provides multinational corporations with opportunities to engage in activities in Caribbean countries that might be illegal elsewhere.[58] Through her

55 Robinson (n 49) n.p.

56 Croall (n 15) 2; Peter Grabosky, 'Globalisation and White-Collar Crime', in Sally S. Simpson and David Weisburd (eds), *The Criminology of White-Collar Crime* (Springer 2009) 136; Peter Gottschalk and Lars Gunnesdal, *White-Collar Crime in the Shadow Economy: Lack of Detection, Investigation and Conviction Compared to Social Security Fraud* (Springer 2018) 4.

57 Esther Figueroa, *Limbo: A Novel About Jamaica* (Arcade 2014) 4. All future references to this edition will be marked in parentheses.

58 Sherrie L. Baver and Barbara Deutsch Lynch, 'The Political Ecology of Paradise', in Baver and Deutsch Lynch (eds.), *Beyond Sun and Sand: Caribbean Environmentalisms* (Rutgers University Press 2006) 5.

portrayal of a multinational bauxite company allowed by the Jamaican state to act with impunity, Figueroa presents environmental harm as state–corporate crime.

The novel opens with a case of sand theft at the construction site of a future luxury beach resort, which Flora is asked to look into by a wealthy Jamaican businessman, Malcolm Krenshaw. In its dramatisation of this case, *Limbo* illustrates how environmental harm is intertwined with other forms of crime and violence. The apparent crime of sand theft is staged by Krenshaw and his associates, whose new 'ten-billion-dollar' development had already failed due to risky financial investments and the collapse of 'pyramid schemes' in the wake of the global financial meltdown (87). They had arranged for their own sand to be stolen so that they could claim insurance on the development. Furthermore, Krenshaw's friend Baxter is involved, in partnership with 'Kid Capone, the number one Mobay Don', who controls the whole coast and the politicians (87), and the unfinished construction site, reduced to a 'wasteland of naked land, razed mangroves, dumped wetlands [...] unfinished buildings and random strewn construction materials', has become 'also conveniently a transhipment point for drugs and guns' (73). Cliff, a diver trying to get footage of coral transplantation taking place in the same location, is killed when he stumbles on these activities.

The details of this multi-layered case raise the question of whether these are separate activities that happen to be taking place in the same location or whether they are interconnected. It is possible that the transformation of the beach, mangrove forest, and surrounding area into an uninhabited 'wasteland' has created ideal conditions for organised crime. However, Flora wonders whether, in fact, 'drug trafficking, gun running, and money laundering [has] always been part of the enterprise' (73). Luxury resort developments may create opportunities for organised crime, but perhaps, she implies here, the commodification of Jamaica's beaches as valuable real estate has always involved shady dealings. As Mason, the lawyer initially assigned to the case, explains to Flora, the tourism industry is a 'good ploy' for money laundering at both national and international levels (87). That Mason has to leave the island, having been pressured to do so 'on the highest authority' (88), and that the sand theft case has not been reassigned, indicates the limitations of the country's justice system in dealing with elite crime.

Featuring dons and gunmen operating alongside and in collaboration with developers, investors, and politicians, Figueroa's novel comments on the fine line between legitimate government and business enterprises and criminal activity. It also explores parallels between contemporary white collar crime and Jamaica's history of colonialism and slavery. Contemplating the damage that will be done by a prospective limestone mining project, Flora reflects: 'The owner was rumoured to be a well-known criminal. But aren't most large landowners, whether from past days of plantation slavery to current days of dons, drug lords, Ponzi schemers, and politicians on the take?' (69). A later scene featuring a public hearing about the project situates the contemporary environmental exploitation of the island in direct relationship to its colonial history. Flora's friend Milton, an investigative journalist, challenges the hollow rhetoric of the government and chamber of commerce representatives:

> [I]t's a damn disgrace that our government permits the digging up of our resources to send off to the richest country in the world. Let them dig up their own backyard. Haven't we learned anything? Are we still slaves or are we a sovereign independent nation?
>
> (81–2)

Milton's comment lays bare the echoes of the colonial past – when Jamaica was a profitable slave colony – in the contemporary dynamics of neocolonial resource extraction. Both then and now, Jamaica functions as a source of wealth for the Global North; *Limbo* presents environmental crime as central to the success of both colonial plantation agriculture and the contemporary mining and tourism industries. In both contexts, environmental harm is 'a necessary by-product of commercial profit and capital accumulation'.[59]

Limbo starts out as a political thriller. As Flora gets caught up in the intrigue surrounding the sand theft case, she is presented as a heroic individual confronting political and corporate power. The questions of who killed Cliff and why initially propel the narrative forward, and the sense of danger characteristic of the thriller emerges when Flora's lover Jerome, to her consternation, embarks on a mission to confront Cliff's killer. However, apart from a throwaway comment that she 'doesn't relish the thought of gunmen barging into her home and killing her' (74), Flora does not spend time fearing for her life. In fact, the political thriller's tendency to subject the protagonist – and by extension, readers – to 'states of fear, anxiety, and even paranoia' is parodied early on in the novel.[60] Flora remembers that after a high ranking politician had warned her about her safety, her attempts at vigilance were half hearted; she had stopped examining her car for bombs because 'she had no idea what she was to look for' and 'the last time she had ripped the seam of her pants.' (4)

If the novel's darkly comic tone is at odds with thriller conventions, Flora's gender also complicates the hero versus conspiracy format. In *The Runnings*, the thrill of physical combat is repeatedly and explicitly associated with the thrill of sexual conquest. By contrast, in *Limbo*, scenes of graphic violence convey not bodily harm but a ravaged island. Correspondingly, while sex scenes are by no means absent from *Limbo*, the novel looks beyond (hetero)sexual conquest and explores a variety of relationships – romantic, platonic, and familial – which take differing forms and, in many cases, resist a masculinist and heteronormative scripting of gender and sexuality. *Limbo* therefore disrupts the thriller genre's well-established and enduring 'masculine codes'.[61]

Limbo also resists thriller conventions in its narrative form. The pace of the narrative is progressively slowed by long passages focusing on themes of belonging,

59 Reece Walters, 'Eco Crime', in John Muncie, Deborah Talbot and Reece Walters (eds), *Crime: Local and Global* (Willan 2009) 174.

60 Castrillo (n 27) 112.

61 Davies (n 35) 132.

community, and conviviality. Towards the end, just when readers might expect the novel to move towards a moment of denouement and regain its focus on the circumstances surrounding Cliff's death, the illness and death of Flora's close friend and mentor Milton derails the novel's thriller plot, sending Flora and Jerome on what she refers to as her 'Milton Pilgrimage' (206), a trip around the island scattering his ashes. Their disorienting journey along mountain roads that 'curve and twist' and go 'up and down' (208) reflects how at this point in the novel the narrative has also gone off course. At the novel's close, Cliff's killer is neither identified nor brought to justice.

Working against the sensationalism of media soundbites, the novel's meandering final section accommodates the long-term, 'incremental', 'accretive', and 'open ended' temporalities of 'slow violence' as defined by Nixon.[62] This is in keeping with the forms of environmental harm that Flora and Jerome encounter on their circuitous journey around the island, such as coastal erosion, the destruction of ecosystems, and the spreading of toxic waste. Yet the novel also confronts readers with scenes of environmental violence that have a spectacular immediacy, such as the 'gaping pits' left by bauxite mining (70). Additionally, environmental crime is shown to be enmeshed with other forms of crime, including homicide, fraud, money laundering, and drugs and arms trafficking. The novel's uneven pace and inconsistent adherence to thriller conventions reflects the complexity of its subject matter; for Figueroa, the topic of white collar crime necessitates a radical reworking of the thriller format.

Conclusion

All three of the texts discussed here, in foregrounding the topic of white collar crime, counter its relative invisibility in the media, popular culture, criminological scholarship, and official crime records and statistics. In different ways, they highlight its prevalence, and its capacity to harm individuals and societies, and cripple economies. In doing so, they debunk the longstanding myth of white collar crime as 'generally victimless, less immediate, and non-violent'.[63] Additionally, they blur the boundaries between white collar crime and organised crime. Finally, in portraying situations where crimes do not result in trials, let alone convictions, these texts emphasise how governments and justice systems, as well as corporations, play a key role in facilitating white collar crime.

Davies claims that the thriller's 'unravellings' necessarily take place 'within the terms and along the grain of the dominant popular codes – sexist, imperialist [and] racist – of masculinity and Englishness'.[64] *Turks and Caicos* operates in line with these codes: its protagonist is a white British man whose appeal

62 Rob Nixon, *Slow Violence and the Environmentalism of the Poor* (Harvard University Press 2011) 2, 6.
63 Kerrigan and Sookoo (n 4) 153.
64 Davies (n 35) 133.

to women is repeatedly emphasised, and the film's critique of capitalism stops short of examining the neocolonial dimensions of the tourism industry in the Caribbean. However, *The Runnings* and *Limbo* both explicitly situate white collar crime in relation to Jamaica's imperial past. Wong Ken's and Figueroa's portrayal of elite crime is also informed by a keen awareness of Jamaica's enduring racially inflected class hierarchies. Yet Wong Ken's endorsement of masculine power and dominance through his characterisation of Chong limits what he can achieve in his critique of politicians' and business executives' abuse of power. By contrast, Figueroa offers a gendered critique of the institutional and corporate cultures that facilitate white collar crime. She thus positions her narrative against the grain of the 'sexist, imperialist, and racist' codes viewed by Davies as fundamental to the thriller genre.

Criminologists have emphasised that there is a lot at stake in conceptualising white collar crime, since the way in which it is defined affects how it is perceived and understood, how it is represented across various media, how it is researched and analysed, and how it is dealt with (or not) by criminal justice systems.[65] Discussion and analysis of aesthetic modes such as fiction and film can contribute to ongoing debates surrounding the definition of white collar crime and in doing so can help to enhance its visibility both within scholarly discourse and in the public domain. While most researchers working with an offender-based definition position white collar crime within a framework of social inequality, focusing on class-based privilege, status, and wealth as key contributing factors, my analysis of fiction and film by Hare, Wong Ken, and Figueroa has illustrated the need to look beyond these class-based factors when analysing the particularities of this phenomenon in the Caribbean, considering too how the causes, characteristics, perceptions, and treatment of white collar crime are impacted by the power dynamics of race, gender, and sexuality and how the history of capitalist exploitation in the region has shaped contemporary white collar offending. Given the increasingly global dimensions of white collar crime, this approach is applicable not just to the Caribbean, but to all countries and regions.

65 Benson, Slyke and Cullen (n 8) ix–x; Levi and Lord (n 24) 2017.

10 Deferred prosecution agreements

A soft touch?

Oliver Charles[1] *and Umut Turksen*[2]

The origins of deferred prosecution agreements (DPAs) can be traced back to the early 1900s in the USA, when juveniles were put on probation for minor offences until they met their probation conditions (short of a prison sentence) whereby they would not be labelled as criminals for the rest of their lives as adults.[3] In contrast to the early use of DPAs, the contemporary use of DPAs is not reserved for vulnerable members of society, but often for rich and powerful companies that have the means to pay the fines and penalties (a common feature of DPAs today).

While the concept of corporate criminal liability was established a long time ago, it was not until the second half of the 20th century when prosecutors decided to utilise pre-trial diversion procedures[4] that have come to be known as DPAs or non-prosecution agreements (NPAs).[5] For instance, in the USA, the Supreme Court in the case of *New York Central Railroad Company vs United*

1 Oliver P. Charles, solicitor and PhD candidate at the Centre for Financial and Corporate Integrity, Coventry University.

2 Professor Umut Turksen Centre for Financial and Corporate Integrity Coventry University, UK Centre for Financial and Corporate Integrity, Coventry University.

3 Eugene Illovsky 'Corporate Deferred Prosecution Agreements' (2006) 21 *Criminal Justice* 36.

4 The US DOJ Office of Attorneys defines pre-trial diversion procedure as 'an alternative to prosecution which seeks to divert certain offenders from traditional criminal justice processing into a program of supervision and services administered by the US Probation Service [...] In the majority of cases, offenders are diverted at the pre-charge stage. Participants who successfully complete the program will not be charged or, if charged, will have the charges against them dismissed; unsuccessful participants are returned for prosecution.' DOJ Pretrial Diversion Programme 9-22.000, https://www.justice.gov/jm/jm-9-22000-pretrial-diversion-program, accessed 30 April 2020.

5 DPAs involve the filing of charges in federal court, as would occur if the prosecutor were taking the case to trial. 'With a DPA, the prosecutor and the corporation agree that although the prosecutor will charge the corporation in federal court, the prosecutor will defer the continued prosecution of the charges until the end of a certain period of time agreed upon by both parties. If, at the end of the term of the agreement, the corporation has followed through on its obligations, the prosecutor will dismiss the charges.' NPAs are not filed in federal courts. See Cindy Alexander and Mark Cohen *Trends in the Use of Non-Prosecution, Deferred Prosecution, and Plea Agreements in the Settlement of Alleged Corporate Criminal Wrongdoing*, April 2015 Searle Civil Justice Institute 8, https://masonlec.org/site/rte_uploads/files/Full%20Report%20-%20SCJI%20NPA-DPA%2C%20April%202015%281%29.pdf, accessed 30 April 2020.

DOI: 10.4324/9781003020813-11

States established corporate criminal liability as early as 23 February 1909, when it held that 'corporations can commit crimes which consist in purposely doing things prohibited by statute, and in such case they can be charged with knowledge of acts of their agents who act within the authority conferred upon them.'[6] This jurisprudence opened the route for many other subsequent corporate criminal liability cases[7] particularly in the 1970s, yet DPAs as an enforcement measure were not codified and used in the USA until the 1990s.[8] Subsequent expansion of the use of DPAs has not only seen an increase in their numbers but also in the scope of corporate criminal liability, inter alia, antitrust, fraud, domestic bribery, tax evasion, environmental violations, as well as foreign corruption cases.

With their increased utilisation, there also ensued increased criticism. One commentator stated that DPAs 'make a mockery of the criminal justice system by serving as a disturbing wellspring of unfairness, double standards, and potential abuse of power'.[9] Uhlman, meanwhile, asserted that 'deferred prosecution and non-prosecution agreements limit the punitive and deterrent value of the government's law enforcement efforts and extinguish the societal condemnation that should accompany criminal prosecution.'[10] Mokhiber, in contrast, interpreted the increased prominence of DPAs as a development that 'has undermined the general deterrent and adverse publicity impact that results from corporate crime prosecutions and conviction', which 'represents a victory for the forces of big business who for decades have been seeking to weaken or eliminate corporate criminal liability'.[11] The UK introduced DPAs (not NPAs) under the Crime and Courts Act 2013, taking effect in 2014.[12] DPAs initially faced a frosty reception,

6 *New York Central R. Co. v United States*, 212 U.S. 481 (1909).

7 For an overview of prominent cases of corporate criminal liability, see V. P. Nanda 'Corporate Criminal Liability in the United States: Is a new approach warranted?' in Mark Pieth and Radha Ivory (eds.), *Corporate Criminal Liability. Ius Gentium: Comparative Perspectives on Law and Justice* (Springer 2011) vol. 9.

8 In 1994, Prudential Securities was the first DPA that involved a public corporation or other major company. See Alexander and Cohen (n 5) 7. The *Salomon Brothers Inc.* case in 1992, in contrast, witnessed the first NPA in the USA where the company agreed to pay a $290 million fine. See US DOJ 'Press Release' (14 September 1992), https://www.justice.gov/archive/atr/public/press_releases/1992/211290.htm, accessed 30 April 2020.

9 Peter Reilly 'Justice Deferred is Justice Denied: We must end our failed experiment in deferring corporate criminal prosecutions' (25 September 25 2014); *Brigham Young University Law Review* 2015; Texas A&M University School of Law Legal Studies Research Paper No. 16-24.

10 David Uhlmann 'Deferred Prosecution and Non-Prosecution Agreements and the Erosion of Corporate Criminal Liability; (2013) 72 *Maryland Law Review*, 1295, 1302.

11 Russell Mokhiber 'Corporate Crime Reporter, Speech Delivered at the National Press Club: Crime without conviction: The rise of deferred and non-prosecution agreements' (28 December 2005), www.corporatecrimereporter.com/deferredreport.htm, accessed 30 April 2020.

12 The UK DPA regime is supplemented by a Code of Practice of the Crown Prosecution Service (26 October 2018), https://www.cps.gov.uk/publication/code-crown-prosecutors, accessed 30 April 2020.

particularly from legislators, judges and prosecutors, as such stakeholders have traditionally taken a sceptical, distrustful view of the use of consensual arrangements and compromises (common features of DPAs) to resolve criminal investigations and prosecutions. Furthermore, a number of judges were openly critical not of the DPA regime per se, but the manner in which it was practised. For instance, in the 2018 case of *XYZ DPA* led by the Serious Fraud Office (SFO), the High Court judges stated that the court had 'real reservations' as to the position adopted by the SFO. It was held that the SFO had not only failed to address relevant considerations but had also 'taken into account irrelevant matters; provided inconsistent and inadequate reasons for its decisions; and, applied an incorrect approach to the law'.[13]

Arguably, over the years, as the authorities have gained experience in how to apply DPAs correctly, the mood in the judiciary seems to have taken a turn. For example, Justice William Davis, who approved the UK's fifth DPA, stated that 'critics who allege that deferred prosecution agreements allow big businesses to evade the full force of the law are guilty of misplaced cynicism'.[14] Those in favour of DPAs and NPAs have also argued that these mechanisms 'enable prosecutors to elicit cooperation and thereby lower the real costs of the investigation to the government and potentially to the company'.[15]

While statements on the pros and contras of DPAs continue, DPAs have become a 'must have' tool in the fight against financial crimes as more and more countries around the world seek to bring them into use.[16] However, as with the utilisation of any legal process or sanction, questions should be raised to ensure the veracity of such a mechanism. At the risk of sounding pejorative given the position of the USA as a country that prides itself on its legal system and its application of justice,[17] the question has to be posed as to whether the use of DPAs by US prosecutors against the artificial person of a company is, in fact, enhancing

13 Max Walters 'High Court Slams "Inconsistent" SFO Over DPA' *Law Society Gazette*, 20 April 2018, https://www.lawgazette.co.uk/law/high-court-slams-inconsistent-sfo-over-dpa-/5065772.article, accessed 30 April 2020.

14 Paul Rogerson 'Serco Fraud: Deferred prosecution critics "cynical", says judge', *Law Society Gazette* (4 July 2019), https://www.lawgazette.co.uk/law/serco-fraud-deferred-prosecution-critics-cynical-says-judge/5070871.article, accessed 30 April 2020.

15 Alexander and Cohen (n 5) 17, citing C. C. Thomas 'The Foreign Corrupt Practices Act: A decade of rapid expansion explained, defended, and justified' (2010) 29 *Review of Litigation*, 439, 451–2.

16 The USA, UK, France, Singapore and Australia have DPA mechanisms in place. For a detailed analysis of the paradigm shift in relation to corporate criminal liability and enforcement via DPAs and NPAs, see Barry Pollack and Annie Reisinger 'Lone Wolf or the Start of a New Pack: Should the FCPA guidance represent a new paradigm in evaluating corporate criminal liability risks?' (2014) 51 *American Criminal Law Review*, 121.

17 A study estimated that up to 10,000 people may be wrongfully convicted of serious crimes in the USA each year. This study shows that the USA has the biggest number of wrongful convictions among all common law jurisdictions and beyond. IAFOR 'Investigating Wrongful Convictions around the World' (14 September 2016), https://iafor.org/investigating-wrongful-convictions-around-the-world-alec-klein/, accessed 30 April 2020.

justice when compared to their application by prosecutors in other jurisdictions such as the UK and France.[18] Furthermore, the actual evidence of DPAs in changing corporate behaviours has to be considered in the light of the prosecution record and fines imposed.[19] In regard to this aspect, the chapter provides various insights from the UK, USA and France.

Following perceived criminal activity, DPAs and NPAs are essentially negotiated agreements between commercial organisations and prosecutors that, in return for an admission of misconduct, generally entail financial and other administrative sanctions but fall short of a criminal conviction.[20] These agreements allow prosecutors to 'enforce sanctions against organisations without bringing a case to trial'.[21] They essentially involve one or more of the following elements that must be performed by the entity subjected to a DPA/NPA: an admission of an unlawful act/guilt (or *nolo contendere*); full cooperation with the authorities without delay (e.g. making available all material facts); payment of fines and penalties; improvement of existing business and management processes or implementation of new protocols and policies for better compliance (e.g. enhanced training of staff, self-monitoring, regular independent audits, etc.); an agreement to prosecution if the terms of the DPA are breached; and an agreement to the statement of facts, as well as admission of guilt, to be admissible should the case go to court.[22]

It is worth noting that DPAs are not the same as plea bargaining processes. A plea bargain is a negotiated agreement between the government and a defendant: if the government sees fit to reduce the charges and/or the severity of the

18 The notion of natural justice used in this context is referring to the fact that enshrined within the US constitution of the Bill of Rights and the Sixth Amendment are a set of rights for a fair trial in the USA, which is underpinned also by the concept of the presumption of innocence. However, there are events in USA legal history where the concept of fairness is considered a relative, not an absolute concept, and the state is given latitude to exercise its powers in ways that UK common law lawyers would find an abuse of process. Legal Information Institute, Fair Trial, Cornell Law School, https://www.law.cornell.edu/constitution-conan/amendment-14/section-1/fair-trial, accessed 30 April 2020.

19 Michael Cross 'Fraud Office Under Fire for Deferred Prosecution After "Not guilty" verdicts', *Law Society Gazette* (23 December 2019).

20 Julie O'Sullivan 'How Prosecutors Apply the "Federal Prosecutions of Corporations" Charging Policy in the Era of Deferred Prosecutions, and What That Means for the Purposes of the Federal Criminal Sanction', (2014) 51 *American Criminal Law Review* 30; Wilson Meeks 'Corporate and White-Collar Crime Enforcement: Should regulation and rehabilitation spell an end to corporate criminal liability?' (2006) 40 *Columbia Journal of Law and Social Problems*, 77.

21 Jonathan Grimes, Rebecca Niblock and Lorna Madden 'Corporate Criminal Liability in the UK: The introduction of deferred prosecution agreements, proposals for further change, and the consequences for officers and senior managers', Association of Corporate Counsel, *Practical Law* (2013/14).

22 William Laufer 'Corporate Prosecution, Cooperation, and the Trading of Favours' (2002) 87 *Iowa Law Review*, 643, 645–7.

sentence, the defendant may then agree to plead guilty to the offence/s concerned.[23] Interestingly, it has been demonstrated that DPAs have not diminished the number of plea agreements in the USA. On the contrary, plea agreements have increased in tandem with DPAs over the last decade.[24]

Between 2000 and 2019 only four companies in the UK were prosecuted and convicted by the Serious Fraud Office (SFO) for economic and financial crimes.[25] Within the UK there have historically been problems with pursuing corporate prosecutions for economic and financial crimes, principally due to lack of resources (the Rolls-Royce investigation, which commenced in 2012 and resulted in the 2017 DPA regarding breaches of the Bribery Act 2010, cost £13 million), the difficulty of proving criminal liability (particularly when dealing with complex financial matters before a jury) and the aspect of *mens rea* when a mental element is required in certain cases such as fraud to prove dishonesty.[26] However, in spite of these issues, the government has shown an increasing appetite to achieve greater corporate accountability for what is termed 'white collar crime'.[27] This has led to the introduction of DPAs within the UK under Schedule 17 of the Crime and Courts Act 2013, providing prosecutors with what is 'seen by the Government as a crucial weapon that has been missing from the prosecution's armoury',[28] following which there have been seven DPAs, whereas in the USA between 1993 and 2007 there had been 102 entered into by federal prosecutors alone, while over the following period of 2008 to 2019 this number increased to 439.[29]

23 Michael Petegorsky 'Note, Plea Bargaining in the Dark: The duty to disclose exculpatory Brady evidence during plea bargaining' (2013) 81 *Fordham Law Review*, 3599.

24 Alexander and Cohen (n 5). For a comparative analysis of plea bargaining between the UK and USA, see Juliet Horne *A Plea of Convenience*, https://core.ac.uk/reader/78941985, accessed 30 April 2020.

25 Serious Fraud Office 'Deferred Prosecution Agreements – Guidance, https://www.sfo.gov.uk/publications/guidance-policy-and-protocols/deferred-prosecution-agreements/, accessed 30 April 2020.

26 The Fraud Act 2006, http://www.legislation.gov.uk/ukpga/2006/35/contents, accessed 30 April 2020.

27 The term 'white collar crime' was famously defined by Edwin Sutherland as: '[A] crime committed by a person of respectability and high social status in the course of his occupation [. . .] The present-day white-collar criminals, who are more suave and deceptive than the "robber barons", are represented [. . .] many other merchant princes and captains of finance and industry, and by a host of lesser followers. Their criminality has been demonstrated again and again in the investigations of land offices, rail-ways, insurance, munitions, banking, public utilities, stock exchanges, the oil industry, real estate, reorganization committees, receiverships, bankruptcies, and politics.' Edwin Sutherland White Collar Crime (Dryden 1949) 9. For a more modern interpretation of white collar crime see Nicholas Ryder The Financial Crisis and White-Collar Crime – The Perfect Storm? (Edward Elgar 2014).

28 Grimes et al. (n 21).

29 Anthony Barkow and Rachel Barkow *Prosecutors in the Boardroom: Using Criminal Law to Regulate Corporate Conduct*, 4 (NYU Press 2011); see also Gibson Dunn *2019 Year End Update on Corporate Non-prosecution Agreements and Deferred Prosecution Agreements*, https://www.gibsondunn.com/2019-year-end-npa-dpa-update/, accessed 30 April 2020.

The extension of the use of NPAs/DPAs within the USA was triggered by the Arthur Andersen case in 2002 following what was perceived as the 'Arthur Andersen Effect', which resulted from the defendant exercising its right to a jury trial with the concomitant suffering of 'collateral consequences'.[30] Arthur Andersen LLP was the ill-fated auditor of Enron, which was convicted of obstruction of justice in 2002, resulting in the collapse of the audit business, only to subsequently have the conviction reversed in 2005. The collateral consequences were the suspension of the organisation's public accounting licence, the laying-off of thousands of employees and the collapse of the business. By the time the conviction was reversed, the collateral damage was so advanced as to be irreversible. This led to a reappraisal as to the obligations and duties of prosecutors when pursuing corporate criminal liability as demonstrated by Assistant Attorney General Breuer in 2012 when he stated: 'I personally feel that it is my duty to consider whether individual employees with no responsibility for, or knowledge of, misconduct [...] are going to lose their livelihood if we indict the corporation.'[31] This resulted in a reconsideration of the 'historical binary option' of whether or not to charge when faced with alleged corporate criminal activity being balanced against the social and economic fallout of criminal charges. However, it could be perceived that this light touch approach where these 'kinds of considerations in white collar crime cases that literally keep [Breuer] up at night, and which must play a role in responsible enforcement',[32] is, in fact, a subjugation of the role of justice. This needs to be put any ideology of a commercial imperative of business. One of the arguments often used in favour of DPAs is that companies are able to avoid criminal conviction and the associated reputational harm. However, in light of the current thinking that 'perception is the new truth' and the public nature of DPAs, the reality is that such an argument is not as strong as it may suggest, given that when a company pays a 'fine' of millions of dollars or pounds under a DPA, the public and media draws the inference of corporate guilt.

It is important to recognise that corporate offences exist and must be tackled. Indeed there have been many substantial and high profile cases such as the Rolls-Royce bribery case (UK) of 2017 resulting in a £497,252,645 payment under a

30 FCPA Professor 'RIP "Arthur Andersen Effect" As FedEx Beats Back the DOJ' (17 June 2016), http://fcpaprofessor.com/rip-arthur-andersen-effect-as-fedex-beats-back-the-doj/, accessed 30 April 2020. It is worth noting that following the *Andersen* case in 2003, Deputy US Attorney General Larry Thompson issued a new memorandum on whether to prosecute corporations. This memorandum confirmed the earlier principles of the 1999 Holder memorandum and expressly conferred the possibility of pre-trial diversion agreements (e.g. DPAs) to entities that are willing to cooperate with the authorities: 'In some circumstances, granting a corporation immunity or amnesty or pre-trial diversion may be considered in the course of the government's investigation.' These memoranda are now codified under the US DOJ Manual for Criminal Prosecutors - 9-27.000 – Principles of Federal Prosecution, https://www.justice.gov/jm/jm-9-27000-principles-federal-prosecution#9-27.620, accessed 30 April 2020.

31 FCPA Professor (n 30).

32 Ibid.

DPA[33] and the 2015 filing of charges in Canada against SNC-Lavalin resulting from a multitude of cases including, inter alia: a $10 million bribe to secure the $1.3 billion McGill Hospital contract; the £2.3 million bribery of Fournier to secure the Jacques Cartier Bridge contract; the decade long bribery of Libyan officials ending in 2011, together with the prosecutions of former company officers Riadh Aissa and Pierre Duhalme.[34]

The principles of a DPA are similar in the UK and the USA, however the UK differs in its procedural application, particularly because of the mandatory involvement or the oversight of the courts, hence the UK's DPA regime has been identified as a 'hybrid' DPA regime.[35] In the UK, the DPA must pass through a series of considerations[36] and procedural steps, commencing with an awareness of the potential for a DPA; being triggered through self-reporting, whistleblowing or a prosecutorial investigation. This is followed by the prosecutor inviting the company to enter into DPA negotiations, which, it is envisaged, will then lead to a potential agreement as to the terms of the DPA. Once terms have been agreed the prosecution institutes formal proceedings that are then automatically suspended by the court. Subsequently, the court determines whether the DPA 'is likely to be in the interests of justice', considering whether the terms reached are fair, reasonable and proportionate. If the court upholds the DPA application, then the court makes the DPA terms public.[37] With the court having approved the DPA, as with most other settlements approved in UK courts, if the terms are breached then the court has the discretion to set aside the DPA and lift the suspension of the proceedings. The importance of the judicial involvement was emphasised by Sir Brian Leveson when he stated that 'the court retains control of the ultimate outcome and, if the agreement is not approved, the possibility of prosecution is not jeopardised.'[38] This is an important element of the UK system with regard to ensuring the integrity and the rule of law compliance of DPAs.

DPAs and NPAs have been used in the USA in relation to corporate criminal activity since 1992, when they were first applied in the Salomon Brothers

33 Serious Fraud Office 'Case Information, Rolls-Royce PLC' (23 December 2013), https://www.sfo.gov.uk/cases/rolls-royce-plc/, accessed 30 April 2020.

34 Alan Freeman *Deferred Prosecution Agreement not Right in* SNC-Lavalin *Case*, https://ipolitics.ca/2018/12/14/deferred-prosecution-agreements-not-appropriate-in-snc-lavalin-case/, accessed 30 April 2020.

35 Michel Perez and Alizee Dill 'The Rise of the American Deferred Prosecution Agreement (DPA) and its European Avatars', (2016) *CHRONIQUE/International Financial and White-Collar Crime, Corporate Malfeasance and Compliance*, 2, 48.

36 For example, pursuant to the Crime and Courts Act 2013, Schedule 17 of the Crime and Courts Act 2013, paragraph 7(1), in order for a DPA to be executed, the prosecutor shall apply to the Crown Court and declare that entering into the DPA is 'likely to be in the interests of justice' and that the proposed terms of the agreement are 'fair, reasonable and proportionate'.

37 Grimes (n 21); see also https://www.sfo.gov.uk/cases/rolls-royce-plc/, accessed 30 April 2020.

38 SFO (n 33).

case.[39] This was a unique situation due to the 'unprecedented cooperation' of the defendant.[40] However, following on from this case the Department of Justice (DoJ) formalised the requirements for the use of DPAs in the United States Attorneys' Manual (ss9-22.0000 (UASM) with the SEC formalising its own rules within its own manual. Within the USA legal system, there exist two variants: the DPA where a prosecution is begun but not proceeded with and the NPA where a criminal action is never filed. The use of DPAs rose to prominence in the USA following the Arthur Andersen case. In contrast, the UK introduced DPAs (not NPAs) in 2014. Both systems share similarities, but there are noticeable differences, not least the court sanctioning within the UK. In 2016, the French government introduced the Sapin II Law, which created the *Convention Judiciaire d'Interêt Public* (CJIP), being the equivalent of a DPA.[41] By contrast, German regulators released only in 2020 the *Verbandssanktionengesetz* (Corporate Sanctions Act) in an attempt to implement a form of DPA. While there are similarities, especially between the USA, UK and France, there are also some marked differences in the interpretation and implementation of these varying regimes.

The application across jurisdictions differs, in spite of there being an intent by governments to formulate a coherent response to international corporate criminal activity. Within the UK, the offences in respect of which a DPA can be applied relate (inter alia) to predicate money laundering offences; the Bribery Act 2010; fraud, theft and other offences under the Fraud Act 2006, Theft Acts and the Forgery and Counterfeiting Act 1981; and various company law and Financial Services and Markets Act 2000 offences, thus creating a defined set of corporate-based offences. By contrast, the USA will apply DPAs/NPAs to any offence save for those involving national security or foreign affairs and to anyone who has two or more prior felony convictions. The French CJIP applies specifically to offences where a company has 'committed corruption, influence peddling, tax fraud or laundering of the proceeds of tax fraud',[42] while the German DPA will potentially apply to a company where either one of the managers or a person 'performing their duties on behalf of the company' has committed a corporate criminal offence.[43] In essence, there is a coherence to broadly capture the corporate crimi-

39 Lynn Paine 'Salomon Brothers, Harvard Business School – Case 305-019' (November 2004 – revised February 2009).

40 Ibid.

41 Created by Law No. 2016-1691 of 9 December 2016 on transparency, fight against corruption and modernisation of the economy, commonly referred to as the 'Sapin II Law', the French Anti-Corruption Agency (alongside High Authority for Transparency in Public Life and the French Financial Prosecutor's Office) has become one of France's tripartite arsenal against corruption and white collar crime.

42 Antoine Kirry et al. *French DPAs – First CJIP Guidelines Published*, https://www.debevoise.com/insights/publications/2019/07/french-cjip-guidelines accessed, 30 April 2020.

43 Ralf van Ermingen-Marbach and Finn Zeidler *The German Corporate Sanctions Act – Heralding a New Era of Enforcement in Germany*, https://wp.nyu.edu/compliance_enforcement/2020/04/14/the-german-corporate-sanctions-act-heralding-a-new-era-for-enforcement-in-germany/, accessed 30 April 2020.

nal activity, however, it is clear that the common law jurisdictions have a wider application than those found in the civil law jurisdictions such as Germany. There is also a further marked difference that applies between the USA and other countries, as the USA will use DPAs/NPAs for individuals as well as corporations, whereas the other countries considered in this study seek to prosecute individuals via regular criminal prosecution processes and specifically do not extend DPAs to individuals.

Procedurally, there is a similarity between the UK and French rules as to obtaining a DPA. The UK guidelines have been set out by the SFO in the Deferred Prosecution Agreements Code of Practice published on 14 February 2014, while the French *Parquet National Financier* (PNF) (a French judicial institution akin to the district attorney, responsible for dealing with serious economic and financial crime) and *Agence Française Anticorruption* (AFA) published joint guidelines on 27 June 2019. In both countries, the process will invariably be triggered by a company self-reporting for a potential offence. Depending on the conduct of the company and its cooperation, the prosecutors will then consider whether to offer a DPA/CJIP and negotiate the terms with the company. In both countries, the final DPA will need the approval of the courts as to the terms agreed and whether the DPA is appropriate and in the public interest. In neither jurisdiction is there a requirement for the formal admission of guilt in respect of the offences. At the time of writing this chapter, it is unclear as to how the proposed German DPAs will be administered.

In the USA, while the process bears similarities to that of its European counterparts, the process is borne of the 'traditional give and take' that has occurred in plea negotiations. The divertees (as they are referred to in the USA) are selected based on eligibility criteria at the pre-charge stage and a proffer discussion ensues. The terms reached between prosecutor and divertee are then set out in a 'pre-trial diversion agreement' that is executed by the parties, with the offender acknowledging responsibility for their behaviour but not being asked to admit guilt.[44]

When providing a self-notification to the prosecutors in any of the jurisdictions there is a requirement for the company reporting to have carried out, or to carry out, a full and thorough investigation. The UK guidance is less clear as to the extent of the pre-reporting investigation, however it does provide clear guidance on the quality of information to be provided, as stated under Rule 4.3 of the UK SFO guidance that if inaccurate, misleading or incomplete information is provided then the prosecutor reserves the right to instigate fresh proceedings for the same offence.[45] Under the French guidance, the company is not required to self-report until it has, within a reasonable time following discovery, conducted its own internal investigation so as to evaluate the facts and confirm to itself if

44 CRM 712 Pretrial Diversion, Department of Justice Archives, https://www.justice.gov/archives/jm/criminal-resource-manual-712-pretrial-diversion, accessed 30 April 2020.

45 SFO, CPS, 'Deferred Prosecution Agreements Code of Practice', Crime and Courts Act 2013.

self-reporting is required.[46] Only if the PNF is satisfied that the investigation has provided sufficient evidence to justify a prosecution will a CJIP be considered.[47] This contrasts with the UK position, where the SFO may offer a DPA either if there is sufficient evidence or where the prosecutor is 'satisfied that sufficient evidence would be forthcoming'.[48] However, the USA rules under the March 2019 Justice Manual 9-47.120 demonstrate that when evaluating self-disclosure, the actual disclosure must occur 'within a reasonable prompt time of becoming aware of the offence' and 'prior to an imminent threat of disclosure or government investigation', thus shifting the onus of disclosure to a point that could occur prior to the conclusion of a full internal investigation. From a multi-jurisdictional aspect, this will place any potentially offending company in a position of having to balance the need for prompt disclosure against carrying out a thorough investigation and thus trying to determine the most suitable jurisdiction within which to self-disclose.

The self-reporting process as noted requires full disclosure and correct information and material. What is also likely to occur with any self-disclosing process is the need for the offending company to engage with its lawyers as to the internal investigation and the disclosure and negotiations with the prosecutors. This requirement places the content of the disclosure into an uneasy position, as it could well include information covered by legal professional privilege (LPP). Within the USA rules pursuant to JM 4-47.120 and JM 9-28.720, it is clear that 'eligibility for cooperation credit [is] not in any way predicated upon the waiver of the attorney-client privilege or work product protection.' These rules go so far as to reinforce the LPP by stating that it 'remains in full force and effect'. However, this is not the case in the UK and France. In the UK, the SFO would seek to challenge any assertion of LPP over disclosure material and places the onus of proving LPP on the self-reporting company. Indeed, the protection of LPP was waived in the DPAs involving Rolls-Royce, Tesco and Serco Geografix. The SFO has sought to show that cooperation credit would be given by waiving LPP and this was supported by the obiter comments of Sir Brian Leveson.[49] The French rules for *secret professionnel* are similar to those in the UK and reinforce the fact that professional secrecy extends to attorneys, not their client companies, although this simplistic view ignores the fact that a privileged dialogue between

46 French National Financial Prosecutor's Office 'Guidelines on the Implementation of the Convention Judiciaire D'interet Public', https://www.agence-francaise-anticorruption.gouv.fr/files/files /EN_ Lignes_directrices_CJIP_revAFA%20Final%20(002).pdf, accessed 30 April 2020.

47 Ibid. The legal regime of the CJIP is outlined in Articles 41-1-2, 180-2 and R. 15-33-60-1 et seq. of the Code of Criminal Procedure.

48 SFO (n 44).

49 *Director of the Serious Fraud Office v Eurasian Natural Resources Corporation Ltd (Law Society Intervening)* (2018) EWCA Civ 2006.

lawyer and client is a two-way conversation.[50] As such the self-reporting company will need to be very circumspect about exactly what information is disclosed.

The use of DPAs/NPAs has grown in the USA with a consistent average of 33.58% over the period 2006 to 2019 (ignoring the 2015 record number of 102),[51] with a total of 541 agreements being settled from 2000 to 2019.[52] Such settlement agreements produce significant revenues for the state and have generated fines of $8.1 billion in 2018 and $7.8 billion in 2019. These figures contrast heavily to those of the UK and France. Over the period 2014 to 2019, the UK entered into six DPAs with a total of £692,565,000 of fines and a total of £1.53 billion including profit disgorgement recovered by the SFO.[53] The reported French CJIPs entered into by the PNF/AFA generated fines totalling €1.6 billion and a total of €2.7 billion including compensation recovery. It is also worth noting in this context the level of prosecutions that are being undertaken in the varying jurisdictions. In the USA in 2019, under the Foreign Corrupt Practices Act (FCPA) alone, there were 73 actual prosecutions, split 54 to the DoJ and 19 to the SEC with 31 DPAs/NPAs being agreed across all corporate fraud cases.[54] Again, this contrasts with the UK: in the same year there were 60 active investigations (not prosecutions), with only two reported DPAs, namely, the Serco and Gurlap cases.[55] In France, there have to date been six reported CJIPs, divided between three agreed by the PNF/AFA and three by the Nanterre Prosecutors Office.[56]

In terms of revenue generated from DPAs – in the form of penalties – the figures from the UK and France are based on all DPAs entered into by the SFO and PNF/AFA since the creation of DPAs in those jurisdictions, whereas, from a comparison of penalties imposed, the USA is generating three to five times the financial recovery in a single year, but correspondingly has a greater volume of DPAs/NPAs to facilitate this. The range of reported fines spans figures from

50 Kathryn Hughes 'French DPAs – Considering the first guidelines' (QEB 6 August 2019), https://www.qebholliswhiteman.co.uk/site/library/articles/french-dpas-considering-the-first-guidelines accessed, 30 April 2020.

51 The unprecedented peak in 2015 was a direct result of the US–Swiss Tax Treaty on pursuing tax evasion cases. See, US Congress 'Ex. Rept. 114-1 – Protocol amending tax convention with Switzerland', https://www.congress.gov/congressional-report/114th-congress/executive-report/1, accessed 30 April 2020.

52 Gibson Dunn *2019 Year End Update on Corporate Non-prosecution Agreements and Deferred Prosecution Agreements*, https://www.gibsondunn.com/2019-year-end-npa-dpa-update/, accessed 30 April 2020.

53 SFO 'News Release – Airbus' (31 January 2020), https://www.sfo.gov.uk/2020/01/31/sfo-enters-into-e991m-deferred-prosecution-agreement-with-airbus-as-part-of-a-e3-6bn-global-resolution/, accessed 30 April 2020.

54 Gibson Dunn (n 51).

55 Jemma Slingo 'SFO Convictions Dwindle as Caseload Shrinks' (31 December 2019) *Law Society Gazette.*

56 Hughes (n 49); J. P. Picca *French Prosecutors Reach First Ever DPAs Settling Bribery Charges* (White & Case 16 March 2018), https://www.whitecase.com/publications/alert/french-prosecutors-reach-first-ever-dpas-settling-bribery-charges, accessed 30 April 2020.

$225,000 through to €2.08 billion. Within the USA and the UK, there are guidelines provided by the state as to the levels of the fines to be set within the criminal system, whereas under the French CJIP system the financial penalty is calculated based on the amount of benefit resulting from the misconduct by looking at the company's gross operating surplus and then applying a cap of 30% of its average annual turnover for the last three years. In addition to this, all three systems apply some form of compensation recovery, whether by profit disgorgement in the UK as a further penalty; victim compensation in France (which was particularly relevant where the French state registered itself as a victim in the HSBC claim thus recovering €86.4 million for the state); or the USA where it can be a mix of profit disgorgement, FCA recovery, restitution and civil claims by victims.

Particularly under the US approach to financial penalties, these additional compensation-type payments can have a direct impact on the level of the financial penalty. For example, the 2019 Celadon Group INC DPA and ContextMedia Health LLC NPA saw a payment of $42.4 million restitution and $70 million compensation respectively and thus, while entering into agreements, did not receive a financial penalty from the DOJ. Table 10.1 outlines penalties imposed in these jurisdictions.

A comparison of DPA/NPA financial penalties across all three jurisdictions demonstrates a synergy of statistical results. It is clear that half of all DPAs/NPAs result in a financial penalty under 10% of company turnover: being split 52% USA, 43% UK and 50% France. The remaining settlement agreement penalties being split between 11% to 20% of turnover (being split 17% USA, 14% UK and 25% France) and 20% plus of turnover (being split 31% USA, 43% UK and 25% France). However, it can be seen that where the total financial penalty is taken as a percentage of turnover, there is a range of 0.07% at the lowest to 58.38% at the highest (ignoring the three anomalous results: (i) Serco Geographix (UK), which had ceased to operate and its financial penalty was met by the parent company, (ii) Unitrans International Inc (USA), which involved a combined civil settlement, and (iii) Tower Research Capital LLC (USA), which involved additional victim compensation payments and CFTC settlements). There is no apparent statistical correlation between the financial penalties and the corporate turnovers and thus, whereas the French CJIP does impose a cap on the calculation hence giving the company a degree of certainty, any company entering an agreement in the USA or UK would be aware of the potential for higher penalties.

This degree of uncertainty within the USA and UK can be argued as a major factor to ensure cooperation of a company with the prosecutors when self-disclosing. There is a disparity between jurisdictions regarding the need for publicly filing annual returns/corporate accounts and as such a direct ratio comparison between USA DPAs/NPAs and UK or French DPAs is not wholly possible. However, where those companies have disclosed their balance sheets it is possible to compare an analysis of financial penalty to asset base, and within this statistic a clearer correlation does begin to emerge. The large multinational corporations with asset bases measured in the billions such as Airbus, HSBC and Monsanto receive financial penalties that range from 0.17% to 1.95% of assets,

Table 10.1 Table of fines and penalties for all UK DPAs and French CJIPs by comparison with those USA DPAs/NPAs for 2019 where company financial data is publically available.

Company name	*Fine*	*Profit Disgorgement*	*Turnover(T/o)*	*Net Current & fixed Assets*	*Ratio fine to T/o*	*Penaltvto T/O*	*Penaltv to Assets*
USA - 2019							
Avanir Pharmacueticals (DPA)	7,800,000.00	5,074,895.00	143,280,000.00	*N/a*	5.44	8.99	
Baton Holding LLC (NPA)	15,540,000.00	15,000,000.00	434,160,000.00	*N/a*	3.58	7.03	
Dannenbaum Engineering (DPA)	1,600,000.00		48,000,000.00	*N/a*	3.33	3.33	
Telefonakiebolaget LM Ericsson (DPA)	520,650,432.00		25,240,000,000.00	30,698,690,000.00	2.06	2.06	1.70
Fresenius Medical Care AG&Co (NPA)	84,715,273.00	147,000,000.00	19,335,850,733.00	36,438,600,000.00	0.44	1.20	0.64
Heritage Pharmaceuticals (DPA)	225,000.00		5,000,000.00	*N/a*	4.50	4.50	
HSBC Private Bank (Suisse) SA (DPA)	192,350,000.00		526,584,739.00	112,000,000,000.00	36.53	36.53	0.17
Hydro Extrusion USA LLC (DPA)		1,800,000.00	1,100,000,000.00	*N/a*	0.00	0.16	
Insys Therapeutics Inc (DPA)	2,000,000.00	28,000,000.00	82,080,000.00	192,530,000.00	2.44	36.55	15.58
Merrill Lynch Commodities (NPA)	25,000,000.00		225,210,000.00	*N/a*	11.10	11.10	
Microsoft Hungary (NPA)	8,751,795.00	16,565,151.00	44,520,000.00	*N/a*	19.66	56.87	
MizrahiTefahot(DPA)	118,000,000.00	24,000,000.00	2,060,000,000.00	77,742,020,000.00	5.73	6.89	0.18
Monsanto Company (DPA)	6,200,000.00	4,000,000.00	14,640,000,000.00	21,333,000,000.00	0.04	0.07	0.05

(*Continued*)

Table 10.1 Continued

Company name	*Fine*	*Profit Disgorgement*	*Turnover(T/o)*	*Net Current & fixed Assets*	*Ratio fine to T/o*	*Penaltvto T/O*	*Penaltv to Assets*
Rising Pharmaceuticals Inc (DPA)	1,500,000.00		12,100,000.00	*N/a*	12.40	12.40	
Samsung Heavy Industries Co Ltd (DPA)	75,481,600.00		6,280,000,000.00	11,614,470,000.00	1.20	1.20	0.65
Tower Research Capital LLC (DPA)	24,400,000.00	10,500,000.00	34,950,000.00	*N/a*	69.81	99.86	
UniCredit Bank Austria (NPA)	1,300,000,000.00		2,129,376,360.00		61.05	61.05	
Unitrans International Inc (NPA)	27,000,000.00		7,270,000.00	*N/a*	371.39	371.39	
UK-all DPAs							
Standard Bank	16,800,000.00	8,400,000.00	172,700,000.00	20,137,500,000.00	9.73	14.59	0.13
Sardad Ltd	352,000.00	6,200,000.00	11,223,000.00	7,596,000.00	3.14	58.38	86.26
Rolls Royce	239,082,645.00	258,170,000.00	14,955,000,000.00	25,538,000,000.00	1.60	3.32	1.95
Tesco	129,000,000.00	106,000,000.00	41,367,000,000.00	26,563,000,000.00	0.31	0.57	0.88
Serco Geographix	19,200,000.00		36,000.00	16,624,000.00	53,333.33	53,333.33	115.50
Giirlap Systems	0.00	2,069,861.00	10,144,000.00	8,358,000.00	0.00	20.40	24.77
Airbus SE	398,034,571.00	585,939,740.00	70,478,000,000.00	114,409,000,000.00	0.56	1.40	0.86
France-all PNF/AFA CJIPs							
HSBC	71,575,422.00	86,400,000.00	526,584,739.00	112,000,000,000.00	13.59	30.00	0.14
Google - France	46,700,000.00		411,016,329.00		11.36	11.36	
Google - Ireland	453,300,000.00		32,159,837,000.00		1.41	1.41	
Airbus SE	1,029,760,342.00	1,053,377,113.00	63,707,000,000.00	114,409,000,000.00	1.62	3.27	1.82

Turnover is taken from the published revenue/sales figure before any cost of sale or other accounting adjustments.
Assets are all current and tangible/fixed asset but with no allowance for balance sheet debtors

whereas 'smaller' companies with asset bases measured within the millions suffer a disproportionate penalty with the ratio measuring anything from 15.58% to 86.26%. This trend naturally cannot be seen as conducive to justice.[57] While the financial penalty should not ostensibly be extracted as a measure of the supposed wealth of the company, as these are the assets on which the company relies to trade, the object of a fine is to exact a measure of punishment that is sufficiently painful to the offender so as to make them adjust their behaviours in future. In industries such as the logistics/transport industry in the UK, where margins can operate as low as 2%, the range of penalties above would have a substantial effect on such a business, however the larger multinational companies identified within these statistics have greater margins and as such the financial penalty could be seen as a mere irritation.

The question thus has to be posed as to whether a company, in fact, has the capacity to enter into a DPA. Prosecuting a company for white collar crime (non-strict liability) such as fraud requires the application of a mental element, which poses difficulties attributing such to an artificial being: 'To attribute a human state of mind, such as intention, to a company is conceptually difficult.'[58] The key corporate textbooks utilised by law and accountancy courses when considering corporate identity initially present the anathema that a company is a legal person, despite its being a 'well-established principle that a corporation is recognized as a distinct legal entity and is considered a legal person separate to those working within the corporation'.[59] Yet in the media and law enforcement circles, we imbue the company with so much legal personality that we almost attempt to breathe life into it as if we are gods, thus giving it a capacity for thought and the ability to differentiate between good and evil. We forget that it is an inanimate creature of the law.

Within both the UK and the USA it has been a long-held legal principle that a corporate body is a separate legal entity and thus a person in law. However, the processes by which each country attaches liability for criminal offences are applied differently, with the USA applying the *respondeat superior* principle that a corporate entity is responsible for all employees' actions (the collective knowledge doctrine), while the UK has until recently applied the test of the directing mind, making the corporate entity liable for the actions of the controlling members of the company (the identification principle). However, with the recent Bribery Act 2010 (Section 7) and subsequent acts, the UK is beginning to erode the current principle by creating offences where the company is liable for the actions of any associated person. Indeed, with the extension of 'failure to prevent' offences that are being increasingly rolled out within the UK, failing to prevent bribery or tax

57 It is worth noting that the Crime and Courts Act 2013 (in para 7(1) and 8(1) of Schedule 17) provides an underlying benchmark whereby entering into a DPA is likely to be and is in the interests of justice and that the proposed and actual terms are fair, reasonable and proportionate.

58 Grimes et al. (n 21).

59 Ibid.

fraud is in itself enough for liability to occur. By contrast, until 2004, a French company could only be held criminally liable if it was expressly provided for under the law, however with Article 121-2 of the French Criminal Code, the scope of liability was extended so that any legal person could be held liable for any criminal offences committed on their behalf by their representatives. This creates an interesting and notable contrast between the legal approaches in the USA and UK and that of France. A company in the USA or UK, as a 'legal person', is imbued with responsibility as if it were a living creature by taking on the actions of its officers, whereas a French corporate entity could be argued to remain an inanimate being to which liability attaches due to the actions of its representatives.

In the recent SNC-Lavalin cases, the company has complained that 'employees and investors are suffering, and that a court case would be a "waste of taxpayers' money and resources".'[60] As a commentator has stated: '[C]oming from a company that ripped off taxpayers for years through bribery and corruption, it's a bit rich' and here again we have the company imbued with the sense of *mens rea* as if it has deliberately set out to commit the offence.[61] The question has to be asked: Who has actually committed the offence? Subsequently, by extension, who is actually protecting the company when entering into a DPA?

Turning to the core principles of criminal justice within common law jurisdictions, the landmark case of Coffin in establishing the presumption of innocence of the accused defined the principle of reasonable doubt not only in the USA but also in the UK for centuries.[62] The concept of reasonable doubt predates common law, being found within the Bible: '[A]nd Abraham drew near and said, "Wilt thou also destroy the righteous with the wicked?"' (Genesis 18:23) and was espoused by the Roman Emperor Trajan who wrote that a person should not 'be condemned on suspicion; for it was preferable that the crime of a guilty man should go unpunished than an innocent man be condemned'.[63] In the Coffin judgment, the court specifically tied the two fundamental principles of the presumption of innocence and reasonable doubt to underpin criminal liability within the USA (and the UK) legal regime.

They demonstrated that these principles cannot exist in isolation: 'The evolution of the principle of the presumption of innocence, and its resultant, the doctrine of reasonable doubt, make more apparent the correctness of these views, and indicate the necessity of enforcing the one in order that the other may continue to exist.'[64] However, with the application of DPAs it could be surmised that this principle is now replaced with a twofold application in criminal justice processes whereby the prosecutor applies their own subjective opinion and the defendant

60 Freeman (n 34).

61 Ibid.

62 *Coffin v United States* 156 U.S. 432 (1895), https://supreme.justia.com/cases/federal/us/156/432/, accessed 28 April 2020.

63 Alexander Volokh 'ASID n Guilty Men' (1997) *University of Pennsylvania Law Review*, 146, 173.

64 *Coffin v United States* 156 U.S. 432 (1895) 460.

carries out a risk assessment. The whole concept of guilt or innocence and the judicial application of testing evidence, and thus the presumption of innocence, is jettisoned in one fell swoop. In dismissing the *FedEx* case[65] (following FedEx's rejection of a DPA offer concerning its alleged conspiracy to traffic drugs in violation of the USA acts), Judge Breyer is reported to have stated: 'The dismissal is an act, in the court's view, entirely consistent with the government's overarching obligation to seek justice even at the expense of some embarrassment.'[66] The comments by Breyer echo the earlier principle established in *Henry v United States* that: '[I]t is better, so the Fourth Amendment teaches, that the guilty sometimes go free than that citizens be subject to easy arrest.'[67]

However, the proponents of DPAs would espouse that the principle of the DPA/NPA is not to punish but rather to change corporate behaviours by bringing them to comply with the law. This may well be the ideology, but it should be borne in mind that the DPA is the response to an alleged breach of the criminal code by the company and in attempting to change behaviour the company pays a substantial financial penalty as a consequence. The corporation is seen as 'too big to jail' (as described by Federal judges), but in reality, how can an inanimate creation of law, by paying a penalty, be expected to change its behaviour? It is akin to expecting one's knife and fork to voluntarily swap their roles while lying on the dining table! This position is evidenced by the *Pfizer* cases in recent years in the USA, where, consecutively, the company was granted three DPAs, yet after each DPA there was no change to its corporate behaviour.[68] To compound this, the issue of reasonable doubt is also being questioned. The safeguarding principle within the criminal system may yet be watered down by the replacement phrase 'satisfied that they are sure' and thus not having to be persuaded of a defendant's guilt with absolute certainty.[69] Such changes have the potential to undermine the standard of proof required when presenting criminal evidence before a court and in the case of DPAs reducing the standard against which the probability of proof would be measured.

The use of the DPA/NPA would therefore seem to undermine the presumption of innocence, a fundamental human right upheld by numerous international and regional legal instruments, inter alia, Article 11 of the Universal Declaration of Human Rights 1948, which states that: 'Everyone charged with a penal offence has the right to be presumed innocent until proven guilty according to law in a public trial at which he has had all the guarantees necessary for his defence.'[70]

65 *United States v FedEx Corp* C14-00380 CRB (2016).

66 FCPA (n 30).

67 *Henry v United States*, 361 U.S. 98, 104, 80 S. Ct. 168, 172 (1959).

68 J. Bostwick 'US vs. UK Deferred-Prosecution Agreements: Somed history and key ifferences', https://ieglobal.vistra.com/blog/2017/8/us-vs-uk-deferred-prosecution-agreements-some-history-and-key-differences#. accessed 28 April 2020.

69 C. Adams 'Judges Told to Stop Using "Beyond Reasonable Doubt" as it Confuses Juries' (*The Telegraph* 26 April 2020).

70 Universal Declaration of Human Rights, http://www.un.org/en/universal-declaration-human-rights/, accessed 28 April 2020.

Indeed the concept of the presumption of innocence was acknowledged as being 'at the foundation of the administration of [USA] criminal law' in the *Coffin* case[71] and under modern law is considered as a universal fundamental right.[72] It is suggested that, to balance this, the defendant still has the right to reject the DPA and proceed to trial, as in the *FedEx* case.[73] However, this merely pays lip service to the commercial realities of any litigation faced by corporations. Following the FedEx dismissal, Patrick Fitzgerald of the company stated that: 'Many companies would not have had the courage or the resources to defend themselves against false charges.'[74] With a DPA, a company is thus being invited to fall on its own sword of guilt based on a risk assessment rather than the testing of evidence. In real terms, if a person accepts a guilty plea, they stand before a judge who verifies the facts and asserts the ability of the defendant to enter their plea before passing a sentence. By contrast the DPA position in fact fosters the increasing application of risk-based assessment in the corporate world, an approach that would be applied by any sensible lawyer when advising their commercial client, with the intent of minimising risk exposure.[75]

In answer to the earlier question (regarding SNC-Lavalin's corrupt past) as to who, in fact, committed the offence, the answer is simple: the board and, at times, the employees. The self-interest of the board of directors or senior managers is served by effectively sacrificing the company at the altar of the DPA so as to avoid corporate liability and the risk of piercing the veil.

The increased use of DPAs in the USA has allowed 'corporate decision makers [to] roll over and play dead [having] forked over millions of dollars in shareholder money to make the DOJ go away'.[76] This leaves the company at the mercy of its officers while ostensibly offering little protection for the shareholders, employees and external third parties such as lenders and suppliers, as the company pays substantial fines to appease prosecutors for the actions of the officers.

The 'majority' are free to commit fraud on the minority or unfair prejudice (s. 994 CA 2006) because, in truth, the application of the rule in *Foss v Harbottle* provides a protection for the 'majority'[77] and thus by extension on occasion, the board in relation to their conduct by maintaining the right of the 'majority'

71 *Coffin v United States* 156 U.S. 432 (1895), 453.

72 The principle is provided and protected by the International Covenant on Civil and Political Rights, 1966, the Rome Statute of the International Criminal Court, 1998, The Convention for the Protection of Human Rights and Fundamental Freedoms of the Council of Europe, 1950, the Charter of Fundamental Rights of the European Union, 2000 and the American Convention on Human Rights, 1969.

73 FCPA (n 30).

74 Ibid.

75 Ibid.

76 Ibid.

77 The principle created being that where a wrong is done to a company the correct claimant is the company and thus by extension where the majority or those in control perpetrate such wrong, they would, in effect, have to authorise action against themselves.

to bind and therefore control the company.[78] With companies becoming ever larger, they are now owned and controlled by institutional investors who, in reality, exercise little control and in today's economic climate would not wish to 'rock the boat'. This position is yet further enhanced by the changes in guidance announced by the US Deputy Attorney General Rod J. Rosenstein on 29 November 2018 modifying the 'Yates Memorandum' of 2015 so that rather than a prerequisite for any cooperation credit being that a corporation must identify *all* individuals responsible and provide *all* facts pertaining to such misconduct, the guidance now reads 'every individual who is *substantially* involved or responsible for the criminal conduct'.[79] This linguistic shift, in fact, creates a gulf as to who was perceived as responsible for misconduct to a smaller pool of responsible individuals. Indeed, the behaviour of the corporate officers within the SNC-Lavalin scenario beggars belief when a company 'in which bribery and corruption was long a mainstay of its business' is now undertaking to lobby the Canadian government to adopt DPAs![80]

The approaches of the USA and the UK/France to DPAs also polarise with this issue, given that under UK and French regulations, while a company may enter into a DPA, the officers and anyone responsible for the criminal activity can still face prosecution as the DPA does not apply to individuals. However, in the USA, DPAs/NPAs can be granted to individuals and thus the corporate officers have the potential to seek personal immunity when a 'deal' is agreed.

In the UK, there exists a body of case law that establishes the principle of the 'directing mind' of the company and, in doing so, criminal liability, thereby the mental element can be established for a company based on the finding in law that 'those individuals who are at the highest echelons of the management of a company must be themselves criminally responsible.'[81] The concept of those individuals with 'the directing mind and will of a company' was further refined in 1972 so as to extend to the 'board of directors, the managing director and perhaps other superior officers of the company' and reaffirmed in 2012.[82] As such if it is possible to establish the mental element for a company based on the actions of its senior 'directing mind' officers, then it must follow that those individuals have also committed the criminal offence in question, because 'a company cannot commit an offence except through the actions of its human agents'.[83] Indeed, this was recognised by Sir Brian Leveson when considering the Rolls-Royce DPA; Leveson stated that it revealed 'the most serious breaches of the criminal law in the areas of

78 *Foss v Harbottle* (1843) 67 ER 189.

79 Gibson Dunn *2018 Year End Update on Corporate Non-prosecution Agreements and Deferred Prosecution Agreements* (10 January 2019), https://www.gibsondunn.com/2018-year-end-npa-dpa-update/, accessed 24 April 2020.

80 Freeman (n 34).

81 Grimes et al. (n 21); *Lennard v Asiatic Petroleum* (1915) AC 705.

82 *Tesco Supermarkets Ltd v Nattrass* (1972) AC 153; *R v Regis Paper Co Ltd* (2012])1 Cr. App. R. 14.

83 Grimes et al. (n 21).

bribery and corruption (some of which implicated senior managements and, on the face of it, controlling minds of the company)'.[84] This view is supported in the USA where the prosecution of companies in the past has rarely been undertaken without a simultaneous prosecution of the managing agents, as explained by US District Judge Jed Rakoff: 'The reasons were obvious. Companies do not commit crimes; only their agents do.'[85]

As such there remains the prospect that, while a company may enter into a DPA, the officers of the company could still be prosecuted for their actions in managing the company. How many officers have, in fact, been prosecuted for the events that have led to a DPA? The answer to this is startling in that very few individuals have faced prosecution within the USA. *The New Yorker* reported in 2017 that 'Federal prosecutions of white-collar crime are now at a twenty-year low',[86] while the use of DPAs within the UK has 'failed to yield individual convictions'.[87]

In the current political and cultural climate, it may be perceived as clever to victimise the corporation and metaphorically beat it for its wrongdoing, much as a farmer might beat his ignorant cow for not doing what it is told. However, it would be wrong to ignore the importance of big businesses that create wealth, advancement and employment; 'In large multi-national companies, the jobs of tens of thousands of employees can be at stake. And in some cases, the health of an industry or the markets are a real factor' (AAG Breuer).[88] In following this current culture of assigning perceived guilt, we avoid the true elephant in the room that is corporate governance.

When considering the discussion surrounding the use of DPAs, much centres on the ability to extricate a form of justice against a purportedly offending company while paying little attention to the legal concepts of; burden of proof, presumption of innocence, corporate personality, corporate governance, piercing the veil and the ephemeral concept of accountability. As such it could be posited that, in the interest of being seen to carry out 'justice', governments have devised a simple tool with which to extract or offset a measure of guilt from corporations and thus be seen to administer judgment. In so doing, they, in fact, ignore the need to pursue the true offenders who are the fraudulent and inept company directors and managers. With the 2019 DPA agreed by the SFO with Gürlap Systems Limited, the company accepted charges of conspiracy and failure to prevent bribery and agreed to pay a penalty of £2 million. However, the three individuals identified as being behind the actions of the company were subsequently

84 SFO 'Rolls-Royce Plc', https://www.sfo.gov.uk/cases/rolls-royce-plc/, accessed 28 April 2020.

85 Rakoff J *The Financial Crisis: Why Have No High-Level Executives Been Prosecuted?* (*New York Review* 9 January 2014), https://www.nybooks.com/articles/2014/01/09/financial-crisis-why-no-executive-prosecutions/, accessed 28 April 2020.

86 Patrick Radden Keefe 'Why Corrupt Bankers Avoid Jail' (*The New Yorker* 31 July 2017).

87 Slingo (n 54).

88 FCPA (n 30).

acquitted in respect of any wrongdoing. This lead to claims by the defence lawyers for the three that it was 'hugely unfair' that the DPA should name and identify the individuals and: 'As nobody at Gürlap Systems has actually been found guilty of any wrongdoing it begs the questions why the company actually admitted to wrongdoing in order to gain a DPA.'[89] The moral indignation of the defence is understandable, but in the court of public opinion the inference must be drawn that the guiding minds behind the company were aware of the wrongdoing and sought to extricate themselves by sacrificing the company through a DPA.

The USA applies a concept of 'wilful blindness' particularly within the corporate setting to infer intent, so that within a 'criminal statute [which] requires proof that a defendant acted knowingly or wilfully' the courts can ensure that the corporate defendant does not escape liability.[90] Within the UK by contrast, there is an increasing list of corporate 'failure to prevent offences' that can create criminal liability as with the Bribery Act 2010 or potential civil responsibility with the proposed *UK Failure to Prevent Mechanism for Corporate Human Rights Harms*.[91] Given the increasing appetite to hold companies responsible yet the failure of prosecutions against the guiding mind/representative individuals, an important question is raised as to whether governments should be reforming corporate governance with ethical imperatives and thereby holding to account company boards and managers. If governments fail to tackle the real issue of bad corporate governance then they risk the same failure to regulate as with the banking sector following the 2008 credit crunch. US DJ Rakoff commented when considering the financial crisis of 2008 that the USA Financial Crisis Inquiry Commission used 157 variants of the word fraud and that it concluded 'that there was a 'systemic breakdown', not just in accountability, but also in ethical behaviour.'[92]

It is clear that DPAs and NPAs have a very important role to play within the arsenal of effective tools for prosecutors when dealing with white collar crime. A number of commentators see DPAs and NPAs as effective tools because they empower the prosecutor to pursue a range of remedies beyond what could be achieved in a criminal prosecution process.[93] However, without a third-party scrutiny of the DPAs and NPAs, as is the case in the USA, the integrity of the regime will always be open to criticism. While the UK legal system is not infallible, the process of checks and balances provide an element of protection for the company. With this in mind, perhaps it is time for the USA to follow the UK lead with the application of judicial appraisal of DPAs to ensure the integrity of these

89 Cross (n 21).
90 *Global-Tech Appliances Inc. v SEB S.A.* 131 S.Ct. 2060, 2068 (2011).
91 Frederick Saugman 'Corporate Failure to Prevent Abuses *Law Society Gazette*, 6 April 2020.
92 Rakoff (n 85).
93 C. Christie and R. M. Hanna 'A Push Down the Road of Good Corporate Citizenship: The deferred prosecution agreement between the US attorney for the Distribute of New Jersey and Bristol-Myers Squibb Co.' (2006) 43 *American Criminal Law Review*, 1043.

agreements when imposed against an artificial person and ensure the accountability of the human officers.

However, it is also clear that while DPAs/NPAs have a critical role to play in combatting offences and the changing of corporate behaviours, they are not a substitute for actual criminal law enforcement. Their use in some cases can be seen, as referenced by US District Judge Jed Rakoff, as leading 'to some lax and dubious behaviour on the part of prosecutors', which has led to his damning commentary 'that the future deterrent value of successfully prosecuting individuals far outweighs the prophylactic benefits of imposing internal compliance measures that are often little more than window-dressing'.[94]

94 Rakoff (n 85).

11 The United Kingdom, organised crime, and money laundering

A critical reflection

Nicholas Ryder,[1] *Dr Samantha Bourton,*[2] *and Demelza Hall*[3]

Introduction

The aim of this chapter is to provide a general overview of the threat posed by serious and organised crime (SOC) in the United Kingdom (UK). The chapter begins by providing a working definition of organised crime and it then moves on to discuss the criminal activities of organised crime groups (OCGs) and the threat they present to the UK. Providing a definition of organised crime is not a straightforward task. The United Nations (UN) Convention on Transnational Organised Crime defines an OCG as 'a group of three or more persons that was not randomly formed; existing for a period of time; acting in concert with the aim of committing at least one crime punishable by at least four years' incarceration; in order to obtain, directly or indirectly, a financial or other material benefit'.[4] The UK Crown Prosecution Service defines organised crime as 'planned and co-ordinated criminal behaviour and conduct by people working together on a continuing basis. Their motivation is often, but not always, financial gain. Organised crime in this and other countries recognises neither national borders nor national interests'.[5] For the purpose of this chapter, the definition adopted by the UK government will be used:

> Organised crime involves individuals, normally working with others, with the capacity and capability to commit serious crime on a continuing basis, which includes elements of planning, control and coordination, and benefits those involved. The motivation is often, but not always, financial gain. Some

1 Professor of Financial Crime, University of the West of England.
2 Lecturer in Law, University of the West of England.
3 Lecturer in Law, University of the West of England.
4 United Nations Office on Drugs and Crime 'Transnational Organised Crime', n.d., https://www.unodc.org/ ropan/en/organized-crime.html, accessed June 3 2021.
5 Crown Prosecution Service 'Organised Crime Strategy', n.d., https://www.cps.gov.uk/organised-crime-strategy#:~:text=Organised%20Crime%20is%20defined%20as, but%20not%20always%2C%20financial%20gain, accessed June 3 2021.

DOI: 10.4324/9781003020813-12

types of organised crime, such as organised child sexual exploitation, have other motivations.[6]

The threat presented by organised crime

The threat posed by OCGs is significant and they are involved in a very wide range of illegal activity. This includes, but is not limited to, counterfeiting currency, firearms supply, organised fraud, organised immigration crime, human trafficking, people smuggling, intellectual property crime, money laundering, cyber-crime, corruption and fraud.[7] In 2013, the Home Office stated that: '[O]rganised crime poses a threat to the UK's national security. However, unlike other national security threats, the effects of organised crime are felt by individuals, communities, businesses and our economy on a daily basis.'[8] Furthermore, the Home Office estimated that: '[I]nternational organised crime syndicates each accumulate in the region of $1.5 billion a year. The international drugs market alone is estimated to be worth £200 billion. The National Security Strategy (NSS) also notes that cyber-crime has been estimated to cost up to $1 trillion per year globally.'[9] Writing in 2015, the HM Government National Risk Assessment (NRA) indicated that money laundering is an important 'enabler of serious and organised crime, the social and economic costs of which are estimated to be £24 billion a year'.[10] In the same report, it was asserted that as of 'December 2014, there were around 5,800 OCGs (comprising approximately 40,600 individuals) operating in the UK'.

Further, it stated: 'The social and economic costs of serious and organised crime are estimated to be £24 billion per year.'[11] By 2016, the total number of OCGs had increased to '5,900 [...] comprising approximately 39,400 individuals'.[12] In 2020, the NRA estimated that the impact of organised crime on the UK economy was approximately £40bn per year.[13] However, it is very important to note that a great deal of serious and organised crime 'remains hidden (child sexual exploitation and abuse, modern slavery), or underreported (fraud, cyber-crime), meaning the true scale is difficult to measure and likely to be much greater'.[14] Therefore, an important part of the UK's efforts to address the threat presented by OCGs is to tackle their proceeds of crime.

6 HM Government *Local to Global: Reducing the Risk from Organised Crime* (HM Government 2011) 8.
7 Home Office *Understanding Organised Crime: Estimating the Scale and the Social and Economic Costs Research Report 73* (Home Office 2013) 15.
8 Ibid. 5.
9 See Home Office (n 4).
10 Ibid. 7.
11 HM Government *UK National Risk Assessment of Money Laundering and Terrorism Financing* (HM Government 2015) 19.
12 Ibid. 20.
13 HM Government (n 8) 26.
14 HM Government *Serious and Organised Crime Strategy* (HM Government 2018) 11.

Organised crime and money laundering

The ultimate goal of OCGs is to generate a profit from their illegal activities. In order to hide or disguise their proceeds/profits of crime, OCGs will embark in a series of innovative and/or elementary laundering mechanisms. This process is crucial because it enables the criminal to enjoy a 'criminal' or 'champagne' lifestyle by laundering the illegal proceeds of crime without jeopardising their source. The money laundering process, which is widely recognised,[15] has three stages – placement, layering and integration. However, the traditional three-stage model of money laundering is outdated and does not represent the modern money laundering process. In order to prevent money laundering, the international community and nation states have adopted a 'preplacement policy', which is based on two concepts: customer due diligence and know your customer. The preplacement policy is heavily reliant on the money launderer using a 'reporting entity' in an attempt to hide or disguise the proceeds of crime. If the reporting entity deems the transaction/activity meets the criteria of a suspicious transaction/activity a suspicious transaction/activity report will be completed, referred to the nominated officer/money laundering reporting officer and sent to a financial intelligence unit (FIU). However, money launderers will place their proceeds of crime in sectors that are not covered by any money laundering reporting obligations, thus making the preplacement policy redundant, or they will use professional money launderers.[16] The money launderer normally attempts to break up the profit into smaller amounts to avoid any cash or currency transaction reporting obligations. This technique is referred to as smurfing, or structured payments.[17]

It is at this stage of the process that financial institutions and many other professions, including for example estate agents, accountants and lawyers, are susceptible to money laundering. The second stage or layering process, involves a large number of financial transactions or conversions. The purpose of this phase of the money laundering transaction is to create as much distance as possible between the initial placements of the proceeds of crime and their original source. It is during this stage that the money could be moved via the purchase of property or shares or simply transferred to several different countries via the internet, thus making it increasingly difficult to detect. The final stage is integration and it is at this stage that the money reappears into the economy. The methods adopted

15 See, for example, United Nations 'The Money-Laundering Cycle', n/d, https://www.unodc.org/unodc/en/money-laundering/laundrycycle.html, accessed 22 November 2018; Financial Action Task Force 'What Is Money Laundering?', n/d, http://www.fatf-gafi.org/faq/moneylaundering/, accessed 22 November 2018.

16 See Financial Action Task Force *FATF Report – Professional Money Laundering* (FATF 2018).

17 See, generally, Nicholas Ryder 'Is it Time to Reform the Counter-terrorist Financing Reporting Obligations? A critical and comparative assessment of the counter-terrorist financing reporting obligations in the European Union and the United Kingdom' (2018) *German Law Review* 19(5) 1169–90.

by money launderers have clearly evolved, yet some money launderers continue to favour the traditional or basic methods including cash couriers, smugglers and professional enablers. A large proportion of the proceeds of crime generated by OCGs are associated with the illegal manufacturing and distribution of narcotics, fraud, cyber-crime and other predicate offences. Other types of illegal activity will include identity theft, human trafficking and terrorism financing. Money laundering is also associated with smuggling, corruption, bribery, extortion, gambling and child exploitation. Money laundering can have a negative impact on the reputation of corporations, it is associated with terrorism financing and it can affect the reputation of regional and national financial centres.

The extent of money laundering

The calculation of money laundering is difficult, if not impossible, because there is no visible data on the amount of money laundered.[18] Any 'economic analysis of money laundering is an area fraught with difficulty [...] [and] in the absence of hard statistical data; studies to date have had to employ indirect methods of estimation'.[19] Nonetheless, there have been claims that money laundering is one of the world's largest industries. For example, the Financial Action Task Force (FATF) claims that the annual amount of money laundered is between $590bn and $1.5tn a year.[20] The UN Office on Drugs and Crime states that the figure was slightly higher, $800bn to $2tn.[21] Conversely, the International Monetary Fund (IMF) estimated that the global amount of laundered money could be between 2 and 5% of the world's gross domestic product.[22] Other studies have suggested that money laundering is $500bn[23] or $1.5tn per year.[24] In the UK, it was estimated that the amount of money laundered ranged annually from £19bn

18 For an excellent discussion and critique of previous attempts to calculate the extent of money laundering, see Michael Levi, Peter Reuter, and Terence Halliday 'Can the AML System be Evaluated Without Better Data' (2018) *Crime Law Soc Change* 69, 307–28.

19 Jackie Harvey 'Compliance and Reporting Issues Arising for Financial Institutions from Money Laundering Regulations: a preliminary cost benefit study' (2004) *Journal of Money Laundering Control* 7(4), 333–46.

20 Financial Action Task Force (n.d.) *Money Laundering FAQ*, www.fatf-gafi.org/document/29/0,3746,en_32250379_32235720_33659613_1_1_1_1,00.html#howmuchmoneyislaunderedperyear, accessed 13 May 2018.

21 United Nations Office on Drugs and Crime 'Money-Laundering and Globalization', n.d., https://www.unodc.org/unodc/en/money-laundering/globalization.html, accessed 19 October 2018.

22 Herbert Morais 'Fighting International Crime and its Financing: The importance of following a coherent global strategy based on the rule of law' (2005) *Villanova Law Review* 50, 583–644, 591.

23 Basia Spalek 'Regulation, White-Collar Crime and the Bank of Credit and Commerce International' (2001) *Howard Journal of Criminal Justice* 40 166–79, 167.

24 Simon Maylam 'Prosecution for Money Laundering in the UK' (2002) *Journal of Financial Crime* 10 157–58, 158.

to £48bn.[25] HM Treasury noted that 'each year £10bn of illicit funds passed through the regulated sector',[26] while Transparency International reported that the figure was £48bn.[27] More recently, the Law Commission reported that money laundering costs every UK household £255 per year,[28] while David Toon (formerly of the National Crime Agency (NCA)) stated that 'hundreds of billions are laundered through the UK annually.'[29] If we take the IMF estimation of between 2 and 5% GDP and base it on the GDP figures for the UK in 2019 (£2.829tn) we are looking at between £55.6bn and £144.5bn. Therefore, if these statistics are relatively accurate, money laundering poses a significant threat to the global economy and national security. The amount of money involved is of epic proportions and requires an effective monitoring and prevention strategy.

Policy background

The origins of the UK's money laundering policy are to be found not in the European Union (EU), but in US President Richard Nixon's declaration of the war on drugs in the early 1970s. Similar campaigns were launched by successive US presidential administrations in subsequent decades. This was hardly surprising, as money laundering was – and remains – inherently linked with the sale, production and manufacturing of illegal narcotic substances, which resulted in its prevention being pushed to the top of the international community's criminal justice agenda in the 1980s. This community, which was led largely by the UN and the EU, introduced a wide range of legislative measures that aimed to tackle money laundering and the problems it creates. These measures included the UN Convention Against Illicit Traffic in Narcotic Drugs and Psychotropic Substances (1988), more commonly referred to as the Vienna Convention. This provides that signatories must criminalise the laundering of drug proceeds, implement instruments to allow for the determination of jurisdiction over the offence of money laundering, permit the confiscation of the proceeds of the sale of illegal drugs and/or materials used in their manufacturing, introduce mechanisms to facilitate extradition and take steps to improve mutual legal assistance.[30] The UK signed the

25 Jackie Harvey 'An Evaluation of Money Laundering Policies' (2005) *Journal of Money Laundering Control* 8(4) 339–45, 340.

26 Financial Conduct Authority *Anti-money Laundering Annual Report 2012/13* (Financial Conduct Authority 2013) 3.

27 Transparency International 'Corruption Statistics', n.d., http://www.transparency.org.uk/corruption/statistics-and-quotes/uk-corruption, accessed 16 June 2016.

28 Law Commission 'Anti-money Laundering', n.d., https://www.lawcom.gov.uk/project/anti-money-laundering/, accessed 19 October 2018.

29 David Toon 'Prosperity Command, National Crime Agency, Treasury Committee Oral evidence: Economic Crime', HC 940, 4 July 2018, http://data.parliament.uk/writtenevidence/committeeevidence.svc/evidencedocument/treasury-committee/economic-crime/oral/86570.html, accessed 22 October 2018.

30 United Nations Convention against Illicit Traffic in Narcotic Drugs and Psychotropic Substances (1988).

Convention in December 1988 and ratified it in June 1991. Its impact is illustrated by the Criminal Justice (International Co-operation) Act 1990, Part 2 of which is entitled 'The Vienna Convention'. It is important to note that the Convention only applies to drug trafficking offences. The scope of the UN's legislative measures was thus extended by the UN Convention against Transnational Organized Crime, otherwise known as the Palermo Convention,[31] to include the 'proceeds of serious crime'.[32] The UK signed the Palermo Convention in December 2000 and ratified it in February 2006.[33] Its influence on UK law is illustrated by the fact that it is referred to in the Serious Organised Crime and Police Act 2005.[34] The scope of the UN's legislative remit to tackle money laundering was also extended by the introduction of its Convention against Corruption in 2003. The UK signed this Convention in December 2003, ratified it in February 2006 and updated its legislation with regard to bribery and corruption via the Bribery Act 2010.[35] In addition to the UN's anti-money laundering (AML) measures, the EU (and its predecessors) introduced a series of initiatives. For example, in 1990, the Council of Europe introduced a Convention on Laundering, Search, Seizure and Confiscation of the Proceeds from Crime.[36] The UK signed this Convention in November 1990 and ratified it in September 1992.[37] Its scope was broadened by the subsequent Council of Europe Convention on Laundering, Search, Seizure and Confiscation of the Proceeds from Crime and on the Financing of Terrorism in 2005, which entered into force in 2008.

As part of the 1990 Convention, the EU requires its member states to implement its money laundering directives. The First Directive was introduced in 1991 and concentrates on what are referred to as 'preventive measures', including client identification, the examination and reporting of suspicious transactions, indemnities to be given for good-faith reporting of suspicions transactions, keeping identification records for five years after the client relationship has ended, cooperation with the authorities and the provision of adequate internal procedures and training programmes. These are based on the 40 recommendations of the FATF and the UK implemented them in 1993.[38] The Second Directive extends the scope of the suspicious transaction reporting requirements and the

31 United Nations Convention against Transnational Organized Crime, G.A. Res. 55/25, UN GAOR, 55th Sess., Supp. No. 49 (UN Doc. A/55/49), Vol. I, 43.

32 Rick McDonnell 'UN Anti-money Laundering Initiatives', in W. Muller, C. Kalin and J. Goldsworth (eds.), *Anti-Money Laundering International Law and Practice* (John Wiley & Sons 2004), 51.

33 See Financial Action Task Force (n 28) 250.

34 Serious Organised Crime and Police Act 2005, s 95.

35 United Nations Office on Drugs and Crime, *Pilot Programme for the United Kingdom* (n.d.) 3.

36 This is more commonly referred to as the Strasbourg Treaty.

37 See Financial Action Task Force(n 28) 250.

38 European Council *Directive on the Prevention of the Use of the Financial System to Launder Money*, 91/308, 1993 O.J. (L 166). This Directive was implemented by Money Laundering Regulations 1993, S.I. 1993/1933.

scope of the reporting obligations to a wider range of professions, thus increasing the scope of the UK's AML obligations. This was achieved in the UK through the Money Laundering Regulations 2003.[39] The Third Directive was implemented by EU member states in 2007. It broadens the scope of predicate offences and provides more guidance on improving customer identification procedures. It applies to all proceeds of serious crime[40] and was implemented in the UK through the Money Laundering Regulations 2007.[41]

In May 2015, the European Parliament agreed on a Fourth Money Laundering Directive that seeks to implement all the FATF's recommendations, which supposedly set a 'global standard for combating money laundering and terrorist financing' following their revision in February 2012.[42] The Fourth Directive goes even further than the FATF's recommendations and addresses a number of important issues, including the development of new rules that apply to electronic money, registers for ultimate beneficial ownership, no distinction between internal and external politically exposed persons, improved cooperation between FIUs and an improved sanctions regime. Furthermore, in January 2020, the UK implemented the EU's Fifth Money Laundering Directive via the Money Laundering and Terrorist Financing (Amendment) Regulations 2019.[43] This Fifth Directive extends the remit of the regulations to include crypto-asset exchange providers, custodian wallet providers, art market participants, a broader definition of estate agents and accountants. Other important changes relate to customer due diligence, beneficial ownership registers, the threshold for prepaid cards, enhanced due diligence and improving communications between FIUs, politically exposed persons and Companies House.[44]

Most recently, the EU published its Sixth Money Laundering Directive, which provides a broader definition of money laundering, extends criminal liability to include companies, increases penalties for those convicted of money laundering and makes improvements to the cooperation between member states.[45] However, given that the UK left the EU in January 2020, it will not implement the Sixth Money Laundering Directive. Nevertheless, the Ministry of Justice maintains that the 'UK already goes much further' than the EU directives.[46] This stance is justi-

39 S.I. 2003/3075.

40 Jonathan Fisher 'Recent Development in the Fight Against Money Laundering' (2002), *Journal of International Banking Law* 17(3), 67–72, 67.

41 S.I. 2007/2157.

42 Joachim Kaetzler and Tanja Kordys 'Fourth Money Laundering Directive: Increased risk management requirements' (2015), *Compliance & Risk*, 4(5), 2–5.

43 S.I. 2019/1511.

44 See HM Treasury, *Transposition of the Fifth Money Laundering Directive: Response to the Consultation* (2020).

45 Directive (EU) 2018/1673 of the European Parliament and of the Council of 23 October 2018 on combating money laundering by criminal law, PE/30/2018/REV/1, O.J. L 284, 12.11.2018, 22–30.

46 Ministry of Justice, *Eighth Annual Report to Parliament on the Application of Protocols 19 and 21 to the Treaty on European Union (TEU) and the Treaty on the Functioning of the*

fied following the publication of the fourth Mutual Evaluation Report from the FATF in 2018, which concluded that the UK has the most comprehensive AML regime in the world.[47]

In addition to the FATF recommendations, further guidelines have been outlined by the Basel Committee on Banking Regulation and Supervisory Principles.[48] This Committee has published a Statement of Principles, which is consistent with the recommendations, as well as a number of best practice papers that aim to prevent the financial system becoming an instrument for financial crime clients.[49] The UK is a member of the Basel Committee and a founding member of the Egmont Group of FIUs. The latter's stated objective is to 'increase and improve the communication between FIUs worldwide to help fight what is recognised as a universal problem'.[50] Moreover, countries are legally obliged to ratify and implement the UN's counterterrorist financing (CTF) measures due to Chapter 7 of the UN Charter. In February 2012, the FATF published its revised International Standards on Combating Money Laundering and the Financing of Terrorism and Proliferation, which amend the 40 original FATF recommendations and introduce nine additional special recommendations with the intention of providing governments with stronger mechanisms to tackle financial crime. Importantly, this means that they now cover both corruption and tax crimes.[51]

The UK is an active member of the FATF and acted as chair of the organisation in 2007. The FATF's influence over the UK's AML policy and legislative framework is well illustrated by the money laundering and terrorist finance strategy of 2007.[52] In the accompanying press release, HM Treasury stated that 'the FATF is central to the UK's international objectives within the strategy'.[53] Meanwhile, in its 2007 *Mutual Evaluation Report*, the FATF concluded that the UK was fully compliant with 19 of the 40 recommendations, largely compliant on nine, partially compliant on nine and non-compliant on only three.[54] Eleven years later, the UK achieved the top rating of over 100 countries when the FATF

Union (TFEU) in Relation to EU Justice and Home Affairs (JHA) Matters (1 December 2016–30 November 2017) (2018), 7.

47 See Financial Action Task Force *Fourth Mutual Evaluation Report United Kingdom* (Financial Action Task Force 2018).

48 For a brief discussion, see N. Ryder *Money Laundering: An Endless Cycle?* (Routledge 2012).

49 Mark Simpson 'International Initiatives', in Mark Simpson, Nicole Smith and Arun Srivastava (eds.), *International Guide to Money Laundering Law and Practice* (Bloomsbury Professional 2010) 202.

50 Ibid.

51 Financial Action Task Force *International Standards on Combating Money Laundering and the Financing of Terrorism & Proliferation* (2012).

52 HM Treasury *The Financial Challenge of Terrorism and Crime* (2007).

53 HM Treasury 'Appointment of the UK President of the Financial Action Task Force', www.gov-news.org/gov/uk/news/appointment_uk_president_financial_action/36083.html, accessed 3 July 2011.

54 See Financial Action Task Force(n 28) 10–15.

reviewed AML and CTF regimes around the world.[55] The FATF has thus concluded that the UK has a far reaching AML legislative framework that fully complies with the UN Conventions.[56]

Furthermore, the UK Criminal Finances Act 2017 introduced a series of wide ranging measures aimed at improving the investigation of the proceeds of crime, including reform of the suspicious activity reports regime, enhanced civil powers to recover the proceeds of crime, provisions to combat terrorism financing and the creation of new corporate tax offences to prevent the facilitation of tax evasion.[57] Also in 2017, the UK government asked the Law Commission to consider some aspects of Part 7 of POCA and the CTF regime in Part 3 of the Terrorism Act 2000.[58] Two years later, the Law Commission published its review, which made a series of recommendations aimed at improving the effectiveness of some aspects of the SARs regime to 'ensure a more proportionate and user-friendly regime; clarify the scope of reporting; reduce the burden of compliance and processing; and produce better quality intelligence for law enforcement'.[59] Moreover, the government has published three NRAs,[60] which have provided an enhanced understanding of the threat posed to the UK by money laundering.[61] In 2019, the government published its Economic Crime Plan, which outlines seven strategic priorities and 52 action points.[62] The last were subsequently updated in April 2021.[63] The UK's AML policy has therefore been strongly influenced by the legislative and preventative measures of the international community and by international best practice and industry guidelines. The policy is managed and

55 Financial Action Task Force *Anti-Money Laundering and Counter-Terrorist Financing Measures United Kingdom Mutual Evaluation Report* (2018).

56 Ibid.

57 HM Government, *Explanatory Notes Criminal Finances Act 2017* (2017). It is important to note that the FATF has attracted a great deal of criticism. See, for example, N. Azinge-Egbiri *Regulating and Combating Money Laundering and Terrorist Financing – The Law in Emerging Cconomies* (Routledge 2021).

58 Law Commission 'Anti-money Laundering', www.lawcom.gov.uk/project/anti-money-laundering/, accessed 7 July 2021.

59 Ibid.

60 See HM Government *UK National Risk Assessment of Money Laundering and Terrorist Financing* (2015); HM Government *UK National Risk Assessment of Money Laundering and Terrorist Financing* (2017); HM Government *UK National Risk Assessment of Money Laundering and Terrorist Financing* (2020).

61 The National Risk Assessments are based on the terminology and methodology used by the FATF. See Financial Action Task Force *FATF Guidance National Money Laundering and Terrorist Financing Risk Assessment* (2013).

62 For more detailed discussions, see Royal United Services Institute 'The UK's Economic Crime Plan: A first step on the road to progress' (24 July 2019), https://rusi.org/commentary/uk%E2%80%99s-economic-crime-plan-first-step-road-progress, accessed 23 October 2020. For efforts to monitor the implementation of the Economic Crime Plan, see Royal United Services Institute 'Economic Crime Plan Online Tracker', www.rusi.institute/ecp/, accessed 5 January 2021.

63 HM Government *Economic Crime Plan – Statement of Progress* (2021).

implemented by several government departments, financial regulators and law enforcement agencies, many of which are considered below.

HM Treasury and the Home Office

HM Treasury is the leading AML authority in the UK as it is responsible for the implementation of money laundering directives and the execution of the UN's financial sanctions regime. It is also the UK's representative on the FATF and sanctions the industry guidelines on compliance with money laundering controls.[64] The importance of its role was well illustrated in its 2007 Money Laundering Strategy,[65] where the stated objective was to create an effective AML framework that would achieve an appropriate balance between tackling money laundering and preventing the imposition of burdensome compliance regulations. The HM Treasury's principal objective was thus to safeguard:

> the integrity of the financial system from exploitation by criminals and terrorists. It does this by deploying financial tools to deter, detect and disrupt crime and security threats. The approach taken is effective and proportionate to the risks posed as well as engaging with business, law makers and law enforcers.[66]

The money laundering strategy also outlined how the government intended to tackle the problems associated with money laundering and the financing of terrorism.[67]

Along with the Home Office, HM Treasury co-chairs the Money Laundering Advisory Committee, which is a meeting place for all relevant stakeholders, including 'financial institutions, trade and consumer organisations, government and law enforcement representatives'.[68] The Advisory Committee 'advises the government on its approach to preventing money laundering in the UK [...] [and] reviews industry guidance before it is approved by the Treasury'.[69] Furthermore, HM Treasury plays a critical role in selecting and appointing controllers in the AML sector. This has resulted in its publication of an annual report that outlines

64 See Financial Action Task Force (n 28) 24.

65 HM Treasury (n 52) 77.

66 Ibid. 78.

67 HM Treasury (n 48).

68 Oxford Analytica Ltd 'Country Report: Anti-money laundering rules in the United Kingdom', in Mark Pieith and Gemma Aiolfi (eds.), *A Comparative Guide to Anti-Money Laundering: A Critical Analysis of Systems in Singapore, Switzerland, the UK and the USA* (Edward Elgar 2004), 271.

69 HM Treasury 'Policy Paper: Preventing money laundering' (5 June 2013), www.gov.uk/government/publications/preventing-money-laundering/preventing-money-laundering#financial-action-task-force-fatf, accessed 1 July 2015.

good practices in the AML arena.[70] HM Treasury also plays a very important role in ensuring that businesses comply with AML regulations. For example, it approves guidelines written by the business sector that the UK courts are obliged to take into consideration. In addition, HM Treasury issues advisory notices on countries that are deemed to have weak AML and CTF systems.[71] The Counter Terrorism Act 2008 provides that firms are obliged to embark on further due diligence obligations with financial transactions involving bodies or persons from such named countries. In this role, HM Treasury is supported by the Home Office, which is responsible for managing police forces in England and Wales, and the NCA, which acts as the UK's FIU. In relation to money laundering, the Home Office also manages the asset recovery scheme and the mutual legal assistance regime.

The Financial Services Authority

Between 1997 and 2012, the Financial Services Authority (FSA) was an integral part of the UK's AML system and as such could be said to have been a key policymaker. The Authority was established following a number of high profile financial scandals between the 1970s and the 1990s, which were arguably caused by poor banking regulation by the Bank of England. The FSA was therefore given extensive rule making and enforcement powers under the Financial Services and Markets Act (FSMA) 2000. Under this Act, the FSA had a duty to reduce financial crime by ensuring that financial institutions had systems and practices in place which protected them against their use as vehicles to launder money by financial criminals. 'Financial crime' is broadly defined within FSMA 2000 as incorporating any offence including fraud or dishonesty,[72] misconduct in (or misuse of information relating to) a financial market[73] or handling the proceeds of crime.[74] The principal objective of the FSA was therefore to focus on the regulated sector's existing AML systems and controls.[75] Under the terms of FSMA 2000, the FSA was empowered to make rules in relation to the prevention and detection of money laundering.[76] These rule making powers were originally outlined in a *Money Laundering Sourcebook*,[77] but were detailed, burdensome and very similar to those in the Money Laundering Regulations 1993. The *Money*

70 See HM Treasury *Anti-Money Laundering and Counter Terrorist Finance: Supervision Report 2010–11* (2011).

71 HM Treasury *Advisory Notice on Money Laundering and Terrorist Financing Controls in Overseas Jurisdictions* (2015).

72 Financial Services and Markets Act 2000, s 6(3)(a).

73 Ibid. s 6(3)(b).

74 Ibid. s 6(3)(c).

75 Members of the regulated sector are defined in the Financial Services and Markets Act 2000 (Regulated Activities) Order 2001, S.I. 2001/544.

76 Financial Services and Markets Act 2000, s 146.

77 Financial Services Authority, *Handbook* (2006).

Laundering Sourcebook was thus replaced by a principles-based approach in the Senior Management Arrangements, Systems and Controls (SYSC) section of the FSA *Handbook*. Arguably, the most important tools that the FSA possessed in the fight against money laundering were its extensive investigative and enforcement powers. It had the ability to demand information from firms,[78] to appoint investigators,[79] to secure the assistance of overseas financial regulators[80] and to provide appointed investigators with additional powers.[81] Furthermore, as confirmed in *R v Rollins*,[82] the FSA became a prosecuting authority in respect of certain money laundering offences.

These powers applied whether or not the entity to be prosecuted was regulated by the FSA.[83] The FSA also had the power to impose a financial penalty where it had established that there had been a contravention by an authorised person of any requirement imposed under FSMA 2000.[84] For example, it fined several firms' money laundering reporting officers (MLROs) and imposed a series of fines on firms that had breached AML rules even when there was no evidence of money laundering.[85] As explained in the next section of this chapter, the FSA was unprepared for the 2007/2008 financial crisis and it was replaced in 2012.

The Financial Conduct Authority

Following the introduction of the Financial Services Act in 2012, the FSA was abolished and replaced by the Financial Conduct Authority (FCA) and the Prudential Regulation Authority (PRA). The origins of the FCA can be traced back to the 2007/2008 financial crisis and the clear failings of the FSA, as graphically illustrated by the near collapse of Northern Rock, one of the then largest UK financial services providers. One of the most important sections of the UK 2010 Coalition Agreement addressed the need to reform the existing system of banking regulation. The Agreement thus stated: '[W]e will reform the regulatory system to avoid a repeat of the financial crisis. We will bring forward proposals to give the Bank of England control of macro-prudential regulation and oversight of micro-prudential regulation.'[86] The existing regulatory system was commonly referred to as the 'tripartite' system as it was jointly administered by HM Treasury, the FSA and the Bank of England. In June 2010, then

78 Financial Services and Markets Act 2000, ss 165–6.
79 Ibid. ss 167–8.
80 Ibid., s 169.
81 Ibid. s 172.
82 *R v Rollins* [2010] UK SC 39.
83 Financial Services and Markets Act 2000, s 402(1)(a).
84 Ibid. s 206(1).
85 FSA Press Release 'FSA Fines Alpari and its Former Money Laundering Reporting Officer, Sudipto Chattopadhyay for Anti-money Laundering Failings' (5 May 2010), www.fsa.gov.uk/pages/Library/Communication/PR/2010/077.shtml, accessed 6 July 2011.
86 HM Government *The Coalition: Our Programme for Government* (2010), 9.

Chancellor of the Exchequer, George Osborne MP, outlined in greater detail the Coalition Government's financial services policy. Of particular relevance to this chapter was the decision to abolish the FSA and transfer its supervisory powers to the Bank of England,[87] create a Financial Policy Committee within the Bank of England, establish the PRA, which would be responsible for the day-to-day supervision of financial institutions, establish the Consumer Protection Markets Authority, which would regulate the conduct of all financial services firms, establish the Economic Crime Agency (ECA), create the Independent Commission on Banking and introduce a specific bank levy.[88] The Financial Services Act 2012 duly resulted in the transformation of the tripartite system into what has been called a 'twin peaks' approach to banking regulation.

In relation to money laundering, the FCA has adopted a very similar approach to that practised by its predecessor, the FSA. According to its website, the FCA is 'the competent authority for supervising compliance of most credit and financial institutions with the Money Laundering Regulations'.[89] In the latest version of the SYSC section of the FCA *Handbook*, the regulated sector is required to have in place systems and controls that are appropriate for firms to conduct their business, including: conducting regular assessments of the adequacy of AML systems to protect themselves from being used to further financial crime;[90] giving a director or senior manager overall responsibility for establishing and maintaining an AML system; and appointing an MLRO.[91] The SYSC regime thus seeks to provide the regulated sector with an even higher degree of flexibility, which allows firms to identify risks and determine how best to divert resources to their most vulnerable areas. This approach seeks to encourage and enable the regulated sector to target its resources most appropriately on activities at risk from money laundering, thus reducing compliance costs. Furthermore, regulated firms are required to:

> [...] establish, implement and maintain adequate policies and procedures sufficient to ensure compliance of the firm including its managers, employees and appointed representatives (or where applicable, agents) with its obligations under the regulatory system and for countering the risk that the firm might be used to further financial crime.[92]

87 See HM Treasury *A New Approach to Financial Regulation: Consultation on Reforming the Consumer Credit Regime* (2010).

88 HM Treasury 'Financial Services Policy Agenda', www.hm-treasury.gov.uk/fin_policy_agenda_ index.htm, accessed 19 July 2011.

89 Financial Conduct Authority 'Anti-money Laundering' (14 November 2011), www.fca.org.uk/firms/being-regulated/meeting-your-obligations/firm-guides/systems/aml, accessed 24 June 2015.

90 Financial Conduct Authority *Handbook* (2006), SYSC 3.2.6 C.

91 Ibid. SYSC 3.2.6 H and I.

92 Financial Conduct Authority (n 86) SYSC 6.1.1.

Additionally, the SYSC section of the *Handbook* requires that a regulated firm:

> [...] must ensure the policies and procedures established under SYSC 6.1.1 R include systems and controls that (1) enable it to identify, assess, monitor and manage money laundering risk; and (2) are comprehensive and proportionate to the nature, scale and complexity of its activities.[93]

Furthermore, a 'firm must carry out a regular assessment of the adequacy of these systems and controls to ensure that they continue to comply with SYSC 6.3.1 R'.[94] The *Handbook* also asserts that: 'A firm must allocate to a director or senior manager (who may also be the MLRO) overall responsibility within the firm for the establishment and maintenance of effective AML systems and controls.'[95] Finally, an authorised firm is required to appoint an MLRO who is responsible for maintaining the firm's compliance with the rules.[96]

The National Crime Agency

The Serious Organised Crime Agency (SOCA) was the UK's FIU and as such administered POCA 2002's assets recovery provisions after inheriting this role from the National Criminal Intelligence Service in 2005. SOCA was created by the Serious Organised Crime and Police Act 2005 and, at that time, it was a major part of the UK government's organised crime strategy. It had three main objectives: to tackle SOC; to gather information relating to crime; and other general considerations. In relation to organised crime, the Act stated that SOCA would prevent and detect SOC while also contributing to the reduction of such crime and the mitigation of its consequences.[97] Furthermore, section 3 provided that it would play a critical role in the 'gathering, storing, analysing and disseminating [of] information relevant to (a) the prevention, detection, investigation or prosecution of offences, or (b) the reduction of crime in other ways or the mitigation of its consequences'.[98]

In May 2010, the newly elected government published its Coalition Agreement, which included a commitment to tackle economic crime. The Agreement proposed that the roles of the Serious Fraud Office (SFO), the FSA and the Office of Fair Trading would be merged into the ECA. The chancellor of the exchequer stated: '[W]e take white collar crime as seriously as other crime and we are determined to simplify the confusing and overlapping responsibilities

93 Ibid. SYSC 6.3.1.
94 Financial Conduct Authority(n 86) SYSC 6.3.3.
95 Ibid. SYSC 6.3.8.
96 Financial Conduct Authority (n 86) SYSC 6.3.9.
97 Serious Organised Crime and Police Act 2005, ss 2(1)(a) and (b).
98 Ibid. ss 3(1)(a) and (b).

in this area in order to improve detection and enforcement.'[99] It was evident that the government's intention was to address the threat presented by financial crime, including fraud, insider dealing, bribery, corruption and money laundering. The government therefore arguably recognised that the existing multiplicity of disparate agencies had led to conflicting priorities and ineffective outcomes. A 'one-stop shop' had been advocated for many years, but the idea was given fresh impetus by a Policy Exchange research note.[100] This argued that the interests of fraud detection, investigation and prosecution would be better served by a unified approach mandated to tackle all aspects of economic crime. The coalition government proposed that the ECA would be led by the Home Office, which historically had adopted a piecemeal approach towards tackling financial crime.[101] To further this endeavour, the Home Office began a consultation process and expected the 'initial elements of the ECA' to be in place by 2011.[102]

However, before this could take place, in June 2010, the new Home Secretary, Theresa May, announced the creation of the NCA, which would tackle organised crime, fraud and cyber-crime, maintain border protection and protect children and young people. This new body was initially divided into four distinct divisions: Organised Crime Command; Border Policing Command; Economic Crime Command; and the Child Exploitation and Online Protection Centre.[103] The Home Office envisaged that the third of these would 'ensure a coherent approach to the use of resources focused on economic crime across the full range of agencies deploying them'.[104] Furthermore, it was hoped that it would 'maintain an overview' across a wide range of economic crime agencies, including the City of London Police and the SFO.[105] The NCA was officially launched following the enactment of the Crime and Courts Act 2013, which tasked the new agency with reducing crime[106] and criminal intelligence,[107] among other functions. In relation to money laundering, the Act states that the NCA will undertake the functions conferred by POCA 2002 as part of its role as the UK's FIU and will also manage the confiscation of the proceeds of crime. According to the NCA's own website,

99 HM Treasury 'George Osborne, Chancellor of the Exchequer: Speech at the Lord Mayor's Dinner for Bankers & Merchants of the City of London, at Mansion House 16 June 2010', www.hm-treasury.gov.uk/press_12_10.htm, accessed 26 June 2010.

100 Jonathan. Fisher and Ted Sumpster *Fighting Fraud and Financial Crime* (Policy Exchange 2010), 12.

101 Home Office 'Economic Crime Press Release (17 January 2011), www.homeoffice.gov.uk /media-centre/news/economic-crime, accessed 22 January 2011.

102 Ibid.

103 Home Office *The National Crime Agency: A Plan for the Creation of a National Crime-Fighting Capability* (2011).

104 Ibid. 20.

105 Home Office (n 99).

106 Crime and Courts Act 2013, s 1(4).

107 Ibid. s 1(5).

it acts as the 'UK Financial Intelligence Unit [and] receives, analyses and distributes financial intelligence gathered from Suspicious Activity Reports'.[108]

Conclusions

Money laundering conducted by or on behalf of OCGs can occur in any country or city in the world, irrespective of the levels of compliance with the global AML legislative and preventative measures. OCGs have always been able to adapt and vary their techniques in response to the increased levels of regulation and the scale of related money laundering is aggravated by a number of important factors such as the increasingly global nature of the financial markets, the inherent link between money laundering and organised crime and the immeasurable number of money laundering mechanisms that exist. The UK's AML policy is generally compliant with the international measures, yet the City of London has widely been acknowledged as a centre for global money laundering.[109] Its policy is managed by HM Treasury, assisted by the FCA and the NCA. The UK has fully implemented the Fifth Money Laundering Directive, with the government asserting that its money laundering regime is the 'gold standard' and continues to exceed the EU's requirements. In spite of possessing the option to use criminal sanctions, it is likely that the FCA will continue to impose financial sanctions on authorised firms that breach its extensive money laundering rules, with criminal prosecutions reserved exclusively for individuals. The most significant modern developments have been the publication of the Law Commission's review of SARs, the publication of the FATF's fourth *Mutual Evaluation Report* and the Economic Crime Plan. Following its detailed review of the SARs regime, the Law Commission made 19 proposals aimed at improving their effectiveness; the FATF's fourth *Mutual Evaluation Report* praised the UK's level of compliance with its recommendations; and the Economic Crime Plan outlined the government's initiatives to tackle financial crime between 2019 and 2022.

108 National Crime Agency 'UK Financial Intelligence Unit', www.nationalcrimeagency.gov.uk/about-us/what-we-do/specialist-capabilities/ukfiu, accessed 25 June 2015.

109 See United States Department of State Bureau of International Narcotics and Law Enforcement Affairs *International Narcotics Control Strategy Report Volume II Money Laundering* (United States Department of State Bureau of International Narcotics and Law Enforcement Affairs 2020) 198; House of Commons Foreign Affairs Committee *Moscow's Gold: Russian Corruption in the UK Eighth Report of Session 2017–19* (House of Commons Foreign Affairs Committee 2018) 11; Intelligence, Security Committee of Parliament *Russia* (Intelligence and Security Committee of Parliament 2020) 11; A. Nice 'The ISC Russia Report Highlighted Problems that Cannot be Solved by the Intelligence Services Alone', n.d., https://www.instituteforgovernment.org.uk/blog/isc-russia-report, accessed 11 January 2021.

Bibliography

Adali A and Lundgren T, *Svenska Rånare* (Lind & Co 2017)

Adams C, 'Judges told to stop using "beyond reasonable doubt" as it confuses juries' (26 April 2020) *The Telegraph*, https://www.telegraph.co.uk/news/2020/04/26/judges-told-stop-using-beyond-reasonable-doubt-confuses-juries/

Adenas M and Cortesi I, 'The creation of a Vatican financial regulatory framework' (2017) 6(2) *Law and Economics Yearly Review* 242

Adler D, 'Silk Road: The dark side of cryptocurrency' (2018) *Fordham Journal of Corporate and Financial Law*, 21 February, https://news.law.fordham.edu/jcfl/2018/02/21/silk-road-the-dark-side-of-cryptocurrency

Adorno T, *Problems of Moral Philosophy* (Polity 2001)

Agamben G, *State of Exception* (University of Chicago Press 2005)

Ahlfort K, *Cashless Future for Sweden?* (KTH 2015)

Alexander C and Cohen A, *Trends in the Use of Non-Prosecution, Deferred Prosecution, and Plea Agreements in the Settlement of Alleged Corporate Criminal Wrongdoing* (April 2015), Searle Civil Justice Institute, https://masonlec.org/site/rte_uploads/files/ Full%20Report%20-%20SCJI%20NPA-DPA%2C%20April%202015%281%29.pdf

Alexander K, Dhumale R and Eatwell J, *Global Governance of Financial Systems: The International Regulation of Systemic Risk* (Oxford University Press 2006)

Allen C, *Islamophobia* (Ashgate 2010)

Allen M, 'Uniting to tackle financial crime' (27 February 2015), *BBA*, https://www.bba.org.uk/news/bba-voice/uniting-to-tackle-financial-crime/#.XyvQWhNKhQI

Allison I, 'Inside the standards race for implementing FATF's travel rule' (4 February 2020) *Coindesk*, https://www.coindesk.com/inside-the-standards-race-for-implementing-fatfs-travel-rule

Amable B, 'Morals and politics in the ideology of neo-liberalism' (2011) 9 (1) *Socio-Economic Review* 3

Ames J, 'Zamira Hajiyeva: McMafia banker's wife could lose her £15m home after court defeat' (6 February 2020) *The Times*

Anagnostopoulos I, 'Fintech and Regtech: Impact on regulators and banks' (2018) *Journal of Economics and Business* 7

Anderson, JL, *Mahogany: The Costs of Luxury in Early America* (Harvard University Press 2012)

Ariel B, 'Disrupting organised crime networks: An evidence based approach to establishing effective interventions' (RUSI 2014)

Armstrong L and Abel G, *Sex Work and the New Zealand Model – Decriminalisation and Social Change* (Bristol University Press 2020)

Aronowitz A, 'Smuggling and trafficking in human beings: The phenomenon, the markets that drive it and the organisations that promote it' (2001) 9 *European Journal on Criminal Policy and Research* 163

Arvidsson N, *Building a Cashless Society: The Swedish Route to the Future of Cash Payments* (SpringerBriefs in Economics, Springer International Publishing 2019) 46

Arvidsson N, Hedman J and Segendorf B, *När slutar svenska handlare att ta emot kontanter? [When will Swedish merchants stop receiving cash?]* (Handelsrådets Forskningsrapport, 2018)

Atkinson C, 'Where were you while we were getting high policing? The consequences of co-location for broader partnership working in tackling organised crime and terrorism' (2019) 29 *Policing and Society* 922

Atkinson R and Rodgers T, 'Pleasure zones and murder boxes: Online pornography and violent video games as cultural zones of exception' (2015) 56 (6) *British Journal of Criminology* 1291

Auer R, 'Beyond the doomsday economics of "proof-of- work" in cryptocurrencies' (January 2019) *BIS Working Papers* 765, 3 https://www.bis.org/publ/work765.htm

Auer R and Boehme R, 'The technology of retail Central Bank digital currency' (March 2020) *BIS Quarterly Review* 85

Auer R and Claessens S, 'Regulating cryptocurrencies: Assessing market reactions' (September 2018) *BIS Quarterly Review* 52, https://www.bis.org/publ/qtrpdf/r_qt1809f.pdf

Australian Transaction Reports and Analysis Centre, 'About the Fintel alliance' (AUSTRAC, 3 March 2017), https://www.austrac.gov.au/about-us/fintel-alliance

Badiou A, *The Century* (Polity 2008)

Bakan J, *The Corporation: The Pathological Pursuit of Profit and Power* (Constable, 2005)

Banai A and Kreide R, 'Securitization of migration in Germany: The ambivalences of citizenship and human rights' (2017) 21 *Citizenship Studies* 903

Barkow A and Barkow R, *Prosecutors in the Boardroom: Using Criminal Law to Regulate Corporate Conduct* (NYU Press 2011) 4

Barshad A, 'The life and death of the "bin Laden" slate', https://slate.com/news-and-politics/2019/08/euros-500-bin-ladens.html

Barton M, '"It's a myth that we can arrest our way out of drug problems" – Mike Barton speech at CDPRG launch' (Conservative Drug Policy Reform Group 2019), https://www.cdprg.co.uk/blog/2019/7/4/its-a-myth-that-we-can-arrest-our-way-out-of-drug-problems-mike-barton-speech-at-cdprg-launch

Baum D, *Smoke and Mirrors: The War on Drugs and the Politics of Failure* (reprint edition, Back Bay Books 1997)

Baver, SL and Lynch BD, 'The political ecology of paradise', in Baver and Lynch (eds.), *Beyond Sun and Sand: Caribbean Environmentalisms* (Rutgers University Press 2006)

Baydakova A, '$2 billion lost in Mt. Gox bitcoin hack can be recovered, lawyer claims' (12 September 2019), coindesk.com, www.coindesk.com/2-billion-lost-in-mt-gox-bitcoin-hack-can-be-recovered-lawyer-claims

BBC News, 'Hundreds arrested as crime chat network cracked' (BBC News 2020)

Beer C, Gnan E and Birchler UW (eds), *Cash on Trial, SUERF Conference Proceedings 2016/1* (2016)

Bell R, 'The confiscation, forfeiture and disruption of terrorist finances' (2004) *Journal of Money Laundering Control* 7(2), 105–25

Benson M, 'Denying the guilty mind: Accounting for involvement in a white-collar crime' (1985) 23 (4) *Criminology* 583

Benson ML, Slyke S and Cullen FT, 'Core themes in the study of white-collar crime' in Slyke, Benson and Cullen (eds), *The Oxford Handbook of White Collar Crime* (Oxford University Press 2016)

Bermingham R, 'Horizon scanning: Crime, justice, policing and COVID-19: What are experts concerned about?' (2020) *POST*, https://post.parliament.uk/ crime -justice-policing-and-covid-19-what-are-experts-concerned-about/

Bernstein R, 'Pope helped bring Poland freedom' (6 April 2005) *New York Times*

Boar C, Holden H and Wadsworth A, 'Impending arrival – A sequel to the survey on Central Bank digital currency' (2020) BIS Paper No.107, www.bis.org/publ/ bppdf/bispap107.pdf

Bonger W, *Criminality and Economic Conditions* (William Heinemann 1916)

Bonnier J, *The Helicopter Heist: A Novel Based on True Events* (Other Press 2017)

Bostwick J, *US vs. UK Deferred-Prosecution Agreements: Some History and Key Differences* (8 July 2017) *Vistra*, https://ieglobal.vistra.com/blog/2017/ 8/us-vs-uk-deferred-prosecution-agreements-some-history-and-key-differences#

Boukli A and Kotzé J, 'Introduction' in A Boukli and J Kotzé (eds.) *Zemiology: Reconnecting Crime and Social Harm* (Routledge 2018)

Boyns D and Ballard JD, 'Developing a sociological theory for the empirical understanding of terrorism' (2004) 35 *The American Sociologist* 5

Brassey J and Burns R, 'Guilty until proven innocent! Unexplained wealth orders: What are they and could they affect you and your clients?' (2020) 26(6) *T&T* 468

Brodeur JP, 'High policing and low policing: Remarks about the policing of political activities' (1983) 30 *Social Problems* 507

Brown D, 'Streatham attack: He grabbed knife near till then ran out and began stabbing' (3 February 2020) *The Times*, https://www.thetimes.co.uk/article /streatham-attack-he-grabbed-a-knife-near-the-till-then-ran-out-and-began -stabbing-b0wtt7tv6

Brown RG, 'When "final" isn't actually final: Cracking blockchain's consensus conundrum' (22 November 2019) *Forbes*, www.forbes.com/sites/ richardgen dalbrown/2019/11/22/when-final-isnt-actually-final-cracking-blockchains-con sensus-conundrum/#c87b74660400

Bullmann D, Klemm J and Pinna A, 'In search for stability in crypto-assets: Are stablecoins the solution?' (August 2019) European Central Bank, Occasional Paper No. 230

Burdis K and Tombs S, 'After the crisis: New directions in theorizing corporate and white-collar crime' in S Hall and S Winlow (eds) *New Directions in Criminological Theory* (Routledge 2012)

Butler E, 'Removing obstacles on the road to economic freedom: 1947–1980' in JB Taylor (ed) *A Special Meeting The Mont Pelerin Society 1980–2020. From the Past to the Future: Ideas and Actions for a Free Society* (Hoover Institution/Stanford University 2020)

Buttigieg CP, Efthymiopoulos C, Attard A and Cuyle S, 'Anti-money laundering regulation of crypto assets in Europe's smallest member state' (2019) 13 *Law and Financial Markets Review* 221

Button M and Tunley M, 'The 2008 financial crisis and fraud: The roles of immoral phlegmatism, deviancy attenuation and de-labelling', in N Ryder, J Tucker and U Turksen (eds), *The Financial Crisis and White Collar Crime – Legislative and Policy Responses: A Critical Assessment* (Routledge 2017)

Cable V, 'Piercing the "silos" in government is challenging – But necessary' (2015) *New Statesman*, https://www.newstatesman.com/culture/books/2015/10/piercing-silos-government-challenging-necessary

CAIN, 'Fact sheet on the conflict in and about Northern Ireland' (2007) *CAIN Web Service – Conflict and Politics in Northern Ireland*, https://cain.ulster.ac.uk/victims/docs/group/htr/day_of_reflection/htr_0607c.pdf

Calderoni F, 'Although there is little truth behind the "godfather" stereotype, mafia infiltration remains a serious problem in Italian politics' (2012) *LSE Blog*, https://blogs.lse.ac.uk/europpblog/2012/11/01/mafia-francesco-calderoni/

Camillus JC, 'Strategy as a wicked problem' (2008) *Harvard Business Review* 11

Campbell-Verduyn M, 'Bitcoin, crypto-coins, and global anti-money laundering governance' (2018) 69 *Crime, Law and Social Change* 283

Castrillo P, 'Towards a narrative definition of the American political thriller film' (2015) 28 (4) *Communication and Society* 109

Chainalysis, 'Chainalysis in action: Department of Justice announces takedown of two terrorism financing campaigns with help from blockchain analysis' (13 August 2020) *Chainalysis*, https://blog.chainalysis.com/reports/ cryptocurrency-terrorism-financing-al-qaeda-al-qassam-brigades-bitcointransfer

Chainalysis, 'The 2021 Crypto Crime Report' (16 February 2021) *Chainalysis*, https://go.chainalysis.com/rs/503-FAP-074/images/Chainalysis-Crypto-Crime-2021.pdf

Chambers T, 'Unstable coins: Cryptoassets, financial regulation and preventing financial crime in the emerging market for digital assets' (5 March 2020) FCA, Speech delivered at The Advancement of Digital Assets and Addressing Financial Crime Risk, New York University School of Law, https://www.fca.org.uk/news/speeches/unstable-coins

Choo A, *The Privilege Against Self-Incrimination and Criminal Justice* (Hart 2013)

Christie CJ and Hanna RM, 'A push down the road of good corporate citizenship: The deferred prosecution agreement between the US Attorney for the Distribute of New Jersey and Bristol-Myers Squibb Co.' (2006) 43 *American Criminal Law Review* 1043

CipherTrace, 'Cryptocurrency Crime and Anti-Money Laundering Report Spring 2020' (June 2020) *CipherTrace* 6, https://ciphertrace.com/spring-2020-cryptocurrency-anti-money-laundering-report/?submissionGuid=9c633339-6b58-43ae-bf15-6c44d3187989

CipherTrace, 'Cryptocurrency Crime and Anti-Money Laundering Report (February 2021) *CipherTrace* 7, https://ciphertrace.com/2020-year-end-cryptocurrency-crime-and-anti-money-laundering-report/

Clancy A, 'Proving the dough: *National Crime Agency v Baker & Ors*' (2021) MLR 84(1) 168

Clatworthy B, 'Don't get stuck with a "bin Laden" €500 note' (18 August 2018) *The Times*

Committee on Banking Regulation and Supervisory Practices, Concordat on Supervision of Banks' Foreign Establishments in IMF, 'International capital markets: Recent developments and short-term prospects' (1981) Occasional Paper No. 7

Committee on Payments and Market Infrastructures, *Distributed Ledger Technology in Payment, Clearing and Settlement*, (February 2017) *CPMI* 16, https://www.bis.org/cpmi/publ/d157.pdf

Cooper V and Whyte D, 'Introduction: The violence of austerity' in V Cooper and D Whyte (eds.) *The Violence of Austerity* (Pluto 2017)

Cortesi I and Adenas M, 'The creation of a Vatican financial regulatory framework' (2017) 6(2) *Law and Economics Yearly Review* 242

Côté-Lussier C, 'The evil, poor, disliked and punished: Criminal stereotypes and the effects of their cognitive, affective and behavioural outcomes on punitiveness toward crime' (London School of Economics 2012) PhD thesis

Council of Europe, 'Moneyval publishes report on the Holy See' (8 December 2017) Newsroom para 65, https://www.coe.int/en/web/moneyval/-/moneyval-publishes-a-report-on-the-holy-seeCouncil of Europe

Council of Europe Communications, 'Council of Europe report calls for Holy See to strengthen supervisory regime', https://rm.coe.int/1680721478

Croall H, *Understanding White Collar Crime* (Open University Press 2001)

Cuervo C, Morozova, A and Sugimoto N, 'Regulation of crypto assets' (10 January 2020) *International Monetary Fund*, FinTech Notes No. 19/03 16, www.imf.org/en/Publications/fintech-notes/Issues/2020/01/09/Regulation-of-Crypto-Assets-48810

Currie E, 'Market, crime and community: Toward a mid-range theory of post-industrial violence' (1997) 1(2) *Theoretical Criminology* 147

Dabrowski M and Janikowski L, 'Virtual currencies and Central Bank's monetary policy: Challenges ahead' (June 2018) Policy Department for Economic, Scientific and Quality of Life Policies, Directorate-General for Internal Policies PE 619.009

Davies T, 'The divided gaze: Reflections on the political thriller', in D Longhurst (ed.), *Gender, Genre, and Narrative Pleasure* (Unwin Hyman 1989)

Davis M and Monk DB, 'Introduction' in M Davis and D Bertrand Monk (eds.) *Evil Paradises: Dreamworlds of Neo-liberalism* (New Press 2007)

De Pascalis F, 'Financial crime prevention and control: The reforms of a 'unique' jurisdiction under EU law and international standards' (2015) 17(4) *European Journal of Law Reform* 528, 532

de Tocqueville A, *Democracy in America* (HarperCollins 1968)

de Waal A et al., 'Silo-busting: Overcoming the greatest threat to organizational performance' (2019) 11 *Sustainability* 6860

Dean J, *Democracy and Other Neo-liberal Fantasies: Communicative Capitalism and Left Politics* (Duke University Press 2009)

Deloitte, 'The future of regulatory productivity, powered by RegTech' (2017), www2.deloitte.com/us/en/pages/regulatory/articles/cost-of-compliance-regulatory-productivity.html

Dews P, *The Idea of Evil* (Blackwell 2008)

Dhumale R, Alexander K and Eatwell J, *Global Governance of Financial Systems: The International Regulation of Systemic Risk* (Oxford University Press 2006)

Ditcham K, 'How COVID-19 is changing the organised crime threat' (2020) *RUSI*, https://rusi.org/commentary/how-covid-19-changing-organised-crime-threat

Dodd V, 'London Bridge attackers bought knives from Lidl for £4 each, say police' (11June 2017) *The Guardian*, https://www.theguardian.com/uk-news/2017/jun/11/london-bridge-attackers-bought-knives-from-lidl-for-4-each-say-police

Don B, 'Network technologies for networked terrorists' (2007) RAND, https://www.rand.org/pubs/technical_reports/TR454.html

Ducan C, 'Boohoo "facing modern slavery investigation"' (2020) *The Independent*, https://www.independent.co.uk/news/uk/home-news/boohoo-leicester-factories-modern-slavery-boohoo-leicester-factories-modern-slavery-investigation-coronavirus-coronavirus-fast-fashion-a9602086.html

Dunn G, *2018 Year-end Update on Corporate Non-Prosecution Agreements and Deferred Prosecution Agreements* (10 January 2019), https://www.gibsondunn.com/2018-year-end-npa-dpa-update/

Dunn G, *2019 Year End Update on Corporate Non-prosecution Agreements and Deferred Prosecution Agreements* (10 January 2020), https://www.gibsondunn.com/2019-year-end-npa-dpa-update/

Eagleton T, *On Evil* (Yale University Press 2010)

Eatwell J, Alexander K and Dhumale R, *Global Governance of Financial Systems: The International Regulation of Systemic Risk* (Oxford University Press 2006)

Edelhertz H, *The Nature, Impact, and Prosecution of White-Collar Crime* (US Government Printing Office 1970)

Ellis C and de Oliveira I, 'Tackling money laundering, towards a new model for information sharing' (September 2015) RUSI Occasional Papers

English R, *Armed Struggle – A History of the IRA* (Macmillan 2003)

Ermingen-Marbach R and Zeidler F, *The German Corporate Sanctions Act – Heralding a New Era of Enforcement in Germany*, https://wp.nyu.edu/compliance_ enforcement/2020/04/14/the-german-corporate-sanctions-act-heralding-a-new-era-for-enforcement-in-germany/

Eurofund, 'Cash register legislation, Sweden' (2013) *Eurofund*

Europa series, (European Central Bank and Suomen Pankki 2015)

European Banking Authority, 'Opinion on "virtual currencies"' (4 July 2014) EBA/Op/2014/08

European Banking Authority, *Report with Advice for the European Commission on Crypto-assets*, January (9 January 2019) EBA, www.eba.europa.eu/eba-reports-on-crypto-assets

European Central Bank, *The Payment System* (Tom Kokkola ed.) (2010) ECB

European Central Bank Crypto-Assets Task Force, *Crypto-Assets: Implications for Financial Stability, Monetary Policy, and Payments and Market Infrastructures* (May 2019) ECB Occasional Papers No. 223, www.ecb.europa.eu/pub/pdf/scpops/ecb.op223~3ce14e986c.en.pdf

European Commission (2017) *Report from the Commission to the European Parliament and the Council on the Assessment of the Risks of Money Laundering and Terrorist Financing Affecting the Internal Market and Relating to Cross-border Activities* Brussels 24.7.2019 COM/2017/0340 final

European Commission, 'Commission Staff Working Document, Analysis of non-conviction based confiscation measures in the European Union' (12 April 2019)

European Court of Human Rights, 'Guide on Article 6 of the European Convention on Human Rights' (updated 30 April 2020), https://www.echr.coe.int/Documents/Guide_Art_6_criminal_ENG.pdf

European Securities and Markets Authority (ESMA), *Advice on Initial Coin Offerings and Crypto-Assets* (9 January 2019) ESMA50-157-1391, para 17, www.esma.europa.eu/document/advice-initial-coin-offerings-and-crypto-assets

EUROPOL Financial Intelligence Group, *Why is Cash still King? A Strategic Report on the Use of Cash by Europol*, 'Crime in the Age of Technology' (2017) EUROPOL EDOC# 924156 v7, https://www.cepol.europa.eu/sites/ default/files/924156-v7-Crime_in_the_age_of_technology_.pdf

Farming UK, 'Report shines light on modern-day slavery in UK agricultural industry' (2018) *FarmingUK*, https://www.farminguk.com/news/report-shines-light-on-modern-day-slavery-in-uk-agricultural-industry_49237.html

Farley P, 'Spotlight on compliance costs as banks get down to business with AI' (4 July 2017) *International Banker*, https://internationalbanker.com/technology/spotlight-compliance-costs-banks-get-business-ai/

FATF, 'FATF guidance on the risk-based approach to combating money laundering and terrorist financing: High level principles and procedures' (June 2007) FATF, Paris, https://www.fatf-gafi.org/publications/fatfrecommendations/ documents/fatfguidanceontherisk-basedapproachtocombating moneylaunderingandterroristfinancing-highlevelprinciplesandprocedures.html

FATF, *International Standards on Combating Money Laundering and the Financing of Terrorism & Proliferation* (2012–2020) FATF, Paris, www.fatf-gafi.org/recommendations.html

FATF, 'Anti-money laundering and counter-terrorist financing measures – United Kingdom, Fourth Round Mutual Evaluation Report' (2018) FATF, Paris, 51, http://www.fatf-gafi.org/publications/mutualevaluations/documents/ mer-united-kingdom2018.html

FCPA Professor, *RIP 'Arthur Andersen Effect' As FedEx Beats Back the DOJ* (17 June 2016), http://fcpaprofessor.com/rip-arthur-andersen-effect-as-fedex-beats-back-the-doj/

Figueroa E, *Limbo: A Novel About Jamaica* (Arcade 2014)

Financial Action Task Force *Money Laundering FAQ*, //www.fatf-gafi.org/document/29/0,3746,en_32250379_32235720_33659613_1_1_1_1,00.html#howmuchmoneyislaunderedperyear

Financial Action Task Force, *International Standards on Combating Money Laundering and the Financing of Terrorism & Proliferation* (2012) FATF

Financial Action Task Force, *FATF Guidance National Money Laundering and Terrorist Financing Risk Assessment* (2013) FATF

Financial Action Task Force, *Virtual Currencies Key Definitions and Potential AML/CFT Risks* (June 2014) FATF Report

Financial Action Task Force, *Guidance for a Risk-based Approach – Virtual Currencies* (June 2015) FATF

Financial Action Task Force, *Anti-Money Laundering and Counter-Terrorist Financing Measures United Kingdom Mutual Evaluation Report* (2018) FATF

Financial Action Task Force, *FATF Report – Professional Money Laundering* (2018) FATF

Financial Action Task Force, *Guidance for a Risk-based Approach – Virtual Assets and Virtual Asset Service Providers* (June 2019) FATF

Financial Action Task Force, 'Money laundering risks from "stablecoins" and other emerging assets' (18 October 2019) FATF, Paris, https://www.fatf-gafi.org/

publications/fatfgeneral/documents/statement-virtual-assets-global-stablecoins.html

Financial Action Task Force, *FATF Report to the G20 Finance Ministers and Central Bank Governors on So-called Stablecoins* (June 2020) FATF

Financial Action Task Force, *12-month Review Virtual Assets and VASPs* (June 2020) FATF

Financial Conduct Authority, *Anti-money Laundering Annual Report 2012/13* (London 2013) Financial Conduct Authority

Financial Conduct Authority, 'Anti-money laundering' (14 November 2011), www.fca.org.uk/firms/being-regulated/meeting-your-obligations/firm-guides/systems/aml, accessed 24 June 2015

Financial Conduct Authority, 'Effectiveness and proportionality: Our financial crime priorities – Speech by Rob Gruppetta, Head of Financial Crime Department', 10 November 2016, https://www.fca.org.uk/news/ speeches/effectiveness-proportionality-financial-crime-priorities

Financial Crimes Enforcement Network, *Application of FinCEN's Regulations to Persons Administering, Exchanging, or Using Virtual Currencies* (18 March 2013) *FinCEN*, FIN-2013-G001

Financial Stability Board (FSB), *Crypto-asset Markets, Potential Channels for Future Financial Stability Implications* (10 October 2018) *FSB* 3, www.fsb.org/wp-content/uploads/P101018.pdf

Financial Stability Board, *Regulatory Issues of Stablecoins* (18 October 2019) FSB, www.fsb.org/2019/10/regulatory-issues-of-stablecoins/

Fisher J, 'Recent development in the fight against money laundering' (2002), *Journal of International Banking Law* 17(3), 67–72

Fisher J and Sumpster T, *Fighting Fraud and Financial Crime* (Policy Exchange 2010)

Fisher M, 'How to kill a zombie: Strategizing the end of neo-liberalism' (2013) Open Democracy, www.opendemocracy.net

Fisher M, *Capitalist Realism: Is There No Alternative?* (Zero Books 2009)

Flemming MH, *UK Law Enforcement Agency Use and Management of Suspicious Activity Reports: Towards Determining the Value of the Regime* (2005) Home Office

Foley S, Karlsen JR, Putniņš TJ, 'Sex, drugs, and bitcoin: How much illegal activity is financed through cryptocurrencies?' (2019) 32 *Review of Financial Studies* 1798

Fors F and Hansén D, 'Pressured to learn? Swedish police experiences of curbing organized crime' (2016) *Forum*

Foster J and Jones C, '"Nice to do" and essential: Improving neighbourhood policing in an English police force' (2010) 4 *Policing: A Journal of Policy and Practice* 395

Frank T, *The Wrecking Crew: The American Right and the Lust for Power* (Random House 2008)

Fredholm M, *Transnational Organized Crime and Jihadist Terrorism: Russian-Speaking Networks in Western Europe* (Routledge 2017)

French National Financial Prosecutor's Office, 'Guidelines on the Implementation of the Convention Judiciaire D'interet', https://www.agence-francaise-anticorruption.gouv.fr/files/files/EN_Lignes_directrices_CJIP_revAFA%20Final%20(002).pdf

Friedman M, 'Neo-liberalism and its prospects' (February 1951) *Farmand*, https://miltonfriedman.hoover.org/friedman_images/ Collections/2016c21/Farmand_02_17_1951.pdf

Friedman M, *Capitalism and Freedom* (40th anniversary edn. University of Chicago Press 2002)

Friedrichs DO, 'White collar crime in a postmodern, globalized eorld' in G Geis and HN Pontell (eds.), *International Handbook of White Collar and Corporate Crime* (Springer 2007)

FSA Press Release, 'FSA fines Alpari and its former money laundering reporting officer, Sudipto Chattopadhyay for anti-money laundering failings' (5 May 2010), www.fsa.gov.uk/pages/Library/Communication/PR/2010/077.shtml

Galeotti M, 'Introduction: Global crime today' in M Galeotti (ed.), *Global Crime Today: The Changing Face of Organised Crime* (Routledge 2014)

Garrison A, 'Terrorism: The nature of its history' (2003) 16 *Criminal Justice Studies* 39

Global Initiative Against Transnational Organised Crime, 'Transnational organized crime and the impact on the private sector: The hidden battalion' (2017) Global Initiative against Transnational Organized Crime, https://www.unodc.org/res/cld/bibliography/ transnational-organized-crime-and-the-impact-on-the-private-sector_-the-hidden-battalions_html/gitoc_tocprivatesector_web-3.pdf

Gogo J, 'Estonia revokes 500 crypto firms' licenses after $220 billion money laundering scandal' (13 June 2020) *bitcoin.com*, https://news.bitcoin.com/estonia-revokes-500-crypto-firms-licenses-after-220-billion-money-laundering-scandal/

Gottschalk P and Gunnesdal L, *White-Collar Crime in the Shadow Economy: Lack of Detection, Investigation and Conviction Compared to Social Security Fraud* (Springer 2018)

Grabosky P, 'Globalization and white-collar crime' in SS. Simpson and D Weisburd (eds.), *The Criminology of White-Collar Crime* (Springer 2009)

Grace J, 'Turks and Caicos; Arena; Whatever happened to Spitting Image? TV review' (21 March 2014) *The Guardian*

Grant T, 'Canadian banks, police following money trail to target human trafficking' (21 February 2017) *The Globe and Mail*, https://www.theglobeandmail.com/news/national/canadian-banks-police-following-money-trail-to-target-human-trafficking/article34093888/#:~:text= Canadian%20banks%2C%20police%20following%20money%20trail%20to%20target%20human%20trafficking,-Open%20this%20photo&text=Project% 20Protect%20is%20a%20partnership,to%20detect%20and%20investigate%20traffickers

Gray O, *Demeaned but Empowered: The Social Power of the Urban Poor in Jamaica* (University of the West Indies Press 2004)

Greeley B, 'The comfort of cash in a time of coronavirus' (16 July 2020) *Financial Times*, https://www.ft.com/

Greer TS, 'The myth of the "securitized Muslim community": The social impact of post-9/11 counter-terrorist law and policy in the West' in C Walker and G Lennon (eds.), *Routledge Handbook on Law and Terrorism* (Routledge 2015)

Griffin SP, 'Caribbean islands', in LM Salinger (ed.), *Encyclopedia of White-Collar and Corporate Crime* (Sage 2005) volume 1

Grimes J, Niblock R and Madden L, 'Corporate criminal liability in the UK: The introduction of deferred prosecution agreements, proposals for further change, and the consequences for officers and senior managers', (2013/14) Association of Corporate Counsel, Practical Law

Gunning J, 'A case for critical terrorism studies?' (2007) 42 *Government and Opposition* 363

Guzman A and Meyer T, 'International soft law' 2010 2(1) *Journal of Legal Analysis* 171–225

Hall S, *Theorizing Crime and Deviance: A New Perspective* (Sage 2012)

Hall S and Winlow S, 'Barbarians at the gate: Crime and violence in the breakdown of the pseudo-pacification process' in J Ferrell (ed.) *Cultural Criminology Unleashed* (Glasshouse Press 2004)

Hall S, Winlow S and Ancrum C, *Criminal Identities and Consumer Culture: Crime, Exclusion and the New Culture of Narcissism* (Willan 2008)

Hallsworth S, *Street Crime* (Willan 2005)

Hare D, *Turks and Caicos* [Film] (Carnival Films/Heyday Films/NBC Universal 2014)

Harney A and Stecklow A, 'Twice burned – How Mt. Gox's bitcoin customers could lose again' (16 November 2017) Reuters, www.reuters.com/ investigates/ special-report/bitcoin-gox/

Harper T, 'From London Bridge to Ariana Grande, UK terror attacks cost just £5000 to execute' (9 September 2018) *The Times*, https://www.thetimes.co.uk/article/ from-london-bridge-to-ariana-grande-uk-terror-attacks-in-2017-cost-just-5-000 -vck5tdttg

Harrison K and Ryder N, *The Law Relating to Financial Crime in the United Kingdom* (Routledge, 2016)

Harvey D, *A Brief History of Neo-Liberalism* (Oxford University Press 2007)

Harvey D, *The Enigma of Capital: And the Crises of Capitalism* (Profile Books 2010)

Harvey J, 'Compliance and reporting issues arising for financial institutions from money laundering regulations: A preliminary cost benefit study' (2004) *Journal of Money Laundering Control* 7(4), 333

Harvey J, 'An evaluation of money laundering policies' (2005) *Journal of Money Laundering Control* 8(4) 339

Hayek F, *The Road to Serfdom* (Routledge & Kegan Paul 1976)

Head B and Alford J, 'Wicked problems: Implications for public policy and management' (2015) 47 *Administration and Society* 711

Headworth S and Hagen JL, 'White-collar crimes of the financial crisis', in SL Van Slyke, ML Benson and FT Cullen (eds.), *The Oxford Handbook of White-Collar Crime* (Oxford University Press 2016)

Heasman W, 'Governments begin to roll out FATF's travel rule around the globe' (14 February 2020) *Cointelegraph*, https://cointelegraph.com/news/governments -begin-to-roll-out-fatfs-travel-rule-around-the-globe

Hendry J and King C, 'How far is too far? Theorising non-conviction-based asset forfeiture' 11 (2015) *IJLC* 396

Henley J, '€500 "Bin Laden" banknotes to be axed' (4 May 2016) *The Guardian*

Hill S, *Deferred Prosecution Agreements: The US experience and the UK Potential*, 14 (July 2014) Lexology, https://www.lexology.com/ library/detail.aspx?g=4f0 cc529-bfdb-49c3-ac8d-e989e87fc84a

Hillyard P, *Suspect Community: People's Experience of the Prevention of Terrorism Acts in Britain* (Pluto 1993)

Hillyard P and Tombs S, 'Towards a political economy of harm: States, corporations and the production of inequality' in P Hillyard (ed.) *Beyond Criminology: Taking Harm Seriously* (Pluto 2004)

HM Government, 'The United Kingdom's Strategy for Countering International Terrorism' (London 2009) HM Government HMSO Cm 7547

HM Government, *The Coalition: Our Programme for Government* (London 2010) HM Government

HM Government, *Local to Global: Reducing the Risk from Organised Crime* (London 2011) HM Government

HM Government, *UK National Risk Assessment of Money Laundering and Terrorism Financing* (London 2015) HM Government

HM Government, *Explanatory Notes Criminal Finances Act 2017* (London 2017) HM Government

HM Government, *UK National Risk Assessment of Money Laundering and Terrorist Financing* (London 2017) HM Government

HM Government, *Serious and Organised Crime Strategy* (2018) HM Government

HM Government, *UK National Risk Assessment of Money Laundering and Terrorist Financing* (London 2020) HM Government

HM Government, *Economic Crime Plan – Statement of Progress* (London 2021) HM Government

HM Treasury, *Combating the Financing of Terrorism. A Report on UK action* (London 2002) HM Treasury

HM Treasury, *The Financial Challenge of Terrorism and Crime* (London 2007) HM Treasury

HM Treasury, 'George Osborne, Chancellor of the Exchequer: Speech at the Lord Mayor's Dinner for Bankers & Merchants of the City of London, at Mansion House 16 June 2010', www.hm-treasury.gov.uk/press_12_10.htm

HM Treasury, *A New Approach to Financial Regulation: Consultation on Reforming the Consumer Credit Regime* (London 2010) HM Treasury

HM Treasury, *Anti-Money Laundering and Counter Terrorist Finance: Supervision Report 2010–11* (London 2011) HM Treasury

HM Treasury, 'Policy paper: Preventing money laundering' (London 5 June 2013), HM Treasury, www.gov.uk/government/publications/preventing-money-laundering/preventing-money-laundering#financial-action-task-force-fatf

HM Treasury, *Advisory Notice on Money Laundering and Terrorist Financing Controls in Overseas Jurisdictions* (2015)

HM Treasury, *National Risk Assessment of Money Laundering and Terrorist Financing* (London 2017) HM Treasury

HM Treasury, 'Economic Crime Plan 2019–2022' (London 2019) HM Treasury

HM Treasury, *Transposition of the Fifth Money Laundering Directive: Response to the Consultation* (London 2020) HM Treasury

HMICFRS, *An Inspection of the NCA* (London 2015)

Hobbes T, *Leviathan* (Hackett 1994)

Hobbs D, 'Professional and Organized Crime in Britain' in M Maguire et al. (eds.) *The Oxford Handbook of Criminology* (Oxford University Press 1994)

Hobbs D, *Bad Business: Professional Criminals in Modern Britain* (Oxford University Press 1995)

Hobbs D, 'Criminal collaboration: Youth gangs, subcultures, professional criminals and organized crime' in M Maguire et al. (eds.) *The Oxford Handbook of Criminology* (2nd edn. Oxford University Press 1997)

Hobbs D, *Lush Life: Constructing Organized Crime in the UK* (Oxford University Press 2013)

Home Affairs Committee, 'Policing for the Future: Tenth Report of Session 2017–19' (House of Commons 2018) HC 515, https://publications.parliament.uk/pa/ cm201719/cmselect/cmhaff/515/515.pdf

Home Office, *Report on the Operation in 2004 of the Terrorism Act 2000* (2004) Home Office 19–20

Home Office, 'Economic crime press release' (17 January 2011), www.homeoffice.gov.uk/ media-centre/news/economic-crime

Home Office, *The National Crime Agency: A Plan for the Creation of a National Crime-Fighting Capability* (2011)

Home Office, 'Definition of policing by consent' (2012) GOV.UK, https://www.gov.uk/government/publications/policing-by-consent/definition-of-policing-by-consent

Home Office, *Understanding Organised Crime: Estimating the Scale and the Social and Economic Costs Research Report 73* (Home Office 2013)

Home Office and HM Treasury, 'Action plan for anti-money laundering and counter-terrorist finance' (Home Office/HM Treasury 2016)

Hong Kong Monetary Authority, 'Fraud and Money Laundering Intelligence Taskforce launched' (26 May 2017) HKMA, https://www.hkma.gov.hk/ eng/news-and-media/press-releases/2017/05/20170526-3/

Hopkins N and Bengtsson H, 'What are the Paradise Papers and what do they tell us?' (5 November 2017) *The Guardian*, https://www.theguardian.com/ news/2017/nov/05/what-are-the-paradise-papers-and-what-do-they-tell-us

Houben R, and Snyers A, 'Cryptocurrencies and blockchain: Legal context and implications for financial crime, money laundering and tax evasion' (July 2018) Policy Department for Economic, Scientific and Quality of Life Policies, Directorate-General for Internal Policies, Study Requested by the TAX3 Committee, European Parliament, PE 619.024, www.europarl.europa.eu/cmsdata/150761/TAX3%20Study%20on%20cryptocurrencies%20and%20blockchain.pdf

Houben R and Snyers E, 'Cryptocurrencies crypto-assets – Key developments, regulatory concerns and responses' (April 2020) Study for the Committee on Economic and Monetary Affairs, Policy Department for Economic, Scientific and Quality of Life Policies, European Parliament, Luxembourg, PE 648.779, https://www.europarl.europa.eu/thinktank/en/document.html?reference=IPOL_STU(2020)648779

House of Commons, 'Report of the official account of the bombings in London on 7th July 2005' (London 2005)

House of Commons, Treasury Select Committee, *Crypto-assets* (12 September 2018) Twenty-Second Report of Session 2017–19

Hudson M, *The Bubble and Beyond: Fictitious Capital, Debt Deflation and Global Crisis* (ISLET 2012)

Hughes K, *French DPAs – Considering the First Guidelines* (6 August 2019) QEB, https://www.qebholliswhiteman.co.uk/site/library/articles/french-dpas-considering-the-first-guidelines

Hurd T, 'Protect and serve: Office for Security and Counter-Terrorism DG Tom Hurd on how government works together to keep the UK safe' (2020) *Civil Service World*, https://www.civilserviceworld.com/in-depth/article/protect-and-serve-office-for-security-and-counterterrorism-dg-tom-hurd-on-how-government-works-together-to-keep-the-uk-safe

Hutton W, *The State We're In* (Jonathan Cape 1995)

IAFOR, *Investigating Wrongful Convictions around the World* (14 September 2016), https://iafor.org/investigating-wrongful-convictions-around-the-world-alec-klein/

Illovsky E, 'Corporate deferred prosecution agreements' (2006) 21 *Criminal Justice* 36

Ingham G, *The Nature of Money* (Polity 2004)

Innes M, Roberts C and Lowe T, 'A disruptive influence? "Prevent-ing" problems and countering violent extremism policy in practice' (2017) 51 *Law & Society Review* 252

Institute for Economics and Peace, 'Global Terrorism Index 2017: Measuring and understanding the impact of terrorism' (2017) 5, http://visionofhumanity.org/app/uploads/2017/11/Global-Terrorism-Index2017.pdf

Institute for Economics and Peace, '2019 Global Terrorism Index: Deaths from terrorism halved in the last four years, but number of countries affected by terrorism is growing' (2019) *News*, https://www.prnewswire.co.uk/news-releases/2019-global-terrorism-index-deaths-from-terrorism-halved-in-the-last-four-years-but-number-of-countries-affected-by-terrorism-is-growing-837142983.html

Institute of International Finance, 'IIF Financial Crime Information Sharing Report' (31 March 2017) IFF, /Publications/ID/952/IIF-Financial-Crime-Information-Sharing-Report

International Consortium of Investigative Journalists, 'The Panama Papers: Exposing the rogue offshore finance industry', https://www.icij.org/investigations/panama-papers/

Jaffe R, 'The hybrid state: Crime and citizenship in Urban Jamaica' (2013) 40 (4) *American Ethnologist* 734

Jaffe R, 'Crime Watch: Mediating belonging and the politics of place in inner-city Jamaica', in H Jones and E Jackson (eds.), *Stories of Cosmopolitan Belonging: Emotion and Location* (Routledge 2014)

Jenkins P, 'Narcotics trafficking and the American mafia: The myth of internal prohibition' (1992) 18 *Crime Law and Social Change* 303

Jensen C, 'Potential drivers of terrorism out to the year 2020' (2015) 59 *American Behavioral Scientist* 1698

JMLIT, 'Introduction to the Joint Money Laundering Intelligence Taskforce (JMLIT Toolkit), http://www.nationalcrimeagency.gov.uk/publications/623-jmlit-toolkit-presentation/file

Johnson J, 'Don't break your silos down – Master them – Services in government' (2020) *Services in Government*, https://services.blog.gov.uk/2020/01/16/dont-break-your-silos-down-master-them/

Jonung L, 'Afterword to "It will soon be 1984 …"' (2020) 17 *Econ Journal Watch* 251

Jucca L and Pullella P, 'Vatican image hurt as JP Morgan closes account' (19 March 2012), Reuters, https://uk.reuters.com/article/uk-vatican-bank/vatican-bank-image-hurt-as-jp-morgan-closes-account-idUKBRE82I0P820120319

Jupp J and Garrod M, 'Legacies of the Troubles: The links between organized crime and terrorism in Northern Ireland' (2019) *Online First Studies in Conflict & Terrorism* 1

Kaetzler J and Kordys T, 'Fourth Money Laundering Directive: Increased risk management requirements' (2015), *Compliance & Risk*, 4(5), 2–5.

Kennedy-Pipe C and Vickers R, '"Blowback" for Britain?: Blair, Bush, and the war in Iraq' (2007) 33 *Review of International Studies* 205

Kerrigan D and Nirmala S, 'White collar crime in Trinidad', in R Seepersad and AM Bissessar (eds.), *Gangs in the Caribbean* (Cambridge Scholars 2013)

King C, 'Using civil processes in pursuit of criminal law objectives: A case study of non-conviction-based asset forfeiture' 16 (2012) *IJEP* 337

Kirby S and Penna S, 'Policing mobile criminality: Towards a situational crime prevention approach to organised crime' in K Bullock, R Clarke and N Tilley (eds.), *Situational Prevention of Organised Crimes* (Routledge 2010)

Kirry A et al., *French DPAs – First CJIP Guidelines published*, https://www.debevoise.com/insights/publications/2019/07/french-cjip-guidelines

Knowles M, 'Priti Patel issues warning to crime kingpins: "We'll come for you!"' (London, 2020) *Express.co.uk*, https://www.express.co.uk/news/ politics/1308104/priti-patel-crime-kingpin-gang-leader-lynne-owens-police-chief

Kochan N, 'How law enforcement is partnering up with banks in AML fight' (9 March 2016) Wolters Kluwer, https://www.wolterskluwer.com/en/solutions/banking-finance-risk-reporting-compliance

Law Commission, *Anti-Money Laundering: The SAR's Regime Consultation Paper* (2018) Law Com No. 236

Law N, CXXVII 'On the Prevention and Countering of the Laundering of Proceeds of Criminal Activities and of the Financing of Terrorism' (30 December 2010), Law N, CLXVI, 'Pontifical Commission for the Vatican City State, Prevention and Countering of the Laundering of the Proceeds of Criminal Activities and the Financing of Terrorism' (25 April 2012)

Law N, XV111, 'On Transparency, Supervision and Financial Intelligence' (8 October 2013) Art 71, hhtps://www.aif.va/eng/pdf/legge_n_XVIII_20131008.pdf http://www.ior.va/content/dam/ior/documenti/media/documenti/DecretodelPresidentedelGovernatorato.pdf

Lazenbatt A, Lynch U and O'Neill E, 'Revealing the hidden "Troubles" in Northern Ireland: The role of participatory rapid appraisal' (2001) 16 *Health Education Research* 567

Leary K and Gohd C, 'Sweden could stop using cash by 2023' (2017) World Economic Forum

Legal Information Institute, 'Fair Trial' Cornell Law School, https://www.law.cornell.edu/ constitution-conan/amendment-14/section-1/fair-trial

Levi M and Lord N, 'White-collar and corporate crime', in A Leibling, M Shadd and L McAra (eds.), *Oxford Handbook of Criminology* (Oxford University Press 2017)

Levi M, Reuter P and Halliday T, 'Can the AML system be evaluated without better data' (2018) *Crime Law Soc Change*, 69, 307–28

Levy A, *The Wiesenthal File* (Constable & Co. Ltd. 1993)

Li X and Whinston AB, 'Analyzing cryptocurrencies' 22 *Information Systems Frontiers* 17

Linklater, 'DPAs à la française: Win:win for companies in France?' (19 August 2019) *Investigations*, https://www.linklaters.com/en/insights/blogs/businesscrimelinks/2019/august/dpas-a-la-francaise-win-win-for-companies-in-france

Lipow J, 'Turn in your bin Ladens' (17 December 2010), *New York Times*, op-ed, https://www.nytimes.com/2010/12/18/opinion/18lipow.html

Lodge HD, *Criminal Finances Act 2017, A Guide to the New Law* (Law Society 2017)

Longstaff S, 'Blockchain: Some ethical considerations' (16 March 2019) *Ethics Centre*, https://ethics.org.au/blockchain-some-considerations/

Lord N, Campbell LJ and Wingerde K (2019) 'Other people's dirty money: Professional intermediaries, market dynamics and the finances of white-collar, corporate and organised crimes' (2019) 59(5) *British Journal of Criminology*, 1217

Lowry B, 'TV review: Worricker Trilogy: Masterpiece's 'Turks & Caicos', 'Salting the Battlefield' (6 November 2014) *Variety*, https://variety.com/2014/tv/ reviews/tv-review-worricker-trilogy-masterpieces-turks-caicos-salting-the-battlefield-1201342866/

Makarenko T, 'Europe's crime–terror nexus: Links between terrorist and organised crime groups in the European Union' (2012) European Parliament, European Parliament's Committee on Civil Liberties, Justice and Home Affairs PE 462.503

Marshall P, 'Does Shah v HSBC Private Bank Ltd make the anti-money laundering consent regime unworkable?'' (2010) *Butterworths Journal of International Banking and Financial Law* 8(9), 287

Marx G, 'High policing' (2012) *MIT.edu*, https://web.mit.edu/gtmarx/ www/highpolicing.html

Marx G, 'High policing' in G Bruinsma and D Weisburd (eds.), *Encyclopedia of Criminology and Criminal Justice* (Springer 2014)

Matchett W, *Secret Victory: The Intelligence War That Beat the IRA* (New Edition 2016)

Maurer B, 'Afterword – Mobile money, money magic, purse limits and pins: Tracing monetary pragmatics' (2011) 4 *Journal of Cultural Economy* 349

Maxwell N and Artingstall D, 'The role of financial information-sharing partnerships in the disruption of crime' (2017) RUSI Occasional Paper

Maylam S, 'Prosecution for money laundering in the UK' (2002) *Journal of Financial Crime*, 10 157–8.

McCallion H, *Undercover War: Britain's Special Forces and Their Secret Battle against the IRA* (John Blake 2020)

McDonnell R, 'UN anti-money laundering initiatives', in W Muller, C Kalin and J Goldsworth (eds.), *Anti-Money Laundering International Law and Practice* (John Wiley & Sons, 2004).

McDowell J and Novis G, 'The consequences of money laundering and financial crime' (2001) U.S. Dept of State, Bureau of International Narcotics and Law Enforcement and Affairs 6, https://www.hsdl.org/?view&did=3549

Medina L and Schneider F, *Shadow Economies Around the World: What Did We Learn Over the Last 20 Years?* (2018), https://www.imf.org/en/Publications/WP/Issues/ 2018/01/25/Shadow-Economies-Around-the-World-What-Did-We-Learn-Over-the-Last-20-Years-45583

Meeks, B, *Envisioning Caribbean Futures: Jamaican Perspectives* (University of the West Indies Press 2007)

Meeks W, 'Corporate and white-collar crime enforcement: Should regulation and rehabilitation spell an end to corporate criminal liability? (2006) 40 *Columbia Journal of Law and Social Problems* 77

Meyer T and Guzman A, 'International soft law' 2010 2(1) *Journal of Legal Analysis* 171–225

Mill JS, *On Liberty and Other Writings* (Cambridge University Press 2006)

Ministry of Justice, *Eighth Annual Report to Parliament on the Application of Protocols 19 and 21 to the Treaty on European Union (TEU) and the Treaty on the Functioning of the Union (TFEU) in Relation to EU Justice and Home Affairs (JHA) Matters (1 December 2016–30 November 2017)* (2018) MoJ

Mokhiber R, 'Corporate crime reporter', Speech Delivered at the National Press Club, *Crime without Conviction: The Rise of Deferred and Non-Prosecution Agreements* (28 December 2005), www.corporatecrimereporter.com/deferredreport.htm

Monbiot G, *Captive State: The Corporate Takeover of Britain* (Pan Books 2001)

Morais H, 'Fighting international crime and its financing: The importance of following a coherent global strategy based on the rule of law' (2005) *Villanova Law Review* 50

Mordecai RL, 'Reading the Jamaican 1970s as political thriller: Lessons from pop fiction' (2019) 23 (1) *Small Axe* 62

Morgan A, 'Review of *The Runnings*', in DN Wong Ken, *The Runnings: A Novel* (Alternative Energy Limited 2003)

Morgan P and Valerie Y, *Writing Rage: Unmasking Violence through Caribbean Discourse* (University of the West Indies Press 2006)

Motu Proprio Fidelis Dispensator et Prudens of His Holiness Pope Francis establishing a new coordinating agency for the economic and administrative affairs of the Holy See and the Vatican City State (24 February 2014), https://w2.vatican .va/ content/francesco/en/motu_proprío/documents/papa-francesco-motu-proprío_ 20140224_fidelis-dispensator-et-prudens.html

Mounk Y, *The People vs. Democracy: Why Our Freedom Is in Danger and How to Save It.* (Harvard University Press 2018)

Muller J, *The Mind and the Market: Capitalism in Western Thought* (Anchor Books 2003)

Murphy C, 'Pecunia non Olet: The case for the €500 banknote' (2016) 24 *European Journal of Crime, Criminal Law and Criminal Justice* 340

Myhill A and Quinton P, 'Confidence, neighbourhood policing, and contact: Drawing together the evidence' (2010) 4 *Policing: A Journal of Policy and Practice* 273

Nance MT, 'The regime that FATF built: An introduction to the Financial Action Task Force' (2018) 69 *Crime, Law and Social Change* 109

Nanda VP, 'Corporate criminal liability in the United States: Is a new approach warranted?', in M Pieth and R Ivory (eds.) *Corporate Criminal Liability. Ius Gentium: Comparative Perspectives on Law and Justice* (Vol. 9 Springer, Dordrecht 2011)

National Commission on Terrorist Attacks Upon the United States, *Monograph on Terrorist Financing* (National Commission on Terrorist Attacks Upon the United States 2004; National Council for Crime Prevention 2008)

National Crime Agency, 'County lines violence, exploitation & drug supply 2017' (London 2017) NCA National Briefing Report, https://www.nationalcrimeagency .gov. uk/who-we-are/publications/234-county-lines-violen-ce-exploitation-dru g-supply-2017/file

National Crime Agency, 'Financial intelligence: The impact of SARs in in reducing financial crime' (London 2018) NCA, https://www.ukciu.gov.uk/(bmhlcii2veploumtsv2ixted)/ Information/Info.aspx

National Crime Agency, 'Joint Money Laundering Intelligence Taskforce' (London 2018) NCA

National Crime Agency, 'The Suspicious Activity Reports Regime Annual Report 2017' (London 2018) NCA

National Crime Agency, 'National Strategic Assessment of Serious Organised Crime' (London 2019) NCA

National Crime Agency, 'The Suspicious Activity Reports Regime Annual Report 2019' (London 2019) NCA

National Crime Agency, 'Annual Plan 2020–2021' (London 2020)

Naylor RT, *Wages of Crime: Black markets, Illegal Finance and the Underworld Economy* (Cornell University Press 2002)

Naylor RT, 'Towards a general theory of profit-driven crimes' (2003) 43 *British Journal of Criminology* 81

Nelken D, 'White-collar and corporate crime', in M Maguire, R Morgan and R Reiner (eds.), *The Oxford Handbook of Criminology* (5th edn., Oxford University Press 2012)

Neocleous M 'Against security' (2000) 100 *Radical Philosophy* 7

Nixon R, *Slow Violence and the Environmentalism of the Poor* (Harvard University Press 2011)

Novis G and McDowell J, 'The consequences of money laundering and financial crime' (2001) U.S. Dept of State, Bureau of International Narcotics and Law Enforcement and Affairs 6, https://www.hsdl.org/?view&did=3549

NPR, 'Ben Franklin's famous "Liberty, Safety" quote lost its context in 21st century' (2015) *NPR.org*, https://www.npr.org/2015/03/02/390245038/ ben-franklins-famous-liberty-safety-quote-lost-its-context-in-21st-century

O'Brien K, 'Review of *The Runnings* quoted in D. N. Wong Ken, *The Runnings: A Novel*' (Alternative Energy Limited 2003)

Office of Public Affairs, 'Global disruption of three terror finance cyber-enabled campaigns' (13 August 2020) United States Department of Justice, https://www.justice.gov/opa/pr/global-disruption-three-terror-finance-cyber-enabled-campaigns

O'Neill S, 'Attracting the megarich while keeping out illicit money' (London 11 October 2018) *The Times*

Orford J, *Power, Powerlessness and Addiction* (Cambridge University Press 2013)

Ortiz-Ospina E 'Trust' (2016) OurWorldInData.org, https://ourworldindata.org/trust

O'Sullivan JR, 'How prosecutors apply the "federal prosecutions of corporations" charging policy in the era of deferred prosecutions, and what that means for the purposes of the federal criminal sanction', (2014) 51 *American Criminal Law Review* 30 OECD

Oxford Analytica Ltd, 'Country report: Anti-money laundering rules in the United Kingdom', in M Pieith and G Aiolfi (eds.), *A Comparative Guide to Anti-Money Laundering: A Critical Analysis of Systems in Singapore, Switzerland, the UK and the USA* (Edward Elgar, 2004)

Paine LS, 'Salomon Brothers (A)' (November 2004, revised February 2009) *Harvard Business School, Case* 305–019

Palan R, 'Futurity, offshore and the international political economy of crime', in J Beckert and M Dewey (eds.), *The Architecture of Illegal Markets: Towards an Economic Sociology of Illegality in the Economy* (Oxford University Press, 2017)

Palmer J, *Thrillers: Genesis and Structure of a Popular Genre* (Edward Arnold 1987)

Pantazis C and Pemberton S, 'From "old" to the "new" suspect communities: Examining the impacts of recent UK counter-terrorist legislation' (2009) 49 *British Journal of Criminology* 646

Pantucci R, 'A contest to democracy? How the UK has responded to the current terrorist threat' (2010) 17 *Democratization* 251

Paoli L, 'The Banco Ambrosiano case: An investigation into the underestimation of the relations between organized and economic crime' (1995) 23 *Crime, Law & Social Change* 345–65

Passas N, 'Anomie and corporate deviance' (1990) 14 *Contemporary Crises*157

Patricca N, 'The Vatican Bank follies' (2013) 29(1) *Windy City Times* 4, Gale OneFile: *News*, link.gale.com/apps/doc/A348647342/STND?u= uniaber&sid= STND&xid=ff161c34

Perez M and Dill A, 'The rise of the American deferred prosecution agreement ("DPA") and its European avatars' (2016) *CHRONIQUE/International Financial and White-Collar Crime, Corporate Malfeasance and Compliance* No. 2

Perrigo B, '"Get Brexit Done." The eslogan that won Britain's Election' (2019) *Time*, https://time.com/5749478/get-brexit-done-slogan-uk-election/

Perry A, 'Organised crime in the UK is bigger than ever before. Can the police catch up?' (2018) The Guardian, http://www.theguardian.com/uk-news/ 2018/ nov/22/uk-organised-crime-can-police-catch-up-national-crime-agency-lynne-o wens

Perry M, 'With new rules, pope aims to reform scandal-ridden Vatican Bank' (13 August 2019) *Organised Crime and Corruption Reporting Project* https://www .occrp. org/en/daily/10465-with-new-rules-pope-aims-to-reform-scandal-rid den-vatican-bank

Peston R, *Who Runs Britain? ... And Who's to Blame for the Economic Mess We're In* (Hodder & Stoughton 2008)

Petegorsky MN, 'Note, plea bargaining in the dark: The duty to disclose exculpatory Brady evidence during plea fargaining', (2013) 81 *Fordham Law Review* 3599

Phayer M, 'Pope Pius XII, the Holocaust, and the Cold War' (1998) 12(2) *Holocaust and Genocide Studies* 233 233–56

Piaggio A, 'The cost and consequences of the war on drugs' (Human Rights Foundation 2019)

Picca JP, *French Prosecutors Reach First Ever DPAs Settling Bribery Charges* (White & Case 2018), https://www.whitecase.com/publications/ alert/french-prosecu tors-reach-first-ever-dpas-settling-bribery-charges

Pol RF, 'Anti-money laundering: The world's least effective policy experiment? Together, we can fix it' (2020) 3 *Policy Design and Practice* 73

Pollack BJ and Reisinger AW, 'Lone wolf or the start of a new pack: Should the FCPA guidance represent a new paradigm in evaluating corporate criminal liability risks? (2014) 51 *American Criminal Law Review* 121

Pontell HN, 'Theoretical, empirical, and policy implications of alternative definitions of "white-collar crime": "Trivializing the lunatic crime rate"', in ML Benson, SR Van Slyke and FT Cullen (eds.), *The Oxford Handbook of White Collar Crime* (Oxford University Press 2016)

Pontell HN, Black WK and Geis G 'Too big to fail, too powerful to jail? On the absence of criminal prosecutions after the 2008 financial meltdown' (2014) 61(1) *Crime, Law and Social Change* 1

Pope Francis, 'Apostolic letter in the form of a *motu proprio*: "On the jurisdiction of the judicial bodies of the Vatican City State in criminal matters"' (11 July 2013), http://www.vatican.va/content/francesco/en/motu_proprio/documents/papa-francesco-motu-proprio_20130711_organi-giudiziari.html

Posner G, *God's Banker* (Simon & Schuster 2015).

Prober J 'Accounting for terror: Debunking the paradigm of inexpensive terrorism' (1 November 2005), Washington Institute, https://www.washingtoninstitute.org/policy-analysis/view/accounting-for-terror-debunking-the-paradigm-of-inexpensive-terrorism

Public Administration Select Committee, 'Strategic thinking in government: Without national strategy, can viable government strategy emerge? – Public Administration Committee' (2012) House of Commons, Select Committee report 24th Report, https://publications.parliament.uk/pa/cm201012/ cmselect/cmpubadm/1625/162502.htm

Pullella P and Jucca L, 'Vatican image hurt as JP Morgan closes account' (19 March 2012) Reuters, https://uk.reuters.com/article/uk-vatican-bank/vatican-bank-image-hurt-as-jp-morgan-closes-account-idUKBRE82I0P820120319

Rakoff J, 'The financial crisis: Why have no high-level executives been prosecuted?' (9 January 2014) *New York Review*, https://www.nybooks.com/articles/2014/01/09/financial-crisis-why-no-executive-prosecutions/

Ramey C, 'Email scammers are savvier, and more successful, than ever' (27 February 2020) *Wall Street Journal*, https://www.wsj.com/ articles/email-scammers-are-savvier-and-more-successful-than-ever-11582808400

Redman J, 'Danske Bank caught using gold bullion to launder illicit funds' (17 November 2020) *bitcoin.com*, https://news.bitcoin.com/danske-bank-caught-using-gold-bullion-to-launder-illicit-funds/

Reichel P, Albanese J and Roth M (eds.) 'Historical overview of transnational crime', in *Handbook of Transnational Crime and Justice* (2nd edn., Sage 2013)

Reilly P 'Justice deferred is justice denied: We must end our failed experiment in deferring corporate criminal prosecutions' (25 September 2014). *Brigham Young University Law Review*; Texas A&M University School of Law Legal Studies Research Paper No. 16-24

Reiner R, *The Politics of the Police* (4th edn., Oxford University Press 2010)

Renard T, 'Counter terrorism in Belgium: Key challenges and policy options' (October 2016) Egmont Paper 89

Riksbank Sedel- och myntutbytet i Sverige: Sammanfattning och utvärdering [Banknote and coin exchange in Sweden: Summary and evaluation] (2018) Sveriges Riksbank, https://www.riksbank.se/globalassets/media/sedlar--mynt/sedel--och-myntutbytet-2015-2017/svenska/utvardering-sedel--och-myntutbytet-i-sverige.pdf

Riksbank, *The Riksbank proposes a review of the concept of legal tender* (Riksbank 2019)

Riksbank, *Så betalar svenskarna 2019 [This is how the Swedes will pay in 2019]* (2019) Sveriges Riksbank, https://www.riksbank.se/globalassets/ media/rapporter/sa-betalar-svenskarna/ 2019/svenska/sa-betalar-svenskarna-2019.pdf

Riksbank, '5,5 miljarder kronor i ogiltiga sedlar – Lös in dem innan avgiften höjs' [SEK 5.5 billion in invalid banknotes – Redeem them before the fee is raised]

(2020) Sveriges Riksbank, https://www.riksbank.se/sv/press-och-publicerat/nyheter-och-pressmeddelanden/pressmeddelanden/2020/55-miljarder-kronor-i-ogiltiga-sedlar---los-in-dem-innan-avgiften-hojs/

Rittel H and Webber M, 'Dilemmas in a general theory of planning' (1973) 4 *Policy Sciences* 155

Robertson G, *The Case Against the Pope* (Penguin Books 2010)

Robinson J, *The Sink: Terror, Crime and Dirty Money in the Offshore World* (Constable 2003)

Robinson T and Fanusie Y, 'Bitcoin laundering: An analysis of illicit flows into digital currency services' (12 January 2018) Elliptic Center on Sanctions and Illicit Finance, https://info.elliptic.co/whitepaper-fdd-bitcoin-laundering

Rogerson P, 'Serco fraud: Deferred prosecution critics "cynical", says judge' (4 July 2019) *Law Society Gazette*

Rogoff K, 'Blessing or curse? Foreign and underground demand for euro notes' (1998) 13 *Economic Policy* 262

Rogoff KS, *The Curse of Cash* (Princeton University Press 2016)

Royal United Services Institute, 'The UK's economic crime plan: A first step on the road to progress' (24 July 2019), https://rusi.org/commentary/uk%E2%80%99s-economic-crime-plan-first-step-road-progress

Rubin M, *Thrillers* (Cambridge University Press 1999)

Ruggiero V, *Organized and Corporate Crime in Europe: Offers that Can't Be Refused.* (Dartmouth 1996)

Ruggiero V, 'It's the economy, stupid! Classifying power crimes' (2003) 35 *International Journal of the Sociology of Law*163

Ruggiero V, 'On liberty and crime: Adam Smith and John Stuart Mill' (2008) 51 *Crime, Law and Social Change* 435

Ruggiero V, 'Networks of greed' (2017) 1 (1) *Justice, Power and Resistance* 3

Ryder N, 'A false sense of security? An analysis of legislative approaches towards the prevention of terrorist finance in the United States and the United Kingdom' (November 2007) *Journal of Business Law* 821–50

Ryder N, *The Financial Crisis and White-Collar Crime – The Perfect Storm?* (Edward Elgar 2014)

Ryder N, *The Financial War on Terrorism: A Review of Counter-Terrorist Financing Strategies Since 2001* (Routledge Research in Terrorism and the Law 2015)

Ryder N 'Is it time to reform the counter-terrorist financing reporting obligations? A critical and comparative assessment of the counter-terrorist financing reporting obligations in the European Union and the United Kingdom' (2018) 19(5) *German Law Review*1169–90

Sandals, https://www.sandals.co.uk/

Sanderson S, 'The scandal at the Vatican Bank' (London 6 December 2013) *Financial Times*, https://www.ft.com/content/3029390a-5c68-11e3-931e-00144feabdc0

Sands P, *Making it Harder for the Bad Guys: The Case for Eliminating High Denomination Notes* (2016) M-RCBG Associate Working Paper Series, https://www.hks.harvard.edu/sites/default/files/ centers/mrcbg/files/Eliminating%2BHDNfinalXYZ.pdf

Sarais A, 'Moneyval and the Santa Sede: Some notes on the recent regulatory provisions for financial transparency in Santa Sede in the Vatican City State' (2014) Iura Orientalia X (135–47), http://www.iuraorientalia.net/IO/IO_ 010_2014/III_06_Sarais.pdf

Satis Group, 'Crypstoasset market coverage initiation: Network creation (11 July 2018) Bloomberg, https://research.bloomberg.com/pub/ res/ d2246jsnqusjYSeacPbQc2IjVIw

Saugman F, 'Corporate failure to prevent abuses' (6 April 2020) *Law Society Gazette*

Saunt R, 'Vatican cardinal resigns from his post amid £180m financial scandal following purchase of London apartment block using Church funds' (25 Sept 2020) Mail Online, https://www.dailymail.co.uk/news/article-8772407/Vatican-cardinal-resigns-post-amid-180m-financial-scandal.html

Schmid A, 'Revisiting the relationship between international terrorism and transnational organised crime 22 years later' (2018) ICCT Research Paper, https://icct.nl/publication/revisiting-the-relationship-between-international-terrorism-and-transnational-organised-crime-22-years-later/

Schneier B, 'Beyond security theatre' (2009) *New Internationalist*, https://newint.org/features/2009/11/01/security

Schott P, 'Reference guide to anti-money laundering and combating the financing of terrorism' (2006) World Bank, http://documents1.worldbank.org/ curated/ en/558401468134391014/pdf/350520Referenc1Money01OFFICIAL0USE1.pdf

Schwartz O, 'The rise of microchipping: Are we ready for technology to get under the skin?' (London 8 November 2019) *The Guardian*, https://www.theguardian.com/technology/2019/nov/08/the-rise-of-microchipping-are-we-ready-for-technology-to-get-under-the-skin

Serious Fraud Office, 'Case information, Rolls-Royce PLC' (23 December 2013), https://www.sfo.gov.uk/cases/rolls-royce-plc/

Serious Fraud Office, 'News Release – Airbus' (31 January 2020), https://www.sfo.gov.uk/2020/01/31/sfo-enters-into-e991m-deferred-prosecution-agreement-with-airbus-as-part-of-a-e3-6bn-global-resolution/

Serious Organised Crime Agency 'The suspicious activity reports regime annual report 2009' (London 2010) Serious Organised Crime Agency

Serious Organised Crime Agency, 'The suspicious activity reports regime annual report 2012' (London 2013) Serious Organised Crime Agency

Shakespeare W, *Hamlet* (Tauchnitz 1843)

Shapiro S, 'Collaring the crime, not the criminal: Reconsidering the concept of white-collar crime' (1990) 55 *American Sociological Review* 346

Sharman JC, *The Money Laundry: Regulating Criminal Finance in the Global Economy* (Cornell University Press 2011)

Shaxson N, *Treasure Islands: Tax Havens and the Men Who Stole the World* (Random House 2011)

Sheller M, 'Natural hedonism: The invention of Caribbean Islands as tropical playgrounds', in S Courtman (ed.), *Beyond the Blood, the Beach and the Banana: New Perspectives in Caribbean Studies* (Ian Randle 2004)

Shover N, 'Generative worlds of white-collar crime', in G Geis and HN Pontell (eds.), *International Handbook of White-Collar and Corporate Crime* (Springer 2007)

Simpson M, 'International initiatives', in M Simpson, N Smith and A Srivastava (eds.), *International Guide to Money Laundering Law and Practice* (Bloomsbury Professional 2010)

Simpson V and Wakefield N, 'Vatican Bank hit by financial scandal … again' (London 19 December 2010) *The Independent*, https://www.independent.co.uk/news/world/europe/vatican-bank-hit-by-financial-scandal-again-2164321.html

Sives A, 'A calculated assault on the authority of the state? Crime, politics and extradition in 21st century Jamaica' (2012) 58 *Crime, Law and Social Change* 415

Skatteverket, *Requirement of cash registers: Impact evaluation* (2013) English Summary of the Swedish Tax Agency Report, https://www.skatteverket.se/download/18.46ae6b26141980f1e2d11b2/138208468720/Summary%20of%20Report%202013_2%20The%20Requirement%20of%20Cash20Registers.%20An%20impact%20evaluation.pdf

Skoczylis J, 'The local prevention of terrorism in strategy and practice: "Contest" a new era in the fight against terrorism' (University of Leeds 2013) PhD thesis

Skoczylis J, and Andrews S 'Can Prevent be saved? No, but ...' (2020) 40 *Critical Social Policy* 350

Slingo J, 'SFO convictions dwindle as caseload shrinks', (31 December 2019) *Law Society Gazette*

Smith DC, 'Paragons, pariahs, and pirates: A spectrum-based theory of enterprise' (1980) 26(3) *Crime & Delinquency* 358

Smith F, 'Introduction: Sexing the citizen', in F Smith (ed.), *Sex and the Citizen: Interrogating the Caribbean* (University of Virginia Press 2011)

Sombart W, *The Quintessence of Capitalism: A Study of the History and Psychology of the Modern Business Man* (Routledge 1915)

Spaaij R, *Understanding Lone Wolf Terrorism: Global Patterns, Motivations and Prevention* (Springer 2012)

Spalek R, 'Regulation, white-collar crime and the Bank of Credit and Commerce International' (2001) *Howard Journal of Criminal Justice* 40 166–79

Ståhl I, 'It will soon be 1984 ... ' (2020) 17 *Econ Journal Watch* 242

Sutherland E, *White Collar Crime* (Dryden 1949)

Sutherland EH, *White Collar Crime: The Uncut Version* (Yale University Press 1983)

Svensson R, 'Bank-, post- och värdetransportrån: En analys av rånen under 1990-talet' [Bank, post and cash-in-transit robberies: An analysis of the robberies during the 1990s], The Swedish National Council for Crime Prevention, 2004, https://www.bra.se/download/18.cba82f7130f475a2f1800014226/1371914729864/2004_bank_post_och_vardetransportran.pdf

SVT, 'Tusentals ungdomar används för att tvätta pengar åt kriminella' [Thousands of youths are used to launder money for criminals] (2019) *SVT Nyheter*, https://www.svt.se/nyheter/lokalt/skane/tusentals-ungdomar-anvands-for-att-tvatta-pengar-at-kriminella

SVT, '108 personer döms i Kasinomålet – Huvudman får åtta års fängelse' [108 people sentenced in the Casino case – principal gets eight years in prison] (2020) *SVT Nyheter*, https://www.svt.se/nyheter/lokalt/uppsala/dom-meddelas-i-kasinomalet-folj-svt-direktrapportering

Sykes GM and Matza D, 'Techniques of neutralization: A theory of delinquency' (1957) 22 (6) *American Sociological Review* 664

Teigland R et al, *The Rise and Development of FinTech: Accounts of Disruption from Sweden and Beyond* (Routledge 2018)

Tett G, *The Silo Effect* (Simon & Schuster 2016)

Thomas CC, 'The Foreign Corrupt Practices Act: A decade of rapid expansion explained, defended, and justified', (2010) 29 *Review of Litigation* 439 451–2

Tinianow A, 'Bitcoin demand drives $1.4 billion ransomware industry in the U.S' (1 July 2020) *Forbes*, www.forbes.com/sites/andreatinianow/2020/07/01/ bitco in-demand-drives-14-billion-ransomware-industry-in-the-us/#78e5c73a32d8

Tombs S and Whyte D, 'Researching corporate and white-collar crime in an era of neoliberalism' in G Geis and HN Pontell (eds.), *International Handbook of White-Collar and Corporate Crime* (Springer 2007)

Tombs S and Whyte D, *The Corporate Criminal: Why Corporations Must be Abolished* (Routledge 2015)

Toon D, 'Prosperity command, National Crime Agency, Treasury Committee Oral evidence: Economic crime' (4 July 2018) HC 940

Transparency International 'Corruption statistics' (n.d.) http://www.transparency .org.uk/ corruption/statistics-and-quotes/uk-corruption

Tudor K, 'Symbolic survival and harm: Serious fraud and consumer capitalism's perversion of the causa sui project' (2019) 59 (5) *British Journal of Criminology* 1237

Tudor K, 'Toxic sovereignty: Understanding fraud as the expression of special liberty within late-capitalism' (2018) 2(2) *Journal of Extreme Anthropology* 7

Tudor K, 'Ponzi Schemes: Illicit Entrepreneurialism in Late-Capitalism' (University of Sunderland 2019) doctoral thesis

U.S. General Accounting Office, 'Money laundering: The volume of currency transaction reports filed could and should be reduced' (15 March 1994) 3, https://www.gao.gov/assets/110/105432.pdf

U.S. State Department, Bureau of International Narcotics and Law Enforcement Affairs, 'International narcotics control strategy report', Volume II Money Laundering and Financial Crime (7 March 2012) 33, https://2009-2017.state .gov/documents/organization/185866.pdf

Uhlmann DM, 'Deferred prosecution and non-prosecution agreements and the erosion of corporate criminal liability' (2013) 72 *Maryland Law Review* 1295

Umellas O, 'EU nation at center of dirty-cash storm cracks down on crypto' (11 June 2020) *Bloomberg*, www.bloomberg.com/news/articles/2020-06-11/eu-nation -at-center-of-dirty-cash-storm-cracks-down-on-crypto?sref=l0bGdXEa

UN Economic and Social Council (ECOSOC), *United Nations Convention Against Illicit Traffic in Narcotic Drugs and Psychotropic Substances* (19 December 1988), https://www.refworld.org/docid/49997af90.html

Unger B, *The Scale and Impacts of Money Laundering* (Edward Elgar 2007)

United Nations 'The money-laundering cycle' (n.d.), https://www.unodc.org/ unodc/en/money-laundering/laundrycycle.html

United Nations Office on Drugs and Crime, 'Money-laundering and globalization' (n.d.), https://www.unodc.org/unodc/en/money-laundering/globalization.html

United Nations Office on Drugs and Crime, 'Transnational Organised Crime', https://www.unodc.org/ropan/en/organized-crime.html

US Congress House of Representatives, 'Identify, disrupt and dismantle: Coordinating the government's attack on terrorist financing' (15 December 2003), House Hearing, 108 Congress, https://www.govinfo.gov/content/pkg/CHRG -108hhrg93428/html/CHRG-108hhrg93428.htm

US DOJ, *Manual for Criminal Prosecutors*, 9-27.000-Principles of Federal Prosecution, https://www.justice.gov/jm/jm-9-27000-principles-federal-prosecution #9-27.620

US DOJ 'Press release' (14 September 1992) https://www.justice.gov/archive/atr/public/press_releases/1992/211290.htm

van Erp J, Huisman W, Vande Walle G and Beckers J, 'Criminology and white collar crime in Europe', in van Erp, Huisman and Vande Walle (eds), *The Routledge Handbook of White-Collar and Corporate Crime in Europe* (Routledge 2015)

Vigna P and Jeong E-Y, 'Cryptocurrency scams took in more than $4 billion in 2019 markets' (8 February 2020) *Wall Street Journal*, https://www.wsj.com/articles/cryptocurrency-scams-took-in-more-than-4-billion-in2019-11581184800

Vuchelen J and Van Hove L, 'An early evaluation of the introduction of euro banknotes and coins' (2002) 29 *Journal of Economic Studies* 370

Wadsley J, 'Money laundering: Professionals as policemen' (July/August 1994) *Conveyancer and Property Lawyer*, 275

Waller L and Harriott A, 'Political corruption and organized crime', in Harriott, *Organized Crime and Politics in Jamaica: Breaking the Nexus* (University of the West Indies Press 2008)

Walters M, 'High Court slams "inconsistent" SFO over DPA' (20 April 2018) *Law Society Gazette*

Walters R, 'Eco crime', in J Muncie, D Talbot and R Walters (eds.), *Crime: Local and Global* (Willan 2009)

Wassermann A and Wansierski P, 'Transparency v money laundering: Catholic Church fears growing Vatican Bank scandal (Hamburg 2 July 2012) *Spiegel International*, https://www.spiegel.de/international/europe/a-growing-vatican-bank-scandal-threatens-catholic-church-image-a-842140.html

Weir M, 'The boom in Benjamins' (2019) 56 *Finance and Development* 60

Wetterberg G, *Money and Power: From Stockholms Banco 1656 to Sveriges Riksbank Today* (Sveriges Riksbank 2009)

Whyte D and Wiegratz J, 'The moral economy of neo-liberal fraud', in D Whyte and J Wiegratz (eds) *Neo-liberalism and the Moral Economy of Fraud* (Routledge 2017)

Whyte D and Wiegratz J, 'Neo-liberalism, moral economy and fraud', in D Whyte and J Wiegratz (eds) *Neo-liberalism and the Moral Economy of Fraud* (Routledge 2017)

Wiegratz J, 'Fake capitalism? The dynamics of neo-liberal moral restructuring and pseudo-development: The case of Uganda' (2010) 37 (124) *Review of African Political Economy* 123

Wiegratz J, 'The neo-liberal harvest: The proliferation and normalisation of economic fraud in a market society', in S Winlow and R Atkinson (eds.) *New Directions in Crime and Deviancy* (Routledge 2012)

Wiener A, 'Why does the Vatican need a bank and what is with the history of scandal?' (10 July 2014) *Foreign Policy*, https://foreignpolicy.com/2014/07/10/why-does-the-vatican-need-a-bank-and-whats-with-the-history-of-scandal/

Williams P, 'Fact check: Have the Conservatives protected police and counter-terrorism budgets?' (2017) *The Conversation*, http://theconversation.com/fact-check-have-the-conservatives-protected-police-and-counter-terrorism-budgets-78782

William SL, 'Corporate prosecution, cooperation, and the trading of favors' (2002) 87 *Iowa Law Review* 643, 645–7

Winlow S and Hall S, 'Realist criminology and its discontents' (2016) 5(3) *International Journal for Crime, Justice and Social Democracy* 80

Winstock AR, Eastwood N and Stevens A 'A new drug strategy for the UK' (2017) 358 *British Medical Journal*, https://www.bmj.com/content/358/bmj.j3643

Wong Ken DN, *The Runnings: A Novel* (Alternative Energy Limited 2003)

World Bank Group, 'Distributed Ledger Technology (DLT) and Blockchain (2017) FinTech Note, No. 1, http://documents1.worldbank.org/curated/ en/177911513714062215/pdf/122140-WP-PUBLIC-Distributed-Ledger-Technology-and-Blockchain-Fintech-Notes.pdf

Wright L, *The Terror Years* (Constable 2018)

Yallop D, *In God's Name* (Constable & Robinson 2007)

Index

For Product Safety Concerns and Information please contact our EU representative GPSR@taylorandfrancis.com
Taylor & Francis Verlag GmbH, Kaufingerstraße 24, 80331 München, Germany

www.ingramcontent.com/pod-product-compliance
Lightning Source LLC
LaVergne TN
LVHW021123300926
849160LV00010B/833

* 9 7 8 1 0 3 2 3 7 3 3 3 1 *